Political Communication in Britain

Previous volumes in this series sponsored by the UK Political Studies Association's Elections, Public Opinion and Parties Group:

Political Communications: The General Election Campaign of 1979/edited by Robert M. Worcester and Martin Harrop. London: Allen & Unwin, 1982

Political Communications: The General Election Campaign of 1983/edited by Ivor Crewe and Martin Harrop. Cambridge: Cambridge University Press, 1986

Political Communications: The General Election Campaign of 1987/edited by Ivor Crewe and Martin Harrop. Cambridge: Cambridge University Press, 1989

Political Communications: The General Election Campaign of 1992/edited by Ivor Crewe and Brian Gosschalk. Cambridge: Cambridge University Press, 1995

Political Communications: Why Labour Won the General Election of 1997/edited by Ivor Crewe, Brian Gosschalk and John Bartle. London: Frank Cass, 1998

Political Communications: The General Election Campaign of 2001/edited by John Bartle, Simon Atkinson and Roger Mortimore. London: Frank Cass, 2002

Political Communications: The General Election Campaign of 2005/edited by Dominic Wring, Jane Green, Roger Mortimore and Simon Atkinson. Basingstoke: Palgrave Macmillan, 2007

Political Communication in Britain

The Leader Debates, the Campaign and the Media in the 2010 General Election

Edited by

Dominic Wring
Reader in Political Communication,
Loughborough University, UK

Roger Mortimore
Director of Political Analysis,
Ipsos MORI, UK

Simon Atkinson
Assistant Chief Executive,
Ipsos MORI, UK

palgrave
macmillan

First published 2011 by
PALGRAVE MACMILLAN

Palgrave Macmillan in the UK is an imprint of Macmillan Publishers Limited, registered in England, company number 785998, of Houndmills, Basingstoke, Hampshire RG21 6XS.

Palgrave Macmillan in the US is a division of St Martin's Press LLC, 175 Fifth Avenue, New York, NY 10010.

Palgrave Macmillan is the global academic imprint of the above companies and has companies and representatives throughout the world.

Palgrave® and Macmillan® are registered trademarks in the United States, the United Kingdom, Europe and other countries.

ISBN: 978–0–230–30145–0 hardback
ISBN: 978–0–230–30146–7 paperback

This book is printed on paper suitable for recycling and made from fully managed and sustained forest sources. Logging, pulping and manufacturing processes are expected to conform to the environmental regulations of the country of origin.

A catalogue record for this book is available from the British Library.

A catalog record for this book is available from the Library of Congress.

10 9 8 7 6 5 4 3 2 1
20 19 18 17 16 15 14 13 12 11

Printed and bound in Great Britain by
CPI Antony Rowe, Chippenham and Eastbourne

Contents

Part IV Parties

Part V Campaigning

Part VI Media

Figures and Tables

Figures

Tables

Preface and Acknowledgements

Since our series of books began with a volume on the 1979 election, political communication is now unquestionably a central facet of the modern democratic process, and one increasingly about strategy and not just tactics. That campaign over thirty years ago proved to be important in signalling the embrace of a more capitally intensive form of electioneering, focused on what was perceived to be an increasingly volatile and more heterogeneous voting public. Following the Conservatives' victory, the Saatchi and Saatchi brothers' agency became Britain's most famous advertisers and were indelibly linked with their client Margaret Thatcher. Intriguingly, by 2010, the same iconic firm was working for a Labour party whose leadership had once denounced the firm for debasing elections and 'selling politics like soap powder'. It should, however, be noted that the founders who had given their name to the company had long departed to form their own rival agency, M&C Saatchi, and once again found themselves advising the Conservatives during this campaign.

So-called spin doctors, image-makers, policy wonks and pollsters now play a major role in the kitchen cabinets that surround every politician aspiring to high office. Underlying this development is a desire to communicate with the public, both through direct persuasion and indirectly via the news media. However, conscious of the growing pervasiveness of what they have often dismissed as spin, journalists routinely doubt politicians as a default position. Tony Blair attacked this attitude when he bemoaned the destructive competitiveness of the contemporary media in a speech he made days before stepping down as Prime Minister in 2007. The seemingly rapacious nature of journalism was something Menzies Campbell also identified as one of the reasons for his own resignation as Liberal Democrat leader later that same year. Campbell's turned out to be a momentous decision that paved the way for the succession of Nick Clegg, a politician their predecessor Paddy Ashdown had supported for the job, citing his abilities as a communicator. The introduction of the Prime Ministerial Debates in this election turned out to be the ultimate gift for Clegg, which he gratefully exploited.

The focus on image and personality regularly informed much reporting of Tony Blair's and latterly Gordon Brown's leadership of the government throughout Labour's third consecutive term in office. Brown's long-awaited succession to the premiership failed to stem febrile media speculation as to whether his position was secure. Inevitably, Conservative leader David Cameron attempted to exploit the Prime Minister's discomfort by presenting himself as a capable, personable alternative. He did so through a carefully orchestrated campaign over five years that was initially overseen by the marketing consultant Steve Hilton and latterly by Andy Coulson, the former editor of the best-selling paper *The News of the World*. Both advisers would join Cameron as key lieutenants overseeing strategy from 10 Downing Street. The proximity of these communications specialists to the Prime Minister is a telling feature of how both governments and elections operate in modern Britain. This volume is devoted to exploring the latter by focusing on the campaigns, debates, polling and mediation of the 2010 General Election.

We are grateful to various people for their help. Philip Cowley, David Denver, Andreas Murr, Anja Neundorf, Paul Whiteley and members of the UK Political Studies Association's Elections, Public Opinion and Parties group provided support that helped make this volume possible. All the authors have made valuable contributions and we would like to put on record our thanks for their work and involvement in producing this book. We would also like to pay tribute to Jane Green, our editorial colleague on the last edition, whose wisdom has continued to inform the series. We are grateful to Michael Cockerell and David Seawright for their support, and Jo Sheriff has been a great help to the project. Special thanks go to Tilly Wring and her friend Diane. Amber Stone-Galilee, Amy Lankester-Owen and Liz Blackmore of Palgrave Macmillan, and Vidhya Jayaprakash and her team at Newgen Imaging Systems have been patient and very helpful from the outset, and we are immensely grateful for their encouragement and dedication to continuing this unique series.

DW, RM and SA

Contributors

Simon Atkinson is Assistant Chief Executive at Ipsos MORI. He has been a member of the company's polling team at every general election since 1992.

Ric Bailey is the BBC's Chief Political Adviser and has represented the BBC in the negotiations over setting up the TV Election Debates.

Jay G. Blumler is Emeritus Professor of Public Communication, Institute of Communication Studies, University of Leeds.

Adam Boulton has been Political Editor of Sky News since the channel's launch in 1989. He has also written extensively for the print media and published a number of books, most recently *Hung Together: The 2010 Election and the Coalition Government* co-authored with his Sky colleague Joey Jones.

Chris Burgess is a doctoral student at the University of Nottingham, who is working in a collaborative partnership with the People's History Museum, Manchester. His research focuses on the development of party political posters in Britain during the twentieth century.

Helen Cleary is Head of Political Research within Ipsos MORI's Social Research Institute. She directed much of the organisation's general election work, including a series of polls in key marginal constituencies for Reuters, ad hoc polls for national media clients and the eve-of-election poll for the *Evening Standard*.

Stephen Coleman is Professor of Political Communication, Institute of Communication Studies, University of Leeds.

Greg Cook has worked for the Labour Party since 1988 and has been the party's Head of Polling and Political Strategy since 1995. He coordinated submissions to boundary review and headed the team that carried out focus group work during the 2010 General Election.

John Corner is Visiting Professor of Communication Studies at the University of Leeds and was formerly at the University of Liverpool. He has written widely on the topics of broadcast journalism, documentary, media audiences, political communication and cultural analysis.

David Cutts is Senior Research Fellow in the Institute of Social Change at the University of Manchester. He has published extensively on electoral geography and other aspects of British politics.

David Deacon is Professor of Communication and Media Analysis at Loughborough University. He pioneered and has worked on each of the media content analyses of every general election since 1992. He has also written widely on other aspects of political communication.

Edward Fieldhouse is Professor and Director of the Institute for Social Change at the University of Manchester, where his main research interests are electoral geography and political participation. He is currently involved in the EPSRC-funded project 'The Social Complexity of Immigration and Diversity'.

Justin Fisher is Professor of Political Science and Director of the Magna Carta Institute at Brunel University. He is joint editor of the *Journal of Elections, Public Opinion and Parties* and has acted as a consultant to various bodies, including the Hayden Phillips review of Party Finance.

Ivor Gaber is Professor of Political Journalism at City University, London. He is an experienced broadcaster, who has worked for all of the major British networks, and has also acted as a consultant to various public bodies, including the UK Government, the EU and the UNESCO.

Andrew Hawkins founded ComRes in 2003 and has advised various politicians in the UK and overseas. He writes for a wide range of publications, including a monthly column for *Total Politics* and is a regular commentator in the broadcast media.

Jennifer vanHeerde-Hudson is Lecturer in Research Methods in the Department of Political Science, University College, London. Her research interests include campaign finance and political communication, and, especially, negative advertising.

Peter Kellner has been President of YouGov since 2007, having previously been its Chairman from 2001. He has also been a political and elections analyst for BBC, Channel Four News and a number of newspapers.

Caroline Lawes joined ComRes in 2007 and managed their political polling during the 2010 General Election work on behalf of various media organisations. She worked on the development of ComRes's automated instant telephone polling following each of the leader debates.

Tomasz Mludzinski is a member of the Political Research team at Ipsos MORI and manages the monthly *Political Monitor*. He was involved in much of the organisation's political polling during the 2010 General Election, including 'the worm' for the BBC used in the Prime Ministerial Debates and also the series of marginal constituency polls for Reuters.

Roger Mortimore is Director of Political Analysis at Ipsos MORI. He has published numerous books and papers on elections and political marketing, including *Explaining Labour's Landslip* (with Robert Worcester and Paul Baines, 2005), and he is Review Editor of the *International Journal of Public Opinion Research*.

Katy Parry is Research Associate at the University of Liverpool, where she works on the Arts and Humanities Research Council-funded project 'Media Genre and Political Culture'. She is co-author of *Pockets of Resistance*, a study of British media coverage of the Iraq invasion.

Chris Rennard was Director of Campaigns & Elections for the Liberal Democrats from 1989 to 2003 and then party Chief Executive until 2009. He is a member of the House of Lords, speaking mostly on issues of constitutional reform.

Kay Richardson is Reader in Communication Studies at the University of Liverpool. She is the principal investigator on the Arts and Humanities Research Council-funded project 'Media Genre and Political Culture: Beyond the News'.

Tom D. C. Roberts is a doctoral candidate at Macquarie University, Australia, where he is researching the life and legacy of Sir Keith Murdoch. Prior to this, he worked for the UK Press Complaints Commission.

Rosalynd Southern is a doctoral student at the University of Manchester. She is researching the impact of new digital media on campaigning and political engagement, using the 2010 General Election as a case study.

Fabro Steibel is a PhD student at the Institute of Communication Studies, University of Leeds.

Joe Twyman is Director of Political and Social Research at YouGov. He has coordinated operations in a number of countries across the world, including working as a project director for the 2001, 2005 and 2010 British Election Studies.

Stephen Ward is Reader in Politics at the University of Salford. He has written widely on the relationship between the internet and politics, both in Britain and in other countries.

Jenny Watson is Chair of the Electoral Commission, a trustee of the Charities Aid Foundation and currently a board member of the charity Money Advice Trust. She was the last Chair of the Equal Opportunities Commission prior to the creation of the Commission for Equality and Human Rights.

Anthony Wells is Associate Director of Political and Social Research at YouGov, running their regular media polling for News International. He also runs the polling blog UKPollingReport.

Alex Wilson joined the Field Campaigning Department at Conservative Campaign Headquarters in early 2008, working on the opinion research and target seats programme. He is also a local councillor in the London Borough of Redbridge.

Dominic Wring is Reader in Political Communication at Loughborough University. He has published widely on press partisanship and the development of election campaigning.

1
Introduction

Dominic Wring

For the first time in a general election since the hung parliament of 1974 no single party emerged as the winner of the 2010 campaign. The Conservatives came first with 36.1 per cent of the vote (306 seats, up ninety-seven), Labour next on 29 per cent (258 seats, down ninety-one), the Liberal Democrats third with 23 per cent (fifty-seven seats, down five) and the rest on 11.9 per cent (twenty-nine seats, down two). In 2005 a 3 per cent margin of victory had been sufficient to enable Labour to form a government with a comfortable working majority. The electoral arithmetic this time meant that, although the Tories' lead was larger, they won fewer than half the seats necessary to govern alone. And, although a hung parliament had been widely predicted, the reality of it still appeared to come as a surprise to some commentators. What followed was a protracted period of negotiations over several days, principally involving the Conservatives and the Liberal Democrats, which ended in these parties agreeing to join together in a formal Coalition, the first of its kind since 1945. If this was a departure from past practice, then so was the campaign itself, given the arrival of the first ever Prime Ministerial Debates.

The UK General Election of 2010 was always going to be a different kind of campaign once the Labour, Conservative and Liberal Democrat parties had agreed to participate in the Debates. That they took place at all was helped by the fact that this would be the first campaign since 1979 in which there would be three politicians fighting their first election as leader. Furthermore, each believed they could gain leverage from these broadcast encounters: David Cameron was widely viewed as the best communicator; Gordon Brown perceived that his party's trailing in the polls might be offset by his explaining his role during the economic crisis; and Nick Clegg needed little incentive to accept the invitation to participate in programmes that would guarantee him more exposure. Long discussed and eagerly awaited – by the cognoscenti at least – the leaders finally got to confront one other in live televised proceedings on the major networks watched by millions of voters. This in turn created a dynamic whereby a key element of the campaign, polling and media analysis focused on the Debates. This commentary dominated a significant proportion of the formal election period, both during the run-up to and after each of the three encounters between the leaders.

The leaders inevitably made careful preparations for their Prime Ministerial Debates, and this resulted in no obvious gaffes. But the broadcasts, and the first in particular, had a notable impact, which was to elevate the status of the third party leader, Nick Clegg, to something resembling that of his opponents. Significantly, this extended beyond the duration of the debate encounters. Clegg's position in this election was, of course, enhanced because expectations of a hung parliament in which he might play a pivotal role were so widespread. But it was the dynamics of the debate format that afforded the Liberal Democrat leader a huge opportunity, which he duly exploited. Prior to the campaign Clegg had, at times, been overshadowed by the skilled media performances of his deputy, Vince Cable, during the economic crisis. The perceived importance to the party of their partnership was underlined by their joint appearance on the official election battle bus. But Clegg's widely acclaimed success in 'winning' the first Debate with a polished performance altered public and media perceptions of him; in sum, he emerged as a formidable political figure in his own right. This was arguably the key discernible change during the campaign, and one that forced the other parties and their supporters to reassess their own strategies. So-called Cleggmania, the term given to the new enthusiasm for the Liberal Democrats, was greeted with derision in Tory-supporting newspapers, which now began devoting more critical attention to the third party than had been the case in past elections. This produced one of the more lurid and controversial press headlines, courtesy of the *Daily Mail*: 'Clegg in Nazi Slur on Britain.' Not all the additional attention was unwelcome, with broadcasters' coverage of the Liberal Democrats appearing far less perfunctory and now informed by an expectation that the party's surge might seriously reconfigure British politics.

The Prime Ministerial Debates featured a significant amount of policy detail. Yet there was a perception that, both during and, more especially, after the election, the campaign did not properly discuss the substantive issues facing the country following the 2008 economic crisis. This was despite protestations from commentators from the left and right of the political spectrum, as well as the Institute for Fiscal Studies, which called for greater clarity as to what the politicians would actually do with the public finances if they took office. Arguably, the parties were keen to avoid the issue of possible spending cuts because they feared that revealing detailed plans might provide their opponents with ammunition. Debate about the economy, such as it happened, was couched in general terms. Thus, the Conservatives blamed the crisis on the former Chancellor of the Exchequer turned Prime Minister, Gordon Brown, for presiding over a spectacular return to a boom and bust cycle he had once boasted of ending. Brown rebutted this claim by arguing that his decisive actions had averted an even worse outcome, which was, in any case, a global rather than a primarily national phenomenon.

Public frustration with politicians over the economic crisis and assorted other issues periodically registered itself during the campaign, though not in the formal Debates programming, because this allowed little meaningful audience participation. The leaders were, however, confronted by ordinary citizens on other occasions, and these encounters generated publicity from news media keen to expose politicians to scrutiny of this kind. Confrontations between leaders and voters, particularly of an impromptu nature, had been widely reported in previous campaigns. 2010 was slightly different in that the most memorable interaction of this kind came when Gordon Brown met Gillian Duffy, who had been invited by his aide to speak with him on a visit to the Lancashire marginal seat of Rochdale. Their onscreen meeting had led to some disagreement, but the two had parted amicably on camera. However, once inside his departing limousine Brown's tone measurably changed, and his dismissal of Duffy as 'that bigoted woman' was recorded courtesy of the microphone still attached to his lapel. Brown was naturally unaware of this, and that his comments would be subsequently broadcast. The ensuing fallout provided much embarrassment and memorable drama, and dominated the agenda for days, with even the most populist Channel Five news leading on the story.

This volume touches on the subjects discussed above, and other topics, from the perspective of academics as well as the various practitioners responsible for different aspects of the campaign. The opening section is devoted to the first ever Prime Ministerial Debates, and features commentaries from those intimately involved in preparing the way for them to happen. Consideration is also given to the debates' impact in terms of how they were reported and how they were perceived by the public. The following two parts of the book discuss polls and voters, including the perplexing issue of why the apparent increase in support for the Liberal

Democrats during the campaign failed to materialize. Consideration is also given to the key so-called battleground seats and the organization of the electoral process itself. The following section considers the election from the perspective of the party organizers themselves. The next chapters consider national and local efforts to win votes through advertising, as well as offline and online forms of constituency-based campaigning. The closing part of the volume is devoted to analysis of the media's role, starting with the major journalistically generated story of the last parliament, the MPs' expenses affair. Other chapters consider how campaign reporting has changed and also what stories did (and did not) dominate the electoral agenda. Finally, consideration is given to the way in which often pervasive non-news media formats represented the election.

Part I
Debates

2
What Took So Long? The Late Arrival of TV Debates in the UK General Election of 2010

Ric Bailey

> Every party politician that expects to lose tries that trick of debates and every politician who expects to win says no.

So spoke a winning John Major of himself and a losing Neil Kinnock in 1992 (Cockerell, 2010). He demonstrated a consistent belief in the theory five years later, when – behind in the polls – he eventually spoke up in favour of election debates between himself and Tony Blair. Perhaps the 'trick' in 2010 was that the debates only happened because none of the party leaders was confident of victory. At least since the legendary encounter between Kennedy and Nixon in 1960, British general elections have tiptoed into the foothills of discussions about holding debates, only for one or more of those involved to trip over the complicated undergrowth, fall out with each other – or simply reassert self-interest. There is no discussion here of the debates themselves, or any conclusion about whether television election debates are right for the UK or not. This chapter looks at the main hurdles that stood in the way of debates for fifty years and how and why they were overcome at this election. In its conclusion, it briefly assesses the impact of the debates from an audience perspective. But it also analyses some of the objectives of both the broadcasters and the political parties and offers a first-hand account of the negotiations which brought about this UK first.

So why did it take so long for the debates to happen? There are two extraordinarily obvious points to be made about the nature of political parties. First, on the whole, they exist because they don't agree with each other. One of the reasons the formation of the coalition government was so surprising for many people is the assumption that the default position for Westminster politics is conflict and disagreement. What chance, then, that common ground would ever be found over election debates? Second, large political parties are in the election game to win: an overwhelming influence on their view of whether to take part in debates, therefore, was not so much 'are they a good thing?' as 'what will be their impact on our electoral prospects?' So the possibility that all the key players might – at the same time – suddenly believe they had something to gain was never a good bet. Without a history of debates in the UK, the negatives still, in 2009, seemed to outweigh any generalised popular sense that their absence here – unlike, say, in Iran, Mongolia and virtually every other Parliamentary democracy – was causing some sort of democratic deficit.

Certainly, the power of the status quo has been a strong factor for most of the last fifty years. So long as debates had not happened before, it was easier to argue that they were not part of the British tradition and that the time was not right. Political parties all realised that, once the duck was broken (to crash the metaphors), it would be very difficult to return the genie to the bottle. Those who now take the arrival of debates for granted, however, should not forget the sixteen-year gap in the US which followed the Nixon–Kennedy encounters. For most of the twelve UK general elections which had taken place since 1960, it's a fairly straightforward task to explain why debates did not happen. Many fall into one of two categories: the 'John Major' principle, which cautions that, if you are in a winning position, don't risk it; and its close relative, the incumbency advantage, which points out that as Prime Minister you already have the upper hand – don't bestow any sense of equality on your opponents. This strategy was most candidly explained by Harold Wilson's political secretary, Marcia Falkender, when talking about the 1970 election against Ted Heath:

> To appear with Heath on TV would have been giving him a lot of exposure as a potential prime minister and Harold's office would in fact have rubbed off on Heath. Harold decided that was not going to happen. (Cockerell, 2010)

But that does not mean that opposition leaders are necessarily in favour of debates – even when they say they are. Wilson himself and Tony Blair both provided textbook examples of opposition leaders who challenged an incumbent Prime Minister to debate when they were actually less than enthusiastic about the idea themselves. For Wilson in 1964, the strategy worked – he challenged Sir Alec Douglas-Home, who dismissed debates as a 'sort of Top of the Pops contest', allowing the Labour leader to present himself as the more attuned to the modern media world. Privately, however, Wilson admitted, 'I was none too keen on the debates. Some small thing might have gone wrong. I might have got hiccups from smoking a dusty pipe' (Cockerell, 2010). Blair's campaign manager, Peter Mandelson, threw down the gauntlet in 1996, urging the broadcasters to start making the arrangements and the Prime Minister to 'go for it'. John Major took pleasure, on this occasion at least, in outfacing his opponent: 'Tony Blair challenged me to a debate, to his dismay I accepted and to everyone's amusement he then chickened out.' To the amusement only of some, it also led to the Tories deploying an actor dressed as a chicken to follow the future Prime Minister's campaign trail – a stunt lifted, apparently, from the 1992 US Presidential election, when Bush Senior seemed reluctant to debate with Bill Clinton.

For any chance of the first UK debate happening, the political planets always needed to be in a certain alignment. The most promising combination of circumstances was evident in 1997, and before that in 1992 and 1979, elections in which the 'incumbency factor' was not so potent and there was less certainty about the result. It was James Callaghan, behind in the polls in 1979, who became the first Prime Minister to sign up for television debates. Margaret Thatcher was tempted, but a combination of Willie Whitelaw, Lord Thorneycroft and – crucially – her influential media adviser, Gordon Reece, persuaded her otherwise (Butler and Kavanagh, 1997). Another of her advisers, Michael Dobbs, who was to lead the Tory negotiations in 1997, related that 'Gordon realised that there was nothing to be gained by a relatively inexperienced woman going on television against a hugely experienced and avuncular opponent like Jim Callaghan – and particularly when she was pretty well ahead in the polls and expected to win.' In political terms, she was advised that the inclusion of David Steel, the Liberal leader, would cost Conservative votes – a fear echoed thirty years later by David Cameron's deputy chairman, Lord Ashcroft (Ashcroft, 2010).

Once in Downing Street, of course, Mrs Thatcher maintained the party's stance and there was no realistic prospect of debates during the 1980s. As we have seen, John Major's pointed observation on Neil Kinnock's challenge stopped in its tracks any incentive to pursue debates in 1992. But five years later the conditions for achieving them were the best they had ever been, and, indeed, negotiations went far further than at any election until 2010. For the first time, the leaders of the two largest parties both appeared to be in favour. And no-one could question Paddy Ashdown's zeal – 'I would have killed for this opportunity,' the former Marine said of his successor's television appearance. Though Labour was well ahead in the polls and went on to win a landslide, the party's absence from office for 18 years meant that few were entirely confident of the predictability of the result. Crucially, there was an incentive – as there had been for Jim Callaghan in 1979 – for the incumbent to seek a 'game-changer' which outweighed the limited credit accrued as the occupant of Number Ten – another foretaste of 2010 (Butler and Kavanagh, 1980). For the first time, there seemed to be momentum behind debates. On the eve of the campaign, a paper for the Hansard Society, proposing a detailed format, firmly made the case that debates would enhance democracy:

> British politics much needs an injection of stimulating public deliberation...Using the medium of television to bring meaningful, live debate between the candidates for the premiership into the homes of millions of voters is but one step towards creating a more deliberative democracy. (Coleman, 1997)

It was, of course, not to be – a 'missed opportunity of epic proportions', according to one of the key broadcasting executives involved (Tait, 1998). The negotiators of 2009–2010 found valuable lessons in what went wrong, including counting no chickens when party leaders are signed up in principle but not in detail. The first learning point was something which became a prerequisite for even the possibility of election debates: the broadcasters themselves need to get their act together, because, although 'breaking the duck' would require all the relevant parties to be at least persuadable to take the bait, there are a host of practical difficulties which allow an ambivalent party to call a halt to the project without losing too much face. If the parties were willing to move anywhere near the hook in 1997, the broadcasters certainly let them off it. With Sky not yet established in the big league, the finger of blame was pointed at the BBC and ITV/ITN. Each of these news organisations submitted its own separate proposals for a series of two debates. Sky's Adam Boulton, a central figure then, as in 2010, fumed afterwards to the *Independent*: 'In their self-serving attempts to secure the kudos of the debates...they failed to live up to their public service remits' (see also Chapter 3 in this volume).

If the broadcasters' lack of unity provided an excuse, it seems clear the two main parties needed little persuasion to seize it. An internal BBC memo in January 1997 hints at the discussions going on within

Downing Street, implying that John Major's private view on debates was never as enthusiastic as his eventual public stance:

> We have had an informal indication from the Prime Minister that he has a strong preference for long one-on-one interviews during the campaign, and is ill-disposed towards a debate – whatever the format. But we know that some of his advisers are keen that he should do it. (Sloman, 1997)

Similarly, as Labour's lead in the opinion polls grew, the appetite for debates appeared to wane. Lance Price, the party's Director of Communications in 2001, looking back on both that election and 1997, was clear about the political reality: 'when you're out in front why take the risk? Why put yourself through the possibility of something going horribly wrong like that?' (Price, 2005). A further lesson of 1997 was the necessity of starting early. Real negotiations did not begin until February of that year – less than two months from the start of the campaign – and continued into the election period itself. There was a strong suspicion by then that the political parties were playing the broadcasters off against each other.

That election also exposed more keenly than before another potential difficulty – how to accommodate the third party. Various possible formats had floated around over the years – three one-on-one debates, a single debate in which the Lib Dems were involved for only part of the time, even a stopwatch check to give the third party proportionately less time. In 1997, the same BBC memo identified inclusion of the Liberal Democrats as 'the key issue' and spelt out that John Major 'has indicated informally that he would be unwilling to take part in a debate that included Paddy Ashdown' (Sloman, 1997). The Prime Minister did not want to be ganged up on, although the Conservative position did soften on this issue during the last-minute talks. Not surprisingly, the Liberal Democrats have been the party most consistently in favour of election debates – providing, of course, they are part of them. As the 1997 campaign started, they fired a friendly warning shot across BBC bows if there was to be any inkling of acceding to the notion of two-party debates. The chairman of the party's campaign, Lord (Richard) Holme, in a letter of 17 March to Director-General John Birt, indicated that the Liberal Democrats were prepared to be 'flexible on time, format, etc.' – conceding that they did not expect equality: 'Let me emphasise that we are anxious to sort this out without resort to legal proceedings if it is possible.' In fact, by then, the BBC had already been convinced that excluding Mr Ashdown was a legal non-starter – this at a time when the Liberal Democrats held barely a third of the seats they were to have as the 2010 election approached.

Taking account of the nationalist parties in Scotland and Wales is more complex. In their respective nations of the UK, they are, of course, significant players competing with the three largest UK-wide parties. In 1997 there was the added complication that Labour's devolution proposals were a central manifesto commitment and, therefore, an important issue for the Westminster election. In the event, the SNP were judged to have jumped the gun by going to court before the broadcasters had firm plans. Ironically, in 2010, another Scottish judge told the party it had come to court too late. By then, devolution meant that the Westminster election was no longer the moment when the electorates in Scotland, Wales and Northern Ireland were exercising their vote on many domestic issues.

These were some of the difficulties and complications stacked up against those hoping for election debates in 2010, even before any consideration of format, number and length of debates, audiences, moderators, questions, themes, who stands where, who goes first, who goes last... and – crucially – how the negotiations themselves were to be conducted. Two more elections had passed in which the perceptive conclusions of Marcia Falkender, John Major and Lance Price had proved decisive – an incumbent Prime Minister with good expectations of victory was unlikely to risk that double advantage. Not that plans weren't prepared by the broadcasters – as they began to see the advantages of working together – but more in hope than in expectation. During the 'election that never was' in 2007, BBC, ITV and Sky had a brief preliminary exchange to establish that they would work together. In September 2009, a meeting was in the diary between the broadcasters to pull together a joint strategy. Two days before, however, Sky's Head of News, John Ryley, writing in *The Times*, declared that Sky would go it alone and hold debates whether all three leaders turned up or not. There followed several days of public disagreement between the broadcasters. BBC and ITV, while clearly in favour of debates, did not feel they could be part of a political campaign to force the issue and would certainly not use a threat of 'empty-chairing' as an opening gambit. They moved quickly to counter Sky's initiative, writing to the *Times* and sending a joint letter to the parties setting out their agreed position. Sure enough, the Conservatives made it clear they were not going to deal separately. It began to feel like 1997. In fact, the debate about the debates that the spat engendered was in itself quite helpful. The past reluctance of some of the parties was feeding into the new atmosphere festering around the expenses scandals, to create a sense that politicians now had more to do if they were to earn votes and that resisting the demands of public opinion over debates was becoming less acceptable.

After trading sharp but not fatal blows on various radio programmes in early September, Adam Boulton and the author bumped into one another in a corridor at the Labour conference in Brighton at the end of the month. Hostilities were called off, a new meeting arranged. From then on, the three rival broadcasters acted with unprecedented unity for the following eight months. A group of six, two from each organisation, was established and quickly agreed broad principles. First rule – to keep it simple. Mark out the broadcasters' territory and the legal and regulatory landscape, and try to step over the more basic hurdles before they could bog down the negotiations. That meant three debates of the same format, one produced by each organisation, live and in peak time. It meant the broadcasters setting out that this would involve the three UK parties, treated equally. It meant each broadcaster dealing separately with the impartiality issues in Scotland and Wales, keeping those difficulties separate from the main discussions. There was some contact with Channel 4 and Five – but again, the three big broadcasters were reluctant to over-complicate matters.

Exploratory talks were held with the parties individually in early November 2009. Both Labour and the Conservatives suggested some sort of 'independent' body to fill the role played in the US by the Commission on Presidential Debates and previously by the League of Women Voters. The American example was further cited by Labour turning up for preliminary discussions with the weighty 'Memorandum of Understanding' from the Bush–Kerry debates of 2004. The collective heart of the broadcasters sank. Although 'US-style' debates were the tabloid shorthand, they were anxious not to follow that model. Not only were those negotiations tortuous and over-detailed, but that sort of agreement would ignore the strong British tradition of the independence and impartiality of the broadcasters themselves. In the US, the TV companies have always had a 'secondary role'. Alan Schroeder, historian of the debates there, points out that 'negotiating sessions for the Kennedy–Nixon debates started off with all parties at the table, but in the second meeting, the politicos asked the broadcasters to leave the room'. CBS News President, Sig Mickelson, reported that 'when we came back in again, [the politicians] laid down the pattern for debates'. This, says Schroeder, has remained the procedure ever since. 'The campaigns hammer out an agreement that suits their own purposes, which then gets presented to the sponsoring institution as a done deal' (Schroeder, 2008).

ITV, Sky and the BBC were adamant that, if negotiations were going to be successful, the broadcasters had to be in the box-seat. They were not willing to hand over editorial independence to some other body to oversee programmes for which they had a responsibility, both to respective regulators and to their audiences. It was the first example of the broadcasters' unanimity and firmness setting the pattern for the negotiations. It is true that there was also some bilateral discussion between Andy Coulson, David Cameron's communications supremo, and Peter Mandelson. In these secret meetings, reports Lord Mandelson, 'the first task was to negotiate the format...Early on, we agreed on most aspects...' This is, of course, accurate, but leaves the strong impression that the debates were sorted out by a carve-up between the two big parties. In fact, what was agreed was the format the broadcasters had already set out.

It was soon felt there was sufficient common ground to bring everyone together in one room – an extraordinary moment in itself. To build trust, such meetings had to be highly confidential. If any differences became embroiled in the normal party political tussle, the talks would be fatally undermined. The first meetings were at the Royal Institute of British Architects in Portland Place, away from the curious eyes of the rest of Westminster. Later, as the logistics of coordinating diaries became more difficult, the unlikely venue, in the heart of Westminster, but appropriately discreet, was the headquarters of the Mothers' Union. In both places, there was space for the classic negotiation layout: a central plenary area with boardroom-style table, plus smaller 'break-out' rooms where each party could retire for private discussion or to phone base camp. Tellingly, these breakout rooms were barely used throughout the negotiations for more than a few minutes, usually while a concession was being ironed out. On only one occasion, outlined below, did the broadcasters have to become involved in 'shuttle diplomacy' when the parties appeared to be intractably in different positions.

What became fairly clear was that each of the parties had entered the negotiations genuinely with the objective of their being successful – itself a first. If the Conservatives, ahead in the polls, seemed to have most to lose, David Cameron had nailed his colours so firmly to debates during his own leadership campaign that retreat would have been difficult, though not impossible. Gordon Brown had seemed less convinced – when challenged by the Opposition leader in the Commons soon after the Obama–McCain debates in 2008, he was still putting the argument used by Labour since 2001 (see Coleman, 2001)– that the British system is different: 'In America they do not have Question Time every week where we can examine what the different policies of the different parties are.'

Assuming the Prime Minister meant 'Question Time' in the Commons and not the Dimbleby version, there is, of course, a rather obvious flaw in this argument: during Question Time in the Commons, only the policies of the party of government are examined, not those of opposition parties. Labour insiders say a decision was taken to go for debates as early as July 2009 – certainly, by the autumn, Mr Brown had been convinced that the debates were in Labour's interests, despite – by his own admission – acknowledging that he 'wasn't a politician for the television age' (Mandelson, 2010). Labour felt that detailed debate on policy would play to Mr Brown's strengths. It was also why, having appeared to be the most reluctant of the parties to sign up to debates, Labour immediately wanted lots of them – not just the leaders and not just during the election period, but a series of debates starting almost straight away among Cabinet ministers and their shadows. Sensing another fatal complication, the broadcasters insisted that these negotiations were only about leaders and the election period – other proposals were normal business and outside the remit of the joint group. But Labour was on board – not least because, according to one senior election strategist, debates were the cheapest way to reach the electorate for a cash-strapped party.

The technique used to sort out the many differences was textbook negotiating. Just before Christmas, there was an announcement of agreement on the general principles. From then on, the media and virtually everyone else assumed the debates were on – though the negotiators themselves were far less certain of success. There were still more than two months of detailed talks to come about many of the issues which had helped to kybosh debates before. But the public expectation created – not accidentally – was by now putting pressure on all sides to make progress. Fifteen drafts of the joint document were produced between New Year and St David's Day. Each meeting would work through the different elements, signing off what was agreed, exploring differences to narrow them down – setting them aside if impasse was reached. The effect was to build agreement and trust and avoid rows, whittling down arguments until they looked isolated and – quite often with time – less crucial than they'd appeared initially. Despite the constant attention of the press, supposed leaks were speculative and often seemed sourced from people not present at the talks who perhaps felt they should be. The BBC's Head of Political Programmes, Sue Inglish, used her brisk and remorseless chairing skills to maintain the momentum until there was a gradual realisation that the debates were actually going to happen.

The most time-consuming element of the negotiations was around the studio audience. There was agreement from the start that there would be one – but its role and composition caused anxiety and was discussed at most of the lengthy fortnightly meetings. From the broadcasters' perspective, there was no desire to reproduce the BBC *Question Time* formula. What would make these debates distinctive was the interaction between the leaders – there would be other opportunities in the campaign for them to be challenged more directly by the voters. At the same time, having them answer questions from professional journalists – the usual US formula – did not seem appropriate either, and contributed to the perception that presidential encounters have often felt more like joint press conferences than genuine debates. The UK broadcasters' objective was maximum engagement between the leaders. It was agreed that the questions would come from the audience, but after many hours it was accepted that questioners would not come back with their own views and – apparently more controversial – that the audience would be asked not to applaud during the debate.

There are arguments in favour of this approach – it saves precious time for the debate itself, allowing as many questions as possible, and it discourages rhetorical flourishes and playing to the gallery. But this was one of a number of areas where some of the parties needed reassurance if progress was to be made. They felt that the viewing audience at home should be able to make up its own mind and not be influenced by the instant reaction of a small, vocal sample. In truth, the restrictions went further than the broadcasters felt appropriate for a television age when the public expect to be more than mute recipients – but these were not objections of principle which encroached on editorial freedom.

Oddly, although the audience's role was very limited, how it was made up was still a matter of acute concern, especially for Conservative and Labour negotiators. If people were going to just sit there and not even applaud, why did it matter so much who they were? After all, the actual questions would be selected by an editorial panel, sifting from those submitted both by the studio audience and by emails. But the parties were exposing their leaders to a new environment in high-risk circumstances and were very familiar with the unpredictability of a studio audience, not least the real terrors of BBC Question Time. Too many silently shaking heads, a relay of raised eyebrows or, worst, maybe even a ripple of mocking chuckles – these were negotiations taking place against a background where the political establishment felt itself at bay from an angry public. The broadcasters had attempted to dilute the parties' fears by delegating selection of the audience to ICM, a polling company which everyone would trust. But there was still much fraught discussion over what 'representative' meant – and some persuasion needed that an initial insistence on an audience of 'undecideds' ran the risk of delivering a studio half full of bored looking 'don't cares'. As the worries over audience make-up threatened to bog down the negotiations, the broadcasters played a trump card. Martin Boon of ICM was brought in to describe in painstaking detail his methodology – fine adjustments made, differential ratios calculated, complex formulae integrated... eyes glazed, Blackberries clicked, discussion eventually moved on.

Much was made of the so-called 76 rules (see Appendix: Prime Ministerial Debates) governing the encounters when the final agreement was published in early March, with fears that they would paralyse debate. Compared with the thirty-odd pages of the US Memorandum of Understanding – 'like the Internal Revenue Code' according to Ross Perot's lawyer in 1992 – the number of rules was actually minimal, barely more than a dozen. The majority of the agreement was made up of clauses simply describing what the debates would look like, how they'd be organised, descriptive details for a format being constructed from scratch after fifty years' gestation. The atmosphere of the negotiations – considering the high stakes and the divergent interests of the participants – was genuinely good-natured and cooperative. There was the sort of bonding that attaches to small groups locked away from the rest of the world – all-party incompetence at operating various coffee machines, competing excuses for lateness and the growth of an exclusive shorthand language ('die-in-a-ditch' indicated an issue on which there would be no compromise). More significant, though, was the slow mutual dawning that something groundbreaking might be within reach.

For some, more than others, the detail could be mind-numbing: Andy Coulson occasionally had the air of a man who wished he was somewhere else – and yet it was he who, following one period of particularly close textual analysis, made quite a stirring speech, reminding everyone of the historic achievement within grasp. The Prime Minister's team in particular began to rather enjoy themselves – astonishingly, this counted as light relief from the pressure-cooker intensity of Downing Street. 'We don't get out much,' said Justin Forsyth, Director of Strategic Communications – only half-joking. There was only one misunderstanding which, for a while, threatened to derail the entire enterprise. The broadcasters had drawn straws (actually bits of paper in a mug) for the order of debates, but also for the themes allocated to half of each debate. There had been much to-ing and fro-ing over how these themes would work – the proportions and timing, what they did and did not include, what they were called. David Muir, the Prime Minister's Director of Strategy and debate negotiator, insisted late in the day that the economy was the most important issue and should, there-fore, be the theme of the first debate. The broadcasters felt the proc-ess had been agreed and the economy drawn for the last debate – the BBC's. By mid-February, it was the only outstanding issue – apart from a largely altruistic and cooperative exploration of the positioning of the leaders' podiums, which would take account of the Prime Minister's restricted vision.

There followed an agonising fortnight, during which the broadcasters began to fret about getting on with the practicalities – such as the com-plicated business of finding the audience in time – and there were real fears that six months' work was heading down the pan, accompanied by much public opprobrium. One constant source of nervousness for everyone but Labour was the inbuilt advantage the Prime Minister had in setting the actual election date. By late February, the announcement could have come any day, with no deal done. Then, on 2 March, the dif-ficulty melted away, as Labour, scarcely covering its retreat on what had hitherto been a 'die-in-a-ditch' matter, accepted that economic mat-ters would be the theme for the third and final debate. Of course, the agreement wasn't perfect. But the priority – given the history – was to make sure the debates happened, and for that compromise was neces-sary, while maintaining the first principles unchanged. Were the policy issues properly explored to the benefit of the electorate? Research by YouGov for the three broadcasters indicated, very consistently across the debates, that more than three-quarters of those polled thought they were a 'positive addition to the democratic process'.[1]

Although there's little dispute the debates had an enormous impact on the campaign, it's less clear-cut whether or not they affected the result. The same research suggests around 10 per cent of those polled changed their vote because of the debates.[2] Clearly, the increase in turnout of 4 per cent cannot be linked directly to the debates, but the relatively higher increase – 7 per cent – among 18 to 24-year-olds is worth putting alongside claims that the debates had more impact on the young than on older voters. Jay G. Blumler, contributing to *Leaders in the Living Room*, contends that the 'youngest voters, those aged 18 to 24 years old, seemed almost to have formed a special relationship with the Prime Ministerial debates' (Coleman et al., 2011). A further series of surveys by YouGov, commissioned for the same paper, makes the case for the debates having a disproportionate impact on young voters: for instance, 55 per cent of 18 to 24-year-olds said they had become 'more interested' in the campaign after the first debate, compared with only 24 per cent of those aged over 55; after the second debate, more than 80 per cent of those aged 18 to 39 – compared with 58 per cent of older voters – felt they had learned more about the parties' policies; half of the 18 to 39-year-olds said the debates helped them make up their minds how to vote – nearly 10 per cent more than the oldest age group.[3] The debates also seem to have encouraged people to discuss the election with each other: 87 per cent of all the respondents to YouGov's post-election survey said they had talked about the debates with others – the figure among the youngest voters (on a relatively small sample) was 92 per cent.

So the debates had an impact on the electorate, but did they properly scrutinise the would-be Prime Ministers? Was the format – much criticised in advance – a hindrance, and were other valuable forms of election journalism 'squeezed' by the debates? (Kavanagh and Cowley, 2010). Those are questions for elsewhere – but certainly, for next time, there will be areas to examine in deciding how debates may play their part. First, an election following coalition government provides an entirely different context; second, the complications regarding Scotland and Wales will be greater still when a general election is due to coincide with the elections to Holyrood and the Senedd; third, the evidence of the broadcasters' post-debate research suggested that viewers felt there should be more of a role for the audience – not so much, it turned out, that applause should be allowed, but that questioners should have the chance to respond to the leaders; journalistically, some felt there needed to be greater flexibility for the moderators to follow up and test arguments, especially in those areas where the leaders themselves may be reluctant to engage with each other; there may also be a case for having more than one format for debates, such as the 'town hall' style, introduced to the US presidential elections in 1996. No doubt there will be arguments both for more and for fewer debates, the latter from those who felt they were too dominant in the 2010 campaign.

But what will be crucially different in 2015 – or perhaps before – is that it will not be the first time voters see Prime Ministerial debates. Consequently, it will certainly be more difficult – though not impossible – for any party leader to turn down the invitation. Public expectation and the strongly positive reaction to the 2010 debates will weigh more heavily against the sort of calculation that made incumbents – or those already confident of victory – reluctant to risk their status in such an unpredictable environment. Although much of the analysis of the debates concentrated on 'winners' and 'losers', performance and style, the debates themselves were overwhelmingly about policy. Four and a half hours of prime-time discussion of the economy, immigration, foreign policy, health, education, crime, etc. – watched by two-thirds of the people who were about to vote. It will not be easy to claim again that such debates should not be part of the British electoral tradition.

Notes

Thanks are due to David Levy and James Painter at the Reuters Institute for the Study of Journalism at Oxford University, where this chapter was researched and written. My thanks also to David Jordan, the BBC's Director of Editorial Policy, for allowing me time away from the office – and to him, Sue Inglish and Tom Bailey for reading earlier drafts and making helpful suggestions. I'm particularly grateful, as ever, to David Cowling and his colleagues in the BBC's Political Research Unit. Special thanks to Professor Vernon Bogdanor for his encouragement and stimulating ideas.

1. The actual approval figures for each of the debate programmes were: ITV 78 per cent, Sky 79 per cent and BBC 77 per cent, according to YouGov polling for the three broadcasters. Fieldwork for ITV was 15–19 April 2010, 1083 adults; Sky 22–26 April, 1092 adults; and BBC 29–30 April, 1028 adults.
2. Figures for each debate were: ITV 12 per cent, Sky 9 per cent and BBC 9 per cent. Fieldwork same as for note 1.
3. These figures are derived from five national internet surveys: pre the debates (1455 respondents, 18+), after each of the three debates (ITV 2018, Sky 2072, BBC 2125 respondents) and after polling day (2113 respondents). For more on this see Bailey, 2011 and Coleman et al (2011).

References

Ashcroft, M. (2010) *Minority Verdict: The Conservative Party, The Voters and the 2010 Election*. London: Biteback.
Bailey, R. (2011) 'The Prime Ministerial Debates – are they here to stay?', Reuters Institute for the Study of Journalism, due Summer 2011.
Butler, D. and Kavanagh, D. (1980) *The British General Election of 1979*. Basingstoke: Macmillan.
Butler, D. and Kavanagh, D. (1997) *The British General Election of 1997*. Basingstoke: Macmillan.
Cockerell, M. (2010) 'Why 2010 will see the first TV leaders election debate', BBC Online, 9 April.
Coleman, S. (1997) *Televised Leaders' Debates – an Evaluation and a Proposal*. London: Hansard Society, March.

Coleman, S. (2001) *Televised Leaders' Debates Revisited: UK 2001 – A Debate Odyssey*. London: Hansard Society, March.

Coleman, S. (ed.) (2011) *Leaders in the Living Room: Prime Ministerial Debates of 2010: Evidence, Evaluation and Some Recommendations*. Oxford: Reuters Institute for the Study of Journalism.

Kavanagh, D. and Cowley, P. (2010) *The British General Election of 2010*. Basingstoke: Macmillan.

Mandelson, P. (2010) *The Third Man*. London: Harper Press.

Price, L. (2005) *The Spin Doctor's Diary*. London: Hodder & Stoughton.

Schroeder, A. (2008) *Presidential Debates: Fifty Years of High Risk TV*. 2nd edn. New York: Columbia University Press.

Sloman, A. (1997) 'Party Leader Debates', internal memorandum, BBC archive, 9 January.

Tait, R. (1998) 'The Debate That Never Happened: Television and the Party Leaders, 1997', in Crewe, I. Gosschalk, B. and Bartle, J. (eds) *Political Communications – Why Labour Won the General Election of 1997*. London: Frank Cass.

3
The Election Debates: Sky News' Perspective on their Genesis and Impact on Media Coverage

Adam Boulton and Tom D.C. Roberts

Britain's General Election in 2010 was unique. For the first time ever the three main UK party leaders took part in live debates on television – fifty years after the first ever televised Presidential debate in the United States between John F. Kennedy and Richard M. Nixon. This chapter falls into two sections. First there is a description of how the television debates came to happen from the perspective of Sky News, which is widely credited with playing a decisive role in bringing them about. This is followed by an examination of the impact of the televised debates on the coverage given to the general election campaign by the rest of the news media, especially the national press.

Over the past fifty years there have been many attempts to organise televised debates between party leaders. All of them were unsuccessful until the 2009/2010 cycle. The failures resulted from an inability of the relevant politicians to agree a suitable format with the broadcasters. For most of this period the chances of agreement were further stymied by the rigidities of electoral law. Under the old Representation of the People Act, equivalent candidates had an effective veto on any debates; by refusing to take part they would render them unbalanced under the terms of the law.

At least one of the candidates usually felt that it would not be to their advantage to facilitate the debate. Most often this was the incumbent Prime Minister, who resisted debating his or her opponents because it would raise them up to an equal level. But, in the run-up to the 1997 election, Tony Blair was so far ahead in the opinion polls that he rejected Prime Minister John Major's challenge with the condescending words 'nice try'. As a result, campaign events were enlivened first by the appearance of Tory chickens (or rather people in chicken suits) outside Labour events and then by Labour foxes to chase them away.

Like the politicians, the broadcasters also had their rivalries. Their competing debate programme bids were skilfully played against each other by party officials to ensure stalemate. Prior to the launch of Sky News in 1989, the BBC and ITV/ITN were the only broadcasters interested in staging debates. For a long time after that, the terrestrial TV companies regarded putative election debates as theirs by right. A key factor in the success of 2010 was that the broadcasters put aside their differences at an early stage to negotiate as a bloc (BBC/Sky News/ITV) across the table with a bloc of political parties (Labour/Conservative/Liberal Democrat). This reflected the recognition by the terrestrial broadcasters of the presence by then of multichannel television and rolling news in the majority of British homes.

It is interesting to note that, in the UK, TV debates have mostly been regarded as a matter for the broadcasters and the politicians to sort out between themselves. This is in contrast to the United States, where civic-minded organisations such as the League of Women Voters had previously taken the burden of responsibility away from the TV networks. In Britain, *The Times* newspaper has probably been the strongest independent champion of leaders' debates at successive elections, including drawing up plans to stage them.[1] Previous attempts to secure debates had also run into difficulty because the negotiations started too late, typically around the time that the election was called. By this stage the parties had already committed their resources to planned campaigns and were reluctant to have them derailed by a major unpredictable factor such as debates. Whether or not candidates were willing to take part also inevitably became a political football in the campaign, just about destroying any chance of agreement.

The Sky campaign

From its launch, Sky News had consistently advocated that leaders' debates should take place at election time. It also judged that agreement would only be achieved in isolation from the political campaign. By early 2009 there appeared to be a window of opportunity, because the next election seemed increasingly likely to be called at full term, more than a year hence. Sky also felt that it needed to reassess its approach to covering the next general election because of the decline in both voter turnout and viewer interest over recent campaigns. On 6 April 2009 John Ryley, the head of Sky News, circulated an internal discussion document by email to the most senior editorial staff involved in political coverage. It ran to eight single-spaced pages and contained the skeleton for what became the Sky News Leaders' Debate Campaign. Ryley proposed mobilising as many Sky News, BSkyB and News Corp resources as possible to create momentum for a televised leadership debate, stressing that this would increase engagement with the electoral process among jaded voters. He argued that such a campaign chimed with a populist sentiment that demanded politicians be held more accountable following the expenses scandal.

Sky envisioned a fresh approach to securing debates to cut through the Gordian knot which had paralysed previous attempts. Initial negotiations should take place *independently* of the parties and be supported by legal opinion. And, while Sky News was keen to be at the vanguard of the campaign, it accepted that any debates would be a public good, most likely facilitated by individual broadcasters but made openly available. Mounting a collaborative approach – Sky, BBC and ITV – from the start would provide the best possible chance of success. Exchanges between the recipients quickly concluded that securing television debates would be the most appropriate way for Sky News to try to enhance voter engagement. And, with the full support of BSkyB at corporate level, it was decided to launch the campaign in early September 2009, when the political year started again after the long summer recess.

Sky also significantly toughened up the tactics it would employ. As a result of the changes in electoral law, party leaders could no longer veto a debate by refusing to take part, provided that they had been invited fairly to do so. It was decided to turn the tables by stating that Sky News was going to stage a leaders' debate, and leaving it up to the individual leaders whether they turned up or not. It was hoped David Cameron and Nick Clegg would take part because both had supported the idea of debates in principle, while Gordon Brown had never been as intractably opposed as his predecessor. During the summer Sky discussed what it was planning to do privately with representatives of all the parties. As an independent twenty-four-hour news channel, Sky News was free to pursue its objective more aggressively than a traditional public service broadcaster. Sky was prepared to take the risk of staging an open leaders' debate, but would anybody turn up? By the end of July Sky had been given private commitments that Clegg and Cameron would debate each other even if Brown refused to participate. The pivotal discussion took place al fresco over lunch at the Inn The Park restaurant, St James' Park, between Andy Coulson, David Cameron's Head of

Communications, and Adam Boulton and Jon Levy, Sky News' Political Editor and Executive Producer for politics respectively.

Coulson committed Cameron unconditionally to the debate, provided that Sky News would state publicly that Brown had been invited to take part should he decline to do so. This presented no problem for Sky News, since it was already dedicated to campaigning for the debate or debates with maximum openness. Coulson also expressed the view that the Conservatives were not interested in negotiating with individual broadcasters. He wanted the TV companies to sort out their differences and to come back with firm proposals as a bloc. Independently, the other parties reiterated this view. Unbeknown to Sky News, the BBC was also in discussions with the parties about staging a series of six BBC exclusive leaders' debates both before and during the election campaign. Only the Brown camp expressed any enthusiasm for this proposal.

In July 2009, BBC and ITV news executives wrote jointly to John Ryley inviting Sky News to discussions about possible debates in October after the party conferences. Ryley accepted, even though it was evident that this invitation was something of an afterthought. He did not inform them of the already well-advanced plans for the Sky Campaign. On 2 September 2009 Sky News launched the Leaders' Debate Campaign – on air, online and in the press. On television we broadcast a number of reports and discussions about election debates. Online we launched a petition to sign up in support of an election debate. John Ryley authored an opinion piece for *The Times*: 'Who'll show up for the TV showdown? Party leaders are cordially invited to take part in the democratic process, they'll be punished by the public if they don't.' Ryley announced: '[T]oday, I have written to Gordon Brown, David Cameron and Nick Clegg, informing them that Sky will be hosting a live debate between them during the election campaign.'[2] He also committed to host separate debates in Scotland and Wales, and confirmed this in writing to the SNP and Plaid Cymru leaders the same week.

Laying out the campaign, the head of Sky News confirmed that it was an initiative in the public interest, not an attempt at 'an exclusive'. 'I also recognise that – however much I might wish it were other – a televisual moment of such importance cannot be "owned" by any one broadcaster. We will, therefore, offer the debate live and unedited to any of our competitors that want to run it. We are ready to sit down with them to discuss the timing and the staging: this debate must be about empowering the British people; egos and self interest must be set aside by us all.'[3] Within twenty-four hours Cameron and Clegg had publicly agreed to take part. Gordon Brown said it was 'not the time' to make the decision. BBC and ITV executives reacted with 'fury', according to news reports. One ITV spokesman described Sky's move as 'childish' and 'a marketing stunt'.[4] The BBC expressed disappointment, arguing that Sky had damaged the notional joint approach by the broadcasters to secure debates. Its invitation to the October broadcasters' meeting was withdrawn. However, informal contacts between broadcasters and with politicians continued through the party conference season. Gradually the BBC and ITV came to accept that Sky wanted to work with them rather than to compete, but that, as Adam Boulton told BBC Radio 4, its campaign had 'kick-started' getting debates.

Gordon Brown's participation in the debates was the remaining holdout, as became clear in an ugly on-air exchange between Brown and Adam Boulton during Labour's 2009 party conference. Many believe that Brown had planned to make a challenge to the other leaders to debate the centrepiece of his Leader's Speech in Brighton. However, there was no such challenge in his address on 29 September – perhaps because he felt the Sky campaign had stolen his thunder. Brown's speech was in any case overshadowed by the announcement at 10 pm that evening by the *Sun*, Britain's biggest-circulation daily newspaper, that it was switching its editorial support from Labour to the Conservatives.

The *Sun* is wholly owned by News Corporation, which has a controlling share of BSkyB plc, Sky News' parent company, but the two are entirely independent of each other editorially. Indeed, the *Sun* only told Sky News of its switch at the same time as it told the BBC, one hour before it was announced. But these subtleties seemed to be entirely overlooked by Brown when he confronted Boulton during a round of live breakfast-time interviews the following morning. Seemingly conflating the *Sun*'s offence with Sky News' questions about the debates, the Prime Minister told Boulton 'You sound like a political propagandist yourself' before storming off without first detaching himself from his microphone. The *Evening Standard*'s front page headline boomed that Brown had suffered a televisual 'meltdown'.[5] But three weeks later Brown's spokesman announced that, subject to negotiations, he would agree to debate with Clegg and Cameron during the upcoming election campaign.

The negotiations

The broadcasters soon managed to form a common front behind agreed proposals for three debates to be held under the same rules. Each organisation nominated two production executives for the negotiating team: Sue Inglish and Ric Bailey from the BBC, Chris Birkett and Jon Levy for

Sky News and Michael Jermey and Jonathan Munro from ITV. Two of Gordon Brown's special advisers, David Muir and Justin Forsyth, represented Labour. The other parties fielded communications professionals: Coulson and Michael Salter for the Conservatives and Jonny Oates for the Lib Dems. Channel Four requested to be part of the group and then withdrew to pursue its own ideas. By general consent, Channel Four subsequently staged the first televised debate of the Election Campaign (actually just before it officially started) between the Treasury spokesmen Alistair Darling, George Osborne and Vince Cable, moderated by Krishnan Guru-Murthy. This left a fairly simple prospect of three debates each to be staged by ITV, the BBC and Sky. Each broadcaster had different objectives, but these were accommodated by their competitors.

Both Sky News and the BBC took a public service approach, making 'their' debate available live to others. ITV had long insisted that it would only surrender prime airtime to a 'live exclusive'. In the event, BBC 2 rebroadcast all three debates the same day at 11.15 pm after *Newsnight*. Sky News and the BBC News Channel each carried the other's debate live, and rebroadcast the ITV debate. It was left to each organisation to honour its obligations to the parties in Scotland, Wales and Northern Ireland. There was some legal sabre-rattling from nationalist parties. In the end all three channels staged live televised debates between these nations' main party leaders nationally: Belfast 22 April (UTV); Belfast 4 May (BBC1 NI); Glasgow 20 April (STV/ITV1); Edinburgh 25 April (Sky News); Edinburgh 2 May (BBC1 Scotland); Cardiff 18 April (Sky News); Cardiff 20 April (ITV1 Wales); and Pontardawe 2 May (BBC1 Wales).

It took from October until mid-February to secure full agreement on the debates with the three main UK parties. Throughout that period, regular weekly meetings took place in secret, first in rooms at RIBA, just up from BBC Broadcasting House, and subsequently at the Mothers' Union in Great Peter Street, close to 4 Millbank, the broadcasters' shared base in Westminster. Most of the discussion was about detail: the nature of the staging, the lighting, the presenters, the audience, the camera shots, the speaking order, and so on. (The full list of guidelines is reproduced in the Appendix.) Perhaps surprisingly, there was little debate about who should participate and on what terms. It was accepted from the outset that there would be three debates, each featuring the Conservatives, Labour and Liberal Democrats on equal terms. With hindsight, Conservatives, led by Lord Ashcroft and Conservativehome.com, have criticised the ceding of parity to Nick Clegg.[6] But this can be taken as an indication of the commitment to hold the debates in all three camps, since any attempt to downgrade a participant would have resulted in a legal logjam.

From one perspective it can be said simply that the leaders' debates happened in 2010 because, for the first time ever, all three of them were willing to take part – greatly to the credit of David Cameron, Nick Clegg and Gordon Brown, in the authors' view. It should also be recognised that a three-way debate reflected the trend towards multi-party plurality in British politics. In 1959, the closest UK general election to the first US televised debate, Conservatives and Labour combined took 93.2 per cent of the votes cast; but by 2005, the last UK election without debates, this had fallen to just 67.6 per cent. It was 65.1 per cent in 2010. In this century around a third of the vote goes to 'third forces'. The presence on the debate stage of the leader of the largest 'third force' was consistent with this trend.

On 21 December 2009, the winter solstice, the debate negotiators, both TV and party political, announced a joint agreement in principle that three Clegg/Cameron/Brown debates would take place during the 2010 General Election campaign. Details of themes, locations and dates were perforce left open, since the Prime Minister had not yet determined when polling day would be. As it turned out, these issues were more than technicalities. There was a hiatus of almost a month on the issue of themes. Labour had consistently favoured themes for debate, while the Conservatives wanted open discussion. A compromise was reached: half of each debate would be devoted to questions on one of three agreed themes – domestic affairs, foreign affairs and the economy. The broadcasters drew lots twice, for order of debates and for order of subjects. This resulted in the sequence of first debate: ITV, domestic; second debate: Sky News, foreign; third debate: BBC, economy. Initially this was endorsed by the three parties, but, after consultations with the Prime Minister, the Labour team announced that the order was now unacceptable – the economy had to be the theme for the first debate. Substantively this only mattered seriously to Brown, but to backtrack at this late stage would have undermined the principles of mutual consent on which the whole debate agreement was based. Neither the Liberal Democrats not Tories were inclined to give way. A four-week standoff ensued before Brown relented and accepted the original order of themes. The announcement of final agreement was made at the beginning of March.

The debates

The first ever UK general election leaders' debate took place on 15 April 2010 at Granada Studios in Manchester, moderated by Alastair Stewart of ITV News. On 22 April, Adam Boulton moderated the Sky News Leaders'

Debate at the Arnolfini Centre in Bristol. David Dimbleby moderated the BBC debate on 29 April at the University of Birmingham. Each debate lasted ninety minutes, without commercial breaks, and accommodated eight questions from an independently selected and demographically representative local audience (plus up to four questioners nominated by the broadcaster). The debates respected the commitment to distinct themes – immigration was the only issue raised explicitly in all three debates. The debates were a spectacular success for British television in terms of impact, audiences and engaging the electorate. The first debate was watched by 9.6 million viewers, the second by 4.2 million and the third by 8.6 million. The debates were also broadcast on BBC and Independent Radio and on C-SPAN in the US. The Sky News debate enjoyed a record audience for the channel; it was broadcast live in HD as well (and watched in HD in 68 per cent of HD-enabled homes). The debate was also recorded in 3D.

Having campaigned so hard for the debates, Sky News took a rigidly disciplined approach to staging the Bristol debate. Unlike the BBC and ITV, Sky located its debate in a relatively small cockpit theatre, the moderator seated with back to the audience directly facing the leaders, each standing behind a podium. This gave a stark intimacy to the Bristol event that was lacking in Birmingham and Manchester. Sky conducted around half a dozen full debate rehearsals in studios mocked up to precisely represent the Bristol theatre.

Sky News also devoted great efforts to question selection, convening around five full meetings of the official certified question selection panel.

The agreed guidelines stipulated that the questions had to be posed by the audience without coaching from the broadcaster. However, the audiences also had to be recruited by an independent body to reflect the electoral demographics of the local area. In spite of the huge public interest in the debates, this meant that many of those who had the privilege of witnessing the event live were comparatively lukewarm about being there and often uninterested in asking questions. Sky News solicited questions from around 300 people who made up the local audience panel.

Each broadcaster was also allowed to add a maximum of four questioners from its general viewership. Sky News also solicited questions via its website, and subsequently went through over 10,000 submitted questions. Questioners chosen in this way took part in the Sky debates in Bristol, Edinburgh and Cardiff.

Even while the programme was live on air, the Sky News producers were still sifting questions to be asked according to the ground already covered by the leaders. The moderator was informed of changes through his talkback earpiece.

In this way the Sky News debate posed probably the most controversial and pointed question of all the debates: the so-called Pope Question – whether the leaders welcomed the upcoming visit to Britain of Benedict XVI. All three leaders commented to Adam Boulton immediately after the debate that they had not anticipated the question and had been momentarily flummoxed by it. At the same time they commented that it was a legitimate issue in the Foreign Affairs debate.

Adam Boulton was on the Sky News question panel. But none of the moderators could raise questions of their own in the way that they would normally as TV journalists and interviewers. Instead, moderating the debates was largely a technical exercise of ensuring that the participants kept to the agreed order and timings – while also trying to make the flowing discussion as accessible as possible to the general viewer.

Boulton tested the limits of the moderators' role when a question was asked on MPs' ethics on the day that the *Daily Mail* and the *Daily Telegraph* both carried negative stories about Nick Clegg.[7] In a full round of answers none of the leaders had dealt with this issue, so Boulton referred directly to the *Telegraph* when bringing in Clegg. The Liberal Democrats did not lodge an official complaint with Sky News, but there were several hundred complaints to Ofcom. Although Ofcom acknowledged that it had little jurisdiction over the debates, it subsequently ruled that Boulton had acted within the relevant guidelines and did not uphold the complaints.

The media reaction

Following Sky News' September 2009 initiative in pushing for the debates, the press reaction was largely supportive, though mixed with reservations as well as some outright attacks. The *Financial Times*, then still supporting Labour, considered that, although the campaign was 'wrapped up in the gimmickry of modern television', it was 'a serious and welcome initiative'. The 'traditional line' of refusal, that televised debates would lead to the 'presidentialisation' of British politics, was 'high-minded, but quaint'. Participation by all three leaders, the hesitant Brown in particular, was required; after all, 'The great British television-watching public deserve better than an empty chair.'[8]

The *Economist* too felt that the 'arguments trotted out against debates are weak' while it was 'amazing that, in 2009, Britain is still debating debates'. Instead, 'a live showdown might help to excite a worryingly apathetic electorate.' Brown should stop 'dragging his feet' – following his disastrous experiments with new media, 'taking on Mr Cameron and Mr Clegg might soften his aloof image.'[9] The Labour stalwart *Daily Mirror* also saw an opportunity for Brown if he decided to participate. Among the '10 things' the Prime Minister had to do to save his party, the paper's political editor, Kevin Macguire, advised him to agree to participate in the debates and call the three broadcasters immediately to tell them so. In Maguire's view, the chance to bash his opponents in the forum of the history-making 'ding-dongs' made the decision a 'no-brainer'.[10]

A more nuanced view was explored by Andrew Rawnsley in the *Observer* under the headline 'Will TV debates change the face of the election?', published the day after Brown, now 'so unpopular that he has nothing to lose', confirmed his participation.[11] The debates were likely to be 'the defining event of the election campaign' for Clegg and Cameron. However, for the electorate they would be a 'mixed blessing' if the electoral coverage trend of recent years towards greater concentration on the 'personalities at the top' continued 'at the expense of everything else'. For both the party machines and media, the debates would become 'the hinge occasions of the campaign, the crucial encounters on which political fortunes will be won or lost'. As to the events' wider success and importance, Rawnsley hedged his bets: 'If we are unlucky, leaders' debates will not be an enhancement of democracy, but a trivialising parody of it' with a focus 'on shallow personality issues, the colour of the candidates' ties, and arguments about whether they should use lecterns or not. If we are fortunate, however, leaders' debates will prove to be a welcome novelty to Britain and a refreshment of voter engagement.' Rawnsley signed off with the hope that the events would provide 'a robust interrogation of the candidates' characters, philosophies and policies, a stress test of those who aspire to govern us that makes a powerful contribution towards helping the electorate to decide...'

The *Independent*'s chief political commentator was having none of it, though. In twelve hundred barbed words under the headline 'The last thing we need is a televised election debate',[12] Steve Richards set out his prediction of broadcaster disagreements and endless negotiating. A focus on the trivialities of the format and events themselves would be the 'only talking point', while the big political issues would not 'get a look in'. The whole process would be 'an anti-climax'. With confidence, Richards signed *his* piece off with the unequivocal assertion: 'Do not believe for one moment that the televised debates would do anything to enhance Britain's fragile democracy.'[13] Fast forward to the day of the election itself, and readers of the *Independent* would be forgiven for scratching their heads as they digested the newspaper's front page. Under a banner headline declaring 'THE PEOPLE'S ELECTION: On Polling Day, 15 reasons to celebrate a campaign that, with your help, could change the face of British politics for ever', listed in pole position were:

1   THE LEADERS' DEBATES

The main party leaders spoke largely in calculated soundbites and platitudes in their three showdowns, yet the effect of their communicating directly to millions of voters was electrifying. Nearly 10 million people watched the first debate – and within 24 hours the British political landscape had been transformed.[14]

Richards had at least moderated his view by then. The debates 'were much better' than he had feared: 'meaty, substantial events that conveyed something about the three individuals and what they represent'.[15]

Readers of the *Guardian* may also have experienced some confusion on picking up their paper the day after the first ITV debate. Marina Hyde, having chosen to watch the debate in a West End sports bar, concluded amongst other criticisms that those who had 'nurtured fantasies of politically re-engaged punters...were in for a disappointment'.[16] These views ran consistent with her original questioning, when Sky News launched its initiative, of whether 'anyone one might care to know socially [would] actually watch the thing?' Hyde had also predicted that 'you'll be weeping with boredom before the first merciful ad break,' espousing the view that the 'whole pointless idea' should be dropped.[17] However, those turning back to the post-debate front page leading paragraph would read Patrick Wintour's account of 'an electrifying, fast-moving, 90-minute primetime broadcast... [that had] focused on domestic issues, especially crime, immigration, education and cleaning up politics – but rapidly spread right across the political canvas'.[18]

For an election campaign period which had, up until the point of the first debate, failed to engage the electorate or communicate issues in an attention-grabbing way, the front pages of 16 April revealed the sudden shift and the re-centring of political debate back into the public sphere. Despite having a crippling volcanic ash cloud as competition, from the *Financial Times* to the *Daily Star* coverage of the debate made the front page. For the *Sun*, everyone was 'PARALYSED BY HOT AIR'. (It is fascinating to note that the *Daily Star*, usually the national daily least likely to deviate from celebrity exposé and human interest front page leads, also gave equally high prominence to reports of the two further debates.[19]) Although, as media commentators wryly stressed, the assessments of who 'won' each debate remained curiously in line with the particular newspaper's political allegiance,[20] the phenomenon that was quickly termed 'Cleggmania' left the press playing catch-up.

Having watched the same live broadcast of the same leaders answering the same questions, each viewer was empowered to make his or her own decision unmediated by comment and editorial skewing. For Channel 4's Jon Snow, not a fan of the 'wretched TV debates' which in his view drained the 'lifeblood' out of the campaign, this typified the 'dreadful election' of the tabloids: 'What did they do? They told their readers that the viewers were wrong. When the viewer had thought that somebody had won they were then told by the media, the tabloids, they were wrong...There was a marvellous moment where the *Daily Mirror* said Brown had won and the *Sun* said that Cameron had won despite the polls saying Clegg had won.'[21]

But it was not just the printed press that would prove to perform below expectations. Before the debates took place, the 2010 General Election was heralded as the occasion when the internet and social media would break through as the most important form of political communication in Britain. Gordon Brown's pollster Deborah Mattinson had declared 2010 as the 'Mumsnet election'[22] and Google and Facebook put commercial rivalry aside to launch the first Digital Debate.[23] Four days before the first TV debate, reporting under the headline 'Web 2.0: the new election superweapon', the *Observer* assessed the 'powerful new ways to engage voters' that technology offered, from 'Twitter and Facebook to viral ads and crowdsourcing'.[24] However, the televised debates would blow such predictions off course, as reflected in the post-mortem studies since.

Nic Newman prefaced his working paper for the Reuters Institute on the role of the internet in the 2010 election by conceding that 'Ironically, the biggest media story of the 2010 election ended up being a television event: a set-piece leadership debate which turned the campaign on its head – with the internet seen as something of a sideshow.'[25] Newman's investigation led him to recognise that 'the TV debates spawned a wide range of complementary activity in the social and digital sphere.' Citing blogger and *Telegraph* digital commentator Shane Richmond's view that 'Social media are at their best and most powerful when they are wrapping around other things,' Newman contended that in the case of the debates 'they enabled an unprecedented sharing of thoughts and opinions about politics...'.[26] Another report seeking to assess the media's role within the 2010 election, which similarly noted that 'Web 2.0 served mostly to amplify and complement news events created on other media, typically television', was undertaken jointly by YouGov and Deloitte.[27] Its findings, drawn from a survey of 2,000 adults, indicated that, despite a final election result which appeared to reflect none of the change in voting intentions during the campaign supposedly stirred by the televised debates, 'television's role in the election was arguably more significant than superficial.' The report found that 'Television was not only a major source of information for voters but it also shaped voting intentions, with its impact often strongest among the younger people.'[28] For the authors: 'Television's biggest impact was to offer, in the form of the debates, a relatively unfiltered view of the leaders to the general public.'[29]

In his roundup of Fleet Street's coverage of the election campaign, Peter Preston acknowledged that, in pushing for the televised debates, 'Ryley has changed elections for all our lifetimes – and, though you wouldn't quite deduce it amid much press snarling, he's given newspapers a circulation transfusion as well.'[30] Preston noted that sales had increased across the board 'between 5% and 10%' on the day following each debate: 'You watched, you chatted, you wanted to compare notes: so you bought a paper.' Despite the swirls of criticism, the simple facts remained: 'Participation went up, not down. So did interest.'[31]

The televised leaders' debates provided a focused forum, devoid of the feared trivialities and easily accessible to the whole electorate. Their great strength lies not only in having generated direct awareness of issues and questions during the live transmission, but also in prompting further discussion and investigation that continued through other media forms, whether press, digital or social – a process which ultimately invigorated newspapers and new media alike. As *Broadcast* magazine stated, the debates 'were transformational, both in the way campaigns will be organised in the future and how broadcasting and other media will report them. Millions of people engaged with the political arguments and political leaders of the day in a way that they had never done before. One thing seems clear: now that we've had the televised debates we will want them again – the viewing and the voting public will demand it'.[32] The debates changed the way the media cover politics and elections in Britain forever. But did they change politics? The question will long be debated.

Labour strategists have subsequently claimed that the debates 'cost David Cameron his majority' by broadening the participation and admitting Nick Clegg. Andy Coulson and David Cameron insist that the widening effect of the debate helped them and prevented Labour from running a focused 'Tory Cuts' campaign of the type that had proved so successful in the past. On the face of it, the Liberal Democrats had most reason to be disappointed by their performance on polling day – but without Cleggmania would Nick Clegg have been accepted so readily as a credible Deputy Prime Minister? Some constituency campaigners claimed they were 'swamped' by the national debates. But others thanked the debates for energising the election. Voters were inspired to stage debates and hustings at constituency and regional levels. And some canvassers reported that for the first time ever they were welcomed when they knocked on the door because voters wanted to discuss the issues raised in the debate. Certainly, audience surveys showed that those who came stayed for the ninety-minute duration of the debates (to paraphrase the Duke of Wellington).

For broadcasters the point surely is that we did what television does best and deployed our unique selling point by staging a series of live mass audience events – this time on the important political issues of the day. It is simplistic to try to trace cause and effect from the debates. What matters is that we increased voter engagement as John Ryley had intended. Voter turnout was up modestly as well. At last television did its job at election time. We have established a firm basis for TV debates at future elections. It will be a brave leader indeed who ducks treading where Cameron, Brown and Clegg have gone before. Of course, refinements are possible. But, as Sue Inglish of the BBC remarked, 'If we have to do it all again on the same template we will.' 2010 was the first British Television General Election.

Notes

1. For one example, see 'Time to Turn On', *The Times*, 14 April 1997.
2. 'Who'll show up for the TV showdown? John Ryley, *The Times*, 2 September 2009.
3. Ibid.
4. 'ITV and BBC accuse Sky News of jeopardising election debate', Leigh Holmwood, guardian.co.uk, 2 September 2009 http://www.guardian.co.uk/media/2009/sep/02/itv-bbc-sky-election-debate
5. 'Brown goes into meltdown on TV', *Evening Standard*, 30 September 2009.
6. See 'Ashcroft exposes Tories' failings', *The Sunday Telegraph*, 19 September 2010 and 'General Election Review: The election debates gave the Liberal Democrats by-election status, and disrupted an already disjointed Tory campaign', ConservativeHome, 12 May 2010 http://conservativehome.blogs.com/generalelectionreview/2010/05/the-election-debates-gave-the-liberal-democrats-byelection-status-and-disrupted-an-already-disjointe.html
7. See the front page stories 'Clegg in Nazi Slur on Britain', *Daily Mail*, 22 April 2010 and 'Nick Clegg, the Lib Dem donors and payments into his private account,' *Daily Telegraph*, 22 April 2010.
8. 'Prime-time politics', *Financial Times*, 4 September 2009.

9. 'Ready for his close-up?', *The Economist*, 12 September 2009.

10. '10 things Brown must do to save Labour', *Daily Mirror*, 26 September 2009.

11. 'Will TV debates change the face of the election?' *The Observer*, 4 October 2009.

12. 'The last thing we need is a televised election debate', *The Independent*, 31 July 2009.

13. Ibid.

14. 'The People's Election', *The Independent*, 6 May 2010.

15. 'What have these showdowns taught us?', *The Independent*, 1 May 2010.

16. 'Bar customers not prepared to give TV election debate a sporting chance', *The Guardian*, 16 April 2010.

17. 'A TV debate is pointless', *The Guardian*, 5 September 2009.

18. 'Clegg the outsider seizes his moment in the TV spotlight', *The Guardian*, 16 April 2010

19. 'Leaders' TV clash is a draw', page 1, 16 April 2010; 'Clegg is pegged back...', page 1, 23 April 2010 and 'Cameron has Gord on Ropes', page 1, 30 April 2010. Although the judgement of the text varied along broadly pro-Cameron lines, equal sized photographs of the three leaders were used in illustration on each of the occasions.

20. See in particular 'Who won the TV debate? Which paper do you read?' Media Monkey, *The Guardian*, 16 April 2010 http://www.guardian.co.uk/media/mediamonkeyblog/2010/apr/16/who-won-which-paper-monkey

21. Report of Jon Snow speaking at the Westminster Media Forum, 20 May 2010, 'Jon Snow: tabloid newspapers had a dreadful election', *The Press Gazette*, http://www.pressgazette.co.uk/story.asp?storycode=45474

22. '2010 – Was it really the Mumsnet election?' http://www.mumsnet.com/politics/mumsnet-election-reviewed

23. 'The YouTube Facebook Digital Debate', 10 April 2010 launch, http://www.youtube.com/watch?v=k-Ua4kPMwrU

24. 'Web 2.0: the new election superweapon', *The Observer*, 11 April 2010.

25. '#UKelection2010, mainstream media and the role of the internet: how social and digital media affected the business of politics and journalism', Nic Newman, Reuters Institute for the Study of Journalism, July 2010, p. 3.

26. Ibid., p. 38.

27. 'Perspectives on Television in Words and Numbers', Deloitte and YouGov. 2010 p.7 http://www.deloitte.com/assets/Dcom-UnitedKingdom/Local%20Assets/Documents/Industries/TMT/UK_TMT_ONTV-Perspectives-on-television2010V3.pdf

28. Ibid., p. 3.

29. Ibid., p. 6.

30. 'Next time, Fleet Street may get the election right', *The Observer*, 9 May 2010.

31. Ibid.

32. 'Broadcast Digital Awards', 18 June 2010.

4
Media Coverage of the Prime Ministerial Debates

Stephen Coleman, Fabro Steibel and Jay G. Blumler

After years of prevarication, non-negotiation and bluster, televised election debates came to the United Kingdom in 2010. For many, this was seen as the worst of times to try such an experiment: in the aftermath of the MPs' expenses scandal, politicians' reputations were at a low ebb; in a period of economic crisis and austerity political leaders were accused of not being straight about their policy intentions. Could the televised prime ministerial debates lead to something like a fresh start – perhaps even serving to reduce or alleviate public disenchantment? Or might the debates fall down the sceptical drain, as it were – be dismissed as just 'more of the same'? With their peak audiences of 10.3 million viewers,[1] the televised debates made possible direct appeals from candidates for the premiership to the immediacy of the domestic audience. While we should not overstate the significance of these events (both the most-viewed first debate on ITV and the second most-viewed debate on BBC attracted smaller audiences than *Britain's Got Talent*, *EastEnders* and *Dr Who*, all shown in the same weeks), there can be little doubt that they reached more voters than any other episode of televised election coverage – and stimulated a considerable amount of reflective commentary and debate both on television and in the wider media.

The effects of the debates cannot be understood in isolation from the wider media coverage, for each of them arrived with its own prehistory of mediated speculations and expectations and was followed by well-orchestrated party spin offensives and journalistic accounts. In many cases, this surrounding media build-up and follow-up reached people who had not seen or heard all, or any, of the debates themselves. As Lang and Lang observed as long ago as 1978 (after the second US televised presidential debates between Ford and Carter), there is an important 'distinction between the direct impact of a communication immediately after exposure and the cumulative effects of communication activity directed toward defining an ambiguous object or situation' (1978: 323). They referred to this as the media 'contamination' of opinion formation. Benoit and Currie (2001: 29) rightly point out that, despite the fact that millions of voters watch the debates, many others only learn about the debates from news coverage. Even those who do watch the debates are exposed to news coverage of them. Thus, media coverage of debates, as well as the debates themselves, is important.

In attempting to make sense of the 2010 British debates, we were concerned to locate them within a wider media ecology comprising print, broadcast and online flows of information and commentary. Our study of the outer regions of that ecology – the virtual space of the blogosphere and other online discussions of the debates – is discussed elsewhere (Coleman, 2011). Our aim here is to report on our research into mainstream media coverage of the debates: our methods of inquiry, key findings and analytical reflections.

Our questions: systemic rather than individual effects

Previous (mainly US) studies of media coverage of televised leaders' debates have tended to focus upon how voters' judgements of candidates were influenced by post-debate reporting. Several scholars have identified differences in responses to the debaters' arguments and performances between people who were asked immediately after watching them live and others who had been exposed to media commentary after the debates. The famous gaffe about Eastern Europe by Gerald Ford in the second 1976 debate is often cited: viewers polled immediately after watching the debate were generally impressed by Ford's debating skills and supported him more than Carter; those polled after the media had devoted sustained negative attention to the gaffe were of the opinion that Ford had clearly 'lost' the debate (Steeper, 1978). Similarly, widespread negative media condemnation of John Kerry's performance in the third 2004 debate against George W. Bush appeared to produce a significant evaluative difference between those exposed only to the debate itself and those exposed to the ferocious media criticism of Kerry's remark about Dick Cheney's daughter (Fridkin et al., 2008).

Like these earlier studies, our research explores how the debates were mediated beyond the period of their live broadcast, but differs from them in three key respects. First, we focused upon how the media depicted the debates as political/democratic events rather than how they portrayed particular candidates or positions. In line with our parallel concern to understand the impact of the debates upon voters as democratic citizens (the extent to which they were seen as real democratic opportunities; raised awareness of issues; stimulated interpersonal discussion; enhanced political efficacy; and encouraged people to vote[2]), the principal aim of our media analysis has been to investigate systemic rather than partisan effects of exposure to media coverage of the debates. So, rather than exploring who the media declared to be debate 'winners' or 'losers', we wanted to establish how far the debates were reported and commented upon as pugilistic exercises, with winners, losers, knockout blows, cunning game plans and gaffes, and how far they were framed as opportunities to understand issues and policies.

Second, in order to study the debates as historically contextualised media events, rather than as a series of discrete ninety-minute spectacles, we decided to monitor media coverage *before* as well as *after* each debate. Post-debate coverage was likely to influence public perceptions in the ways we outlined above, but pre-debate media framing was likely to shape public expectations. For example, if, before the first debate, there was media anticipation that it would be 'a damp squib' (too controlled, no audience voice, too scripted, too Americanised, too personalised), this would be likely to affect the public mood differently from media anticipation that it would be 'a big deal' (historic first ever, possible game changer, stimulus for public enthusiasm). By charting the expressed expectations of the media, we were better able to understand how the debates evolved as public dramas, in which the scene of the leaders' confrontation was inseparably linked to the build-up of public anticipation and the frenetic sequel of retrospective evaluation.

Third, while much of our content analysis revolved around a key distinction between media coverage that focused upon the debates as a game and that which emphasised policy substance (see next section for definitions), we proceeded from the assumption that these characterisations were not mutually exclusive. The political communication literature has tended to discuss game and substance as if they were either–or entities. Rather than replicate the previous game–bad, substance–good dichotomy, we decided to reopen the question of how these orientations coexisted empirically and normatively within the debate coverage. As will become clear from our analysis, this mix was rather more subtle than previous studies of televised debates have tended to suggest.

Method of inquiry

We collected all direct press and broadcast media references[3] to the debates between 6 April (the first day of the 2010 General Election campaign) and 12 May (one week after polling day). The media sample analysed comprised the following materials:

- Four 'quality' newspapers (*Guardian, Independent, Telegraph* and *Times*)
- Three popular newspapers (*Daily Mail, Mirror* and *Sun*)
- Six BBC programmes (*BBC News at Ten, Breakfast, Newsnight, The Politics Show, Andrew Marr Show* and *This Week*)
- Four non-BBC programmes (*ITV News at Ten, Channel 4 News*, Sky's *Decision Time, GMTV*)

The media content listed above was collected for every day of the monitoring period, but we only include in this analysis the print editions or broadcasts that appeared on the day before each debate and the Fridays and Sundays after each debate.[4]

We analysed the content in two stages. First, we coded all direct references to the debates.[5] Second, we constructed a coding index to measure the extent to which each press article or TV feature referred to the debates in terms of game or substance. We defined game references as those which focused upon the debates as strategic performances that could be described and evaluated in terms of rhetorical style, impression management, winners and losers. We defined substantive references as those which focused upon policy challenges, intentions and solutions, party records and leadership qualities. Using a scale from 1 to 5, in which 1 denoted articles or features characterised by a solely game orientation, 2 mainly game with some reference to substance, 3 a balance of game and substance, 4 some game, but mainly substance and 5 solely substance, all 778 articles and features in our sample were coded as individual units of analysis.[6] The aim of our coding index was to investigate the degree of mix and balance within the media coverage.[7]

We wish to point out that our research does not provide a comprehensive account of media coverage of the 2010 campaign as a whole. It focuses on the debates, not the rest of the campaign. It deals only with certain media outlets, not a different spread of them. It focuses only on certain days, not all of them. And it deals only with a certain aspect of the coverage – the substance–game dimension – and not others. Since, however, the debates were frequently reported in the media (according to Scammell and Beckett (2010) they were mentioned more often than any other campaign topic in the national press), our results are likely in many respects faithfully to reflect the larger picture.[8]

A profile of press–broadcast coverage

We collected all press articles and broadcast features (hereafter referred to separately as *articles and features*[9] and jointly as *coverage*) that related directly to the debates, rather than ones that only mentioned them in passing. A total of 778 articles and features were coded. In the pre-debate period there were sixty-eight press articles and thirty-one TV features (13 per cent of all coverage in our sample), looking forward to the debates. The first and second debates precipitated the largest amount of coverage: 136 articles and ninety-five features immediately before and after the ITV debate on 15 April (30 per cent of all coverage) and 130 articles and 107 features immediately before and after the Sky debate on 22 April (30 per cent of all coverage). The third, BBC, debate, on 29 April, was preceded and followed by 114 articles and eighty-two features (25 per cent of all coverage) and in the period after the third debate there were only fifteen press articles and no TV features that referred directly to the debates (2 per cent of all coverage).

More press articles (463) than TV features (315) referred directly to the debates (Figure 4.1). This was to be expected, given the greater volume of press to broadcast news journalism. In the print sample, articles from the quality press (317) are significantly more represented than popular articles (146). *The Guardian* covered the debates more than any other newspaper (102 articles), followed by the *Telegraph* (ninety-seven), *The Times* (eighty) and *The Independent* (thirty-eight) (45 per cent of *The Independent's* articles on the debates were before or after the first one, but after that they seemed to lose interest, with only 11 per cent of its debate-related articles appearing by the time of the third debate). Of the popular newspapers, *The Sun* and the *Mirror* had the highest number of debate-related articles (fifty-three each), while the *Mail* published forty.

We categorised all articles and features in our sample by genre. The most common genre was 'opinion' (journalists or other commentators expressing their own views on the debates), which accounted for 63 per cent of all press coverage and 40 per cent of all TV coverage. The second most common genre was 'news' (factual reports), comprising 22 per cent of press and 27 per cent of TV coverage. A third genre, 'vox pop' (where the words of members of the public were cited), accounted for 8 per cent of all debate coverage.

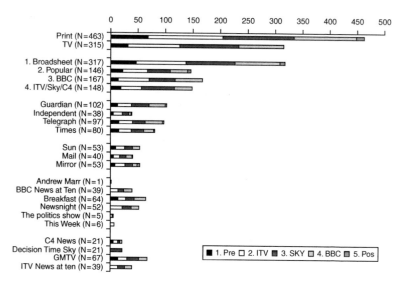

Figure 4.1   Distribution of coded articles per type of media and per media name (in counts)

Game–substance balance

A persistent concern of political communication scholars, not only in relation to debate coverage but to all reporting of politics in the media, has been a tendency towards reduced focus upon the reporting of candidate/party policy positions and leadership records, while more time and space are devoted to matters of style, strategy and process. Excessive emphasis upon the game reinforces an image of elections as passing shows in which 'candidates are seen as performers, reporters as theatrical critics, [and] the audience as spectators' (Jamieson, 1992: 166). Patterson (1994: 59), for example, has shown how between 1960 and 1992 the ratio of game to substance election news stories on the front page of the *New York Times* increased from 45:52 to 80:15. A similar pattern has been observed in the British media's electoral coverage (Blumler and Gurevitch, 2001; Deacon et al., 2006; Harrison, 2001).

A series of nationally televised leaders' debates, broadcast during the heat of a short, three-week election campaign, was bound to be seen as a dramatic contest in which rhetorical performances mattered and the risk of visible failure would be regarded by politicians as a zero-sum game. It would be churlish to expect the media to report debates as if they were academic seminars characterised by dispassionate disputation. But, if such attention to the game were to overwhelm coverage of substantive policy presentation and contestation, the more educative and civically nourishing aspects of the debates could be obscured. For this reason, a main focus of our media content analysis was to explore in some detail the balance between game and substance in the coverage of the 2010 debates.

Eighty-four per cent of all articles and features in our sample referred to the game aspect of the debates, while 75 per cent had some reference to substance. This confirms our expectation that media coverage would be mainly game-centred, but qualifies it by observing that most coverage also included references to substance. The coexistence of game and substance can be found in all of the categories that we analysed. In the print sample, 87 per cent of the articles included game references, while 78 per cent referred to substance. In the TV sample, the respective percentages were 80 per cent and 70 per cent. The gap between game–substance references was higher in the populars (86 per cent – 71 per cent) and in the non-BBC TV channels (84 per cent – 68 per cent). The ratio of game to substance references was lower in the quality press (87 per cent – 82 per cent) and BBC (77 per cent – 73 per cent) coverage.

In order to gain a more detailed understanding of the ways in which game and substance were invoked in the media coverage, we explored four variables that were central to the construction of game and substance orientations. The first two variables refer to what it means to have a debate; the second two refer to the characterisation of leadership.

Debating metaphors

The debates themselves were relatively rich in policy substance and participant interaction. They projected a symbolic image of what it means to have a debate. But the media coverage complicated this image, focusing sometimes on a game-oriented representation of what debate entails and at other times focusing upon a more substantive notion of debate.

One way to think of a televised debate is as a gladiatorial contest in which the most adept fighter steals victory from the 'losers'. It is a story best told through the metaphorical language of sport ('the horse race' – 'own goal' – 'winners/losers'), war ('battleground' – 'pincer movement' – 'all guns blazing') or the mysterious dark art of 'spin'. As in reports of sport and war, debates are described as short bursts of energy in which victory is to be won and the visibly wounded will find it hard to recover. The other way to conceive debate has more in common with the rules of deliberation: the main function of the debaters is to present the clearest possible articulation of their position, while at the same time listening and responding to other positions. Seventy-seven per cent of all articles and features employed a metaphor referring to the debates in terms of sport, war or spin. Although there were no formal votes at the end of the debates, and evaluations of success were inevitably somewhat partisan, approximately half of all the coverage made reference to who won or lost the debates. Quality and popular newspapers employed such metaphors in more or less equal proportions (49 per cent – 46 per cent), while the BBC (43 per cent) did so much less than the other TV channels (61 per cent). Half of all quality newspaper articles invoked metaphors relating to sport or war – more so than the populars (38 per cent), the BBC (38 per cent) and non-BBC TV channels (22 per cent). One-third of all coverage referred to 'spin' and associated metaphors describing post-debate attempts by the parties to claim victory.

Seventy-two per cent of all articles and features referred to policies discussed in the debates, but this does not mean that most coverage reported or examined the leaders' specific policy positions. When policy was mentioned in the media coverage, it tended to be in general terms: the debaters argued about 'cutting the deficit' or 'controlling' immigration. These very general policy references occurred in 72 per cent of articles and features, but only 24 per cent referred to the three leaders' specific policy objectives, for example, X proposed to cut the deficit by doing Y or A proposed to control immigration by adopting policy B. While quality newspapers referred to policy issues more than did the popular newspapers (42 per cent – 38 per cent), it was the populars that were more likely to set out the candidates' specific policy objectives (29 per cent – 26 per cent). This is partly explained by the populars' strong focus on the differences between the leaders on immigration policy and partly by the populars' reasonable belief that their readers might not have come across these differences in policy objective before (the extent to which quality newspaper editors were justified in believing that their readers were cognisant of such distinctions is another matter). In the TV coverage, BBC features were more likely to refer to specific policies (20 per cent) and to outline specific policy objectives (16 per cent) than were features on other channels (36 per cent and 27 per cent respectively).

A clear illustration of how game and substance coverage were subtly mixed relates to the reporting of polls. In the 2010 election polling remained a central barometer of the fluctuations of public opinion, with the added feature that this time polls were conducted and reported within minutes of the three debates ending. While the notion of a 'poll' may seem to convey the notion of a 'game' with winners and losers, full stop, it was not quite as straightforward as that. A significant amount of poll coverage referred not only to 'who won', but how particular messages as articulated in the debates succeeded or failed to appeal to viewers, alongside explanations for dramatic changes in post-debate opinion, such as the Liberal Democrat surge. Other poll reporting resembled the instant feedback of TV talent shows like *X-Factor*, with the debates depicted as little more than ninety-minute performances, to be judged on the basis of game-based criteria. Some of the best poll coverage combined both approaches, drawing upon the simplicity of the game framework, while at the same time using that as a springboard for the introduction of more substantive psephological analysis.

Representing the leaders

As with the idea of debate, so with the evaluation of leadership: there were ways in which the struggle to appear as the most impressive, sensible, honest, genuine leader could be represented as a game, not unlike TV shows in which the least convincing 'characters' are voted out by the public, or as a substantive test of measurable qualities. The game–substance tension here should not be thought of as a simplistic division between 'personality politics', as it is sometimes called, and dispassionate, impersonal issue politics. As has already been stated, one expects debates to focus upon the personal qualities of their participants. Critics of televised debates have raised this as a major objection: by placing so much focus on the words and gestures of leaders, broader issues of democratic politics are forgotten (Ibrahim, 2010; Mangan, 2010). Worthy of debate though such an objection may be, it was not the aim of our research to criticise the media for commenting on leaders' qualities in relation to debates that were designed to test the qualities of would-be national leaders.. It was *how* these qualities were discussed (in stylistic–game or substantive–political terms) that interested us. That is why we decided to code two separate personality-related variables: one identifying game-related references to stylistic and strategic performance within the debates and the other identifying more substantive references to the individual leaders' political records, skills and ideas.

Game-oriented representations of the leaders focused upon their performances as debaters. The debate was depicted as a public test in which the 'authentic' personalities of the leaders would be forced into visibility. Forty-two per cent of the coverage referred in some way to the leaders' body language or rhetorical style. Newspapers seemed to be fascinated by this, inviting 'experts' to comment on photographs of leaders' body movements and other indicators of charisma. Forty-nine per cent of press articles addressed these matters, compared with 32 per cent of TV features. This was not, incidentally, confined mainly to the popular press: 53 per cent of quality newspaper articles referred to body language or rhetorical style, compared with only 42 per cent in the populars. Again, references to leaders' personality traits as assets or hindrances to their debating performances were much higher in the press (31 per cent) than in TV coverage (12 per cent). Thirty-four per cent of all popular references alluded to personality characteristics, usually with an emphasis upon defects. Finally, around one in five (17 per cent) of all the articles and features referred to leaders' supposed gaffes and knockout blows. This seemed to have been more of a preoccupation of the quality newspapers (21 per cent) than the populars (15 per cent).

In contrast to the 42 per cent of the articles and features that referred to the leaders' rhetorical–stylistic debating performances, only 28 per cent referred to their performances in terms of conventional political qualities and records. These references tended to focus upon the debaters' activities before and beyond their participation in the debates. Of these substantive references, press articles were significantly more common (35 per cent) than broadcast features (18 per cent). Only one in ten articles or features (11 per cent) referred to personal achievements of any one of the leaders – and these few examples tended to focus on the leaders' private lives: challenges overcome / misfortunes borne. Only one in twenty of all articles and features in the sample referred to any achievement by a leader in the sphere of politics.[10]

Concocting a civic mix: a realistic assessment

Had most media coverage focused solely upon the debates as a strategic political game, the substantive richness of the debates themselves might have been swamped by an ocean of mediated froth. If, on the other hand, the media coverage had simply attended to the dry substance of the leaders' declared positions, the rhetorical force of the debates as dramatising moments in the campaign might have been undermined. For democratic citizenship to be well served, a sensitive mixture of coverage was needed: one that reported and made sense of distinctive policy differences, while representing and augmenting the symbolic energy of agonistic democracy. How well did the media do that?

Overall, nearly all of the media coverage (95 per cent) included some elements of game or substance,[11] but the tendency to represent the debates as a game was clearly more pronounced than the tendency to provide substantive accounts. There was twice as much coverage that was solely or mainly game-oriented (45 per cent) as solely or mainly substance-oriented (22 per cent). This skew towards game-oriented coverage was partly qualified by two important factors: first, the divergence that existed between different types of media and, second, the movement towards a greater focus upon substance as the debates went on.

Differences between types of media

When we look at how different types of media produced mixtures of game and substance, it becomes clear that TV coverage was both more likely to be solely game-oriented and at the same time more likely to be solely substance-oriented than press coverage. Twenty-seven per cent of TV coverage adopted an entirely game-related orientation, compared with only 17 per cent of press coverage. At the same time, TV had twice as much coverage that focused solely upon substance (17 per cent) as the press (8 per cent) (Figure 4.2).

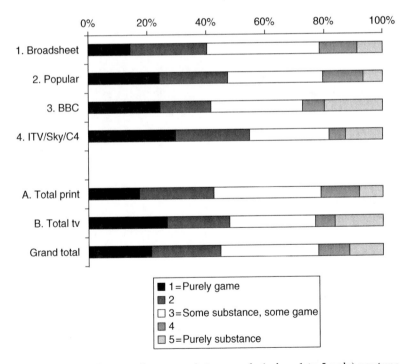

Figure 4.2 Distribution of game – substance scale (values 1 to 5 only) per type of media

Some newspapers and broadcasters tended more towards one extreme or the other, but few avoided any balance between game and substance. The BBC broadcast a significantly higher number of features that were purely substance-oriented (20 per cent) than other TV channels (13 per cent), the quality newspapers (9 per cent) or the populars (7 per cent). The breakfast programme GMTV had more solely game coverage of the debates (41 per cent) than any other media outlet, followed by *Channel 4 News* (32 per cent) and the *Mirror* newspaper (27 per cent). The fewest solely game references were in the *Independent* (9 per cent), Sky's *Decision Time* (14 per cent) and *The Guardian* (14 per cent).The BBC *News at Ten* included the highest number of solely substance reports on the debates (24 per cent), followed by ITV *News at Ten* (21 per cent) and *Newsnight* (16 per cent). The fewest solely substance references were in *Channel 4 News* (5 per cent), the *Daily Mail* (5 per cent), *The Times* (6 per cent) and *The Guardian* (6 per cent).

This differentiation between types of media coverage augurs well for future televised debates. There was a sense in which the media were searching for their roles during the period of the campaign; that the BBC was warming to its role as a public-service explainer of substantive positions; that the populars were seeking to make sense of the policy differences for their readers; and the quality press was satisfied to perform the role of a post-event commentariat. As the UK becomes more accustomed to televised leaders' debates, the media may well establish an even clearer division of responsibilities.

Emergence of substantive content over time

A key finding from our research was that substantive references within all media coverage increased as the campaign went on. At the outset of the election campaign, before the first debate took place, both press and TV seemed to be obsessed by the debates as strategic performances. Looking to the US presidential debates as a reference point, journalists seemed to be obsessed by the potential theatricality of the forthcoming events, anticipating the risk of major gaffes, knockout blows and show-stealing rhetoric. In the pre-debate period the overall ratio of game to substance was 2–5.

After the first debate the ratio reached 2.6; 2.7 after the second debate; and 3.4 after the third debate. If we analyse the evolution of the game:substance ratio from the pre-debate period (1) up to the third (BBC) debate period (4), we can see that the ratio of game to substance increased towards substance across all the media categories (Figures 4.3 and 4.4, Table 4.1).[12] The overall movement towards more substantive

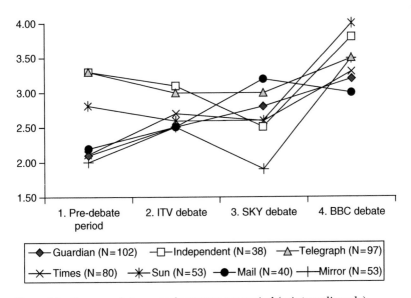

Figure 4.3 Game – substance scale average per period (print media only)

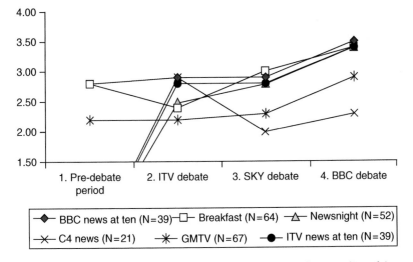

Figure 4.4 Game – substance scale average per period (broadcast media only)

Table 4.1 Game – substance scale distribution and average per media name

| | Broadsheets | | | | Populars | | | BBC | | | ITV/Sky/C4 | | | |
	Guardian (N=102)	Independent (N=38)	Telegraph (N=97)	Times (N=80)	Sun (N=53)	Mail (N=40)	Mirror (N=53)	BBC News at Ten (N=39)	Breakfast (N=64)	Newsnight (N=52)	C4 News (N=21)	Decision Time Sky (N=21)	GMTV (N=67)	ITV News at Ten (N=39)
	%	%	%	%	%	%	%	%	%	%	%	%	%	%
A. Game/Scale substance (1–5 only)														
1 = Purely game	14	9	16	15	25	18	27	18	23	25	32	14	41	18
2 = Mainly game	27	34	17	32	17	24	29	13	21	16	32	38	22	21
3 = Some substance, some game	39	40	39	35	35	39	24	34	30	31	26	29	25	29
4 = Mainly substance	14	9	15	12	15	13	14	11	3	12	5	10	02	11
5 = Purely substance	6	9	13	6	8	5	6	24	23	16	5	10	11	21

B. Game/Scale (extremes grouped)

1–2 = Mostly or purely game	41	43	33	47	42	42	57	32	44	41	63	52	63	39
3 = Some game, some substance	39	40	39	35	35	39	24	34	30	31	26	29	25	29
4–5 = Mostly or purely substance	20	17	28	18	23	18	20	34	26	27	11	19	13	32

C. Game/Scale (pure extremes)

1–4 = Any game mention	94	91	87	94	92	95	94	76	77	84	95	90	89	79
2–5 = Any substance mention	86	91	84	85	75	82	73	82	77	75	68	86	59	82
Grand Total	100	100	100	100	100	100	100	100	100	100	100	100	100	100
Scale average per election period[13]	$\bar{x}$	$\bar{x}$	$\bar{x}$	$\bar{x}$	$\bar{x}$	$\bar{x}$	$\bar{x}$	$\bar{x}$	$\bar{x}$	$\bar{x}$	$\bar{x}$	$\bar{x}$	$\bar{x}$	$\bar{x}$
1. Pre-debate period	2.1	3.3	3.3	2.1	2.8	2.2	2.0	.	2.8	.	2.8	.	2.2	.
2. ITV debate	2.5	3.1	3.0	2.7	2.6	2.5	2.5	2.9	2.4	2.5	2.9	.	2.2	2.8
3. Sky debate	2.8	2.5	3.0	2.6	2.6	3.2	1.9	2.9	3.0	2.8	2.0	2.6	2.3	2.8
4. BBC debate	3.2	3.8	3.5	3.3	4.0	3.0	3.5	3.5	3.4	3.4	2.3	.	2.9	3.4
Overall scale average	2.8	3.0	3.2	2.7	3.0	2.8	2.5	3.2	3.0	2.8	2.6	2.6	2.4	3.0

coverage of the debates suggests that the media were initially excited by the prospect of high drama – some of which they certainly got – but that, as the campaign proceeded and the debates came to seem less exotic, journalists calmed down and turned their attention to a more balanced game–substance mix.

The politics–democracy balance

Our argument throughout this analysis has been that citizens were likely to benefit most from a mixture of game and substance-oriented debate coverage. Another way of putting this would be to say that the televised debates encompassed both Politics (with all of its well-known character-istics of partisan competitiveness, strategic impression management and manipulative techniques) and Democracy (with its normative emphasis upon the inclusion of the widest number of citizens in informed and well-reasoned deliberation and decision-making). As political events, it behoved the media to treat the leaders' debates with some scepticism; to delve critically beyond the surface images and rehearsed phrases; and to reflect upon the consequences of debate performances in the blunt terms of opinion poll ratings and voting projections. Indeed, 60 per cent of all media coverage did refer in some way to the political impact of the debates, with 28 per cent discussing probable or actual polling effects and 24 per cent reflecting upon how the parties' campaigning would be or was affected by the debates. As important moments in the history of British democracy, one might have expected the media to focus on the debates as opportunities to create a more informed electorate, while stimulating a more deliberative election. Almost one in five (19 per cent) articles in the quality press alluded to the debates in these democratic terms (populars: 13 per cent; BBC: 9 per cent; other TV channels: 11 per cent) and almost one in 20 of all articles and features (4 per cent) dis-cussed the possible effects of the debates upon turnout.

In considering the game–substance mix, our normative concern has been that the political dimension of the debates should not be reduced to a cynical emphasis upon gamesmanship, to the exclusion of the real policy choices at stake, while the democratic dimension of the debates should not be so marginalised as to squander the potentially energis-ing effects of an unprecedented innovation in party-leader communi-cation. Overall, neither of these negative outcomes transpired. Despite much pre-debate media scepticism about the over-regulated design of the debates, the limited differences between the three participating leaders and the aftermath of a very corrosive expenses scandal, the

British media rose to the occasion in one key respect: they helped to capture the public imagination by offering a broad and compelling mix between substantive and game-based narratives. We recognise, however, that much could have been done better according to other criteria of evaluation. In particular, much of the debate coverage in the press was manifestly partisan to the point of being unfair. But, in terms of the civic mix that has been the focus of our evaluation, the media's performance could have been much worse.

There can be no certainty about how well the media will perform in future elections, once debates have become a more routine electoral feature; about how far the coverage of these debates will compare with the reporting of other important political events; or about how much of the mix we have identified was noticed by readers and viewers. But, as we found in our study of public responses to the debates,[14] voters – who are always at the same time newspaper readers and TV audiences – seem to have felt that the 2010 election was one in which television played a vital civic role.

Notes

The research reported here was conducted as part of a wider project, funded by the Reuters Institute for the Study of Journalism, University of Oxford, involving the Universities of Leeds, Oxford and Wolverhampton. A comprehensive study of public, mainstream and new media responses to the televised leaders' debates can be found in Coleman, 2011.

1. The audience for the first debate, shown on ITV1 on 15 April, was 9.6 million, with a peak of 10.3 million, equivalent to 37% of the TV audience. The second debate, shown on Sky on 22 April, had an audience of 4 million (2.1 million watching the Sky News and the rest watching live transmission on the BBC News channel). This low figure was not surprising, considering the odd decision to air it live on non-terrestrial channels only. The audience for the third debate, shown on BBC1 on 29 April, was just under 8.6 million.
2. This was a separate strand of our research, published as chapter 3 in Coleman, 2011.
3. These dates were selected because Friday is the immediate day after the debates and Sunday is the day that the media generally summarise the main events of the week. Nevertheless, we included some exceptions to this rule: We also included news broadcasts immediately after each debate (thus coding Thursday evening's news on three occasions); we replaced the first Friday of the elect ion campaign (when no debate had yet taken place) with the Thursday immediately before the first debate. After applying the sampling criteria and making the adjustments outlined above, we grouped the days of coding into five periods, which are distributed in the following order:
   - Week 1 (Pre-debate period): Sun 11/Apr (print and TV sample) and Thu 15/Apr (print sample and pre-debate TV sample only)

- Week 2 (ITV debate): Thu 15/Apr (TV post-debate only), Fri 16/Apr (all), Sun 18/Apr (all)
- Week 3 (Sky LD period): Thu 22/Apr (TV post-debate only), Fri 23/Apr (all), Sun 25/Apr (all)
- Week 4 (BBC LD period): Thu 29/Apr(TV post-debate only), Fri 30/Apr (all), Sun 02/May (all)

4. This is a problematic term. Our two categories – quality and popular – are intended as commonly-used descriptions rather than judgements on journalistic standards.

5. A direct reference was defined as any article or feature in which the debates were described or discussed. Passing references comprised articles or features on a separate subject in which the debates were mentioned, e.g. a press article on the war against the Taliban in which the writer suggests that this subject should have been raised more prominently in the debates.

6. Although the scale ranged from 1 to 5, it also admits the value 6, which denotes cases in which the article or feature refers neither to game nor substance (e.g. coverage in which the qualities of a particular moderator or TV channel were discussed. These cases accounted for approximately 5% of the coverage).

7. The game/substance index is not a linear scale, but more like a hyperbolic curve in which the value of 3, referring to the co-presence of game and substance, represents an empirical norm at the bottom of the curve.

8. See chapters by Harrison and Scammell and Beckett in Kavanagh and Cowley (2010) for further analysis.

9. Press articles comprised any discrete text, ranging from full-page reports or opinion pieces to five-line snippets. 45% of all articles coded were between a quarter and half a page in length. TV features comprised any single programme or part of a programme, ranging from news reports and live post-debate coverage to interviews and expert commentary. There were several lengthy TV reports and discussions about the debates, but 35% of all TV features in our sample devoted no more than one minute to debate coverage.

10. It is worth noting that the relative absence of references to leaders' qualities might in part be a consequence of our coding method. We based our analysis only on explicit references to the coding variables, discarding implicit or semiotic references, such as those from photographs, cartoons or video images.

11. The remainder of the coverage in our sample focused upon the design of the debates and their impact upon turnout.

12. If we analyse all the media labels independently, the scale averages registered during all the phases range from a minimum of 1.9 (The Mirror, phase 3) to a maximum of 4.0 (The Sun, phase 4). Considering only the overall average, the GMTV is the media label with the index most skewed to game (2.4), followed by the Mirror (2.5) and C4 news (2.6), while the BBC News and the Telegraph are the only ones with an index skewed to substance (3.2 each). The Independent, the Sun, Breakfast and the ITV News at Ten have a non-skewed index of 3.0 each. The pattern of average index variation per period

considerably varies from one media label to another. Some of the samples
for example present a general increase in the average index across time (i.e.
The Guardian, The Times, The Mail, the BBC news, Breakfast, Newsnight,
GMTV, ITV News); while other samples present a general decrease in the
average index when analysed per period of coding (i.e. The Independent,
The Telegraph, The Sun, and the C4 news). At the same time, the Mirror is
the only one with no clear pattern of average index variation across time.
13. The phase 5 period (post-debate) has too few articles coded (N=15 in total,
or 9 qualities, 6 populars and none from the TV sample) and was not
included.
14. See chapter 3 of Coleman, 2011.

References

Benoit, W. L. and Currie, H. (2001) 'Inaccuracies in Media Coverage of the 1996
and 2000 Presidential Debates', *Argumentation & Advocacy*, 38: 28–39.
Blumler, J. G. and Gurevitch, M. (2001) ' "Americanization" reconsidered: U.K.-
U.S. campaign communication comparisons across time', in Bennett, W. L. and
Entman, R. M. (eds) *Mediated politic: Communication in the future of Democracy*.
NY: Cambridge University Press, 380–406.
Coleman, S. (ed.) (2011) *Leaders in the Living Room: Prime Ministerial Debates of
2010: Evidence, Evaluation and Some Recommendations*. Oxford: Reuters Institute
for the Study of Journalism.
Deacon, D., Wring, D. and Golding, P. (2006) 'Same Campaign, Differing
Agendas: Analysing News Media Coverage of the 2005 General Election',
British Politics, 1(2): 2006.
Fridkin, K. L., Kenney, P. J., Gershon, S. A. and Woodall, G. S. (2008) 'Spinning
Debates: The Impact of the News Media's Coverage of the Final 2004 Presidential
Debate', *Harvard International Journal of Press Politics*, 13(1): 29–51.
Harrison, M. (2001) 'Politics on the air', in Butler, D. and Kavanagh, D. (eds) *The
British General Election of 2001*. London: Palgrave.
Ibrahim, A. (2010) 'Leaders' Debates Will Dumb Down our Democracy', http://
www.politics.co.uk/comment/general-election-2010/comment-leaders-
debates-will-dumb-down-our-democracy-$1364183.htm, 8 March (accessed
on 5 November 2010).
Jamieson, K. H. (1992) *Dirty Politics: Deception, Distraction, and Democracy*.
Oxford: Oxford University Press.
Lang, K. and Lang, G. (1978) 'Immediate and Delayed Responses to a Carter-Ford
Debate: Assessing Public Opinion', *Public Opinion Quarterly*, 42(3): 322–341.
Mangan, L. (2010) 'A critic's view of the TV debates', *The Guardian*, 7 April.
Patterson, T. (1994) *Out of Order*. NY: Vintage Books.
Scammell, M. and Beckett, C. (2010). 'Labour no more: the press', in Kavanagh, D.
and Cowley, P. (eds) *The British General Election of 2010*. Basingstoke: Palgrave
Macmillan.
Steeper, F. (1978) 'Public response to Gerald Ford's statements on Eastern Europe
in the second debate', in Bishop, G. F., Meadow, R. G. and Jackson-Beech M.
(eds) *The presidential debates: Media, electoral and political perspectives*. NY:
Praeger, 81–101.

5
The Polls, The Media and Voters: The Leader Debates

Caroline Lawes and Andrew Hawkins

A general election first

The 2010 General Election saw a new phenomenon, which defined the election campaign and is likely to play a significant role in future election campaigns. The introduction of the debates between the three main party leaders, over the final three weeks of the campaign, gave millions of voters the chance to see the possible Prime Ministers up close and personal.

In analysing how the debates were likely to affect the campaign, Labour and Conservative strategists could have done with seeing a preview of Michael Cockerell's excellent BBC2 programme *How to win the debate*. The programme, aired just days before the first debate, charted how John F. Kennedy hit Richard Nixon for six in the first-ever US Presidential debate in 1960. If nothing else, it showed how disruptive the debates could prove in baring politicians before the public. Unsurprisingly, a senior source within the Liberal Democrats declared afterwards that they couldn't believe their luck, and dared not believe the debates would actually happen until all the details had been agreed in writing.

Rumours abounded that the two main parties had drafted in expensive American debate consultants to groom their leaders. Electric Airwaves, who trained Nick Clegg and gave him the advice to look straight into the camera – obvious in hindsight but apparently missed by the Americans – trumpeted their man's success afterwards with a well-placed advert in the PR industry press. Perhaps the other parties should have demanded their money back.

Once the details of the three debates – on ITV1, Sky News and BBC1 respectively – were finalised, the pollsters got to work designing a suitable methodology to measure immediate reaction, in an attempt to provide the fastest and most accurate insight once the credits began to roll. The speed of the polls was vital in order to set the tone of the commentary and analysis following the debates, as well as providing some reality for the spin room. ComRes and YouGov ran instant polls for publication within minutes of the end of the debates, and the other reaction polls followed over and the next day.

This chapter examines the different approaches to the five instant polls that were conducted, focusing particularly on the challenges facing the pollsters, and explores some of the implications of the instant polls for the conduct of the campaign. Being most familiar with the new methodology utilised by ComRes, this chapter particularly addresses our experience and lessons learnt through polling the leadership debates. The three central challenges this new spectacle brought are:

- **Technical** – how were we to complete a large sample of interviews in the shortest time possible?
- **Methodological** – what was a 'right' sample going to look like?
- **Reactive** – what were the challenges of managing the media's expectations, understanding and reporting of the results?

Following this, an analysis of the results and its impact on the final election result is considered.

The players and the games

Before addressing the finer points, we take a brief look at the players in this new game. Five polling companies rose to the challenge of competing to run instant polls or reaction polls: Angus Reid, ComRes, ICM, Populus and YouGov. Three methodologies were used, with three different weighting models. ComRes used a computerised programme to conduct instant automated telephone surveys; ICM used the traditional Computer Aided Telephone Interview (CATI) approach, from a pre-recruited panel; and Angus Reid, Populus and YouGov conducted online polls among pre-recruited panels of viewers.

The methodologies are summarised in Table 5.1.

As soon as the party leaders began their summing up at the end of each debate, the race started for the pollsters to gain reaction from a representative sample of the audience as quickly as possible. As such, it is perhaps not surprising that the sample sizes are reflective of different methodologies employed. The traditional CATI approach, used by ICM, is the slowest methodology, and so they achieved 500 interviews following each debate. The three online pollsters achieved samples of 1,000–2,000 responses and, in some cases, demonstrated some very fast turnarounds. Finally, the ComRes automated telephone poll took six minutes to complete from start to finish and could manage large volumes, including achieving a sample of more than 4,000 after the first debate. The sample sizes of each poll are given in Table 5.2.

The first challenge highlighted above is the technical one – how do we achieve a robust sample in as fast a time as possible? Methodology has a key role to play. ComRes used an automated telephone methodology. Similarly, YouGov used an online methodology with a survey that

Table 5.1   Instant poll methodologies

Pollster	Methodology	Recruitment	Timing	Weighting
ComRes	Automated Telephone	Online panel	Immediately after the debate	Nationally representative and past vote recall
ICM	CATI	Telephone omnibus	Evening of the debate	Estimated viewer profile
Angus Reid	Online	Online panel	Evening of debate and following day	Nationally representative
Populus	Online	Online panel	Immediately after the debate	No weighting
YouGov	Online	Online Panel	Immediately after the debate	Estimated viewer profile

Table 5.2   Instant poll sample sizes

	Sample size		
Pollster	Debate 1	Debate 2	Debate 3
ComRes	4,032	2,691	2,372
ICM	505	504	510
Angus Reid	1,524	935	1,264
Populus	1,004	1,067	1,929
YouGov	1,091	1,110	1,151

was fast to complete and so also had a fast turnaround. In the instant and reaction polls, sample was pre-recruited to minimise fieldwork time. Often respondents were reminded in advance of the opportunity to participate in the poll, and so at the end of the debate were expecting a phone call or email invitation to the survey. This helped increase the response rate, which therefore sped up fieldwork.

In the two weeks leading up to the first debate, ComRes recruited a panel of just over 10,000 people who indicated they were likely to watch the debates and would be willing to be contacted by telephone immediately afterwards. Data were collected on their age, gender, region, social group, 2005 General Election vote and current voting intention (in the week before the first debate). This information was used so that we could ensure that the sample was representative and provide additional insight and analysis by demographics and political allegiance.

Similarly, the three online pollsters used pre-recruited online panels who were screened to target those who were likely to watch the debate. Demographic and political information was gathered about the respondents, or was already available from the panel, in order to ensure the sample could be defined and weighted as necessary.

The week before the first debate ComRes ran a full trial, following tests conducted over the prior months. ComRes tested the full system and the computerised automated weighting system and tabulation. The system ran to plan, and the response rate and achieved sample were slightly higher than expected. However, it was important to ensure there was plenty of sample available for the first poll, which enabled a record 4,032 responses to be completed in just six minutes.

Who is the target population?

As a UK first, one of the key questions was 'who will watch the debates?' A number of companies conducted polls in the run-up to the debates to try to understand the audience profile and demographics that were most likely to watch them. While there was a general trend indicating that the viewer profile was likely to be more Conservative identifiers, older age groups and people in social group AB, the viewing figures were generally overestimated in most polls in the weeks preceding the debates.

The second challenge is to decide what a 'right' sample looks like. While there may be a philosophical argument for a sample that is representative of the audience who viewed each debate, there is a political case for modelling the sample as a sub-set of the national voting population and trying to understand what the impact would be on the wider population. In addition, while the viewing audience could be estimated from previous research, the actual numbers would only be released after the debate, and each broadcaster would be likely to attract a slightly different audience.

ComRes decided to model the sample to be nationally, and politically, representative, and following the instant polls we extrapolated the impact on the wider population, having determined the viewing figures. As such, our aim was to look at what impact the debates had on the wider population and to anchor the results to an objective measure. But it was also vital to ensure a political weight, since this tends to have a more significant impact than demographic weighting. Since the debates were so high-profile, the impact of secondary and media coverage in the 24 hours following each debate, especially the first, is vital to understand their impact. The instant polls published on the night explicitly did not, and indeed could not, seek to measure the secondary impact, but polls that were not instant, which ran over the next 48 hours, began to pick up the national impact. Indeed, this was seen particularly strongly in the first voting intention polls after the first debate.

With hindsight, we can look back at the actual profile of the viewers and see where different assumptions about what the sample might look like were right or wrong. The actual viewing figures for each debate are given in Table 5.3.

As well as providing an interesting insight following the polls, these figures provide an inevitable starting point in planning for the next election debates, possibly in 2015 if the Coalition stays the course.

After looking at some of the topline results, we shall scrutinise the different weightings in further detail. But, initially, we can see from the viewing figures that the ITV and BBC debates did have a skew towards older age groups, although the Sky debate had a skew in the other direction. Similarly, each audience had a majority of people in social groups AB and C1 – the higher income earners – but the gender divide was more even than some pre-debate polling had suggested.

Who won the debates?

Each poll addressed different questions, but one headline figure was common among them all: who viewers perceived to have won the debate. Before looking at the results, there are a few important considerations.

Table 5.3 Audience viewing figures

Debate Profiles (per cent)	Audience numbers	Gender		Social Group		Age					
		Male	Female	ABC1	C2DE	18–34	35–44	45–54	55–64	65+
ITV Debate 1	9,679,000	45.7	54.3	60.5	39.5	19.6	16.6	16.1	16.3	31.4
Sky Debate 2	2,212,000	51.9	48.1	73.9	26.1	29.6	18.6	19.8	15.3	16.7
BBC Debate 3	7,428,000	47.5	52.5	65.5	34.5	24.2	15.3	16.5	15.3	28.7
UK adult population	48,675,000	48.6	51.4	55.1	44.9	28.5	18.5	17.2	15.0	20.8

Source: BARB (audience figures); Office of National Statistics 2009 midyear population estimates and National Readership Survey (population figures)

First, when asking who has won the debates, what are pollsters actually measuring? Essentially, it is likely to be judged on performance, rather than meeting a particular tenet that has been laid out, and so respondents are making a judgement about who performed the best during the debate. However, in addition to this top 'who won?' question – which was what dominated media coverage – further questions were included, such as who was the most honest, who gave the most straight answers, who was best on key policy areas and finally, who actually changed their vote.

Second, what was being measured depended on the timing of the post-debate polls. The secondary coverage and commentary about the debates followed immediately after the debates ended. So, without delay, members of the public were being fed with wide-ranging opinions and analysis, which, as time passed, would affect their views of the outcome. As a result, the fastest polls aimed not to be influenced at all by secondary media coverage, but the later polls will have been influenced by those already released within the first hour after the debate. This feeds into what was discussed above, that shortly after the debates even those who did not watch them were inundated with the media analysis and responses – including from the party spin rooms.

The charts and analysis below sum up the key results to the question of 'who won?'

In the first debate, the polls were unanimous – Nick Clegg won outright (Figure 5.1). As had been expected, this amount of profile could

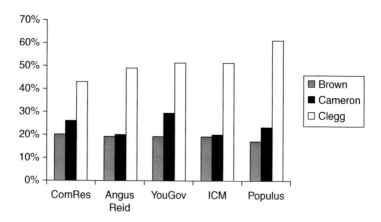

Figure 5.1   Who won the first debate?

only be good for the Liberal Democrats. Even just having that amount of media coverage meant that members of the public could put a face to a name. Although expectations were low, Nick Clegg exceeded them – primarily by being there, looking at the camera and not being Gordon Brown or David Cameron. It was significant that, in the weeks leading up to the campaign, polls had shown consistently that many people who had hitherto supported Labour had made up their mind not to, but equally they struggled to bring themselves to vote Conservative. As a result, the Lib Dems received a massive boost in the polls and showed themselves to be a party to be taken seriously.

However, just because the polls came to the same conclusion – that Nick Clegg won – they did not all give the same result. The range of percentages of those who thought Nick Clegg won was between 43 per cent and 61 per cent – far beyond any margin of error. Clearly the timings, methodology, sampling and weighting must have played their part. The two pollsters who weighted their samples to be nationally representative showed the lowest scores for Nick Clegg, followed by those weighting to an estimated viewer profile. Populus showed the highest figure (61 per cent) with their quotaed but unweighted sample.

Debate two was much harder to call, and the three leaders all came fairly close, with the vote split between them. After Nick Clegg's performance in debate one, Labour and Conservative strategists – stunned by the impact – ordered their leaders to look directly into the camera much more. Gordon Brown had had a dismal first debate, so it was little

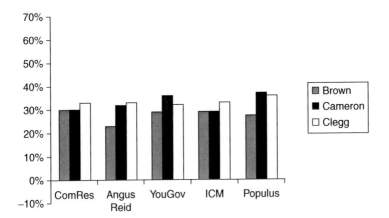

Figure 5.2   Who won the second debate?

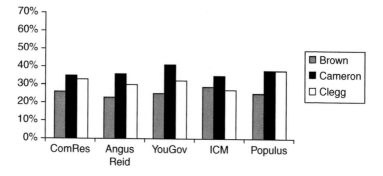

Figure 5.3   Who won the third debate?

surprise that he was deemed to have performed 'better than expected' in the second one. This time the pollsters came much closer in their findings, but did not agree on who took first position (Figure 5.2). ComRes, Angus Reid and ICM put Nick Clegg just ahead of David Cameron, while YouGov and Populus had David Cameron marginally in the lead. As will been seen later, small changes in weighting methodology have a significant impact on who is judged to have won.

At the final hurdle, David Cameron sneaked narrowly into pole position, with between 35 per cent and 41 per cent of the voters agreeing that he had won the third debate (Figure 5.3).

Weighting and waiting

The question of how to get the right sample was addressed in different ways by different pollsters. Following the debates, and once viewing figures were available, ComRes examined what the impact of different weightings would have been. To repeat, we weighted by nationally representative demographic and political rim weights. Once demographic viewing figures had been obtained, we reweighted the data to test whether weighting to actual viewing figures would result in a different outcome. The reweighted results of the lead question of who won each debate are compared in Table 5.4. It is clear that the different weights generally produce results within the margin of error of the first results.

However, it is interesting to note that the closest debate – the second one – is neck and neck between David Cameron and Nick Clegg when this new weighting is applied.

Table 5.4 Impact of actual viewer figures weighting on ComRes instant polls

	Nationally representative weighting	Viewer profile weighting
Debate 1		
Cameron	26%	27%
Clegg	43%	43%
Brown	20%	19%
Debate 2		
Cameron	30%	32%
Clegg	33%	32%
Brown	30%	30%
Debate 3		
Cameron	35%	38%
Clegg	33%	30%
Brown	26%	27%

Source: ComRes

The political impact

After identifying the winners and losers in each debate, ComRes looked at the impact on the voting intentions of those who watched the debate. At recruitment, ComRes collected past vote recall in 2005, propensity to vote on a scale of 1–10 (where 1 = 'certain not to vote' and 10 = 'certain to vote') and current voting intention (collected approximately a week before the first debate). Those 'shy voters' who refused to state a party, but stated they were certain or likely to vote, were reassigned a party based on their party identification at the time of recruitment. While political identification will have some impact on the attitudes of who won the debate and some of the key political issues, how did the debates influence the voting intention of those who watched them?

The voting figures in Table 5.5 are the ComRes results for the *viewers'* voting intentions before and after each debate. The key figures are the percentage point change in each sample's voting intention from before to after each debate. As can be seen, the Liberal Democrats appeared to get a boost following Nick Clegg's performance in each debate, although it did decline over the three weeks, and it is important to remember that is just among the viewing audience.

Table 5.5 Viewer voting intention changes

	Sample voting intention		
	Before debates	**After debate 1**	**Percentage change**
Conservative	39%	36%	−3%
Labour	27%	24%	−3%
Liberal Democrat	21%	35%	+14%
Other	13%	6%	−7%
	Sample voting intention		
	Before debates	**After debate 2**	**Percentage change**
Conservative	37%	35%	−2%
Labour	26%	24%	−2%
Liberal Democrat	25%	36%	+11%
Other	12%	5%	−7%
	Sample voting intention		
	Before debates	**After debate 3**	**Percentage change**
Conservative	38%	36%	−2%
Labour	24%	24%	0%
Liberal Democrat	27%	36%	+9%
Other	11%	4%	−7%

Source: ComRes

The media learnt the hard way, as will be addressed later, that these figures need to be treated with caution. They are for a *subsample* of the population and therefore cannot be compared with regular voting intention polls.

It is particularly useful to look at where exactly this movement was coming from. Table 5.6 shows the 'switchers' from their vote before the debates to after each debate. The shaded boxes in the tables show the percentage of people who before the debates were voting Conservative, Labour, Lib Dem or another party and who would, following the debate, now vote Liberal Democrat.

It is interesting to see that, following each debate, about 15 per cent of the Liberal Democrats' vote among viewers came from those who had previously stated they were voting for other parties. Around 15 per cent of Labour or Conservative voters were suggesting they would vote Liberal Democrat, but, interestingly, around a third of people voting for

Table 5.6   Switching voting allegiance

| Vote following debate 1 | Recorded (pre-debate) voting intention | | | |
	Conservative	Labour	Liberal Democrat	Other
Conservative	82%	3%	5%	16%
Labour	3%	81%	8%	8%
Liberal Democrat	14%	16%	87%	39%
Other	1%	1%	1%	36%

| Vote following debate 2 | Recorded (pre-debate) voting intention | | | |
	Conservative	Labour	Liberal Democrat	Other
Conservative	83%	5%	4%	18%
Labour	4%	76%	9%	7%
Liberal Democrat	12%	19%	87%	29%
Other	1%	0%	0%	46%

| Vote following debate 3 | Recorded (pre-debate) voting intention | | | |
	Conservative	Labour	Liberal Democrat	Other
Conservative	84%	2%	6%	25%
Labour	4%	79%	10%	8%
Liberal Democrat	11%	19%	83%	36%
Other	1%	1%	1%	31%

Source: ComRes

other minor parties were looking as if they might switch to the Liberal Democrats as a consequence of the debates.

Beyond the instant polls, what was the impact on the wider campaign? Figure 5.4 shows the average daily voting figures during the campaign. The so-called Lib Dem surge can be seen as a consequence of the first debate, but after that it steadily decreased towards polling day. However, the hype surrounding the debates began before the first debate, and then the subsequent polls demonstrated the impact. It quickly became evident that the debates were going to massively disrupt the election campaign – they dominated the three weeks leading up to 6 May. Rather than running with policy themes each day, as had been the case in previous elections, the leaders and their advisers would go to ground in the run-up to each debate to rehearse and prepare as best they could.

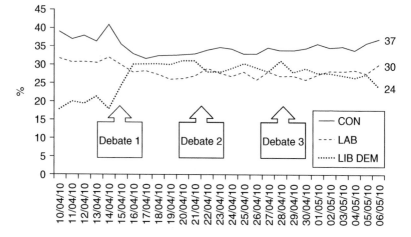

Figure 5.4   Average daily voting intention polls during the campaign

So, while the debates appeared to be the defining points of the campaign, and indeed ensured that personalities, above policies, seemed to define the mood, by the end of the campaign the Lib Dem rise was muted. If we look back at previous general elections, the Lib Dems' vote share tends to increase a little over the final six months as election day approaches, but this year the pollsters all overestimated the impact of the Clegg effect that resulted from the first debate. (This issue is explored further in the chapter by Roger Mortimore and Simon Atkinson.)

Further findings from the leadership debates

Debate one: the Clegg effect

As seen above, after the first debate Nick Clegg was the clear winner. However, the Conservatives, closely followed by the Lib Dems, were seen to have the best policies on immigration, and this topic became increasingly important during the campaign. While it was not a leading policy in any of the manifestos, this debate and Gordon Brown's mishap at 'Bigotgate' two weeks later meant that immigration, an issue close to the heart of many voters, took a higher profile.

Another key concern among the public, both during the campaign and leading into autumn 2010, was the issue of spending cuts. Voters considered who was the safest pair of hands when it came to making decisions about spending cuts. After debate one David Cameron and Nick Clegg were equal, with 36 per cent of viewers considering each to be the best bet. Nick Clegg emerged from the debates as being considered trustworthy and the most likely to give straight answers. At the end of a year that had been tarred with the consequences of the expenses scandal, the public were looking for a politician they felt they could trust. The debates positioned Nick Clegg as this person. However, looking back now, it seems that this helped sow the seeds of his later unpopularity as Deputy Prime Minister, as a result of policies such as the increase in tuition fees, and a view held among a majority of the public that he had lied to them.

Debate two: nervous consolidation

By debate two, expectations had been set. Indeed, 47 per cent of viewers thought that Gordon Brown performed better than expected in this debate, compared with just 21 per cent of people for Nick Clegg and 27 per cent for David Cameron. For Gordon Brown, while he was not considered to have won, the expectations for him had been set so low that he could hardly fail to overcome them.

Following the expenses scandal in 2009, the issue of trust and honesty from politicians was a key factor during the campaign. With an uncertain economic future and politicians having hit rock bottom on truthfulness ratings, who would be considered the most honest during the debates?

Forty-three per cent of viewers thought Nick Clegg gave the most honest answers – compared with 29 per cent for David Cameron and 23 per cent for Gordon Brown (Figure 5.5). Nick Clegg had the advantage of being less tainted by expenses than the other parties and also

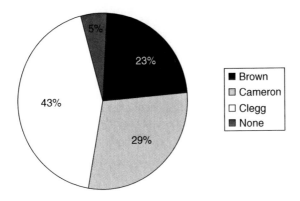

Figure 5.5 Who gave the most honest answers?

being the third party – hence setting himself apart from the others was a clear advantage when it came to truthfulness.

Debate three: Cameron narrowly triumphs

By debate three, David Cameron was ahead in winning the debate, and had also crept ahead on 'most trusted to make decisions on spending cuts' – 36 per cent compared with 33 per cent for Nick Clegg and 31 per cent for Gordon Brown, but it was still close.

Other instant polls tracked 'best prime minister': the Populus figures are shown in Table 5.7.

The results for best Prime Minister mirror the results of who won the debates, with Nick Clegg being the clear winner after debate one and David Cameron and Nick Clegg being fairly level after debates two and three. However, David Cameron did not manage to regain the position he held before the debates.

YouGov also tracked who viewers thought was the 'most evasive and least willing to give straight answers'(Table 5.8). Despite winning the last debate, David Cameron was considered the most evasive and only Gordon Brown managed to improve his ratings on this negative factor.

This poll backs up a ComRes poll for the *Independent* in February 2010, showing that most of the public saw David Cameron as a 'slick

Table 5.7 Best PM from debates

Best PM	Pre debates	Post first debate	Post second debate	Post third debate
David Cameron	47%	35%	37%	37%
Gordon Brown	30%	22%	26%	25%
Nick Clegg	23%	43%	37%	38%

Source: Populus

Table 5.8 Most evasive and least willing to give straight answers

	Debate 1	Debate 2	Debate 3
Gordon Brown	48%	30%	29%
David Cameron	44%	45%	49%
Nick Clegg	4%	21%	19%
Don't know	4%	4%	3%

Source: YouGov

salesman' and worried about what he was like underneath. In the months before the election campaign, David Cameron struggled to demonstrate clear policy messages, and the public overall were unclear what he stood for. These results demonstrate that this feeling continued during the campaign.

The media reaction

Four out of the five instant and reaction polls were commissioned by media outlets: ComRes polled for ITV News, ICM polled for the *Guardian*, Populus polled for *The Times* and YouGov for the *Sun*. This brought in a competitive angle and positioned each of the separate methodologies into the context of practical politics.

Following the first debate, 16 April will be remembered in the ComRes office. Just after 11 am on that morning, the day after the night of the first debate, was what Gary Gibbon, Political Editor of Channel 4 News, dubbed 'the ComRes Hour'. A journalist inadvertently tweeted data from the viewers' voting intention figures in the instant poll, assuming it to be a nationally representative sample. The figures suggested the Lib Dems had increased their vote share from 21 per cent to 35 per cent – in second place, just one percentage point behind the Conservatives. As excitement spread, it precipitated turmoil on the currency markets. Political journalists travelling with Gordon Brown and David Cameron, were offered the opportunity of challenging the two main party leaders to respond to the surge.

The interest in the poll results was so significant that at the ComRes office a queue of Westminster journalists gathered at the door and the website received such high volumes of traffic that it temporarily crashed. As soon as it became apparent what had happened, a clarification statement was released and the media frenzy died down again, but it demonstrated just how potent poll results could be in driving the media agency in the wake of the debates.

It also highlights the importance of addressing the final challenge listed at the start of the chapter – how to report and analyse the results in the heat of a fast-moving election campaign and an even faster-moving world of social media.

Conclusion

What was a new phenomenon, and defined the whole election campaign, is now likely to be a permanent fixture. The genie cannot be put back in the bottle now. In a year when there were more polls than ever before, and five pollsters gauging instant reaction, what can we take away to learn for next time?

First, the importance of knowing the audience – in future debates, the viewing figures and results from 2010 are likely to prove useful. It is debatable whether a viewer-profiled sample or a nationally representative sample is ideal, as both have their advantages and disadvantages, but this needs to be carefully considered. On the one hand, a nationally representative sample demonstrates the impact on the whole voting population and provides an objective measure to anchor the results to. However, it does not take into account the demographic skew of the viewer profile, to generally higher income groups and older age groups. A viewer-profiled sample does take this into account, and yet the exact profile of viewers is unknown until after the debates.

Second, the importance of timing – if you poll too early then the debate is still going, but if you poll too late the secondary coverage, and indeed other polls, could influence the outcome.

Finally, the lesson of interpretation. While more than nine million people watched the debates, and millions more will have been influenced by the coverage afterwards, pollsters still face the challenge of how to model this impact, and how to manage media expectations and analysis under the tight timing and pressure that come with a fast-paced election campaign. Debates are likely to be a permanent feature of elections from now on.

There is a real need for the instant polls. They provide a clear indication of results, which are impossible for the parties to spin; the media is hungry for real and immediate feedback; and the pundits can easily get it wrong – so public opinion is vital. However, there is the wider impact to take into account. Instant polls do risk misinterpretation and do not measure the real immediate impact on the wider population of non-viewers.

After the debates, ComRes looked into the change in national voting intention in our polls. Table 5.9 shows ComRes's national voting intention poll results on 14 April and 18 April – before and after the first election debate.

So what happened in the middle to viewers and non-viewers? ComRes recorded the voting intention of viewers in the instant debate poll on the evening of 15 April. Given that 9.9 million people viewed the debate and 37.4 million people did not view the debate, ComRes used the figures for national voting intention after the debate and the figures for

Table 5.9 National voting intention before and after the first debate

	ComRes voting intentions 14 April	ComRes voting intentions 18 April
Conservative	35%	31%
Labour	29%	27%
Liberal Democrat	21%	29%
Other	15%	13%

Source: ComRes

Table 5.10 Voting intention of viewers of the first debate

	Instant poll viewers' voting intentions 15 April	Extrapolated non-viewers' voting intentions
Conservative	36%	30%
Labour	24%	28%
Liberal Democrat	35%	27%
Other	6%	15%

Source: ComRes

viewers' voting intention after the debate to extrapolate the impact on non-viewers.

As we can see, the impact on the Lib Dem vote among viewers was vast, moving up to 35 per cent, while the Conservative vote share fell to 30 per cent (Table 5.10). However, the Liberal Democrat vote share increased from 21 per cent nationally to 27 per cent among non-viewers, as a result of that secondary coverage. So, while the Lib Dem surge was particularly pronounced among debate viewers after the first debate, it is clearly evident among non-viewers as well.

The conclusion to be drawn, therefore, is that, while the impact of that first debate was very strong among viewers, there was a profound shift in opinion among non-viewers in the hours following it. Of course, the debate can only *directly* influence the people who watch it. There are many more who do not but whose opinions of the race are transformed by the reporting of the debate. The instant polls are an important and revealing element, and they set the tone of that post-debate analysis.

Part II
Polling

6
Were the Polls Wrong about the Lib Dems All Along?

Simon Atkinson and Roger Mortimore

Introduction

Opinion polls in modern elections serve several purposes. From the amount of attention that tends to be paid after the election to analysing the accuracy of the final 'predictions', it might seem that this rather trivial game of trying to give the newspapers news of the result a few hours ahead of the vote-counting is the only important one. But of course it is not.

In theory the polls are only intended to measure; but inevitably, as the results are published, they also affect what they are measuring. The media coverage of the election is much influenced by the flow of the narrative, as indicated by the polls, and parties and public alike react to them. As Chapters 5 and 7 demonstrate, the potential for the polls to affect the campaign was perhaps greater than ever in 2010, with more polls than ever before and the new element of the leaders' debates and the polling that went with the reporting of them.

During recent British elections, the pollsters have particularly concentrated their efforts on correctly measuring the Conservative and Labour shares of the vote. This is partly in reaction to the election of 1992, when all the pollsters were seen as having 'got it wrong', over-predicting Labour's share of the vote and under-predicting the Conservative share, and were roundly criticised as a result. As worrying as the fact that all the polls were 'wrong' was that, within very narrow margins, they all agreed. As Kellner et al. explain in Chapter 7, several separate sources of error were uncovered (Market Research Society, 1994). After 1992, all the pollsters changed their methods, in some cases radically, and made further refinements after subsequent elections, as their predictions proved better but not perfect. Some companies retired from the business altogether, while other new ones joined the fray.

By 2005, the third general election after 1992, the polling industry looked close to having solved this perennial problem, producing the best performance in its history with not a single poll more than two percentage points out in predicting any party's vote share. Yet some misgivings remained. Critics pointed out in particular that the remaining errors, tiny as they were, still seemed to be systematically in favour of Labour and against the Conservatives.

The 2010 election might seem, therefore, as if it should be triumph and vindication for the pollsters. The average predicted lead was within a point of the final outcome and, this time, the error was slightly in the Conservatives' favour rather than Labour's. Better still, almost all the polls were in close agreement: of the nine final polls from British Polling Council (BPC) affiliated companies,[1] eight had the Conservatives on between 35 per cent and 37 per cent of the vote, and all had Labour on between 27 per cent and 29 per cent.[2] All but one put the lead between 6 and 9 points, a fine prediction of the real 7.2-point lead and pointing unerringly to a hung Parliament in which the Conservatives were the largest party (see Table 7.2 in Chapter 7 for the detailed figures).

The problem, though, was that they proved noticeably less accurate at predicting the Liberal Democrat share: all nine BPC polls put the Lib Dems on between 26 per cent and 29 per cent, whereas in the event they secured only 23.6 per cent. Of course, this did not occur because of any lack of effort to measure the Liberal Democrat share correctly. It was entirely unforeseen. In no previous British election have the polls ever seemed to have any serious difficulty in measuring the strength of the Liberal Democrats or their predecessors; there is no record at all of over-predicting the party's strength (see Table 7.1 in Chapter 7).

Nevertheless, in 2010 the polls – with a convincing show of unanimity – predicted one thing, and when the ballot boxes were opened the voting showed another. Arguably, an error of this scale in measuring Lib Dem share is much less serious than an error in the relative strength of Labour and the Tories. Because Liberal Democrat success tends to be much more locally concentrated than that of the two larger parties, their national vote share is a relatively poor predictor of the number of seats the party will win. (In fact, in 2010 they lost seats despite gaining votes, and precisely the converse had been true in 1997.) In any case, within fairly broad limits the number of Lib Dem seats does not affect the main outcome of the election – with 20 more or 20 less than they actually won they would still have been the third party in any coalition negotiations, and equally powerless if either the Conservatives or Labour had won a majority. So it could be said that the error in the Lib

Dem share could not be in any real way misleading about the likely outcome of the election, and was therefore only a blow to the pollsters' professional pride.

On the other hand, errors in the final poll predictions raise questions about the credibility of the polls earlier in the campaign. In 2010, the story of the Liberal Democrat vote share was the story of the campaign. The apparent impact of Nick Clegg's debate performance on the intentions of voters, the perceived possibility that the Liberal Democrats might overtake Labour to take second place; these were the factors that to a great extent drove the way the election was seen and was reported, and perhaps the way it was fought. If the polls were wrong about the Lib Dems come polling day, had they been wrong all along? What was the real state of public opinion when the polls were showing a dramatic, though slowly fading, 'Lib Dem surge'? Was everybody being misled?

Since the only systematic evidence of the course of public opinion during the election is the polls themselves, we can only interpret what they have to tell us if we can understand why they were 'wrong' at the last moment, which may also indicate how reliable their measures were earlier in the campaign. Thus in this chapter we approach the question of why the polls failed to predict the result not in a spirit of pure curiosity, nor as pollsters trying to ensure that we can avoid any recurrence of the problem next time around, but with the hope of reconstructing the real course of the parties' fortunes during the campaign, and thereby understanding better the interaction between the polls, the parties and the public in 2010.

The polls and their methods

This is not the place to attempt a detailed methodological post-mortem of the 2010 polls. Suffice to say that the evidence that has emerged from the companies' own investigations and those of the academics has been, so far, inconclusive and to some extent contradictory. However, it is at least possible to say that some interpretations of the polls during the campaign seem much likelier than others. To understand this, we need to take on board two important points.

The first is that the 'error' in the final polls was not random but systematic. Random sampling error could explain a single poll missing the mark in this way; it cannot explain nine separately making the same mistake in unison. We need to treat these nine poll results as a single phenomenon to be explained rather than as nine isolated events. Furthermore, the agreement in the polls was not merely a last-minute convergence: the five companies (ComRes, ICM, Ipsos MORI, Populus and YouGov) that had been publishing regular polls throughout the parliament had been generally in step with each other in their voting intention measures for almost all of this period.[3]

It therefore seems reasonable to assume that all the final polls were making the same mistake or were afflicted by the same distorting phenomenon. However – unlike in 1992 – the polls were not all reaching their conclusions by the same methods: there was a considerable divergence in sampling, weighting and data interpretation. Some of the companies used telephone samples with random digit dialling (RDD), though with different methods of deciding which household member to interview when the phone was answered; others had recruited a panel of internet users, and could use information collected from them in previous surveys to help in drawing the sample; one still used the traditional face-to-face quota sampling method. All companies weighted their data demographically, but, while some also used some form of 'political weighting' (on the basis of either reported past vote or party identification), others did not. Some used a 'squeeze question' to persuade don't knows and refusers to volunteer a voting intention; some imputed a voting intention to those not giving one; some did both. Most made some adjustment on the basis of respondents' expressed likelihood of voting, but varied considerably in the stringency of this adjustment and hence in the difference it made to voting intentions. In fact, no two of the regular pollsters used essentially identical methods.[4]

This is the second important point. The cause of the overestimation of the Liberal Democrat vote in 2010 must rest in something common to the models underlying all the polling methodologies, not in the detailed nuts and bolts of particular methodologies where we are more used to searching for errors.

What might have happened

With this context understood, let us turn to considering the course of the 2010 election campaign. The heavy line in Figure 6.1 tracks the rolling three-day average of the Liberal Democrat share of the vote in the published national polls (grouping polls by fieldwork date rather than by publication date, and taking each as a measurement of the share halfway through its fieldwork). This can be taken as a rough representation of the Liberal Democrats' election as measured by the polls, though, being a rolling average, it understates the suddenness of the increase in support after the debate on 15 April. The black square at the

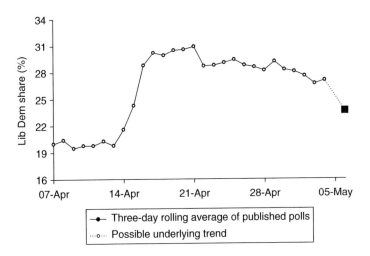

Figure 6.1 Late swing scenario

right hand edge of the chart indicates the 23.6 per cent of the vote the Liberal Democrats eventually achieved.

So what was really happening while the polls told the public that the trend was as shown by the heavy line? The simplest possibility is that the polls were right all along, and that the Liberal Democrats simply lost support in the final 24 hours or so, after the last opinion poll was complete. This, which we can call the **late swing scenario**, is shown by the dotted line in Figure 6.1. It might have involved a direct swing of voters from the Liberal Democrats to other parties, or simply a lower turnout by Liberal Democrats, or a combination of both. (Bear in mind, though, that the polls attempt to allow for differential turnout – their 'predictions' are intended to measure the proportions of the public who will vote for each party, not simply the proportions of supporters regardless of turnout. So, in this scenario, 27 per cent of those fully intending to vote at the time of the final polls were Liberal Democrats, and if the change depended on turnout it involved some of these changing their minds and not voting, rather than their already being less likely to vote than their Labour and Conservative counterparts.)

A last-minute swing is not, on the face of it, impossible or even improbable; after all, it is a much less dramatic movement than the apparent leap in support earlier in the campaign. Furthermore, as can be seen from the graph, there was already some evidence of a modest downwards trend over the previous few days. Moreover, it is clear that public opinion in the 2010 election was unusually volatile: in Ipsos MORI's final poll, 30 per cent of those giving a voting intention said they might still change their mind who to vote for, many more than at any previous election, and in our post-election poll 14 per cent of those who said they had voted told us that they had decided which party to vote for within the final 24 hours.

This possibility would, of course, answer all reasons for concern about the polls earlier in the campaign. But, comfortable as this scenario would be for the pollsters, it is perhaps unlikely. The direct evidence from the polls is limited and inconsistent. The final polls found a slight uptick in Liberal Democrat strength compared with those of the previous few days, arguing against a continual slippage of support. And, while Populus found lower support for the Liberal Democrats on the Wednesday than the Tuesday in their final poll, YouGov found support similar on the Tuesday and Wednesday (Wells, 2010), and Ipsos MORI's callback on Wednesday of respondents contacted on Tuesday (specifically designed to detect any late swing) found no evidence of one. The evidence from post-election surveys re-contacting respondents from the pre-election polls (Boon and Curtice, 2010) and those interviewing fresh samples also seems to be mostly against a late swing, though the British Election Study (BES) campaign study found significant evidence of a lower turnout by Liberal Democrats than by Conservative or Labour supporters (Whiteley et al., 2010). In any case, the strength of this post-election evidence depends on how far we trust people's after-the-event reports of their voting behaviour. So there is room for disagreement on how to interpret the post-election polls.

Another simple explanation would be that there was a **long-term bias** in the poll findings – caused presumably by the composition of their samples, the way that their questions were answered or the way that the pollsters interpreted the data, so that they systematically overestimated Liberal Democrat strength throughout the election campaign and perhaps long beforehand. Figure 6.2 shows how the real course of public opinion might have looked in this scenario.

There are several convincing reasons for finding this suggestion highly unlikely. First, all the polls made the same prediction despite their diversity of methodologies, which would suggest they must all be making the same error. One could imagine, for example, how this might arise if all the polls were weighted on the basis of reported past vote and set their weighting targets to the wrong level, so as to artificially inflate the number of Liberal Democrats in their weighted samples; but, in

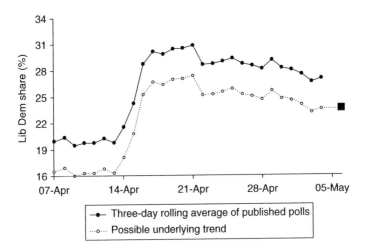

Figure 6.2 Long-term sampling bias scenario

2010, the companies that did not use political weighting had similar high measures of Liberal Democrat strength to those that did.

Second, it must be remembered that the polls have never previously had any problem predicting Liberal Democrat strength: on the contrary, during the 2005 General Election the established pollsters – using essentially the same methods as in 2010 – estimated the Lib Dem vote correctly. The distorting factor must have been new, and one that would equally affect all the different sampling methods and projection models used by the different companies.

What, then, might in theory cause such an error? Perhaps some new sampling bias may have arisen since 2005. Or perhaps an existing and unnoticed bias in the samples, which had previously had no partisan effect, might have started to distort voting intentions for the first time: if some group were greatly over-represented in the polls, and if in 2010 they disproportionately supported the Liberal Democrats whereas previously their votes had been evenly spread, this might produce such an outcome. Or perhaps for some reason a significant part of the adult population began consistently telling pollsters that they intended to vote Liberal Democrat even though they did not intend to do so. However, there has never been anything to suggest that any of these possibilities were true.

The strongest argument against the long-term bias scenario, perhaps, is Occam's Razor (the philosophical principle that asserts, in essence, that simplest explanations are best). In the 2010 election we saw two unusual and unexpected phenomena in Liberal Democrat voting intentions – a literally overnight leap of unprecedented size in recorded support after the first debate, and a significant over-prediction of final vote share – whereas in other respects the polls behaved as expected. Common sense suggests that there is probably a link between the two. For Liberal Democrat support to be overestimated for the first time because of a previously unsuspected existing bias, and entirely coincidentally at the same election for Liberal Democrat support to undergo the sharpest movement ever seen in the polls during a British election campaign, with no connection between them, is a little hard to swallow. (It is much easier to believe in a bias that only began to take effect after and because of the impact of the first debate; but that involves a different scenario, a different shape to our dotted line, and is therefore considered below.)

However, assume for a moment that the long-term bias scenario is correct. In that case, although the exact level of Liberal Democrat support would always have been wrongly measured, the story of the campaign as shown by the polls would have been essentially true. There would still have been an unprecedented surge of 'Cleggmania', the Lib Dems would still at their high point have been challenging Labour for second place (if not quite so strongly as supposed), and there would have still been a subsequent slow leaking of support from this peak in the following three weeks. If this was the real story, the public were not materially misled by the polls.

The third of the straightforward possibilities is that which we might characterise as **'the phantom surge'** – in other words, the spike in Liberal Democrat support that the polls detected after the first debate was completely spurious, and bore no relation to reality. In that case, the real shape of Liberal Democrat support was probably something like the dotted line in Figure 6.3.

Now, whatever the trend in real voting intentions, all the pollsters found a rise after the first debate in the proportion of the public saying that they intended to vote Liberal Democrat. So, if the surge did not really exist, either a great many people were suddenly telling the pollsters that they intended to vote Liberal Democrat when they did not, or existing Liberal Democrats were suddenly much more likely to be interviewed and so skewed the poll samples.

Here we need to introduce a concept already familiar to students of the polls, the 'spiral of silence'. Stated simply, the spiral of silence theory suggests that, when a party is seen to be unpopular, this will

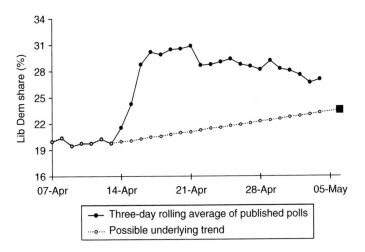

Figure 6.3   Phantom surge scenario

discourage its remaining supporters from admitting their loyalties: they may decline to take part in polls altogether, may refuse to answer voting intention questions, or may say they are undecided or unlikely to vote when in fact their voting intentions are clear. There is a good deal of evidence that this does indeed occur on occasion, and that it was one of the factors in the error in the polls in the 1992 election.

But the converse is probably true as well. Support for a party felt to be popular and fashionable – the Liberal Democrats in 2010 after Nick Clegg's performance in the first debate? – might be exaggerated. A supportive social atmosphere could have caused Liberal Democrats to be more willing than before to take part in polls, to exaggerate their likelihood of turning out (maybe to themselves as well as to the polls), and the don't knows or won't votes might have felt more comfortable by appearing to be part of a newly flourishing Liberal Democrat consensus among their peers than by remaining non-committal.

However, this sort of reverse spiral of silence would surely need some sort of trigger. If Liberal Democrat support was being inflated by an impression that the party was popular and fashionable, where was this impression coming from? Not from the polls – it is the very first polls showing a Liberal Democrat surge that this theory is trying to explain away. From the impression that Nick Clegg had won the first debate? But (as Andrew Hawkins and Caroline Lawes show in Chapter 5) the instant reaction debate polls were already finding a swing among those who had watched the debate, before they had had any chance to absorb the wider reaction. Moreover, that was a real swing, of identifiable respondents changing the voting intention they had given before the debates, not just a sampling error caused by Liberal Democrats suddenly becoming unusually willing to take part in polls.

This does not rule out the possibility of a more subtle effect, in which the excitement and 'buzz' around Nick Clegg's performance caused the public to exaggerate, to themselves as well as to the pollsters, how much impact it was having on their opinions. It may be that for a short period many voters felt they would probably vote Liberal Democrat, even though their underlying loyalties to other parties were too strong and this was never really likely to happen, or even if they were never likely to turn out at all despite believing at that moment that they would. But, in opinion polling terms, such a movement would be 'real' – except perhaps in the final 'prediction' poll, we would never claim to measure what voters *will* do, only what they think they will do.

This movement in voting intentions looks just too sudden to be wholly attributable to a spiral of silence type explanation. As the name implies, the classic view of such spirals is that they build gradually; an initial peak in support from which all subsequent movement was downwards simply does not fit the shape we should expect from such a cause. There must have been some sort of real spike in opinion, and the completely phantom surge does not seem a realistic possibility.

However, it is less easy to dismiss the possibility of some 'reverse spiral of silence' process at a slightly later stage, once the initial surge to the Liberal Democrats was an established fact and a positive climate of opinion towards the party had had a chance to spread. This gives us our fourth possible scenario, in which voters feel reluctant to admit that their enthusiasm for the party making the momentum in the election is fading, so preventing the polls from accurately measuring how quickly support for the party fell away again. We might call this scenario a '**spiral of noise**'. Two alternative possible underlying trends, with support falling away steadily from the first peak until polling day (4A) or falling away more sharply (4B), are shown in Figure 6.4.

However, this scenario is purely speculative – we do not know of any positive evidence, conclusive or inconclusive, pointing towards this being the case. Moreover, there are two arguments that suggest this explanation is unlikely, although neither is strong enough to prove it impossible. The first concerns the nature of 'spiral of silence' and 'spiral of noise' effects, which are simply a special case of a phenomenon well known to survey researchers, 'social desirability bias'. There is good deal

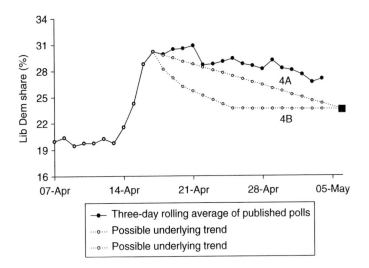

Figure 6.4 'Spiral of noise' scenario

of general evidence that social desirability bias tends to be lower in self-completion surveys than when the respondent is interacting directly with an interviewer. This would suggest that we might expect this effect to be less strong in the internet polls, which use self-completion questionnaires, than in the telephone or face-to-face polls. However, the internet polls found no signs of the Liberal Democrat surge being smaller or less robust than did the other polls.

Secondly, we would expect a significant part of any exaggeration of Liberal Democrat share in this scenario to come from Liberal Democrats becoming disproportionately willing to take part in surveys. But we can test this to some extent with the internet polls, because their samples are drawn from panels and there is, therefore, contemporary information recorded about their previous political views. Anthony Wells of YouGov has reported in his Polling Report blog (Wells, 2010) that after the first debate response rates in their panel rose among (pre-debate) Liberal Democrat identifiers, but no more than the rise among Conservative and Labour identifiers; so there is no evidence of a spiral of noise or of silence where we would most readily expect to find it.

But, once again, let us suppose that this scenario gives the best approximation of the underlying trend. In that case, did the polls give a misleading impression? If the real trend was line 4A, a gradual but steady falling away of support from the Lib Dem peak, it is hard to argue that the impression was very different from reality: true, the degree to which support fell off may have been slightly underestimated and the eventual discrepancy wider than is normally expected in allowing the polls a 'margin of error', but the broad story was in fact faithfully reflected.

Arguably, though, the polls would have been more materially misleading if the collapse in Liberal Democrat support had been sharper, as line 4B suggests. If this was the truth, then the Lib Dem 'surge' was only a short-lived spike in opinion, and not the lasting step-change that the polls seemed to indicate. This would mean that the very nature of the impact of the first debate on the election was misunderstood, and possibly that both the media narrative and campaigning priorities were based on a misconception about the debate's importance. This would, certainly, be a worrying possibility.

However, it should be borne in mind that, if this is what happened, a substantial part of the overstating of Liberal Democrat support after the first debate probably came from people sympathetic to the party exaggerating their likelihood of turning out. In this case there is, perhaps, a very fine line between the polls being 'wrong' and the polls being 'right' but eventual turnout not living up to voters' own expectations. Certainly, the parties should not have been taken by surprise if this was the case: the support that the Liberal Democrats apparently picked up came disproportionately from groups with historically low turnouts – the young and those who had not voted at the previous election – and seemed (at least on the basis of Ipsos MORI's polls) to have been drawn very largely from people who up to the time of the first debate had not been sure that they would vote at all, rather than from those who had previously been determined to vote for other parties. Even if the polls were absolutely accurate at this stage, cautious observers should have had the possibility of Liberal Democrat support not fully materialising on polling day well in mind. But perhaps the pollsters could do more to put across to the media the element of uncertainty that fluctuating turnouts give to levels of party support in modern elections.

Finally, let us consider a fifth scenario, that the polls measured the *shape* of the trend in Liberal Democrat support accurately but that they overestimated the *size* of the movement that had taken place – in other words a scenario of **exaggerated swing**. (In Figure 6.5 the possible underlying trend has been calculated simply by taking the Lib Dems' pre-debate support as the baseline, and assuming that the real excess of support above this line was a constant fraction of the increase indicated by the polls.)

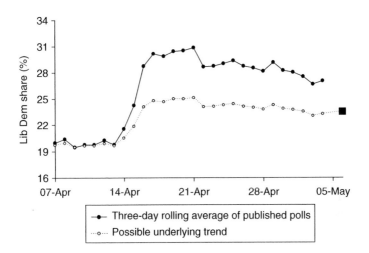

Figure 6.5 Exaggerated swing scenario

There is at least limited, though perhaps inconclusive, evidence for this scenario, in that it appears that the parties' canvass returns reported a significantly smaller surge than did the polls (Kavanagh and Cowley, 2010: 238). As it happens, the exaggerated swing scenario as a theory of the real trend in Liberal Democrat support fits several entirely distinct theories explaining the reason for the error.

The first of these possibilities is that, starting from the time of the first debate, there was a sampling bias – those intending to vote Liberal Democrat were systematically over-represented among those people who were interviewed by the polls. Perhaps there was some group of the public that, unnoticed by the pollsters, has always been over-represented in samples but has not previously been politically distinctive and therefore has not distorted poll findings; if this group swung especially strongly to the Liberal Democrats after the first debate, since they were over-represented the polls would exaggerate the size of the swing.

But why should any group be over-represented, and is it likely that they would swing more than average to the Liberal Democrats in 2010? One suggestion that has been made might answer both those objections. People who take a greater than average interest in politics might well be over-represented, since they will probably be more likely to agree to take part in polls if asked. Such people would also be more likely to have watched the debates and therefore be more likely to have been affected by them; certainly the poll evidence from the campaign showed that those who watched the debates were more likely to support the Liberal Democrats than those who did not.

An entirely different possibility is that the samples were representative of the adult public, and that the polls accurately measured what the public *believed* they would do, but that the polls did not succeed in making an adequate adjustment for turnout – in other words, the 'real' swing was exaggerated because many of those swinging to the Liberal Democrats were never really likely to vote at all, and did not do so when it came to the point.

As already noted, there is some evidence that may point in this direction in Ipsos MORI's polls. Comparing the pre- and post-debate polls, there was no sign of any net movement from Conservative or Labour to Liberal Democrat: there were as many respondents 'certain to vote' and intending to vote Conservative and Labour as there had been before the start of the campaign. But the number 'certain to vote' *and intending to vote Liberal Democrat* had increased massively, at the expense of those who had not previously said they were certain to vote at all. This also seems to make intuitive sense: we would expect those previously less interested in politics to have less strong commitments to any party and therefore to be more susceptible to a campaign element such as the debates; and also it would be unsurprising if their eventual turnout was lower than that of those who were already committed to voting before the campaign got underway.

But again we need to bear in mind that, should this be the true explanation, there is room for more than one interpretation of what should be considered the 'real' situation that the pollsters were trying to measure. If the voters themselves believed they would vote Liberal Democrat, though in reality they were unlikely to do so, should they be thought of as 'really' Liberal Democrats at that point in time or not?

Another variation of this theory would incorporate the spiral of silence possibilities already outlined. In this case, in addition to any honest but over-optimistic inflation of likely turnout by genuine Liberal Democrats, the 'Cleggmania' atmosphere following the first debate might have encouraged those leaning towards the Liberal Democrats to express their support, while some Conservatives or Labour supporters might have been inhibited from doing so. This could involve both conscious exaggeration or playing down of likelihood of voting, and Conservative or Labour supporters recording themselves as 'don't knows', while some genuine 'don't knows' were counted as intending to vote Liberal Democrat. Such a process might well produce an outcome similar to scenario 5, and would certainly be considered a more clear-cut case of the polls being 'wrong'. That said, however, it should be remembered that several of the polls make explicit adjustments to protect against a spiral of silence, and they were no more accurate in predicting the Liberal Democrat share than those that do not. While this explanation is possible, there seems to be no evidence that clearly points towards it.

If the exaggerated swing scenario is true, the polls may have encouraged everybody to accord the debates more importance than they deserved, and to take seriously an outcome that was never realistic: the Liberal Democrats finishing ahead of Labour in votes. But it would imply that the impact of the first debate was still real, giving a very real boost to Liberal Democrat strength, so that the course of the campaign was perhaps distorted but not totally misrepresented. The media would still have been right to focus on Nick Clegg as the main story of the election, albeit not to the extent that the polls suggested that he was. The overall impression would certainly to some extent have been misleading, but much less so than in the spiral of noise scenario where a spike in support was misunderstood as a step change.

Conclusion

We remain unsure what caused the discrepancy between the polls' final 'prediction' of the Liberal Democrat vote and the party's actual share of the vote in 2010. Yet, despite this, it is possible to narrow down what really happened during the campaign to a relatively small number of likely possibilities. It is certainly not impossible that the polls were right all along. If they were not, the likeliest possibilities seem either the exaggerated swing hypothesis (Figure 6.5, where the polls overstated the scale of the Lib Dem surge but otherwise reflected the course of events accurately) or the first spiral of noise hypothesis (line 4A in Figure 6.4, where the falling off of Lib Dem support after the surge was understated but, again, the rough shape of the public's opinions was not misrepresented too drastically). If that is the case, the polls did not tell a wholly inaccurate story. But they will hope to do better next time, of course, and a big challenge will be working out whether the 2010 experience was peculiar to this campaign, or exposed weaknesses that will need to be addressed in what is likely to be a very different electoral climate come the next general election.

The 2010 campaign has underlined the need for polling organisations to explain what is happening alongside their regular voting intention figures, which are given so much prominence. In particular, there is a clear need to report on how intentions to *actually vote on the day* are changing and among which groups – something that was less necessary before the 2000s, when turnouts of between 70 per cent and 80 per cent were the norm.

Nevertheless, looking at the campaign as a whole, it does not seem unreasonable to say that the polls made more of a positive than a negative contribution to the election. In their absence, with only the media pundits and the party spin rooms to map the course of the campaign, the likelihood of misunderstandings and misconceptions would have been far greater.

The only exception to this, perhaps, is the second spiral of noise scenario, in which the polls accurately recorded a huge pro-Clegg surge, then failed to notice that the bubble had burst immediately (the lower line on Figure 6.4). If this were the case the polls would, perhaps, have more to answer for. However, none of the evidence seems to suggest that this was true; unless something subsequently emerges to revive the theory, we can probably conclude with relief that the impact of the polls' inaccuracy (assuming, of course, that they were inaccurate) was small. Nevertheless, the possibility should be a reminder of why accuracy in the polls is important and why the polling organisations will never be able to conclude that they have found the perfect method; as so often in life, as one set of problems appear to be solved, new ones lie in wait.

Notes

1. Throughout the chapter, we confine ourselves to consideration of the polls published by these nine companies, all of whom publish detailed results and methodology, and have enough of a track record of previously published polls to put their findings into context. (Of the companies whose polls are listed in Table 2, Chapter 7, this excludes BPIX, RNB India and OnePoll.)

2. Note that percentages apply to share of the vote in Great Britain only – Northern Ireland is not included in the voting intention polls.

3. For example, the average of all the polls published by the five companies in 2009 showed the Conservatives on 41 per cent, Labour on 27 per cent and the Liberal Democrats on 18 per cent, and no single company's average was more than a point away from this for any of the three parties.

4. Of the five companies polling regularly between the elections, YouGov samples from an internet panel, weights on the basis of a party identification question asked in a previous survey, and makes no adjustment for certainty of voting except in the immediate run-up to the election. Ipsos MORI uses RDD with quotas to find a telephone sample, uses only demographic weighting, and includes only the responses of those who say they are 'absolutely

certain to vote' in the headline voting intention figures. ICM, Populus and ComRes all use RDD samples without quotas, but weight them on the basis of their reported vote at the previous general election, and use a less drastic adjustment for certainty of voting than Ipsos MORI. ICM and Populus also impute voting behaviour to a proportion of refusers and don't knows, while Ipsos MORI and ComRes both use 'squeeze' questions to persuade refusers and don't knows to offer a voting intention. Ipsos MORI also impute a vote for refusers (though not for don't knows), but only in their final pre-election poll. ICM, Populus and ComRes differ further in the details, for example in how the targets for past vote weighting are set. (None of the three weights recalled vote directly to the actual election result, as experience has shown that representative samples of British voters consistently misreport their past votes.) The four other BPC companies polling at the election add further variations to the mix: face-to-face quota sampling (TNS BMRB), and three other internet panels (Angus Reid, Opinium and Harris Interactive), each with different weighting strategies.

References

Boon, M. and Curtice, J. (2010) 'General Election 2010: Did the opinion polls flatter to deceive?', http://www.research-live.com/comment/general-election-2010-did-the-opinion-polls-flatter-to-deceive?/4003088.article, accessed 7 December 2010.

Kavanagh, D. and Cowley, P. (2010) *The British General Election of 2010*. Basingstoke: Palgrave Macmillan.

Market Research Society (1994) *The Opinion Polls and the 1992 General Election*. London: Market Research Society.

Wells, A. (2010) 'Why the polls got the Lib Dems wrong in 2010', blog post 10 October 2010, http://ukpollingreport.co.uk/blog/archives/2831, accessed 7 December 2010.

Whiteley, P., Clarke, H., Sanders, D. and Stewart, M. (2010) 'Polling and forecasting the general election of 2010', *International Journal of Market Research*, 52: 687–91.

7
Polling Voting Intentions

Peter Kellner, Joe Twyman and Anthony Wells

Polling companies have tracked public opinion in every general election since 1945. This paper reviews their performance and discusses some of the issues facing polling organisations today. In particular it examines the recent performance of YouGov and other online polling companies, the challenge of achieving politically representative samples and the advantages and disadvantages of different research modes.

The record of the polls since 1945

On 4 July 1945, the day before that year's general election, the *News Chronicle* published the results of a Gallup poll. It showed Labour on 47 per cent, six points ahead of the Conservatives. It caused little stir. Polls were a novelty in Britain. True, Gallup had accurately predicted the result of a by-election in Fulham in 1938; but this general election poll seemed utterly ridiculous. Everyone 'knew' that Britain's wartime leader, Winston Churchill, would lead the Conservatives to a comfortable victory. Even the *News Chronicle* itself seemed to downplay its own figures, describing the outcome of the election as unpredictable.

In fact, Gallup's figures were close to the result. Labour won by 9.5 points; Gallup's average error in the share of vote of the three main parties was just 1.6 points. In the Nuffield study of the election, R. B. McCallum and Alison Readman (1947) predicted that 'in future, no doubt, more attention will be paid by journalists and others to Gallup Polls and other similar devices for estimating public opinion' (p. 243).

And so, of course, it proved. At every general election since then, polls have been published. They now play a central role in media coverage and party strategy. It is inconceivable to imagine a general election

94

campaign these days without virtually daily polling data. What lessons can be learned from the polls' record in the eighteen elections since 1945?

Table 7.1 shows how face-to-face and telephone polls collectively have performed in those eighteen elections. It compares the average of the final polls with the outcome of each election (using the figures for Great Britain, and excluding Northern Ireland).

Overall, the polls can claim to have performed well in eight of the eighteen elections; that is, their average final figures deviated from the final result by two points or less for each of the three main parties. That leaves ten in which the polls, collectively, deviated by more than two points for at least one party. There is no sign of a long-term trend towards greater (or for that matter lesser) accuracy.

However, there are some patterns that are worth noting. Only three times in the last fifty years (February 1974, 1983 and 2010) has Labour's

Table 7.1 Opinion polls since 1945: variations in the average of final polls from the result

Year	No. of polls	Con	Lab	Lib*
1945	1	+1.5	−2.0	+1.3
1950	2	+0.9	−2.3	+1.5
1951	3	+2.0	−4.0	+1.8
1955	2	+1.8	0	−1.0
1959	3	−0.3	+1.1	+0.1
1964	4	+1.7	+1.5	−0.8
1966	4	−1.3	+1.8	−0.8
1970	4	−1.6	+3.8	−1.3
1974 Feb	4	+1.4	−1.8	−1.0
1974 Oct	4	−2.7	+2.8	−0.6
1979	4	+0.3	+1.6	−1.0
1983	5	+2.4	−2.2	0
1987	5	−1.1	+2.7	−1.4
1992	4	−4.0	+4.1	−1.6
1997	5	−2.1	+2.6	−1.2
2001	5**	−1.8	+4.0	−1.1
2005	4**	−0.7	+1.3	−0.6
2010	6**	−0.9	−1.7	+3.6

Notes: *Lib/SDP in 1983 and 1987; Lib Dem since 1992
** Excluding internet surveys

Sources: derived from (a) Butler and Butler (2000) British Political Facts, 1900–2000. Macmillan; (b) Butler and Butler (2006) British Political Facts since 1979. Palgrave; (c) House of Commons Library

polling average understated its actual vote share. On the other eleven occasions its share has been overstated. Polling figures for the Liberal Democrats (previously Liberals or Liberal/SDP Alliance) have erred with much the same consistency in the opposite direction, understating their vote share in eleven of the last fourteen elections. (In two others, the polling average was almost exactly right: 2010 is unique in that every poll *overstated* Lib Dem support by at least two percentage points.) The long-term pattern for the Conservatives is not quite as clear-cut, but its polling share has understated its vote share in each of the past six general elections.

On four occasions the polls told the 'wrong' story, in that the political outcome of the election was not what their figures foretold.[1] In 1970, all the polls bar one predicted that Labour would remain in office. Instead it lost. The one exception was ORC, whose final poll for London's *Evening Standard* detected a late swing to the Conservatives, which appears to have taken place after the other polls ended their fieldwork.

In February 1974, the polls (this time, trying to learn from 1970, polling until the eve-of-election) indicated that the Conservatives would be re-elected. Instead, they lost. To be fair to the polls, their figures were not badly wrong – this was one of the eight elections in which their average figures were within two points of the votes obtained by each party – but Labour ended up with more seats, even though the Tories narrowly won more votes. The *Daily Mail*'s election day headline – 'A HANDSOME WIN FOR HEATH' – was wrong, although, statistically, its NOP data was close to the figures that each party obtained.

In both of those elections, the polls could offer a reasonable defence: their figures were reasonably accurate at the time they did their field-work; they were undone by late swing (in 1970) and the fact that the party with the most votes failed to win the most seats (February 1974).

No such excuses can be offered for two later 'bad' elections for the pollsters. In October 1974 they predicted a nine-point win for Labour – enough to give Harold Wilson a three-figure majority. In the event, Labour's lead in the popular vote was just 3.5 points, and Labour's overall majority was just three.

Then, in 1992, came the pollsters' *annus horribilis*. Their average final-poll predictions were four points too high for Labour and four points too low for the Tories. The Conservatives won by eight points. None of the polls came close to predicting that they would remain in power with a clear overall majority.

This very public failure provoked a great deal of heart-searching, inquiry and the beginnings of a reform in polling methods. The Market

Research Society set up a commission to investigate what had gone wrong. Its report (1994) identified two sets of issues. First, the pollsters, who used very similar sample designs, all produced weighted samples that were too downmarket: too few ABC1, and too many C2DE, electors; too few two-car owners and too many council tenants. The latest available census data was eleven years old; and more up-to-date survey-based data had underestimated the growth of Britain's middle classes. This problem may have been exacerbated by the consequences of the poll tax, which led to some less well-off (and thus normally Labour) people not registering to be electors at all.

The second set of problems could be readily identified in principle, but these were hard to measure separately. There was differential turnout: Conservative supporters were keener to vote than Labour supporters. There was a 'spiral of silence': some voters were unwilling to admit to strangers that they would vote Conservative. And there may have been very late decisions by some voters either to vote Conservative or not to vote at all.

Good pollsters have long been aware of the risks they ran. In the early Seventies Humphrey Taylor, who ran the Opinion Research Centre in London before heading across the Atlantic to run Harris Polls in America, told Peter Kellner that all polls were liable to contain a number of errors. What pollsters hoped was not that they would be eliminated, which was not possible, but that they would cancel out, so the overall numbers would be right. In 1992 all the errors were in the same direction, and compounded each other.

1992 to 2005

Subsequently, the uniformity of polling methods broke down, as each company devised different ways to correct the errors they had made in 1992. They all agreed that their samples needed to be more upmarket; but that was about it. Different ways were devised to deal with differential turnout and the spiral of silence. ICM made the most radical changes. As well as using more sophisticated demographic weights, and reallocating 'don't knows' to counter the spiral of silence, it also weighted its data by past vote. That is, it asked respondents how they had voted in the previous general election, and weighted their data to ensure the correct political balance in the published results.

Past-vote weighting has remained a topic of controversy among pollsters ever since. The problem is easy to state, but hard to solve. There is plenty of empirical evidence to show that many people suffer false memory syndrome, and misremember whether, and how, they voted.[2] In particular, many Liberal Democrat voters, and some non-voters, have in the past 'remembered' voting Labour. This means that it is not necessarily right to weight recalled past vote to the actual result of the previous general election. Indeed, the first company to conduct general election polls by telephone for the media – Audience Selection (ASL) in 1983 – came unstuck because it weighted its data to actual past vote, instead of correcting for false memory syndrome. Its prediction for Labour was five points too low and for the Liberal/SDP Alliance three points too high. Had ASL made allowances for misremembering, it would have been more accurate. ASL's failure probably delayed the widespread use of telephone polling in British elections by a decade (both ICM and Gallup made the switch from face-to-face to telephone in the mid-1990s).

If the biases were constant, then it should be possible to estimate the 'correct' past-vote figures (i.e., not the actual result of the last election, but the distribution of answers that would be given if every elector in Britain were interviewed). But, though past-vote data appears to be reasonably stable in the short term in normal times, there can be no guarantee that the memories of millions of voters won't suddenly change in response to some major political event. Precisely because of this danger, Ipsos MORI, alone among the companies publishing regular polls, takes the purist view: it asks about past vote, but does not use the responses to weight its data. All other companies do weight by past vote, but they use a variety of methods to estimate it.

In the three elections that followed the nightmare of 1992, the pro-Labour biases were reduced, but did not disappear. By 2005 conventional polls were still prone to overstate Labour support, though usually by less than in 1997 or 2001, and (though less often) to understate Conservative support. 2005 was also the first election in which online surveys were widely reported. (YouGov had tested the water in 2001 with some success, but its polls appeared only in the little-read, and subsequently defunct, *Sunday Business.*) YouGov, Harris and BPIX all produced final polls that came close to the election result. Unlike the conventional polls, their figures did not show any sign of systematically overstating Labour or understating the Tories.

In short, the conventional polls did better in 2005 than in the previous three elections, but they did not entirely eliminate their pro-Labour bias; and they did not agree completely on the best way to convert raw data into accurate published results. In contrast, the three internet polling companies had a good election.

The 2010 election – polls' performance

The General Election of 2010 was unprecedented in the numbers of polls published and the number of companies conducting national voting intention polls. New entrants at general elections are, of course, not a new phenomenon. In 2005 there was a single poll by Harris Interactive alongside the established companies, in 2001 YouGov's online and Rasmussen's automated telephone polls entered the market, and in 1983 and 1987 there were phone polls by Audience Selection. The difference in 2010 was the sheer number and scale of new companies attempting to conduct voting intention polls.

During the election campaign twelve different polling companies released opinion polls. Angus Reid, an established online Canadian pollster, conducted regular British polls for the website www.politicalbetting.com and eventually for the *Sunday Express*. Opinium, a new online company, conducted regular polls for the *Daily Express*. Onepoll, a company that had previously specialised in PR polls, carried out voting intention polls for the *People*.

Harris Interactive conducted regular polls for the *Metro* freesheet, while TNS-BMRB (a newly merged company that included System Three, previously known for conducting regular Scottish voting intention polls) conducted regular face-to-face polls without a client. There were also two telephone polls by an unknown Indian company, RNB Research.

The influx of polling was presumably partly the result of what was expected to be a more exciting campaign than the previous two elections, and partially due to the low barriers to entry and low costs for conducting online polling. In 2005 the only online polling was YouGov, BPIX polls carried out by the British Election Study team on the YouGov platform, and a single Harris poll. In 2010 YouGov and BPIX continued to poll, but Harris now conducted regular polls and were joined by Opinium, Angus Reid and OnePoll. Lower costs also allowed the previously unusual sight of pollsters producing regular polls without a client. MORI carried out their monthly political monitor without a client for several years between losing their contract with *The Times* and signing up with Reuters, but this was a large company continuing a long-standing data set. In 2010 TNS-BMRB and Angus Reid put out regular voting intention polls with no regular paying client, presumably purely in the hope of getting publicity and winning a future client. If it hadn't been for the sheer volume of polling, it would probably have worked. In practice, the number of polls being published meant that polls from newer entrants received relatively little media pickup.

Ipsos MORI shunned national voting intention polls for most of the campaign, instead conducting weekly polls of key Labour marginals for Reuters. This approach was last tried by NOP back in 1987, which failed to attract much attention because it could not be easily compared with other polls. In 2010 marginal polls received much more attention, and the Ipsos MORI/Reuters polls of marginal seats were joined by marginal seat polls by ICM and YouGov. They gathered more attention because of the widespread belief that the Conservatives would struggle to get the 7 per cent national swing they needed on paper, but might hope to do better in marginals as a result of Lord Ashcroft's targeted campaigning there.

Among the new companies only Angus Reid attempted any particular innovations, using both mocked-up ballot papers specific to the constituency and 'micro-weighting' by small groups of similar constituencies. Any benefit this brought to them was probably cancelled out by a failure to account for false recall in their past-vote weighting, which led to them underestimating Labour's vote by six percentage points. Table 7.2 compares the final polls from each company with the actual result.

Two big conclusions emerge from Table 7.2. The first is that every poll overstated the Liberal Democrats' share of the vote, and by at least 2.4 percentage points. (This is discussed by Roger Mortimore and Simon Atkinson in Chapter 6.) The second is that every poll bar one produced a reasonably accurate figure for the Conservative lead over Labour. Eleven out of the twelve companies predicted a Conservative lead of between 6 and 9 percentage points. It was, in fact, 7.2 points. In terms of swing, all the polls bar one predicted a swing to the Tories of between 4.5 per cent and 6 per cent; it was in fact 5.1 per cent. The conventional figures for average error tend to miss this point. All the polls overstated the Lib Dems: therefore they were bound, collectively, to understate the combined support of the other parties. That appears to be the sole systematic reason why nine out of twelve polls understated the Tories and all twelve understated Labour. In terms of the battle between the two main parties, most polls had a good election. On the morning of election day, the final batch of polls pointed to the near-certainty that the Conservatives would be, by some margin, the largest party in the new House of Commons, but that they might not secure an overall majority. The *Sun* on 6 May reported YouGov's final prediction that the Conservatives would win between 300 and 310 seats; they won 307.

In terms of average error, the two most accurate polls were those produced by ICM and RNB Research. The least accurate, by some margin,

Table 7.2 How the polls performed in 2010

Poll	Con	Lab	Lib	Dem	Others	Mean error	Con lead Error on Over Lab lead
Established polls, traditional methods							
ICM	36	28	26	10	1.2	8	0.8
Ipsos MORI	36	29	27	8	1.7	7	0.2
Populus	37	28	27	8	1.8	9	1.8
ComRes	37	28	28	7	2.5	9	1.8
TNS-BMRB	33	27	29	11	3.3	6	1.2
AVERAGE	35.8	28.0	27.4	8.8	1.9	7.8	0.6
Established polls, online							
Harris	35	29	27	9	1.7	6	1.2
YouGov	35	28	28	9	2.2	7	0.2
BPIX	34	27	30	9	3.2	7	0.2
AVERAGE	34.7	28.0	28.3	9.0	2.4	6.7	0.5
New entrant, traditional method							
RNB research	37	30	26	9	1.3	7	0.2
New entrants, online							
Opinium	35	27	26	12	2.3	8	0.8
Angus Reid	36	24	29	11	3.3	12	4.8
OnePoll	30	21	32	17	7.8	9	1.8
AVERAGE	33.7	24.0	29.0	13.3	4.5	9.7	2.5
RESULT	*36.9*	*29.7*	*23.6*	*9.9*	*7.2*		

was by OnePoll for the *People*. All four of their figures (for Conservative, Labour, Liberal Democrats, Others) were adrift by seven points or more. While in 2005 online companies generally performed better than companies conducting their research offline, telephone polling generally ended up with a better record than online research in 2010. However, when new companies are excluded, and the data from established companies alone are compared, the gap was not large.

2010 General Election – innovations

The arrival of live television debates among the three main party leaders transformed the campaign – and had a marked effect on the role of the polls.

As these were the first debates of their type in the UK, it naturally followed that the approach for all the inevitable polling surrounding them had yet to be defined. It was widely expected that most, if not all, of the established pollsters would attempt some sort of post-debate analysis to identify the 'winner', but there was no agreement about how it would be done or exactly what form it should take.

One thing was certain, however, and that was that traditional polling methods would not be able to operate fast enough. Data would be needed within minutes of the end of each debate (the first and third ended at 10 pm, the second at 9.30). This was for two reasons. The first was to provide newspaper clients with results in time for their main editions. The second was a matter more of professional pride than commercial calculation. We wanted to make public the unmediated verdict of the viewers before the inevitable spinning process that followed each debate could influence public perceptions. In short, each of us was engaged in three contests: against time, against each other, and against the spin doctors.

Five companies reported viewers' verdicts within an hour of the end of each debate. All used pre-screened samples, so they could question people who were likely to have actually watched the debate. Angus Reid, Populus and YouGov conducted their surveys online, ComRes used an automated telephone system (which had been employed by Rasmussen in 2001 in their sole foray into British election polling), and ICM held to the traditional method of polling by interviewers over the telephone.

As experienced internet pollsters, it was perhaps little surprise that YouGov were the fastest in all three debates, with results from just over 1,000 respondents announced by the media in around ten minutes. ComRes came a close second in all three, with Populus, ICM and Angus Reid following. This meant that subsequent media coverage about who won – and, in particular, Nick Clegg's clear victory in the first debate – was shaped by the polls; the spin doctors quickly admitted defeat.

Regardless of speed, the most important methodological difference emerging among the pollsters was the profile of who it was they were actually sampling. YouGov decided in advance of the first debate on 15 April to sample and weight the data to the profile of those intending to watch. To help achieve this, between 8 and 13 April YouGov used its panel to conduct a large establishment survey that produced a profile of all viewers of the programme, as indicated by those saying that they were 'absolutely certain' to watch the first debate.

Using that target profile and the establishment survey, a representative sample of respondents who were certain to watch were contacted again. These respondents were informed they would be invited to take part in a survey immediately after the debate finished. The final data were then weighted to the overall profile of viewers.

In contrast to this approach, other pollsters, most notably ComRes, conducted polls that were weighted to nationally representative targets. YouGov's analysis of the establishment data showed that the profile of debate viewers tended to be more likely to be from the top three social classifications and also more likely to identify with the Conservatives when compared with a nationally representative sample.

These differences in approach, which were numerically significant but not vast, go some way to explaining why the results themselves differed from pollster to pollster – a point of some discussion among commentators at the time. While Nick Clegg was unanimously crowned the winner of the first debate, the results of the next two were less clear-cut, as Table 7.3 shows.

Table 7.3   Post-debate polling results for 2010 General Election campaign

	Brown	Cameron	Clegg
15th April – ITV – Domestic Affairs			
Angus Reid	18%	20%	49%
ComRes	20%	26%	43%
Populus	17%	22%	61%
YouGov	19%	29%	51%
ICM	19%	20%	51%
22nd April – Sky News – Foreign Affairs			
Angus Reid	23%	32%	33%
ComRes	30%	30%	33%
ICM	29%	29%	33%
Populus	23%	37%	26%
YouGov	29%	36%	32%
29th April – BBC – Economic Affairs			
Angus Reid	23%	37%	29%
ComRes	26%	35%	33%
ICM	29%	35%	27%
Populus	25%	38%	38%
YouGov	25%	41%	32%

The striking thing is that all five polling companies, despite using different methods and operating at great speed, told broadly the same story. Nick Clegg easily won the first debate, while Gordon Brown trailed in third place. Both Cameron and Brown gained ground in the second debate, which produced no knockout victory for any of the leaders; and, according to four of the five companies, Cameron narrowly won the third debate, with Clegg second (the fifth company, ICM, called it a tie between Clegg and Cameron).

Of course it will never be possible to know the 'true' result; but as leader debates increasingly establish themselves as part of the electoral landscape, the decisions pollsters make when deciding on their strategy for post-debate polling will come under more scrutiny. It remains to be seen whether the approaches adopted in 2010 will still be used come the next election.

The prospect of the TV debates prompted another innovation by YouGov. They might have a big impact on voters. How big would it be – and how long would it last? Or would a weak or strong performance by any of the leaders leave voters unmoved? At YouGov we felt that the only way to chart the ebbs and flows of the campaign properly was to conduct daily polls. In 2001 and 2005 six different agencies had been polling during the election campaign. The result had been that somebody was releasing new data virtually every day. In 2010 the number of agencies would eventually rise to twelve, with ever more data available, but YouGov's intention was to take things a stage further and ensure that it was releasing results for new surveys with fresh samples every single day of the campaign.

The general concept was by no means revolutionary, but the idea of a new, self-contained, nationally representative survey for publication running every day had never been achieved in the UK before – or, as far as we know, provided to the media in any of the world's democracies.

Forms of daily polling had been tried before: by Harris for TV-am in 1987, by Gallup for the *Daily* and *Sunday Telegraph* in 1997 and by Populus for *The Times* in 2005. But in each case these had been 'rolling' polls, combining three or four days' worth of data. In 2005, Populus suffered the misfortune of a clearly rogue sample during the final weekend, which happened to be a Bank Holiday weekend. The outcome was implausibly large Labour leads for three painful days. In 2010, ComRes also opted for the rolling poll approach, but only for three days a week, for ITV News. YouGov instead conducted discrete daily polls with separate samples of around 1,500 each day.

YouGov adapted and expanded the rolling cross-sectional approach it had developed for the British Election Study (BES) Campaign Survey in 2005. Then, YouGov's panel for the online component of the BES was evenly split so that on each day of the campaign the same number of respondents were invited to take part in the second wave of the study. Obviously not all respondents read and then took part in the survey on the day their email invite was sent out. Instead a proportion would answer on that day, while others took part a day after receiving the invite, some a day after that, and so on. At the end of each working day a data file containing all the previous days' results was produced and sent to the BES Principal Investigators at the University of Essex. Weight variables were appended to the file that allowed results from each given previous twenty-four-hour period to be weighted, and then a separate variable for each given previous seventy-two-hour period. The sample size was around 270 respondents per day, meaning that a reasonable number could be aggregated over three days.

The principle of some people replying on the first day of receiving the email, some on the second and so on was maintained for Daily Polling in 2010. However, the intention was to increase significantly the sample size for each individual day, with the aim of achieving a unique sample of around 1,500 respondents per survey. The resulting data would then not need to be aggregated across a number of days. Instead, each survey would be published on its own.

The advantages of such an approach were numerous. Naturally, during any election campaign specific events (dear boy, events) can prove crucial, but predicting when these moments of importance will take place is not always possible. Only through polling sufficient numbers of nationally representative respondents every single day do you ensure that the immediate impact of any and all such unforeseen occurrences is measured, along with the possible aftermath over subsequent days.

While such short-term fluctuations can be observed, so too can longer-term trends. The large number of responses coming in was then combined with the speed of polling via the internet to ensure our clients received the results from that day's polling for publication in the paper the next day. The end result was unrivalled insight across the duration of the campaign.

YouGov began Daily Polling in February 2010. Figure 7.1 plots the fortunes of the parties as they moved through the long campaign towards election day.

Figure 7.1 clearly demonstrates what anyone with more than a vague, passing interest in the election campaign knew: the first debate was

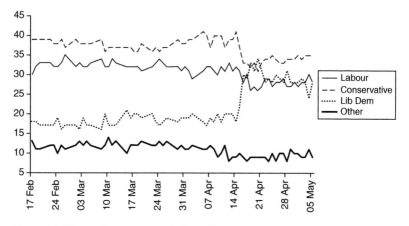

Figure 7.1   Voting intentions in daily polls

what Lord Ashdown described as a 'game changer'.[3] Twenty-four hours after the first TV debate, the lead stories on BBC News, ITV News and Sky News all reported YouGov's first post-debate voting intention poll for the *Sun*, showing the Liberal Democrats surging into second place. Other companies subsequently showed the same surge, with some of them briefly putting the Lib Dems in first place. For the rest of the election, Nick Clegg and his party's policies received far more attention than had any third party in living memory. The combination of the first TV debate and the subsequent polls transformed the campaign. Had there been no polls, the campaign would almost certainly have played out very differently; and had the polls taken two or three days to assess the debates (the normal turn-round time in past decades) the Clegg bandwagon might not have taken off so dramatically. The immediate post-debate polls, and YouGov's daily polls, produced a form of almost real-time voter feedback that unquestionably influenced the progress of the 2010 campaign, and is likely to affect all future general elections.

Conclusions

As this chapter has shown, the record of polls over the past 65 years has been mixed. At different times, problems have arisen and been tackled – only for new problems to subsequently arise. In 1970 most polls missed a late swing to the Conservatives – so most companies have continued polling until as late as possible in subsequent elections.

In 1992, all polling companies used inaccurate demographic data; ever since they have worked hard to apply more up-to-date and more sophisticated weighting methods. As we have seen, most pollsters made other changes after 1992 in order to correct for a 'spiral of silence' that appeared to lead to an understatement of Conservative support; but either this problem was not fully solved in the following three elections, or some new bias appeared that caused Conservative support to continue to be understated, and Labour support to be overstated, by telephone polls.

In 2010 the polls generally did remarkably well in reporting the balance of support between Labour and Conservative. Support for both parties tended to be understated, typically by one or two percentage points. But, as some understatement of the total support for Labour and the Conservatives was the inevitable consequence of the consistent overstatement of the Lib Dem share, it is likely that the specific pro-Labour, anti-Conservative bias of the elections from 1992 to 2005 did not reappear this time.

As for the Liberal Democrats, perhaps the polls suffered from an opposite effect to the 'spiral of silence' that led some people in previous elections not to admit that they would vote Conservative. Could there have been this time a 'spiral of eloquence' which led some people to say they would vote Liberal Democrat because it seemed to be the trendy, socially acceptable answer, once Clegg had been declared the winner of the first TV debate? It may be that some of them, come the day, did not vote at all or, faced with a ballot paper, changed their minds. (In YouGov's case, we found that rim-weighting our sample left us, in the event, with too many highly educated voters under 30 who were strongly pro-Lib Dem. A more sophisticated weighting system would have reduced our eve-of-poll Lib Dem rating from 28 per cent to 26 per cent, but this would still have been 2.4 points too high.)

Whatever the particular explanation, the broader point is that each election seems to throw up new polling challenges. We try to root out old errors – with some but not always total success – only to be threatened by new ones. What distinctive challenges will pollsters face at the next election, and how well will we deal with them? We shall let you know – shortly afterwards.

Notes

1. Technically there was a fifth wrong call, in 1951, when the final polls showed a clear Tory lead, but Labour ended up winning more votes. However, the

Conservatives won more seats than Labour and returned to office, so this was not generally regarded as a polling 'mistake'.

2. For example, in April 1998 ICM re-interviewed 1,000 people it had questioned on the day of, or the day after, the general election the previous year. The 1998 survey asked whether and, if so, how they had voted in May 1997. Seventeen per cent gave different answers from those at the time of the election. Of the 158 who told ICM in May 1997 that they were about to vote Liberal Democrat or had just done so, only eighty-seven 'remembered' voting Lib Dem a year later; forty-five 'remembered' voting Labour, while nine 'remembered' voting Conservative. Overall, 53 per cent of those who a year later recalled voting said they had voted Labour, compared with its actual support of 44 per cent, while 31 per cent recalled voting Conservative (31 per cent in 1997) and 13 per cent recalled voting Lib Dem (17 per cent in 1997). (*Observer*, 26 April 1998).

3. http://news.bbc.co.uk/1/hi/uk_politics/election_2010/8624317.stm, accessed 22 March 2011.

References

R. B. McCallum and Alison Readman (1947) *The British General Election of 1945*. Oxford: Oxford University Press.

Market Research Society (1994) *The Opinion Polls and the 1992 General Election*. London: Market Research Society.

Part III
Voters

8
The Campaign As Experienced by the Voters in the Battleground Seats

Roger Mortimore, Helen Cleary and Tomasz Mludzinski

Introduction

This chapter explores the election campaign from the point of view of the voters in some of the key Labour–Conservative battleground constituencies, where the eventual outcome of the election was likely to be decided and where we might expect the election to have been hardest fought. We consider the potential importance of the campaign here (as measured by the size of the floating vote), how many people the campaign reached and what those on the receiving end thought of it. We also look at how far the voters here were aware that they were in strategically important constituencies, how many claimed to be voting tactically, and how far these decisions seem to have been well informed and well judged. Finally we consider the impact of the leaders' debates – here, as elsewhere, an influential factor, despite Nick Clegg's performance being arguably an irrelevance in these constituencies that his party had no chance of winning.

The constituencies on which we concentrate are those in which Ipsos MORI conducted a series of five cross-sectional surveys for Reuters before and during the election campaign.[1] These were the fifty-seven constituencies won by Labour in 2005 where the Conservatives needed a swing of between 5 per cent and 9 per cent to gain the seat (that is, where the Labour lead over the Conservatives was between 10 per cent and 18 per cent of the vote).[2] These were constituencies where the result was likely to be close if the Conservatives were anywhere near to securing an overall majority in the Commons, where they might hope to gain extra seats if only they could slightly outperform the national swing, and presumably the sort of constituencies targeted by Lord Ashcroft's target seats

Table 8.1   Survey details

Survey	Fieldwork dates	Sample size
1	19–22 March 2010	1,007 residents aged 18+
2	30 March – 5 April 2010	1,008 residents aged 18+
3	16–19 April 2010	1,001 residents aged 18+
4	23–26 April 2010	1,018 residents aged 18+
5	30 April – 2 May 2010	1,004 residents claiming to be registered to vote

campaign. They were also the type of constituencies in which, from January 2010, Labour concentrated its greatest efforts (Kavanagh and Cowley, 2010: 231). For an overall majority, the Conservatives would need to win around half these seats.

The surveys were not designed, of course, to make measurements in each of these constituencies separately, but to measure attitudes and experiences across the whole group collectively. They were conducted by telephone, with numbers selected by random digit dialling and quotas set based on constituency (ensuring a roughly equal number of interviews in each of the fifty-seven eligible constituencies), sex, age, social grade and working status. Sample sizes and fieldwork dates are given in Table 8.1.

Campaign reach

As is usually the case, television was the dominant medium by which voters in these marginal seats gained information about the election. More than half, 56 per cent, said in the final week that they had been getting most of their news about the election campaign from television, far ahead of newspapers (16 per cent), the internet (13 per cent) and radio (10 per cent). As television is the least localised of these media and least likely to be a regular source of detailed local information, this plainly puts on the parties the onus of getting across any constituency or candidate-specific details that they wanted voters to take into consideration.

On the whole, it seems that the party machinery in these key seats remains effective. Almost all the public here, 95 per cent, told us on 30 April – 2 May that they had had political leaflets through their letterbox in the previous week,[3] and 62 per cent that they had received a letter individually addressed to them and signed by some senior party figure. But only one in six had been called on by a party representative and one in ten had been telephoned (Table 8.2). These levels of leafleting and of personal canvassing were much the same as we found reported elsewhere. One in five (20 per cent) said in Ipsos MORI's final eve-of-poll national survey that a representative had called on them, but in that case they were asked about 'the past few weeks' and the survey was some days later than that in the marginals, so, allowing for the longer timescale, this probably suggests a slightly higher level of contact in the key seats.

However, reported telephone canvassing was much lower nationally than in the marginals, only 5 per cent, which suggests that this more expensive and more closely coordinated method of campaigning was much more clearly focused where the votes were needed most. We also found that those in the marginals who had not been canvassed by telephone over the previous week were twice as likely to say that they had changed their mind about which party to vote for as those that had been (15 per cent compared with 7 per cent). This presumably points to such canvassing having been targeted at bolstering the loyalties of already committed voters in preference to winning over floating voters, rather than to its being actively counterproductive.

Table 8.2 Campaign penetration
Q. **During the past week, have you ... ?**

		Yes	No	Don't know
... had any political leaflets put through your letterbox?	%	95	5	1
... seen any political advertisements on billboards?	%	74	26	*
... received a letter signed by a senior party figure individually addressed to you?	%	62	36	2
... been called on by a representative of any political party?	%	18	82	*
... visited other websites for information on candidates or parties?	%	18	82	0
... seen any reference to a political party on a social networking site (e.g. Facebook, Twitter, MySpace etc)?	%	17	82	*
... met any of your local candidates?	%	15	85	0
... been telephoned by a representative of any political party?	%	10	90	*
... visited official party websites?	%	10	90	0
... received an email from a political party?	%	8	89	3

Note: *Figure less than 0.5 but greater than zero

Source: Ipsos MORI/Reuters Base: 1,004 GB residents aged 18+ in key marginal seats who said they were registered to vote, 30 April – 2 May 2010

Perhaps contrary to expectations, it does not seem that the Conservatives had achieved a significant head start here before the campaign, for all the widely discussed funding of their pre-election campaigning by Lord Ashcroft. Populus polled for *The Times* before the election got underway (on 5–7 March) in a differently defined, slightly wider, band of Labour–Conservative marginal constituencies (Populus, 2010). They found that 42 per cent reported having had leaflets or newspapers delivered by the Conservatives in recent months and 40 per cent by Labour, while 21 per cent had had a personally addressed letter from the Conservatives and 16 per cent from Labour. But, while 7 per cent said Labour had knocked on the door and 5 per cent that they had telephoned, the figures for the Conservatives were 6 per cent and 3 per cent.

It seems that candidates were working hard in the target seats. In the final week, we found that almost as many people (15 per cent) said that they had met one of their local candidates as had been personally canvassed. Even if we assume that respondents were not answering literally when saying this had happened 'during the past week', this is pretty good going, amounting to more than 10,000 people in the average constituency having met one of the candidates. Although it seems likely that many of these were in fact council rather than parliamentary candidates, it implies that the parties are still putting more effort into pounding the streets before polling day than they are sometimes given credit for.

One surprising aspect was that Labour voters were far likelier than supporters of other parties to say they had met a local candidate (23 per cent, compared with 13 per cent of Conservative voters and 7 per cent of Lib Dem voters). This may mean that both parties had chosen to especially target areas with Labour voters, or perhaps simply that Labour voters were more likely to be in when candidates were canvassing (though, intriguingly, the same difference is not apparent in reported calls by other party representatives).

Three-quarters of the public had seen political advertisements on billboards within the previous week. Intriguingly, despite the fact that older voters are generally thought to pay more attention to election phenomena, it was the young who were more likely to say they had seen such posters: 86 per cent of 18–34-year-olds, 78 per cent of 35–54-year-olds and 61 per cent of those aged 55+ said that they had done so. Even allowing that the older respondents may be less mobile on average, and, particularly if retired, may be less frequent users of the busy roads beside which these posters are often placed, the difference is surprising. Perhaps the form or content of the parties' advertising was better suited to catch the attention of the young than of the more elderly.

As has been widely reported elsewhere, and despite the apparent precedent of the Obama election in 2008, this once again failed to be 'Britain's first internet election'. For all the importance many politicians and journalists placed on Twitter, Facebook and other social networking sites, just one in six (17 per cent) of the public in the marginal constituencies saw any reference to a political party on them. A similar number, 18 per cent, had visited non-party websites to gain election information, and 10 per cent had visited an official party website. Nevertheless, those touched by new media were too big a minority to be safely ignored, and were less easily reached than other voters through more traditional channels. Of those who said they had visited a non-party website for information about candidates or parties, more named the internet as their *most* important source of election information (41 per cent) than television (36 per cent). Further, those who had made such a visit in the previous week were twice as likely to have changed their minds about how to vote over the same period as those who had not. This is a volatile group. Presumably those of the parties that do not address this need will be unable to communicate effectively with this small but growing group of voters.

Those who used the internet to get election information were strongly concentrated in the youngest third of the population (aged under 35), and were much more likely to be middle-class (ABC1) than working-class (C2DE). These groups were also the strongest source of Liberal Democrat support, both nationally and in the marginal constituencies. Unsurprisingly, therefore, Lib Dem supporters were the most likely to have visited the official websites of political parties, and to have visited other websites to get information about the election (30 per cent had done so, compared with 17 per cent of intending Labour voters and 14 per cent of Conservatives). But it is nevertheless at odds with the expectation that the internet might play an especial role in promoting tactical voting and furnishing the information necessary to do so intelligently: these respondents were all still intending to vote Liberal Democrat, a week before polling day, in constituencies the party had no chance of winning.

Size of the floating vote

There was certainly scope for the campaign to make a decisive effect by swinging votes. In the first of the surveys (19–22 March), we found that 46 per cent of those who expressed a voting intention said they might change their mind, while just 52 per cent had 'definitely decided' to vote for the party they were supporting (Table 8.3).

This is an extraordinary level of vacillation, and did not change significantly until the final week of the campaign. However, it was not peculiar to the marginals, as we found almost identical figures (50 per cent 'definitely decided', 49 per cent 'may change mind') in our national poll on 18–19 April. This uncertainty far exceeded anything we had ever found in previous elections, though there have long been signs of a trend towards later decision-making. In MORI's national polls, using the same question at an equivalent stage of the 2001 and 2005 elections, the proportion saying they might change their minds was 32 per cent and 35 per cent respectively; but it had been 17 per cent or 18 per cent at three successive elections from 1983 to 1992.

But not all parties' votes were equally 'soft'. In March, those in the key marginals supporting Labour or the Conservatives were very much more likely to have definitely decided who to vote for (60 per cent and 59 per cent respectively) than Liberal Democrats (23 per cent), implying considerable scope for vote switching. By the final week, the Conservative vote had firmed up somewhat, with 73 per cent of Tories saying they were definitely decided, but Labour certainty was still at only 65 per cent and that for the Liberal Democrats just 51 per cent, with 48 per cent still saying they might change their minds with less than a week to go. As might be expected, those saying at this stage that they had not yet 'definitely decided' who to support were also less certain that they would vote at all – 89 per cent of those who had definitely decided but only 71 per cent of those who (though having a voting intention) might change their minds felt 'absolutely certain to vote'.[4]

Why did so many decide so late? It does not seem to be that the increasing targeting of modern elections on key voters has meant that both parties have secured their own core votes while making less

Table 8.3   Indecisiveness of the voters
Q. **Have you definitely decided to vote for the...party, or is there a chance you may change your mind before you vote?**

	19–22 March %	30 March– 5 April %	16–19 April %	23–26 April %	30 April– 2 May %
Definitely decided	52	54	51	53	63
May change mind	46	46	47	46	36
Don't know	2	1	2	1	1

Source: Ipsos MORI/Reuters Base: c. 1,000 residents aged 18+ in key marginal seats

impact in the middle ground: those who had been contacted by the parties in various ways were not significantly more likely to have made up their minds than those who had not. All the competitors had failed to achieve a decisive advantage through their campaigning even with those that they successfully contacted.

Marginality and tactical voting

Both Conservatives and Labour needed to ensure awareness (at least among their own supporters) of the marginality of these constituencies, the need for a high turnout and the case for tactical voting. Given the extensive boundary changes in England and Wales, this was perhaps even more needed in 2010 than in most elections. The surveys showed scant signs that any of these had been achieved.

In each of the five surveys, residents were asked whether they lived in a marginal constituency or not. Strictly speaking, the constituencies included in the surveys were not 'marginal' in the normal sense – the winning candidate at the previous election had won by a minimum of 10 per cent of the vote and by 18 per cent in the most extreme cases. Nevertheless, when most media commentators spoke of 'marginal seats' it was this sort of constituency, where the outcome was expected to be close, to which they were referring. In March, only a quarter (25 per cent) said that they lived in a marginal constituency, while 45 per cent admitted they didn't know. This awareness of the closeness of the contest did not seem to increase significantly over the course of the campaign, and in the final poll we still found only just over a quarter, 27 per cent, saying that they lived in a marginal constituency (Table 8.4).

Throughout the campaign, those who said they were certain to vote were at least as likely to think that their constituency was not marginal

Table 8.4 Awareness of marginality
Q. As far as you know, do you live in a marginal constituency? By marginal constituency I mean a constituency where the current MP has only a narrow majority?

	19–22 March %	30 Mar– 5 Apr %	16–19 April %	23–26 April %	30 April– 2 May %
Yes	25	31	30	30	27
No	30	30	30	29	33
Don't know	45	40	40	41	40

Source: Ipsos MORI/Reuters Base: c. 1,000 residents aged 18+ in key marginal seats

as those who thought they might not vote. So the impression that the constituencies were not marginal ones was rife among those who were taking an interest in the election, not just among those we might expect to be less well informed, and there is no sign that awareness of a likely close contest was increasing determination to turn out.

Nor did we find signs of raised tactical voting. This was not because the electorate was entirely unwilling to consider it. On 16–19 April, 26 per cent said either that they were voting tactically or that they would do so if they thought their preferred party did not stand much chance of winning in their constituency, and an ICM poll (ICM, 2010) of Labour–Conservative marginal seats[5] in early April, using a differently worded question, found that three in ten (30 per cent) said they were *prepared* to vote tactically. This left ample scope for tactical voting to determine the result.

But there was apparently confusion about the tactical situation. On 23–26 April, people were fairly evenly divided on whether 'a vote for the Liberal Democrats in my constituency is a wasted vote' (45 per cent agreed, 41 per cent disagreed), though those intending to vote Liberal Democrat were naturally much less likely to think so (18 per cent agreed).

Perhaps understandably, therefore, the number who said their voting intention was a tactical one rather than a vote for 'the party that most represents your views' (Table 8.5) was comparatively low, measured at 12 per cent on 16–19 April and 9 per cent in the final two polls.[6] This

Table 8.5   Prevalence of tactical voting

Q. (To all expressing a voting intention) **You said you would vote for [INSERT PARTY]/ are inclined to support [INSERT PARTY]. Which of the following statements comes closest to your reasons for intending to vote for the [INSERT PARTY] party?**

	16–19 April %	23–26 April %	30 April–2 May %
It is the party that most represents your views	85	87	86
The party you support has little chance of winning in this constituency so you vote for the (INSERT) party to try and keep another party out	12	9	9
Other	3	3	4
No opinion	1	1	1

Source: Ipsos MORI/Reuters Base: c. 1,000 residents aged 18+ in key marginal seats

was in line with the 10 per cent who said they were voting tactically in Ipsos MORI's final national poll, conducted of course mainly in safe seats where tactical voting was unlikely to affect the result. The parties seem to have failed, therefore, to achieve a higher level of tactical voting in constituencies where it could do them any good.

Nor was the tactical voting that did take place in the battleground constituencies necessarily rational or well informed. In our marginals poll on 16–19 April, as many of those intending to vote for the Liberal Democrats (13 per cent) as for Labour (10 per cent) and the Conservatives (13 per cent) said that this was a vote 'to keep another party out', suggesting that many had little real knowledge of the tactical situation in their constituency. More than half of those who claimed to be voting tactically for the Liberal Democrats – in constituencies where the Liberal Democrats realistically had no chance – said they would actually prefer either the Conservatives or Labour to win.

It is true that, during the course of the campaign, tactical voting intentions that did not fit the local situation fell significantly: in the last of the five surveys, 11 per cent of those intending to vote Labour but only 7 per cent of Conservatives and 6 per cent of Liberal Democrats said they were voting tactically. Perhaps, therefore, voters' level of information improved or they took time to consider their options more carefully and, to this extent, the campaign worked. Even so, one in six of those still intending to vote Liberal Democrat said that they would switch their vote if they thought their own party could not win in their constituency. Not enough bar charts in the leaflets, perhaps. (In the event the Liberal Democrats came third or fourth in every one of the 57.[7])

As far as the partisan effect is concerned, a higher proportion of Labour than of Conservative votes were apparently tactical, so it seems the eventual balance of advantage from tactical voting was slightly in Labour's favour; but the net effect would have amounted to less than a 1 per cent swing. Labour's tactical votes came mainly from those who would ideally have preferred the Liberal Democrats to win; most of those tactically voting for the Tories were from minor parties.[8] However, those who said they would vote tactically if their party could not win, yet still intended to vote Liberal Democrat, split five-to-one in favour of Labour rather than the Conservatives as the party to which they would switch. Even allowing for the very small numbers in these subsamples, therefore, it seems probable that Labour failed to squeeze quite all of the juice out of tactical votes that was potentially available for them.

The television debates

While Nick Clegg's success in the debates was a surprise to voters in the marginal seats as it was everywhere else, it was no surprise that the debates played an important part in the campaign. At the start of April, three in five adults in the battleground seats thought that the performance of the leaders in the debates would be 'very important' or 'fairly important' in helping them decide how to vote, very similar to the figures in a national Ipsos MORI survey in February. Of those who said that they might change their minds about their voting intention, 70 per cent rated the debates as at least 'fairly important'.

It was widely expected that David Cameron would win the debates: 45 per cent picked Cameron as the leader they expected to 'gain most public support as a result of the debates', while Gordon Brown trailed third on 17 per cent behind Clegg on 22 per cent, even in those Labour-held constituencies where he still retained a voting intention lead.

Claimed viewing figures were high: 53 per cent said they had watched all or some of the first debate live, 38 per cent said the same of the second debate (screened on a channel to which not all voters would have had access) and 49 per cent the final debate; many others missed the debates but saw news coverage of them afterwards (Table 8.6). These figures were slightly higher than was indicated by polling across the country: 47 per cent said they watched some or all of the first debate in Ipsos MORI's national poll the following weekend, which was a considerable overstatement of the official viewing figures, which put the audience between 9 and 10 million (roughly 20 per cent of adults). Assuming that the figures in the marginals include a similar level of overclaim, the debates nevertheless reached a substantial part of the electorate.

Around half of those who said they saw each of the debates or some coverage of it – amounting to a third of the entire electorate – said it affected their voting, though for the biggest number of these it had encouraged them to vote for the party they already supported rather than persuading them to change their vote or to make up their minds (Table 8.7). In the final survey we also asked, before mentioning the debates, 'In the last week have you changed your mind about which party to vote for, or not?' Almost half of those who said they had changed their minds and who had watched the final debate said the debate had encouraged them to switch their vote.

Nick Clegg was overwhelmingly perceived as winner of the first debate: 59 per cent felt Clegg performed best in the debate, 7 per cent that David Cameron had and 8 per cent that Gordon Brown had. A

Table 8.6 Reported debate viewing

Q. *(16–19 April)* **As you probably know, for the first time in a general election campaign the leaders of the three main parties recently debated key issues live on television. Did you watch the debate, either live or reported on the news afterwards, or not?**

Q. *(23–26 April, 30 April – 2 May)* **As you probably know, the second/last of the three televised leader debates took place recently, in which the leaders of the three main parties recently debated key issues live on television. Did you watch the most recent debate, either live or reported on the news afterwards, or not?**

	16–19 April %	23–26 April %	30 April– 2 May %
Yes – all of it on the night	28	21	29
Yes – some of it on the night	25	17	20
Didn't watch the debate but saw news coverage of it afterwards on television	16	20	19
Didn't watch the debate but saw news coverage of it afterwards in newspapers	5	4	5
No – didn't watch it	26	33	25
Watched the first or second debate but not the third	n/a	4	3
Don't know	*	0	0

Note: *Figure less than 0.5 but greater than zero
Source: Ipsos MORI/Reuters Base: c. 1,000 residents aged 18+ in key marginal seats

Table 8.7 Reported impact of debates on party support

Q. *(To those who had watched or seen coverage of the debate)* **Which of these statements do you most agree with?**

	16–19 April %	23–26 April %	30 April– 2 May %
The (latest) debate has encouraged me to vote for the party I already support	25	33	26
The (latest) debate has encouraged me to switch my vote from one party to another	14	7	11
The (latest) debate made me change from being undecided to choosing one of the parties to vote for	9	8	9
The (latest) debate has put me off voting for any party	2	1	2
The (latest) debate has had no impact on how I intend to vote	47	47	48
None of these	3	2	4
Don't know	1	2	1

Source: Ipsos MORI/Reuters Base: c. 1,000 residents aged 18+ in key marginal seats

quarter (most of whom didn't watch the debate) said they didn't know. Of those who said they had watched the whole debate, rather than only part of it or relying on news coverage, 80 per cent picked Clegg as the winner. In the two weeks since the previous poll, the Liberal Democrat voting intention share in these constituencies had doubled, from 11 per cent to 23 per cent, and almost half of these supporters said the debate had encouraged them to switch support either from another party or from being undecided, so virtually all of this swing apparently came from the debate effect.

Clegg's perceived victory in the second debate was narrower (33 per cent thought he performed best, while 19 per cent picked Cameron and 11 per cent picked Brown), and the reported impact on voting intentions was correspondingly less. Only 7 per cent said they had switched their allegiance from one party to another – and, intriguingly, as many of these had switched to Labour as to the Liberal Democrats, although it was the Lib Dems who once more made the biggest gains from the previously undecided.

The final debate, however, was apparently watched by as many people as the first had been, and had a similar level of impact, with the bulk of those who reported either that their vote had been swung, or that they had made up their minds after having been previously undecided, intending to vote Liberal Democrat. But these gains were clearly not big enough to compensate for the losses the Liberal Democrats were sustaining for other reasons, since their share of the vote fell slightly between the third and fifth surveys.

The voters' verdict on the campaign

The voters seem to have been interested by the election but less impressed by the campaign. They were divided on how well the parties had put across their policies. Towards the end of April, they were asked how clearly they felt each of the three main parties had explained their plans to reduce the deficit: the Conservatives rated marginally best (50 per cent said they had explained 'very' or 'fairly' clearly, 40 per cent 'not very' or 'not at all' clearly), Labour (49 per cent to 43 per cent) and the Liberal Democrats (42 per cent to 45 per cent) coming just behind.

Perhaps these figures are not as bad as might be expected, given the widespread criticism that the campaign was a negative one. Questioned after the first leaders' debate, two-thirds (64 per cent) felt the campaign was being fought by the parties pointing out what was wrong with the policies and personalities in other parties, and only 25 per cent that the parties were putting forward their own policies and personalities. But there was little dissent that the election *should* be fought by parties putting forward their own policies and personalities, preferred by 80 per cent compared with the 14 per cent who backed the more negative tactic. (But, of course, this is a perennial complaint, and the parties would reply that, while the voters may not like negative campaigning, it does seem to work.)

Reaction to the novelty of the debates was also equivocal. Overall, there was a feeling that they had promoted interest in the election but only at the expense of increased 'presidentialisation'. Four out of five (79 per cent) said they thought that the debates had helped to get more people interested in the election campaign, but barely half that number (42 per cent) admitted that it had made them personally more interested; and 73 per cent agreed that the debates had led to too much emphasis on the personality of the leaders, and not enough on policies.

Conclusion

Of course, we can hardly judge the campaign in the abstract, with no reference to its effects. But, judged by voting intentions, its effects were minimal. Labour's lead over the Conservatives did not move significantly at any point in the campaign, and remained steady until polling day. The only noticeable movement was to the Liberal Democrats after the first debate, gaining from both major parties, then subsequently fading slightly, exactly as in the national polls (Table 8.8). If we assume the final poll was exactly accurate, the movement in the last week from

Table 8.8 Voting intentions (marginal constituencies)
Q. **How do you intend to vote on May 6th?** *(If undecided or refused)* **Which party are you most inclined to support?**

	Notional result 2005 %	19–22 March %	30 Mar– 5 Apr %	16–19 April %	23–26 April %	30 April– 2 May %	RESULT 6 May %
Conservative	31	37	38	32	35	36	36
Labour	45	41	41	36	38	36	39
Liberal Democrat	17	11	11	23	21	20	16
Other	7	11	10	9	6	8	9
Labour lead	14	4	3	4	3	0	3

Source: Ipsos MORI/Reuters Base: c. 700–800 residents aged 18+ in key marginal seats expressing a voting intention and 'absolutely certain to vote'

the Liberal Democrats slightly favoured Labour over the Conservatives, but the difference is within the margin of error and may be illusory. Either way, Labour hung on and lost only 23 of these 57 seats.

How, then, should we assess the campaign in the marginals? The parties succeeded well in reaching voters, but it is not clear how persuasive they were. Significant numbers changed their voting intentions over the campaign, but with no significant net gain for either major party, and many voters kept open minds until the last minute. This may simply be a sign of a stalemate between two equally effective campaigns, rather than that both were ineffectual. But low awareness of the marginality of these constituencies, levels of tactical voting no higher than in safer seats and a Liberal Democrat share of the vote that was higher at the end of the campaign than at the beginning suggest the latter rather than the former.

The general impression is that, even in these constituencies where the local campaign should have been paramount, the national campaign overrode it. Television was the most used source of information, and the TV debates swung votes to the Liberal Democrats, even in the seats that the Liberal Democrats could not win. If the message got across, we saw few signs of it.

But what stands out above all is how great a proportion of the electorate remained uncertain in their vote for so long. Whatever the reason, it changes the nature of the election in these key seats. This floating vote is pivotal to the constituency outcome, and in almost every case the result must have been in the balance almost to the very end. The campaign could have been crucial. There was the scope in these seats alone, had they swung only a little differently, to give David Cameron a majority or to keep some form of minority Labour government in Downing Street. The coalition government that emerged from the election owes much to the failure of either major party to achieve a decisive campaigning win in these marginal seats.

Notes

1. Further details of all these surveys, including the full questionnaires, can be found at www.ipsos-mori.com.
2. This, of course, refers to the 'notional result' allowing for boundary change, not to the real result in a sometimes much-altered constituency.
3. We did not attempt to distinguish between those that were hand-delivered and those sent by post.
4. Certainty of voting was measured on a ten-point numerical scale 'where 10 means you would be absolutely certain to vote and 1 means that you would be absolutely certain not to vote'. Only those giving an answer of 10 or saying that they had already voted by post were regarded as 'certain to vote'.

5. The ICM poll was conducted in constituencies where the Conservatives needed a swing of between 4 per cent and 10 per cent to win.
6. The fall from 12 per cent to 9 per cent was not statistically significant.
7. Although the Greens came through from third place to win in one case, Brighton Pavilion.
8. These tactical votes from the Tories came mainly from UKIP. (Not a single respondent in our final poll said they had switched tactically from the BNP, although 2 per cent of those giving a voting intention said they intended to vote for the BNP.)

References

ICM (2010) Poll for the *News of the World*, conducted 7–8 April 2010, http://www.icmresearch.co.uk/pdfs/2010_apr_notw_marginals_campaign_poll1.pdf, accessed 17 November 2010.

Kavanagh, D. and Cowley, P. (2010) *The British General Election of 2010.* Basingstoke: Palgrave Macmillan.

Populus (2010). Poll for *The Times*, http://populuslimited.com/uploads/download_pdf-070310-The-Times-The-Times-Marginal-Seats-Poll---March-2010.pdf, accessed 17 November 2010.

9
Public Confidence in Elections
Jenny Watson

Introduction

Casting a vote on election day is one of the most important things we do as citizens in a democracy. Everyone who is entitled to should be able to register to vote and vote. We want people to know voting is as straightforward, accessible and secure as possible. We want to make sure people receive a consistently high-quality service wherever they live.

The 2010 UK Parliamentary general election was the first UK general election since my appointment as Chair of the Electoral Commission. International observers for the first time were officially allowed to observe a general election in the UK. What was striking to some of them was the culture and tradition of trust and honesty that underpins our election process.

Our system trusts that people are who they say they are when they turn up at the polling station. Hundreds of individual Returning Officers are trusted to deliver elections on the ground with no central authority managing them.[1] Elections staff are trusted to transport ballot boxes from polling stations to count centres. All of this dates from a time when communities were closer-knit, and when mass participation was not sought or expected because far fewer people had the right to vote.

It is, therefore, a system overwhelmingly dependent upon those running elections on the ground. It is also based on complex layers of legislation as well as a multiplicity of elections and voting systems – all of which places greater strain on it. Maintaining public confidence in an electoral system based on trust takes a huge amount of hard work and commitment.

It also means, as we have witnessed, that it can take a long time to rebuild trust when things go wrong. In Scotland in 2007 there were a high number of rejected ballot papers, and across some parts of England in 2010 people were left standing in queues at some polling stations at 10 pm on polling day and were unable to vote. Fraud, although not widespread, also plays a part in undermining public confidence in the system. Without the right structure, systems and checks and balances, the risk of something going wrong is always there. You can't therefore presume that a system built on trust will work in perpetuity. The UK is a successful, thriving democracy, with proud traditions on which to draw. But we must be realistic enough to ask how we can best keep that legacy secure in the future, and this year's election gave us another warning that the question should not wait too long for an answer.

This chapter looks at the Electoral Commission's assessment of the 2010 elections, including the challenges faced on polling day. It also provides an analysis of the levels of public satisfaction with, and confidence in, the electoral system – including perceptions of electoral fraud – as measured through Electoral Commission surveys.

Building on this assessment, it will consider the crucial issues which the Commission believes need to be addressed for the 2011 elections and beyond to make sure that the interest of voters comes first. These include effective management and coordination of Returning Officers, transparent funding of electoral administration, strengthening of security for postal votes, whether there is any role for advance voting and the potential for ID requirements at polling stations as in Northern Ireland. We also want individual electoral registration to be implemented across Great Britain in a way that ensures complete and accurate electoral registers.

The 2010 experience

Registering to vote

This was the first UK general election in which voters could register to vote after the election had been announced, following changes introduced in the Electoral Administration Act 2006 (EAA) and argued for by the Electoral Commission.[2] Previously, the deadline for new or changed registration applications had been up to a month and a half before polling day; a time when far fewer people are engaged with the impending election. This was also likely to be the last general election to be based on electoral registers created using the system of household registration across Great Britain. A system of individual electoral registration already exists in Northern Ireland and has done since 2002. We welcome the

Government's plans to introduce individual electoral registration for Great Britain in 2014.

Before the election, the Commission ran public awareness campaigns across Great Britain and Northern Ireland to promote electoral registration for both the UK general election and the English local government elections. These were aimed at increasing the number of eligible people registered to vote, particularly under-registered groups such as young people, home movers and certain black and minority ethnic groups. The campaign was successful in raising awareness of registration among the target audience, initiating and prompting requests to be registered. There were over two million visits to our website www.aboutmyvote.co.uk and more than 500,000 registration forms downloaded.

We also worked with Facebook, who created a Democracy UK hub (www.facebook.com/democracyuk) which featured polls, links and feeds to political parties, videos forums and games about democracy. Users could register using the 'register to vote' tab which brought up an aboutmyvote.co.uk page on Facebook. There were 13,800 visits to the register to vote page on Facebook.

According to the Central Office of Information, our campaign for the 2010 General Election was the most cost-effective of the more than forty recent campaigns in their benchmarking database, using the measure of cost per active response (for our campaigns, an active response is defined as a download or order of a voter registration form).

On polling day the electoral registers for the 2010 UK General Election included nearly 45.6 million entries, an increase of over 1.3 million since the last general election in 2005.

Thursday or Friday counts?

In the weeks leading up to the election there had been significant debate over the timing of the election counts. For the Electoral Commission the most important issue was the accuracy of the result. Our guidance to Returning Officers made it clear that convenience was not a good enough reason to delay the count. There was a debate in the House of Commons and a high-profile campaign to ensure that votes in the vast majority of constituencies were counted and the results announced during the evening and early morning following the close of poll on 6 May.

Following this the Constitutional Reform and Governance Act received Royal Assent on 8 April 2010. This required all Returning Officers to take steps to begin counting votes within four hours of the close of poll. Those who did not were required to publish a statement explaining why they were unable to begin counting within this timescale.

Some of the reasons given by Returning Officers for delaying a count included the challenges presented by local geography to the safe transportation of ballot boxes from polling stations to the count centre, longer than anticipated verification of postal votes and the availability of suitable and experienced staff.

In the event, twenty-three constituencies reported that they began the count on the Friday morning following election day. For the first time, all the Northern Ireland constituencies counted overnight.

Administering the election

A total of 29.7 million valid votes were cast at the UK general election, a turnout of 65.1 per cent. Nearly 24 million votes were cast in approximately 40,000 polling stations with 5.8 million valid postal votes received. Over 140,000 people were appointed a proxy. Local government elections were held on the same day across parts of England. A total of 13.6 million valid votes were cast at these elections, a turnout of 62.2 per cent.[3]

Overall, our analysis of the 2010 elections found that for the most part they were well run without any major problems (Electoral Commission (2010b)). Our performance standards, which monitor the performance of Returning Officers across Great Britain, show there has been an overall improvement since 2009 across all standards.

- **Planning and organisation** – skills and knowledge of the Returning Officer; planning processes in place for an election; and training
- **Integrity** – maintaining the integrity of an election
- **Participation** – planning and delivering public awareness activity; accessibility of information to electors; and communication of information to candidates and agents.

Eighty-two per cent of (Acting) Returning Officers met all standards, an improvement of 17 percentage points from last year.[4] Particular progress has been seen in both delivering public awareness activities and maintaining the integrity of elections. Both of these were identified in 2009 as the weakest areas of performance, and we have been encouraged by the willingness of Returning Officers and their teams to use the performance standards framework as a basis for continued improvement.

Our full report on performance standards can be found on the Commission's website (Electoral Commission, 2010c). We intend to develop these standards further in the next few years, building on the baseline of knowledge which we have developed.

While there is no formal coordination between Returning Officers for UK general elections, there was evidence of good national and regional planning and coordination. In Scotland, Wales and Northern Ireland, Returning Officers and electoral administrators used existing coordination and planning groups, which contributed to well-run elections in these areas.

Scotland deserves particular mention. The (then) interim Electoral Management Board established in November 2008 in Scotland led the planning and delivery of the election. Immediately prior to the general election it consisted of one Returning Officer who was the Convener, another four Returning Officers, two Electoral Registration Officers and four Deputy Returning Officers. There were discernible benefits from its efforts and work in relation to preparations for the general election: in particular, its discussions with Royal Mail, additional guidance on recounts and adjudication of doubtful ballots, and its work to achieve a greater consistency in election materials.

But elsewhere there was evidence of poor administration, such as the highly publicised issue of people queuing outside polling stations on election night in local authorities including Manchester, Sheffield and Hackney. This variation in practice across England is perhaps inevitable given that 319 (Acting) Returning Officers are making individual decisions with no overall coordination.

Polling station queues

The Commission launched an immediate investigation into queues outside polling stations. We published a report (Electoral Commission, 2010a) within weeks of the election setting out what went wrong and what needs to happen to make sure those particular problems are not repeated. We found that just over 1,200 people were left queuing outside some twenty-seven polling stations and were unable to vote when polls closed at 10 pm on 6 May. So why did this happen?

In these constituencies, there was clear evidence of poor and inadequate planning processes. In some places, contingency plans were in place but were not triggered by staff at particular polling stations.

Unrealistic and inappropriate assumptions had been made about the number of electors who would turn out to vote, especially later on polling day, despite the Commission encouraging staff to plan for a higher turnout. This meant that some polling stations were left understaffed. Although extra polling station staff were brought in to provide support, it was sometimes too late to manage the queues and ensure that everyone was able to vote.

Some polling stations were found to be too small and cramped to deal with the steady stream of voters. Returning Officers are sometimes restricted by the current rules that determine what can be used as a polling place, meaning more suitable premises were not always available to them. But this was made worse by the fact that too many electors had been allocated to a particular polling station in the first place. Ideally the number of electors allocated to one polling station should not exceed 2,500, as set out in the Electoral Commission's guidance (Electoral Commission, 2009). However, in some of the areas where voters experienced problems, in excess of 3,000 and as many as 4,500 electors were allocated to a particular polling station.

In areas where local government elections were also held, some polling station staff said that the need to explain the different ballot papers to voters meant that the issuing of ballot papers took longer. During busy periods this meant that queues formed in and outside the polling station. Almost all of these problems could have been foreseen in the planning process.

In the year preceding the elections the Commission had issued guidance to (Acting) Returning Officers which highlighted the need to plan on the basis of higher turnout than in recent elections, including the 2005 General Election. Yet the Commission has no power to direct Returning Officers to follow our guidance, nor any power to make individual Returning Officers think differently about their actions beyond what might be described as 'naming and shaming'. We will need to find ways to address these shortcomings through the way we monitor performance in the run-up to future elections.

On top of administrative challenges, Returning Officers had to work within the confines of the legislation. Crucially, there is no scope within the existing legislation to extend polling hours beyond 10 pm.[5] The detail of electoral legislation in other countries varies, but in general the rules are more inclusive than in the UK. Take three democracies with similar traditions to that of the UK as examples. At federal elections in Australia and parliamentary elections in New Zealand, all electors who are present inside the polling place at the close of poll are entitled to vote. At parliamentary elections in Canada, electors who are in the polling station or in a queue at the door of the polling station at the close of poll are entitled to vote. There is no reason why this should not work in the UK.

We believe that there would be clear benefits for voters if the rules for all UK elections were revised to provide clarity that those who are present, or in a queue, at a polling station at the close of poll are entitled to vote. We first recommended a change to this rule following the November 2003 Assembly elections in Northern Ireland, but the recommendation has still not been addressed.

Other issues arising

There were a raft of other things that should have gone better. While limited in number, we feel they represented unacceptable levels of service to the voter. These included:

- polling stations not opening on time and having insufficient staff
- inappropriate polling places
- wrong ballot papers or electoral registers being delivered to the polling station
- polling stations where supplies of ballot papers ran out before stocks could be replenished
- errors in printing poll cards and ballot papers

While these problems need to be identified and addressed, we must acknowledge the efforts made by Returning Officers and electoral administrators for the work they do locally to make our democracy work, with some going the extra mile. Many did so without incident, and their efforts were overshadowed by polling station queues; yet they deserve our thanks. And in one case, in Northern Ireland, election staff responded with complete professionalism to an attempt by dissident republicans to disrupt the count in Londonderry with a car bomb. Despite the count being suspended while staff were safely evacuated, it was successfully completed after only a short suspension. Effective planning and coordination between the Deputy Returning Officer and the Police Service of Northern Ireland prior to the election ensured that the integrity of the electoral process was maintained.

So what impact does all this have on public confidence in the electoral process? Do the public trust the current system, and what damage do high-profile problems do to public confidence and satisfaction?

Public confidence in elections?

The public's overall satisfaction with the voting process remains fairly high and relatively stable. In May 2010, 75 per cent of people described themselves as satisfied with the procedure of voting. That is down from 80 per cent after the 2009 elections but similar to the 74 per cent and 75 per cent recorded in England and Wales after the 2007 elections. However, 13 per cent of people are not satisfied, which means there is work to be done to ensure greater satisfaction for future elections.

Satisfaction was notably higher among those who voted at the election (80 per cent) compared with those who did not (51 per cent). In addition, voters were significantly more likely to say they were very satisfied (36 per cent) than non-voters (15 per cent). However, dissatisfaction with the voting process does not appear to be a contributing factor to non-voting. An individual's circumstances play a much more significant role, with 21 per cent saying they were too busy on the day, 8 per cent indicating that specific circumstances on the day prevented them from voting and 5 per cent being away from home.

Those who have been voting for longer were more positive about the voting process, with those aged 55 and over significantly more likely to be satisfied (83 per cent) than 18–34-year-olds (67 per cent). We can't assume that those younger voters will just 'get used to it' and learn to love the system and that they will continue to vote. Those who always vote in general elections are also more likely to be satisfied (81 per cent) than those who sometimes do (66 per cent) or never do (35 per cent).

Our research suggests that, for those who do vote, their direct experience of voting is usually very positive. In 2010, 93 per cent of polling station voters and 99 per cent of postal voters were satisfied with their chosen method for casting a vote. Furthermore, 94 per cent of people indicated that they felt confident when filling in a ballot paper (with 67 per cent very confident). This is supported by the small number of ballot papers rejected at the count (0.28 per cent of all those cast), which may include both deliberately and accidentally spoilt ballots.

However, while a majority of voters (69 per cent) in 2010 were confident the elections had been well run, this was 23 percentage points lower than in the 2009 elections (92 per cent). More strikingly, the percentage who said they were very confident fell from 54 per cent to 25 per cent. This is a clear indication that, even if their individual experiences remain positive, voters' confidence in the system can be quickly shaken by reports of problems elsewhere.

In addition, the public still have concerns about electoral fraud. The results of tracking research from 2005 to 2010, which is not carried out at election time, shows that the percentage of people who think electoral fraud is a problem has remained around one-third – ranging from 37 per cent to 27 per cent. Only one in five of those responding to our survey after the 2010 general election believed that the voting system is very safe from fraud or abuse. One-third of people were concerned that fraud took place at the general election.

We will publish a full analysis and assessment of data relating to cases of electoral malpractice at the 6 May 2010 elections in early 2011. The report will provide information on the number of cases reported to police and the proportion of these cases that end in a prosecution once investigated by the police.

It is clear that there is still work for the Commission and the UK government to do to reassure the public that their vote is safe. This is an important issue for people. When asked what is most important to them in relation to voting – safety, secrecy, convenience or choice – people have indicated, in every Electoral Commission survey since 2006, that the most important element is either safety or secrecy.

The Commission also surveyed candidates standing at the election. Most (80 per cent) were satisfied with the administration of the general election in their constituency. A total of 41 per cent declared themselves very satisfied, and a further 39 per cent fairly satisfied. However, candidates were less positive than voters on the issue of fraud and abuse. Only 62 per cent of candidates said that they thought voting was fairly or very safe from fraud, with 28 per cent saying they thought it was very or fairly unsafe. More encouragingly, concern among candidates that malpractice had actually occurred in their constituency was somewhat lower. Forty-six per cent said that they were not very concerned that this had happened, and 30 per cent that they were not at all concerned.

We will continue to encourage them to follow the Code of Practice agreed by all parties on the handling of postal votes, and to report fraud whenever they suspect it. Candidates and their local agents and campaigners on the ground are a vital source of evidence in relation to fraud.

So what now – 2011 and beyond

So where does all this leave us? 2011 is a big year for electoral events. There will be a referendum on the powers of the National Assembly for Wales on 3 March. There are scheduled elections to the Scottish Parliament,

National Assembly for Wales and Northern Ireland Assembly, and local government elections in England and Northern Ireland on 5 May 2011. It is our current assumption,[6] subject to UK Parliamentary approval, that a UK-wide referendum will be held on a change to the voting system for the UK Parliament alongside these scheduled elections. The first and only UK-wide referendum was held in 1975 on Britain's membership in the European Community. There could also be by-elections at any time.

2011 is also a big year for the Commission. Not only will we be reporting on the devolved elections but, unlike with elections, we will be responsible for running the Wales and UK-wide referendums. Preparations are currently on track for the proposed referendum and scheduled elections on 5 May next year, but it will still be a significant challenge to make sure they are well run.

I will be the Chief Counting Officer (CCO) responsible for the conduct of the referendum and ensuring the accuracy of the overall result. So what do I think needs to be in place by then to ensure that both the elections and referendums are properly run, and that voters, campaigners and candidates will be able to participate in these with confidence?

From the outset the Commission has said that all those involved in running the polls on 5 May should approach them from the point of view of the voters, many of whom will be casting their votes in elections as well as referendums. It is imperative that the government works with us to put a robust process in place to plan for those polls so that the interests of voters across the UK are considered as a priority.

For the UK-wide referendum, the rules on how the referendum will be conducted must be clear from at least six months in advance so that everyone taking part or involved can be clear about their roles and responsibilities and can undertake the necessary planning and preparation for the polls. The legal framework must make provision for the formal combination of the referendum poll with the scheduled elections.

The Chief Counting Officer has powers of direction for the Wales and UK-wide referendums to be held in 2011. This will mean that at these referendums, unlike at elections, the CCO will have the power to direct Counting Officers in the discharge of their functions, including directions requiring them to take specified steps in preparation for the referendum, and can require Counting Officers to provide any information that they have or are entitled to have. The CCO also has a power of direction in relation to Regional Counting Officers and the discharge of their statutory functions.

As such we will adopt a more directive approach to performance monitoring. Our instructions will take the form of modules with Counting Officers asked to follow the instructions using the supplied templates. We will actively monitor the conduct of the referendums to enable us to certify the referendum result with confidence.

For the referendums, we will provide templates to Counting Officers for some of the key voter-facing forms and notices that voters use when voting. These will be based upon our *Making your mark* design guidance aimed at improving the usability and accessibility of voter materials used at elections.

Under the Political Parties, Elections and Referendum Act 2000 the Commission is required to assess the intelligibility of proposed referendum questions, and we have carried out this exercise for both referendum questions. We wanted to ensure that voters are able to understand the wording of the questions they will be voting on. As part of our question assessment process for both the Wales and the UK-wide referendums we undertook public opinion research[7] with voters. We have recommended changes to the question in both cases – substantial in the case of the proposed question for the Wales referendum – and in both cases the revised wording has been accepted.

There also needs to be proper provision for public awareness activity so that voters can understand the different events, the ballot papers and the voting systems. Voters must be able to vote easily and confidently, knowing that their vote will be counted in the way they intended.

The Commission will run public awareness campaigns ahead of the Welsh referendum in March 2011 and the UK referendum and elections in May 2011. It will ensure that voters are aware of the events taking place, and how they can take part in them. Alongside advertising on television, radio, press and websites, a booklet will be delivered to all 28 million households. The booklet will explain what the referendum is about, what will happen in the event of a 'yes' or 'no' vote to the referendum, and different ways to cast your vote (polling station, postal, proxy). Specifically for the May polls, the booklet will include details on the elections taking place in each part of the UK and what the first past the post and alternative vote systems are.

For May, where the polls are combined with scheduled elections, there must be an appropriate level of funding available for the delivery of the referendum and the elections together. This will enable Returning Officers and Counting Officers to ensure that both polls are well run. The UK Government has indicated that it intends to use the framework used for the 2009 European Parliamentary and 2010 UK General

Election, to provide appropriate funding for the delivery of the polls. The Commission will continue to monitor whether local authorities have sufficient resources and staff in place to deliver these polls.

It is essential that robust planning is in place for the referendum and elections. The Commission has established a Steering Group – including representatives from the Commission, Regional Counting Officers, the Association of Electoral Administrators and the UK Government – to coordinate delivery of the referendum and elections and ensure robust planning for 5 May.

As part of our planning for and delivery of the referendums in 2011, we will be drawing upon lessons learned from previous elections. We do not want to see a repeat of any of the problems faced by voters at the 2010 elections, such as queuing to get into polling stations. As a result, our instructions to Counting Officers will include a realistic assessment of turnout and limits on the number of electors allocated to each polling station. But we are clear that turnout is in the hands of those standing for election, and those campaigning on either side in the referendums. Only they can generate the excitement that means that people want to participate.

Beyond 2011

The UK coalition government has set out an ambitious programme of democratic reform, which is likely to mean more opportunities for voters to express their views. It will also, inevitably, mean more pressure on the machinery of electoral administration, particularly at a time when financial pressures are increasing across the public sector. It may not attract the same degree of attention as the politics of reform, but the role of electoral administration in delivering these changes must not be overlooked.

The Commission has set out its agenda for what we would like in place to ensure that elections and referendums are well run in the future. The current system is in need of long-term reform. It is insufficiently robust and coordinated to meet the challenges of elections in the twenty-first century.

We urge the UK Government to bring forward proposals for a comprehensive modernisation strategy. This should include fundamental, long-term changes to the way we run elections across the UK. At the same time it is crucial that the interests of electors are kept at the heart of electoral policy and decision-making. The electoral system cannot afford any further decline in public confidence, and the problems encountered by voters in England on 6 May 2010 must never be allowed to happen again.

The proposal for fixed term parliaments should make planning for and administering UK general elections easier. All those involved, electoral administrators, candidates and voters, will know well in advance when it is taking place and will be able to plan accordingly. For example, administrators will know when postal votes will be issued and will have longer to find suitable premises for polling stations. It also presents an opportunity to consider lengthening the timetable for UK general elections and the key deadlines within it. However, this will not address all problems with the current electoral system.

Effective management and consistency in the delivery of elections

The experience of the 2010 elections, with inconsistent service provided to voters, especially in those areas that had highly publicised problems, demonstrates that there must be appropriate mechanisms to hold Returning Officers to account for the delivery of their statutory functions.

We want the UK Government to respond to recommendations we have made in the past to ensure consistency in the delivery of future elections. There must be effective coordination of the delivery of statutory functions by Returning Officers across the UK – including a power of direction exercised by the Electoral Commission or by other Electoral Management Boards responsible for coordinating elections.

We hope that local government scrutiny in areas where there were problems in May 2010 will lead to greater scrutiny of electoral services across the board, and hope to work with local government associations across Great Britain to help this happen in a way that is appropriate.

We are pleased that the Local Electoral Administration (Scotland) Bill, introduced in the Scottish Parliament on 7 October 2010, provides for the Electoral Management Board to be established on a statutory basis for its work in relation to local government elections in Scotland. This would include giving the Convener of the Board a power to direct other ROs and EROs, and is an excellent example of how a new system of coordination might operate. We still urge the Scottish Government and UK Government to consolidate this for all elections.

The costs of running elections must also be properly met with comprehensive and transparent funding mechanisms. There needs to be greater consistency in funding elections across local authorities. This will result in a more consistent service for voters regardless of where they live.

The current funding arrangements are complex and do not deliver accountability. The UK government is responsible for the legal and funding frameworks for UK general elections, European Parliamentary elections and elections to the Scottish Parliament and the Northern Ireland Assembly. An Order is laid in Parliament which sets out the maximum amounts that can be recovered by Returning Officers. Elections to the National Assembly for Wales are funded by the Assembly themselves.

Although the UK Government is responsible for the legal framework for local government elections in England, including the Greater London Assembly, the funding of these elections is directed by local authorities themselves. Electoral registration is also largely funded by each local authority. It is up to the discretion of the local authority how much money is allocated to running the registration process and these elections, meaning that there are inconsistencies across the country in the amount of resources available and ultimately the service received by the elector.

Security and accessibility of voting

Voting must be safe and secure, but it should not prevent the voter from being able to vote successfully.

More and more people are choosing to vote by post, finding it a more convenient way to cast their vote. In the 2010 elections, 15 per cent of eligible electors were issued with a postal vote, compared with 4 per cent in 2001 and 12 per cent in 2005. Eighty-three per cent of people returned their postal vote, which represented almost one-fifth of all votes cast at the general election.

Security is clearly an issue in relation to postal voting. Our research has shown that, while there has been a ten percentage point increase in the proportion of people who consider voting by post to be safe from fraud or abuse since 2005, only 46 per cent of respondents thought postal voting was safe from fraud and abuse in 2009. This compares unfavourably with the 87 per cent who thought voting at a polling station was safe.

The introduction of new security checks on postal votes through the use of Absent Voter Identifiers (AVI) has led to a reduction in the scale and volume of allegations of postal vote fraud. However, to strengthen the security of postal voting further we want to see 100 per cent checking of personal identifiers on returned postal voting statements. At the election, 476 out of the 632 constituencies in Great Britain conducted verification of the identifiers on 100 per cent of postal votes returned. A further ninety-five constituencies conducted verification of between 90 per cent and 99 per cent. However, that means that nearly 10 per cent of constituencies verified fewer than 90 per cent, with some verifying only the minimum required 20 per cent.

With measures in place to enhance the security of postal voting and the registration system in Great Britain moving towards the system, already in operation in Northern Ireland, 'in person' voting may become the weak link to which those inclined towards abusing the system gravitate. In Great Britain, when a person votes in a polling station it is trusted that they are who they say they are. Unlike in Northern Ireland, no identification or written proof is required.

We want the Government to review the case for requiring ID for voters at polling stations. Research undertaken by the Commission indicates that requiring photographic ID when going to vote would broadly be well received by the public. Over half (55 per cent) of the British public say it would increase their confidence in electoral security and only 7 per cent that it would decrease their confidence, although 37 per cent say it would make no difference (Ipsos MORI, 2009).

Alongside increasing security, we would like the Government to consider more flexible options for people wanting to vote. This may include advance voting, which would allow people to vote in their electoral area between one and seven days before traditional polling day. The system we envisage would allow electors to cast their vote at one or more conveniently located polling stations within the constituency.

Our support for a form of advance voting is based on evidence drawn from pilot schemes which ran in a number of local authority areas in 2006 and 2007. Our evaluation found that, despite low take-up ranging from 0.5 per cent to 7 per cent of votes cast, 'advance voting has the potential to enhance the accessibility and convenience of the electoral process.' Furthermore, findings from our post-election survey suggest that more flexibility with voting arrangements would be welcomed by some non-voters; just under a third said that they would have been more likely to vote at the 2010 elections if they could have voted at the weekend.

Challenging elections

The system of challenging an election by election petition has been relatively the same since 1868. Following the 2010 election, there were two petitions to parliamentary seats which had been heard at the time of writing: Oldham East and Saddleworth, and Fermanagh and South Tyrone. The petition in Fermanagh and South Tyrone was dismissed, and the implication of the successful petition in Oldham East and Saddleworth, and the wider impact this might have on election conduct and the willingness of candidates to challenge the result of an individual election, is unknown.

The system has been given more visibility due to such high-profile election petitions. However, the system remains complex and inaccessible, and risks deterring a candidate from lodging a justified petition for fear of personal financial loss.

Petitions have to be presented within twenty-one days after the election and in a prescribed manner, providing specific information. The petitioner must pay a fee of £180 on issue of the election petition and a further sum as a security against costs (up to £5,000 for a parliamentary election and £2,500 for a local election). While this security for costs will not be more than the fixed maximum amount, the total costs to the petitioner will almost certainly exceed the cost of the security, should the petition be unsuccessful. In addition, legal aid is not available in connection with election petitions. A balance therefore needs to be struck between allowing access and deterring abuse.

Similar arguments about accessibility can be made about the process for issuing an election petition. It is a technical and legally complex area of law known well by only a few specialists. Many candidates find the process daunting without specialist advice, and not all can call on specialist lawyers employed by the political parties. Even if this does not deter them, a large proportion of election petitions fall on technicalities relating to the process of issuing the petition rather than on the point at issue. Moreover, the size of the winning candidate's majority is a further factor in determining whether a petition is successful. A challenge can only succeed if the breach of rules was significant and would have affected the result.

In 2007 we held discussions with interested parties and issued a briefing paper, calling for a wider debate on the current methods of challenging the result of an election. Any electoral modernisation proposals would be incomplete if they did not address the outdated and complex method of challenging elections where poor-quality administration has had an impact on the result.

Conclusion

We want to see free and fair elections where voters are confident that when they cast their vote it will be safe and it will be counted. We want a system that serves us well and continues to do so in the future; a system that is fit for the twenty-first century, which is voter-friendly and preserves the secrecy and integrity of the ballot. The basic building blocks of electoral administration need long-term reform, support and maintenance.

As demonstrated, we cannot rely upon a system that trusts that the machinery of electoral administration will always work well and deliver elections to a consistently high standard. Trust may have been a sufficient anchor for the system in the past, but, while trust is good, caution and deterrent controls are better. As international observers at the 2010 General Election stated, the UK system is not corrupted, but it is certainly corruptible.

Notes

The author would like to thank Katy Bere and Phil Thompson of the Electoral Commission for their assistance in writing this chapter.

1. In Northern Ireland elections are overseen by the Elections Office for Northern Ireland.
2. Previously, electors had to be on the register when Parliament was dissolved before the election. In effect this meant electors would have had to be on the register as it stood at 1 April for an election that was called in April, and held in May.
3. The coincidence of the general and local elections makes comparisons with turnout at previous local elections misleading.
4. This is based on returns received from all 372 (A)ROs in Great Britain.
5. Except in the case of riot or open violence, where polling would be adjourned to the following day – Rule 42 Schedule 1, Representation of the People Act 1983.
6. Writing in November 2010.
7. Reported in http://www.electoralcommission.org.uk/_media/response-submission/commission-responses-to-external-consultations/Question-assessment-report-English-FINAL-no-embargo.pdf and http://www.electoralcommission.org.uk/__data/assets/pdf_file/0006/102696/PVSC-Bill-QA-Report.pdf (accessed on 31 October 2010).

References

Electoral Commission (2009) *Essentials of effective election management: Planning for a UK Parliamentary general election*, http://www.electoralcommission.org.uk/__data/assets/electoral_commission_pdf_file/0020/81362/UKPGE-Essentials-WEB.pdf (accessed on 31 October 2010)

Electoral Commission (2010a) *2010 UK Parliamentary general election: Interim report: review of problems at polling stations at close of poll on 6 May 2010* (20 May 2010), http://www.electoralcommission.org.uk/__data/assets/pdf_file/0010/99091/Interim-Report-Polling-Station-Queues-complete.pdf

Electoral Commission (2010b) *Report on the administration of the 2010 UK general election* (27 July 2010), http://www.electoralcommission.org.uk/__data/assets/pdf_file/0010/100702/Report-on-the-administration-of-the-2010-UK-general-election.pdf

Electoral Commission (2010c) *Report on performance standards for (Acting) Returning Officers in Great Britain: UK general election 2010* (December 2010), http://www.electoralcommission.org.uk/__data/assets/pdf_file/0018/106623/Analysis-of-RO-Performance-final-no-embargo-29Nov.pdf

Ipsos MORI (2009) *Electoral Commission Winter Research 2009*, http://www.electoralcommission.org.uk/__data/assets/pdf_file/0009/84609/Ipsos-MORI-public-opinion-research-winter-2009-survey.pdf

Part IV
Parties

10
The Conservative Campaign

Alex Wilson

Introduction

The General Election of 2010 was one of great historical interest, resulting in the defeat of Britain's longest-serving Labour administration and the formation of the first coalition government since the Second World War. It was also the first since 1992 to be genuinely competitive – previous elections in 1997, 2001 and even 2005 had been, rightly or wrongly, largely seen as foregone conclusions, with few seriously expecting anything other than a Labour victory in each. 2010 was different, but at no stage was a Conservative victory – either as a majority or as simply the largest party – an inevitability. In order to return to government, the Party faced a number of serious challenges, which it had hitherto repeatedly failed to overcome.

Starting point – the uphill struggle

1997, 2001 and 2005 marked the three worst performances by the Conservatives, in terms of both national vote share and number of seats won. On every previous occasion that the Party had returned from opposition to power, it had done so from a much stronger starting point than it faced in 2010.

Rallings and Thrasher's estimated 2005 results for the new boundaries gave the Conservatives a notional total of 210 seats – still barely more than Labour had achieved under Michael Foot in 1983, at the nadir of their post-1979 decline. With John Bercow now sitting as the Speaker rather than as a Conservative, this meant we needed to gain 117 further constituencies – far in excess of any result achieved since the very different context of the National Government in 1931. The number of gains required exceeded the previous greatest achievement under normal circumstances – eighty-seven in 1950 – by a third.

To realise these gains, an estimated uniform national swing (UNS) of 6.9 per cent from Labour was necessary. This too would be a requirement of historical standards – again the greatest since 1931, and significantly greater than that achieved when we last returned to power in 1979 (5.3 per cent). The only occasion since the war in which *either* party has succeeded in both votes and seats to the extent now required was Tony Blair in 1997, and to be guaranteed becoming Prime Minister David Cameron needed to exceed the electoral achievements of both Winston Churchill and Margaret Thatcher.

Repairing the brand

When in 2005 the Conservative Party asked the electorate 'Are you thinking what we're thinking?' the response was a resounding 'No.' Our vote share increased by just 0.5 per cent and, while some gains were made, these often resulted largely from Labour voters moving to the Liberal Democrats or other parties rather than switching directly to the Conservatives.

A political party's brand image – how it presents itself and (more importantly) how it is perceived by the wider electorate – is crucial to its potential electoral success. The brand is created not only by the 'shopping list' of pledges and promises put forward in a manifesto, the detail of which few voters will digest in full. While specific policies are undoubtedly important in constructing a workable programme for government and their announcement is vital for seizing media attention, the brand is something far deeper. It reflects the Party's values, themes and priorities, judgements of its character, credibility and competence, and assessments of its leading figures and their ability to empathise with and deliver on the concerns of those they seek to represent.

When David Cameron became leader of the Conservative Party in December 2005, despite eight years having passed since the humiliation of 1997, public perceptions of the party had not materially improved. We were still seen as out of touch and out of date, more concerned with representing the better off than the whole of society, and failing to share the aspirations or desires of ordinary people.

Cameron knew from the outset how the Party was, and had been, perceived on a range of 'brand attributes'. Measures of the perception of the party's values, priorities and competence – and the extent to which they corresponded with those of the electorate – were central to the Party's analysis of both public and private polling throughout the Parliament. At this early stage, on nearly every measure, the Conservatives scored less favourably than both Labour and the Liberal Democrats, and on none of them was the Conservative score better than Labour's.

Research also showed that, while many were by now disappointed with the Labour government, they were still unsure about a Conservative alternative. The old adage 'oppositions don't win elections, governments lose them' does not ring true – change will only occur when the electorate is both dissatisfied with the incumbent administration *and* confident that the opposition represents a credible alternative. In the public's eyes, this second condition was not yet satisfied – an overwhelming majority felt the party had either not changed at all since 1997, or had even changed for the worse.

David Cameron recognised the scale of this challenge – his leadership campaign had been mounted on the platform of 'Change to Win' – and his Blackpool Conference speech, which electrified the contest, placed great emphasis on the need to be 'relevant to people's lives today' and 'comfortable with modern Britain'.

As leader, Cameron's early actions would set the tone for the remainder of his tenure as Leader of the Opposition. Policy commissions were established to initiate a wide-ranging review of the Party's approach to the six key challenges he set out in his acceptance speech. As well as tackling issues such as economic competitiveness and national/international security, the establishment of these commissions and the results that followed demonstrated an ambition to take the Party into areas that were not traditionally seen as Tory territory – public service improvement, quality of life, globalisation / global poverty and – most important of all – social justice. Cameron's interpretation of social justice went deeper than the simple redistributive approach favoured by the Left – with Iain Duncan Smith in the chair, this group would examine in detail the causes and consequences of poverty, family breakdown, addiction, care for the elderly and the role the voluntary sector could play in providing new and imaginative solutions – and, in doing so, paved the way for important areas of the Government's programme on welfare reform and the Big Society.

He also placed concerns about the environment at the heart of the Party's thinking, as evidenced by the 'Vote Blue Go Green' message first employed in the 2006 local elections, and raised issues of corporate responsibility. Both in tone and substance, David Cameron was clearly a different kind of Conservative leader.

As well as changing the approach and themes associated with the Party, he aimed to broaden its public face – if we wanted to represent modern Britain, we must ourselves first become more representative of modern Britain. Changes to candidate selection procedures, including the 'priority list', have been discussed at length elsewhere but it is worth acknowledging the great efforts that went into attracting a more diverse selection of prospective Conservative MPs than ever before.

Most importantly, David Cameron avoided the trap his predecessors had been accused of falling into – a narrow, 'core vote' campaign focused on issues such as Europe, immigration and tax, which had not delivered success in either 2001 or 2005. That is not to say we ignored these issues, but to have made them the sole focus of the campaign would have only served as a reminder to the electorate of the party they had so decisively rejected. Instead, as polling day drew near, the economy and public services – particularly the NHS – would provide the backdrop for much of our campaigning efforts.

This approach meant we were campaigning most vigorously on those issues that polling indicated were most salient to voters. Pursuing these campaigning priorities also helped tackle two of the principal weaknesses the Party had faced since 1992 – the loss of our reputation for economic competence, and concerns over whether we could be trusted to look after public services. The 'NHyeS' campaign, and our commitment to protect health spending even in an era where government in general would have to make savings, was both right for the country and politically essential.

The result of these efforts gradually became apparent in both quantitative and qualitative research. By the summer of 2008, our position relative to Labour on key brand attributes, and performance on a range of direct comparisons between David Cameron and Gordon Brown, had improved significantly. We were now also trusted by the electorate to deal with a much wider variety of issues than previously. In December 2005, the only issue on which the Conservatives held a lead over Labour was immigration (a lead that MORI's polling suggested we had even in 2001). By June 2008 the lead on immigration was still commanding, as it was on crime. But there were also comfortable leads on the economy, taxation and education, and even a narrow lead on the NHS. Of course, this poll had been conducted when the Conservative lead in published voting intention (VI) polls was at its height, but, while the position on issues weakened slightly before May 2010, published and private polling still showed large Conservative leads on immigration and crime and clear leads on the economy and education. Labour had retaken the lead on the NHS, but the issue remained significantly more competitive than it had been prior to David Cameron's leadership, when Labour's lead had appeared insurmountable.

Target seats

Repairing the brand played an essential part in ensuring the Party could once again be competitive in the national, media-driven 'air war'. But it could only ever be half of the story – general elections are not won or lost on a headcount of national vote share. The outcome is determined not just by *how many* votes a party receives, but also by *where* those votes are distributed in particular constituencies. It was therefore necessary to build strong local campaigns on the ground and focus resources accordingly to maximise the number of Conservative MPs returned for any given vote share. This would prove to be particularly important in a close election where every seat could potentially make the difference between a majority and a hung parliament, or influence the balance of the parties within a hung parliament. It was also important in attempting to partially mitigate the impact of bias, which persisted in the electoral geography. The new constituency boundaries notionally gave the Conservatives an extra twelve seats and Labour seven fewer, but it remained the case that, for an equal vote share, Labour would continue to win significantly more seats than the Conservatives (in 2005 we won the popular vote in England but ninety-two fewer seats) and that to achieve a parliamentary majority we required a double-digit lead in national vote share.

The 2005 campaign, as well as being saddled with a tarnished national appeal, had suffered from an over-ambitious targeting strategy that meant resources were spread too thinly to be of real benefit. Originally, a realistic aim of reducing Labour's majority had been set – and a list of around ninety target seats drawn up to reflect this. However, the decision was later taken to almost double this number, based on the optimistic premise that we could actually win the election. This optimism was ultimately misplaced, and it is probable that we actually made fewer gains than would have been the case had we adhered to the original strategy.

For 2010, with the Party faring much better on a national level, winning outright *was* a realistic possibility, and therefore the target seats list would need to be a large one. However, it was also essential to devise a structure that would prevent the 2005 mistake of overstretch happening again.

The target seats list was not simply a collection of the 117 small-est opposition majorities – there were some seats we felt would fall to us anyway without a significant national swing, and some where Conservative incumbents looked vulnerable. Also, to achieve a *workable* majority rather than a majority of just one, we would need to gain more than just the 117 most marginal seats. We estimated that approximately 130 constituencies would determine the outcome of the election, and, as the battleground shifted slightly over time, up to 200 benefited in some way from being part of the project.

Seats were originally placed in one of five categories:

- Consolidation – held by potentially vulnerable Conservative MPs, usually where their constituencies had been adversely affected by the Boundary Review
- Best Placed To Win – mainly new seats with notional Conservative majorities
- Battleground – which received the most attention
- Development – not really winnable now but where we aimed to become more competitive so they could be in future
- Long Shot – self-explanatory!

The list was kept under regular review, so seats could be 'promoted' or 'relegated' in light of the changing national situation and the meet-ing of strict performance targets for local political activity. In order to qualify for financial or other support from Conservative Campaign Headquarters (CCHQ), constituencies had to demonstrate detailed, well-structured campaign plans – arguably, it was this level of account-ability, and with it the more professional approach it brought to local campaigns, that would turn out to be of greater long-term benefit than the funds themselves.

Instead of structuring the campaign on a purely geographical basis as had traditionally been the case, we divided seats into clusters according to the characteristics of the constituencies themselves. Geography would remain an important factor, but we also took into account the demo-graphic profiles of similar kinds of seats in devising the target clusters:

- Inner/Outer London
- East/West Pennines
- Central/West Midlands
- New Towns
- Seaside Towns

- Thames Gateway
- Wales
- Lib Dem seats (these were treated separately throughout)
- Miscellaneous (seats which didn't neatly fit with any of the other clusters)

Battleground Directors were appointed for each cluster, with teams of Campaign Directors working under them to make sure campaign strategies were delivered on the ground. Selecting candidates early was also important to give them time to build their local profile and reputation, and to build strong, committed campaign teams around them.

Target voters

Having chosen the constituencies that would comprise the electoral battleground, the Party went further than ever before in targeting particular groups of voters within those constituencies to highlight particular themes and messages that would resonate most strongly. To do this we made full use of MOSAIC, Experian's powerful classification tool, which divides the entire population into 61 types, within eleven wider groups, based on a vast array of demographic, geographic and lifestyle data. It was already possible to use MOSAIC to highlight groups that might be concerned about particular issues such as schools or pensions, and this we did to great effect in our direct mail campaigns. But we also went beyond this existing function, seeking to use the data to maximum effect.

In an era when traditional socio-demographic variables have become increasingly poorer drivers of party choice, we used MOSAIC to build a more sophisticated model of voting behaviour which we could use to inform our campaigning approach in both air and ground wars. We set about combining MOSAIC data with results from extensive private polling, and by February 2008 we had a large enough sample for a robust model to be estimated. In addition to the standard Voting Intention question, our polling had asked respondents how likely on a scale of 1–10 they might be to vote for each party – in this way it was possible to measure those voters who, while giving a current voting intention for one party, could nonetheless be persuaded to switch their support. Accordingly, each MOSAIC type was then allocated to one of five target tiers:

- Solid Conservative
- Reassurance

- Top Targets
- Tug of War
- Solid Labour

Solid Con/Lab groups displayed much higher than average tendencies to be strong supporters of either party, with fewer undecideds. Top Targets showed an above average Conservative lead but a greater tendency to be wavering, while Tug of War were evenly split and with a much higher level of undecideds. The Reassurance category was introduced after the second round of research in Summer 2008 had shown – in line with national VI polls – a much increased level of Conservative support, but also that much of this was more out of protest at the Labour government than firm commitment to the opposition. The new tier largely included groups that had risen from Top Targets but would still require significant attention to be turned into definite Tory voters. As with the target seats list, the target voter tiers were kept under review, although the cost of polling a large enough sample meant it could only be fully updated twice.

Battleground and Campaign Directors were able to use the data for their constituencies to aid their targeting within particular wards and polling districts to great effect in identifying potential supporters in parts of their seats that had hitherto been ignored as 'no go areas'.

Direct mail and literature campaigns

MOSAIC truly came into its own in forming a key component of our direct mail strategy, which played a larger part in our campaign than ever before. Key groups – in terms of both likely issue interest and voter tiers – were relentlessly targeted with personally addressed letters, lifestyle magazines and postcards covering a wide range of subjects such as the NHS, schools, crime, jobs, pensions, civil liberties, immigration and the environment, to the extent that seventeen million pieces of centrally driven direct mail were issued in the five months leading up to polling day. In most direct mail we also included surveys, the feedback from which we used to refine the next waves to target particular people who, for example, were undecided but preferred David Cameron to Gordon Brown, or were especially concerned about particular issues such as immigration, Europe, crime or the NHS.

During the campaign itself, we repeatedly polled voters in our key battleground clusters, including questions measuring campaign penetration. In every cluster we polled, over half of respondents reported that the Conservatives 'have written a personally addressed letter to you' – significantly outstripping the other two parties (indeed, we outperformed the opposition on this measure to a greater extent than on the other measures of campaign penetration such as leaflet delivery, door knocking or telephone calls).

The target seats project was also responsible for producing seventy-four million pieces of CCHQ-driven literature – leaflets, newspapers, magazines, postcards, and so on – between October 2007 and polling day, over and above what local associations themselves were creating. The Battleground polling showed that here, too, we were at least matching and in most cases exceeding the output from our rivals.

Almost inevitably, given its scale and rigour, the target seats operation was called into question by some of the Labour MPs who were its intended victims, and the myth that 'Ashcroft's millions' were being used to 'buy seats' gained some traction in certain sections of the media. The allegation was untrue – the Party's spending was on a very modest scale compared with the huge sums Labour received from the trade unions, and, in any case, where we were fighting incumbent Labour MPs we were effectively starting at a huge disadvantage. Through the newly introduced Communications Allowance, the ability to transfer funds from staffing allowances to communications budgets and a further pot of taxpayer-funded cash in the 'Incidental Expenses Provision', incumbent MPs were in effect able to spend up to £40,000 of public money a year on communicating with their electorate. As the party with most seats, Labour were, of course, the main beneficiaries of this, and we had to work doubly hard in our target constituencies just to level the playing field.

Target seats campaign – a success?

The success of the target seats operation should be judged both on its own merits, and also in the context of our efforts in previous elections. In 1992 John Major's Conservatives polled more votes than any party previously or since, yet were rewarded with a slender majority of just twenty-one. The swing to Labour had been comparatively small (and certainly smaller than the polls had predicted!), but Labour made significant gains in key marginals, denying the Tories the larger majority that uniform national swing would have given. Five years later, in 1997, we lost a further twenty-four seats over and above what the already massive swing would have suggested. 2001 saw us make ten fewer gains from Labour than the (admittedly minor) swing should have delivered. 2005 was slightly better – we outperformed UNS by eight seats. This time, we gained thirty-two seats with swings greater than that achieved nationally: twenty-three from Labour and nine from the Lib Dems. Without these gains, Labour would have remained the largest party in the House of Commons, and a putative Labour / Lib Dem coalition would have had a majority of forty-four. Of course, there were also some seats we *didn't* gain that required less than the national swing, and three seats we *lost* to the Liberal Democrats. But, even taking those into account, the Conservatives outperformed UNS by sixteen seats – enough to make the vital difference to the parliamentary arithmetic that a Lab / Lib Dem coalition was not viable at all.

Of the target clusters outlined earlier, we outperformed national swing in nine. One of the main disappointments of the election was the extent to which the Labour vote held up in London, but even here, while the swings in the Inner/Outer clusters were lower than the national swing, they were still greater than for London as a whole.

While we could feel reasonable satisfaction with our performance in many clusters, there was real disappointment that we couldn't quite secure an overall majority, notwithstanding the historically low starting point. To win the election we faced some major challenges, which we fought and overcame to a large extent – but not completely. Returning to government will itself bring further challenges, but also fresh opportunities. The political and organisational changes we have made to our party, and the lessons learned on this campaign, will ensure we tackle and seize these with greater relish than ever before, and put us in a strong position for delivering future success.

Reference

Rallings, C. and Thrasher, M. (2007) *Media Guide to the New Parliamentary Constituencies*. Plymouth: Local Government Chronicle Elections Centre.

11
The Labour Party's Road to 2010

Greg Cook

Any serious analysis of the result of the 2005 election led most observers to conclude that the likely outcome of the next contest was a hung parliament. The two major parties combined had received barely more than two out of three votes cast, and Labour's 36.5 per cent was the lowest ever to produce an overall majority of seats. Despite the 5.5 percentage point drop in Labour's share of the vote compared with 2001, the Conservatives had made just thirty-three net gains, leaving them still short of 200 of the 646 seats in parliament. The Liberal Democrats' 22.6 per cent had provided them with sixty-two seats.

So the barriers to either Labour or the Conservatives being able to reach an overall majority in 2009 or 2010 were formidable. The Labour majority comprised thirty-two constituencies, whose largest majority was just 1,839, leaving it vulnerable to a swing of just 1.8 per cent to the challenging party. Boundary changes, while having only a modest impact overall, nevertheless reduced that margin still further. Labour's internal calculations[1] were that, on the new boundaries, the majority in 2005 would have been fifty, with the twenty-sixth most marginal seat, Cardiff North, having a majority of just 1,146 (2.5 per cent) over the Conservatives, and therefore vulnerable to a swing of 1.3 per cent.

Against that, the scale of the Conservatives' task remained formidable. In order to reach the 326 seats required for an overall majority of one in the new parliament they would need to make 118 gains. The 118th target seat (Oxford West and Abingdon) was held by the Liberal Democrats with a majority of 5,992 (11.8 per cent). That their baseline of seats was far below what Labour's had been in 1997 (a notional 274 of 659 seats from 35% of the vote in the 1992 election), was partly because of their accumulated losses to the Liberal Democrats. While at any level of national swing there could be an expectation that most

Labour seats vulnerable to that swing would be gained, that could not be said for those held by the Liberal Democrats, where personal votes tended to have much more influence. Of the 118 gains required by the Conservatives, twenty-five were held, at least notionally, by the Lib Dems. Every one of those that they failed to gain would therefore need to be compensated by another with a larger majority.

Furthermore, the swing to the Conservatives in 2005 had been almost entirely due to the net effects of a shift from Labour to the Liberal Democrats and to minor parties, rather than an improvement in the Tories' own performance. Their share of the vote had increased by just 0.5 percentage points compared with 2001, and, while they had done well in certain constituencies, notably in affluent parts of London and some rural areas, in many parts of the country their advance had been insignificant, and in the North of England their share of the vote had actually fallen slightly. Alarmingly for them, the election had seen further new losses to the Liberal Democrats,[2] suggesting that, even after two parliaments in opposition, their own heartlands remained under threat. It seemed that they remained a party disproportionately reliant upon the voters of the south of England, and their representation in Scotland, Wales and most of the larger conurbations remained sparse. While Labour's national share of the vote had fallen precipitately, the battle for the middle ground had been decisively won. What may be loosely termed the new Labour coalition in the smaller towns and suburbs of England that had carried Labour to victory in 1997 and 2001 had basically held together.

Indeed, there was much evidence that the relatively narrow margin of Labour's national lead understated the advantage in the two-party balance with the Conservatives. Polling both pre- and post-election among defectors from Labour indicated that, among those who did not switch to the Conservatives, there was a strong preference for Labour over Conservative government. The misleading media coverage which projected modest polling leads into three-figure Labour majorities had encouraged many of them to switch away from Labour in protest on the assumption that Labour would win anyway. Labour's protestations in the latter part of the 2005 election campaign that the switch of small proportions of Labour voters to the Lib Dems could result in the election of a Conservative-led government, furiously rejected at the time by Lib Dem leader Charles Kennedy and derided by some academic psephologists, were fully vindicated. If, as many believed, this argument persuaded some back to the Labour camp, then it is reasonable to suggest that it saved Labour's majority, given that the total Labour lead in the thirty-two most marginal seats amounted to just 25,174 votes.

A net total of about one million switched from Labour to Liberal Democrat between 2001 and 2005 and they became labelled as 'Iraq' voters, shorthand for a stereotype of educated urban liberals motivated predominantly by their opposition to the war but also by a range of other issues including tuition fees, civil liberties and public service reform. Undoubtedly there was considerable truth in this analysis, as the swing was exaggerated in seats containing large numbers of those sharing this demographic profile, leading to losses of constituencies[3] well beyond the national projections. However, the picture was more complicated. Internal post-election polling among lost Labour voters indicated that, of those who defected from Labour to the Liberal Democrats, only about one in four cited their opposition to the Iraq war as a motivation, and hardly any mentioned tuition fees. Instead, asylum and immigration, as well as health and education, all featured as significant. So, in addition to what may be regarded as an ideologically coherent swing, the Lib Dems were also the beneficiaries of old-fashioned broad-ranging protest, and what was telling was that those voters had not felt able to support the Conservatives.

All of this suggested that, despite the narrow margin of Labour's victory in 2005, it was far from inevitable that the next election would bring defeat. However, any strategy for success had as its premise the need to grow the Labour vote. It was highly unlikely that circumstances would again organise themselves to convert 36 per cent of the vote into a parliamentary majority. Therefore the aim must be to add to both the number of Labour voters and the share of the vote. Such an achievement would have been against the usual trend for governments to lose support from election to election, but it was certainly possible to envisage a scenario where it became credible.

Central to this was the fact that the next election would almost certainly be the first since 1992 when the outcome would be likely to be in doubt. Not only would that place the Conservatives under greater scrutiny; it would potentially alter the dynamics of the election. Specifically, it offered the possibility that additional Labour votes might be gained from two sources:

1. Increased turnout
2. A squeeze on Liberal Democrat and nationalist voters

There had been many theories as to why turnout had dropped from the pre-1997 norm of 75 to 80 per cent to just 60 per cent, with five million fewer voters taking part in the 2001 election than in 1997, but by far the most compelling explanation was that Labour's victory was regarded as a foregone conclusion. So in both 2001 and 2005 we had seen the evidence of how the drift away from habitual support for the major parties could mean that voters would also lose the habit of voting at all. With an almost unbroken lead in the opinion polls stretching back to 1993, the subliminal assumption of the media was that a Labour victory was assured, and that conveyed itself to the electorate, along with the logical conclusion both that individuals' votes would make little difference to anything and, more importantly, that there was not really a contest in which to take sides. Worse, it meant that to an extent Labour was its own opposition, with a focus on its supposed failures rather than a comparison with its opponents.

There was much less justification for this interpretation in 2005 when the polls were closer, but the media convinced themselves through their reliance on the theory of a uniform swing that any kind of lead in votes would deliver a landslide victory for Labour. That, however, was highly unlikely to pertain in 2009 or 2010. The prospect of a competitive election and of a change of government might well galvanise more electors into taking part, as it had done in close elections in the United States, Italy and France in recent years. All the evidence suggested that low turnout disproportionately affected Labour, with an ICM BBC poll of non-voters after the 2001 election showing that 53 per cent of them, had they voted, would have voted Labour and 19 per cent Conservative. Quite what electoral impact a higher turnout would have, however, was more uncertain. If it were to reach 75 per cent or more it would inevitably have been concentrated in safer Labour seats, rebalancing the alleged Labour bias in the electoral system rather than securing more Labour MPs, but any reduction in the differentials would be likely to assist Labour to some extent.

Likewise, the balance of Liberal Democrat voters seemed much more favourable to Labour than to the Conservatives, so if a competitive election resulted in any squeeze on their support it would again probably be helpful. The so-called Iraq defectors were an obvious source of potential new voters were they to believe, as many had not in 2005, that their support for the Lib Dems might contribute to the election of a Conservative government.

Labour's strategy for the 2009 or 2010 election was thus one of political expansion rather than retrenchment and defensiveness. Its ambition was not just to increase the vote and the share of the vote but to win additional seats. This task was complicated by the boundary review which had not only abolished a number of (mainly Labour) seats but had created others and in some cases produced some notional bonus gains and losses. So in theory Labour was 'defending' a number of seats that it had lost in 2005 because on the new boundaries it would probably have won them,[4] and vice versa.[5] In reality, the incumbency bonus due to new MPs was likely to make most of these notional Labour seats much harder to win than those where a Labour MP was defending a notionally Conservative seat. The best prospects for capturing new seats were clearly those where there had been aberrational swings to the Liberal Democrats that might unwind in different political circumstances.

One problem was the party's constrained financial position, which limited the amount of money that could be devoted to supporting local campaigning activity. However, given the concern about the potential advantage that some Conservative candidates might accrue from so-called Ashcroft money,[6] this was made a priority, and considerable investment was made in the party's IT infrastructure to support local parties and to centralise databases to make targeting more effective. The true impact of 'Ashcroft' money and the difference it made to marginal seat results was a matter of some controversy in 2005 and in 2010, and is impossible to quantify, given the number of variables that have to be taken into account. A number of beneficiaries did no better and sometimes worse than the average, but nevertheless the sums were apparently large, and it was obviously designed to give the Tories a competitive advantage in the local campaign. The response, therefore, was to try to make Labour's campaigning smarter by using all the available data to identify the voters who would make a difference and matching them to the party's strongest messages.

The political strategy was, of course, founded on the unique circumstances of having a leader and Prime Minister who had fought the election on the promise that he would stand down during the parliament. This opened up the opportunity for what became known as 'renewal in office', the reinvention of the party's strategic message and policy under a new leader while in power. Inevitably, subliminal parallels were drawn with the experience of the Conservatives in 1990, who had on an identical timescale replaced their leader, and in the subsequent election won an unexpected victory with the largest number of votes ever cast for any party. Of course, the circumstances were very different and possibly even more propitious for Labour, who would be able to accomplish the handover without the rancour associated with the removal of a leader against that leader's wishes.

The precise timing of that handover, however, was clearly likely to be politically sensitive. Many believed that the new leader would require and deserve a significant period in office in which to establish his or her political credentials with the electorate. An equally, if not more, powerful argument could be made that, in pure electoral terms, the later the change was made the better, and that any new leader would gain the maximum benefit from the favour which the electorate always tends to show until hard political choices tend to alienate more and more people and tarnish the novelty value. A further consideration was that of mandate, for, however much the British people had known at the election that under Labour at some point a new Prime Minister would take over, there would always be an issue of legitimacy attached to any leader who had not yet faced the electorate in his or her own right.

All of these factors came into play in the autumn of 2007, when speculation about an early poll reached the point where Gordon Brown effectively had to cancel an election that had never been called. Having taken over roughly at the halfway point of the parliament, a decision had to be made as to whether to seek a new mandate. Obviously that decision was also taken in the context of the lead Labour had built in the opinion polls over that summer, which peaked with a YouGov survey published in the *Daily Telegraph* on 29 September, during the Labour Party Conference, which showed an 11 percentage point advantage over the Conservatives.

The Nuffield Election study (Kavanagh and Cowley, 2010) devotes a whole preliminary chapter to the 'election that never was', such is the political importance which they attach to it. That would seem amply justified by the trends in published opinion polls, where Labour's rating plunged from this point onwards, never to recover to that level again before the 2010 election. Many have suggested that Labour would have won an election at that time had it been called.

The fact remains, however, that Labour's support in the opinion polls was clearly at an artificial and unsustainable high as Gordon Brown enjoyed the 'honeymoon' period with the electorate, and indeed the media, that is common to most new leaders and may be magnified when that new leader is Prime Minister. It reached its peak in Labour Party Conference week, consistent with the usual boosts which all parties tend to receive in the polls during their conferences. Importantly, the polling figures had begun to turn well before the announcement that there would be no election, with one[7] showing Labour and Conservative neck and neck. If, as it was suggested, this was a direct response to the announcement by the Conservatives of their plan to increase the inheritance tax threshold, it precisely demonstrated the febrile and unstable nature of Labour's rating that such a relatively trivial event might bring such dramatic shifts. The debate about whether Labour would have won that election, or even just done better than it did in 2010, is, of course, completely unanswerable. It is true that this episode triggered a shift in the media's attitude towards the Prime Minister and the government and that it marked a sharp dip in Labour's poll rating. However, that stabilised between November and April in the same range as for most of 2006, so in that sense it could be argued that the non-election simply marked a dramatic and sudden ending of the honeymoon period that would have come about in one way or another anyway. That is probably to understate its significance, for at the very least it meant that some of the other controversies of the autumn, such as the loss of the Child Benefit data disc and a row about party funding, were portrayed by the media in a much less favourable context and therefore were more electorally damaging.

Of longer-term significance to the politics of the 2010 election was the collapse of Northern Rock, the first real indicator of the economic turmoil that was to dominate the latter half of the parliament. Prior to this the assumption had been that the next election would be held in the context of low unemployment, rising house prices and increasing prosperity and that the debate would focus on the distribution of public spending and the possibility of tax cuts. The Conservatives had alluded to the latter in their new mantra 'sharing the proceeds of growth', but had otherwise adopted the government's spending plans. If there were to be no growth then the likely battleground between the parties became much more uncertain.

There is a lazy assumption among much of the media, and indeed many politicians, that a downturn in the economy will be damaging to a government's electoral prospects. Any survey of recent history alone will demonstrate that there is very little correlation between the state of the economy and the ability of a government to win an election. Indeed, if anything, it would appear to be easier for opposi- tions to win elections when the economy is doing reasonably well. So, while the economic crisis transformed the political debate, it did not necessarily work against Labour. In fact, on the basis that tougher economic circumstances might make voters more cautious, there was an opportunity to develop a message of experience against inexperience.

By the start of 2008 the Conservatives had re-established the lead in the opinion polls that they had gained immediately following the election of David Cameron and maintained through to the accession of Gordon Brown. During this period they had reached an estimated national share of the vote of 40 per cent in the 2006 and 2007 local elections, their best performance since 1992. The Scottish National Party had won the most seats in the Scottish Parliament and Labour had held just twenty-six of the sixty seats in the Welsh Assembly. However, although these were Labour's worst mid-term results since 1997, they were not dissimilar to those in the 2004 local and European elections, and there was no reason to believe that the position was not recoverable.

In 2008, however, the level of protest and hostility towards the government became much more intense, focusing on the row about the abolition of the 10 per cent tax banding and its cost to lower-income households. The outbreak of the controversy in March was reflected in a further sharp decline in Labour's opinion poll ratings, with the Conservative lead typically in the range of 15–20 percentage points. In the May local elections the Conservatives were estimated to be on 44 per cent of the vote to 25 per cent for the Liberal Democrats and 24 per cent Labour, and soon afterwards they won the Crewe and Nantwich by-election on a swing of 17 per cent. This was the first time that the Tory performance was in any way comparable to that of Labour in the mid-1990s, and appeared to reflect a new depth of alienation from Labour. In July Labour lost the Glasgow East by-election to the SNP, a seat in which there had never before been any serious opposition even at a local council level.

The period between that low point for Labour and the 2010 General Election result was marked by three further upheavals, which brought about significant and immediate shifts in the partisan balance.

The first was the crisis in the banking sector resulting in the bailout of October 2008. The widespread approbation for the actions of the Prime Minister and Chancellor transformed Labour's popularity in the polls, which rose on a similar gradient to that of the summer of 2007 and was borne out in the Glenrothes by-election in November when, against the odds and all expectations, Labour not only held the seat but increased its vote, a feat almost unheard of for a governing party. It may well have been that the location of the contest in the Prime Minister's 'backyard' in Fife was significant, for it seemed that his credibility as a manager of the economy and his reputation as a successful Chancellor were working to his advantage in comparison with the inexperienced and untried Conservative leadership. So, from having benefited from a successful growing economy in 2005, it seemed that his experience and knowledge would provide a political advantage in the contrasting circumstances of a recession. Brown and Darling were trusted to run the economy with a lead over Cameron and Osborne that exceeded Labour's voting intention.

There may, however, have been a sense that all of this was partly a product of the sense of national crisis brought about by the near-collapse of the major banks and the measures in the pre-budget report, which were introduced to respond to what was widely anticipated to be a steep downturn. The usual response of the electorate to a military conflict is, at least for a time, to show solidarity with the government, and it may be that some of the same instincts were to the fore here. The improvement in the polls was only sustained until the end of the year and in January there was another rapid decline, punctuated by a recovery at the time of the G20 summit in April but then completely undermined by the second major upheaval, the MPs' expenses scandal.

The politics of this period were hard to interpret. On the face of it the Conservatives, who were as much implicated in the details of the expenses revelations, found it hard to make it work to their advantage, and their popularity also suffered. Inevitably, though, Labour was much more vulnerable as the incumbent and establishment party, and in that the seeming decadence of the politicians concerned underlined the Conservatives' message 'Time for a Change'. In electoral terms, the big winners were the minor parties, and in particular the United Kingdom Independence Party, whose good fortune it was that the scandal dominated the run-up to the European Elections, in which they duly took 16 per cent of the vote and pushed Labour into a dismal third place. It is quite possible that they might have done this anyway, but the awfulness of the results was compounded by the success of the British National Party in winning list seats in the North West and in Yorkshire and the Humber. In the parallel local elections Labour's estimated 23 per cent of the vote was its worst ever performance, and it led to the loss of two out of every three seats being defended. The councils concerned were mainly the shire counties in England, which are anyway Labour's weakest territory, and with just 166 seats from the 2,316 being elected it was almost a wipe-out. All four Labour county councils were lost. The next month the Conservatives gained Norwich North in a by-election in which Labour retained a lower proportion of its vote than it had in Crewe and Nantwich.

The period up to the start of the election campaign saw the slow re-establishment of the political balance, as Labour's rating steadily recovered to its seeming default mid-term level of around 30 per cent, at the expense of the minor parties. The political debate focused more and more on the politics of the recession and increasingly the reductions in spending that seemed to be the consequence of the budget deficit. While Labour never regained the lead, attention became more and more focused on the Conservatives and their ability to win a majority of seats. With their opinion poll rating never significantly above 40 per cent, the mathematics of uniform swing indicated that they would struggle to win an overall majority.

By the time the election campaign began in April, the Conservative lead was typically no more than five percentage points, and then that balance too was upset by another upheaval following the first of the leaders' debates.

A snapshot of the polls just before the debate almost precisely predicted the final result. The Conservatives were at that time on about 37 per cent, exactly what they achieved in the election. Labour was on 31 per cent and the Lib Dems 21 per cent, which on the trends of previous elections would have probably over-stated the former and understated the latter in comparison with the likely outcome. The conclusion could then be drawn that the Liberal Democrats' take-off in the polls following that leader's debate was a mirage, an outburst of fantasy politics fuelled by the novelty of the debate and the media's relentless focus on it. With hindsight it is hard to argue against that analysis. It was though, a real phenomenon. For the rest of the campaign there was a sector of the electorate, which the polls suggested was mainly among those under the age of 35, that seemed more motivated to vote and much more likely to vote Liberal Democrat. The final polls showed some erosion of that new support, but still pointed to a possible breakthrough.

Perhaps the best comparison that can be made is with the short-term bubbles in the polls that have tended to follow Liberal Democrat by-election victories. With the diminishing numbers of committed adherents to the two main parties, the Lib Dems have always had an appeal as the 'honest' alternative, and many have always claimed that they were put off voting for them because they did not feel that they could win. The debate offered a perfect opportunity for these sentiments to surface again, especially among younger people who have the lowest level of loyalty to Labour and the Conservatives. So, the fact that ultimately that breakthrough did not materialise may be a matter of some concern for the Lib Dems: with the coverage concentrating on their second place in the polls and the near-certainty of a hung parliament, the argument that they had no chance was redundant. Yet that supposed support melted away. Rather than the difficulties of making themselves electorally credible, it may have been the lack of clarity about who or what they stood for that was their undoing.

There was considerable confusion on election night about the apparently contradictory results from individual constituencies, and in particular

Labour's retention of seats such as Birmingham Edgbaston, Westminster North and Hammersmith – all of which should have been routine wins for the Conservatives. In some cases local organisation seems to have made a significant difference, and there was a discernible correlation between the results and the strength of the local campaign, especially as measured by the level of voter id[8] and the number of contacts made with target voters; in some cases incumbency (or lack of it) was decisive.

There were, though, clear demographic trends that underlay most of the differentials. The map of the country that emerged showed Labour representation in England hugely concentrated in the large conurbations and, within those conurbations, still very few non-Labour seats. In other words, Labour support clearly held up much better in more multi-ethnic constituencies and those where the middle class may have more of a public sector bias. These patterns are reminiscent of those Labour faced in the late 1980s, when the electoral map was similar. In 1987 Labour won 229 seats with a higher share of the vote. In 2010 the additional thirty seats came mainly from the outskirts of London and other large cities where the proportion of Black and Asian voters has transformed their demography.

The Conservatives compensated for the seats they failed to gain from Labour by winning several more that required above-average swings. In fact, they made as many gains from Labour as they needed for an overall majority. They fell short mainly because of those that the Liberal Democrats held, and indeed some that they gained. Perhaps more seriously, their failure to make any progress in Scotland or the large industrial and multi-ethnic cities impeded their efforts to be a truly national party and acted as a ceiling on their share of the vote and their ability to secure a majority of seats.

So, five years on, a hung parliament duly materialised, but after one of the most extraordinary sequences of events, which brought successive short-term reversals in the fortunes of the parties. At the end of it the outcome turned out to be consistent with the important psephological trends of the last thirty years. It seemed like an election where none of the parties was popular. No party could be satisfied with the outcome, and all face major challenges next time, even without the implications of coalition government.

Notes

1. All references to notional constituency results are based on internal labour party analysis.
2. Solihull, Taunton and Westmorland and Lonsdale

3. e.g. Cambridge, Hornsey and Wood Green, Manchester Withington
4. e.g. Croydon Central, Northampton South, Rugby, Wellingborough
5. e.g. Finchley and Golders Green, Rochester and Strood, Sittingbourne and Sheppey, South Thanet
6. The funding of certain candidates by Conservative Deputy Chairman Lord Ashcroft
7. ICM in *The Guardian*, fieldwork completed 4 October 2007.
8. Labour Party term for information on voting intention gathered from speaking to voters.

Reference

Kavanagh, D. and Cowley, P. (2010) *The British General Election of 2010* (Basingstoke: Palgrave Macmillan).

12

From Protest to Power – The Progress of the Liberal Democrats

Chris Rennard

The rocky road to 2010

The fifth general election since the Liberal Party and the SDP merged to form the Liberal Democrats provides an opportunity for some longer-term reflection on the party's electoral progress. These five campaigns took place over a twenty-two-year period since the 'Alliance' parties headed by David Steel and David Owen became the Liberal Democrats, first led by Paddy Ashdown.

The consolidation of the party's position in the 2010 General Election should be seen in the context of the many points during these twenty-two years when the party made progress in spite of relatively frequent forecasts of imminent demise. In the early days, this demise was even feared by those within the party. Two years after the party was formed, Paddy Ashdown would often jokingly refer to the asterisk next to the party's name in opinion poll listings. This indicated that the party might not have any support at all – or that it might be below the 3 per cent margin of error in those polls.

The new party struggled at first to establish itself, while the media were able to make fun of it for saying that it claimed to know how the country should be run but did not know what to call itself. Former supporters of the Liberal/SDP/Alliance could not understand the new 'Social and Liberal Democrat' party name or the short-lived 'Democrat' tag. David Owen led a rump of the SDP that rejected the majority pro-merger view of its members. This group sought to retain the name of the Social Democrat Party formed in 1981 and stood its own candidates in opposition to those of the merged party. These interventions had a significant effect in parliamentary by-elections between 1988 and 1990[1] and prevented the new party from making the sort of early breakthroughs that could have launched it successfully.

Electoral success at national level eluded the party in its first two years, and it finished the 1989 European Elections with just 6 per cent of the vote and in fourth place, well behind the Greens. Its first leader, Paddy Ashdown, suffered some very poor ratings in those early years (–18 at one point) and it was generally thought that the traditional 'two-party squeeze' had reasserted itself after what was considered to be the 'aberration' of some success for the Alliance in the 1980s. This era had come to an end after the disappointment of only winning twenty-two seats in the 1987 General Election. It is a shame that the only major work on the SDP (Crewe and King, 1995) was published when it looked as though the SDP–Liberal merger might have been a failure, rather than at a later point, after 1997, when it proved to be much more successful.

It was at the very low point of the party's fortunes that I became its Director of Campaigns and Elections in August 1989. Any suggestion then that by 2010 the party would have secured between 17 per cent and 23 per cent in all five general elections, elected around fifty or sixty seats in the last four of them and entered Government with the party leader becoming Deputy Prime Minister would have seemed fanciful. The start of the post merger recovery was the Eastbourne by-election in October 1990[2] when a 16,000 Conservative majority was overturned to become a 4,550 Liberal Democrat majority. Lib Dem poll ratings increased from around 8 per cent to 18 per cent after the by-election.

The progress towards 2010 was certainly along a very rocky road. The Liberal Democrats survived the 1992 General Election with twenty seats and a nascent strategy for targeting seats (Denver and Hands, 1997). But the effect of that campaign was for the Conservatives to appear to be invincible, having won a surprise fourth term victory. After a year in which the Liberal Democrats appeared invisible, back-to-back parliamentary by-election victories in Newbury and Christchurch led the Liberal Democrats to rise to within 3 per cent of the Conservatives in the August 1993 ICM poll.

Following the election of Tony Blair as Labour leader, for a few years it looked as though the Liberal Democrats could be made irrelevant, as 'New Labour' took much of the support available for a centre-left party as well as much of the disillusioned Conservative vote. The Lib Dem victory in Littleborough & Saddleworth in 1995, however, showed that the party's campaign skills could still lead the party to capture Conservative seats despite high-profile Labour challenges. These skills brought about the party's big breakthrough in the 1997 General Election campaign when its number of MPs rose from eighteen (estimate based on the new boundaries if they had existed in 1992) to forty-six. This was in spite of the fact that the Lib Dems were on just 9.5 per cent in an opinion poll in the December before the 1997 General Election and began that campaign with another poll rating of just 11 per cent. The national campaign increased support to 17 per cent of the vote on polling day (Holme and Holmes, 1998).

The resignation in 1999 of Paddy Ashdown, who had transformed his image to become the most popular party leader in the country, caused another crisis of confidence for the party. In his early years as leader, Charles Kennedy struggled to assert any sense of authority without the hugely increased media profile that comes to a Lib Dem leader with a general election. Confidence that the party could retain its newly won seats came from the Romsey by-election, when a seat that was very safe for the Conservatives, even in 1997, went Liberal Democrat in 2000. Charles Kennedy became the outstanding leader in the 2001 General Election and the national campaign raised the party's share of the vote from around 13 per cent in polls at the start of the campaign to a respectable 19 per cent of the vote in June 2001 (Rennard, 2002).

The 2005 General Election proved to be the party's most successful in terms of seats won. Parliamentary by-election successes at Brent East and Leicester South in 2003 and 2004, the Iraq War and protests over Labour's introduction of tuition fees helped the party to begin that campaign at around 20 per cent in the polls. But the party failed to build significantly on this position during the campaign. It struggled to recover from the Manifesto launch that became a media disaster for Charles Kennedy two days after the birth of his son. But this struggle succeeded in the last two weeks of the campaign with another series of strong TV performances by Charles Kennedy and more identification of the Lib Dems with popular policies than had been the case in previous elections. The national campaign eventually added 1 or 2 per cent to the starting position so that the party reached an eventual vote share of 22 per cent. The party won a record sixty-two seats at Westminster with a net loss of just two seats to the Tories, twelve gains from Labour and one from Plaid Cymru (Rennard, 2007).

The party's crisis management capability was severely tested in the aftermath of the 2005 campaign. Charles Kennedy resigned in January 2006 amid much turmoil in the party and another slump in poll ratings.

Bitter divisions among the MPs were widely reported over how and why Charles Kennedy resigned.[3] Early 2006 was another period in which many commentators considered the party to be more or less finished. A YouGov poll rating of 13 per cent was widely reported. But the party's fortunes again appeared to be restored in the classic way of the party by winning an astonishing parliamentary by-election in Dunfermline and West Fife. This by-election probably helped neighbouring MP Sir Menzies Campbell to become leader in March and restored confidence and support for the party. Preparations for a potential 2007 General Election began in earnest during the summer of 2006.

The Liberal Democrat strategy for survival and growth

Before looking at the start of Liberal Democrat preparations for the general election that eventually came in 2010, it is worth reflecting on the factors that enabled the party to survive and prosper at national level during this period.

I would point to the following four factors:

1) *The party's local government base.* The Liberal Party had only a handful of Councillors in the 1960s, building to just over 1,000 by 1979. But the early pioneers of what the party called 'community politics' also paved the way for an effective electoral advance in local government. The growth to over 4,000 Councillors representing around 20 per cent of the local council seats in Britain gave the party something to focus on in most areas, a taste of electoral success and a demonstration of how effective campaigning and organisation, based on target campaigns, could produce a breakthrough. The party gained credibility and profile from winning seats and then taking over control of local councils. There was a very strong correlation between local government success and the twenty-eight seats gained in the 1997 General Election.

2) *The parliamentary by-elections.* It was the 'shock' win at Eastbourne in October 1990 that saved the merged party – and probably also triggered the downfall of Mrs Thatcher as Prime Minister six weeks later when Conservative MPs panicked in response to the Lib Dem success. The 16,000 Conservative majority was overturned with a 20 per cent swing by a party with just 8 per cent support in the polls at the time. The eleven Liberal Democrat parliamentary by-election victories between 1990 and 2006 almost all gave the party very significant boosts to profile, poll ratings, credibility, morale and funds.

Newbury in 1993 re-established the party after 1992, and the crushing 22,000 majority with a 28 per cent swing, followed by an even greater swing of 35 per cent in Christchurch, showed the party to be a challenger to the other two main parties. The gain of Romsey from the Tories in 2000 took the wind out of William Hague's sails. Brent East and Leicester South in 2003 and 2004 showed how the party could advance against Labour. The gain of Dunfermline & West Fife in 2006 rescued a party that otherwise appeared to face oblivion after the resignation of Charles Kennedy.

3) *The target seat approach.* The old political science textbooks assumed that the constituency campaign made little difference to the result in a general election. Most of the people in senior positions in all the parties agreed. But a study of some very diverse constituencies showed how a handful of Liberal MPs, such as David Penhaligon in Cornwall, Richard Wainwright in Yorkshire and David Alton in Liverpool, had consistently defied national swings and expectations. The campaign which I ran for David Alton in the Liverpool Mossley Hill constituency in 1983 saw a 14 per cent swing to the party (at a time when the Conservatives won a 144 seat majority nationally). Liberals and Liberal Democrats had elected Councillors and won parliamentary by-elections by concentrating resources (skills, people and money) on their target council wards, and in the 1990s began to develop this approach to target parliamentary constituencies. There were, of course, sceptics in the party, but the authority that came with overseeing the successful by-election campaigns helped persuade the party to invest much of its limited resources towards the target seats. A huge differential developed between the results that would have been suggested by a uniform national swing and the results achieved in the seats that were most closely targeted. The highest swing from Conservative to Lib Dem in 1997 was the 18 per cent achieved in Sheffield Hallam. The target seat strategy was the basis of the twenty-eight gains in 1997, eight further gains in 2001 and sixteen gains in 2005.

4) *The leaders.* The crucial role of the leader is perhaps even more important to the standing of the Liberal Democrats across Great Britain than it is to other parties. Liberal Democrat leaders (like Liberal leaders before them, such as David Steel) have all struggled to establish significant public profiles prior to their first general election campaign. But the first election campaigns of David Steel (1979), Paddy Ashdown (1992), Charles Kennedy (2001) and Nick Clegg (2010) were tremendously successful in establishing them with very positive

profiles. The public standing that they established in these campaigns has given a much clearer and more prominent profile to the party generally. This has meant that they have been used extensively to promote the party's candidates in Parliamentary by-elections and in general elections. The leader's national tours have been the main focus of the party's national campaigns and provided most of the positive coverage for the party that has helped to raise the party's level of support during those campaigns.

Much, of course, was also owed to some outstanding individuals among the party's parliamentarians (at every level), candidates, Councillors, staff and generous donors.

The party elected Members of the Scottish Parliament and Welsh Assembly who exercised power in coalition, Members of the European Parliament (who sometimes acted as regional leaders for the party) and Councillors who demonstrated the capacity to run their local authorities with majority administrations or in balance of power situations. Their efforts, and those who worked in their election campaigns and the parliamentary by-elections in particular, often rescued the party when it was in difficulty and provided the sense of momentum required for it to prosper.

The 2010 campaign

Liberal Democrat general election campaigns have always been planned on two levels – but with an aim of successfully integrating the main messages. What I termed, for internal party purposes, the 'ground war' was all about the target seat campaign (identifying the seats and candidates, training, leaflets, local media, funding and concentrating efforts). The 'air war' was about the national media campaign and messaging guided by market research, including the manifesto, press conferences, speeches and election broadcasts. National policy messages were made relevant locally and local campaign issues identified and made the focus of attention for the constituency campaigns.

Since the party nationally began taking a very serious approach to targeting at the Westminster level in 1994, efforts in many key constituencies remained continuous. The aim following the 1997 breakthrough was to focus on 'incumbency protection' as well as future gains. Only two of the twenty-eight gains made in 1997 were lost in 2001,[4] although three more of them were lost in 2005. Resources to fund key seat operations had always run dry in the year or two after a general election. The effective start of the 'ground war' for 2010 was therefore not until 2006 but a full four years before the eventual polling day. With much more limited resources than those available to other parties, it was necessary to plan carefully the national expenditure that supported key seats (held and target) in 2006 and 2007 in anticipation of a general election in 2007. The level of support for these seats was far greater and over a much longer period of time than in any previous Parliament. Major training events for MPs and target seat candidates were held during this period. Around two dozen Campaign Officers supported clusters of held and target seats to promote best practice, and a record number of professional agents (over eighty) were employed in the key seats from this period through to polling day.

The party's new Director of Campaigns, Hilary Stephenson, oversaw the introduction of Key Performance Indicators to carefully monitor progress in the key seats. Regular review meetings enabled the party to promote the best campaigning approaches that had been developed over the last fifteen years or so. But it also became plain that the other parties had now shifted their attention and much greater resources to the sort of key seat strategy that the Liberal Democrats had pioneered in the previous three general elections. Liberal Democrats no longer enjoyed an effective monopoly on literature and direct mail delivered in these battleground seats. MPs from other parties that were under threat followed many aspects of the model incumbency protection techniques used so effectively by their Liberal Democrat rivals (some of these tactics having always been the policy of very good constituency MPs).

In some respects, Liberal Democrats felt that the 'ground war' battles of the 2010 General Election were like those of the First World War, in that it proved very difficult to make substantial progress when MPs from other parties were effectively well dug in. The national campaign and Nick Clegg's charismatic leadership gave a big boost to all Liberal Democrat constituency campaigns. But the appearance of such success also made it harder for the party to keep its activists focused on a realistic number of winnable seats as unrealistic hopes of victory rose in very many other seats.

Preparations for a better general election 'air war' strategy also began soon after the 2005 General Election. The relative success of the 2005 campaign had brought more resource into the coffers of the parliamentary party (the party's 'Short' money increased as a result of the additional MPs and number of votes). A lack of integration between the Leader's operation, the party's policy function, the MPs' collective research team and the overall coordination of Policy and Communications with a much too slender media team were identified as problems to address. The result of a review that I initiated was the merging of Policy and Research functions, a significant expansion of the media team and the appointment under me as Chief Executive of an overall Director of Policy and Communications.

This restructuring could not prevent the damage done to the party's reputation by the internal splits following the 2005 General Election. But it did help to provide a much sharper focus for how the party would eventually approach the 'air war' in the 2010 campaign. In the meantime it was fully tested as the party geared up for an Autumn 2007 General Election and quickly produced a campaign plan, draft manifesto, leader's tour schedule, election budget, press conference schedule, drafts of all election leaflets, and so forth.

If there had been a general election in 2007 or 2009, I would have remained in place to oversee it. But, having overseen all of the preparations for the general election campaign until then, I handed over my responsibilities as Chief Executive to Chris Fox in the summer of 2009. I had initially appointed him as Director of Policy and Communications. John Sharkey (whom I had made my Deputy Chair of the general election campaign) was asked in the autumn to Chair the Campaign and Jonny Oates (whom I had also first appointed as Director of Policy and Communications) returned as Director of General Election Communications.

The post-2007 financial crisis inevitably meant that there was a quite different Manifesto, produced by a team led by Danny Alexander, than would have been the case previously. The party focused on four clear themes ('Four Steps to Fairness') based on making the tax system fairer for those on middle and lower incomes, the pupil premium to boost education spending on children from the most deprived backgrounds, moves to a much more sustainable and greener economy, and measures of political and constitutional reform. These were simultaneously the basis for a negotiation with any other party in the event that no party achieved an overall majority.

The launch of the Manifesto was probably the party's most successful ever. Its timing on the eve of the first leaders' debate helped, in my view, to warm up the electorate for the charms of Nick Clegg the following evening. Nick's performances in the leaders' debates were no surprise to me. I had met him in the 1990s before he had thought seriously about becoming an MEP or MP. I had been convinced then that he would one day be the leader of the party, and my view is that he won the party leadership election in December 2007 because of his performances at the members' hustings meetings. The launch of 'Cleggmania' and the effective use of 'I agree with Nick' posters and stickers appeared to transform the election.

It is my view that Nick would probably have done just as well during the course of the campaign even without the leaders' debates. His standing was rising before the first one took place, and I believe that it would have increased steadily with daily press conferences and the sort of national tour that had boosted Paddy Ashdown and Charles Kennedy previously. The first debate accelerated this process massively, but the resulting attacks from most of the print media made it hard to sustain. The nature of the three debates also meant that much of the policy focus was on areas such as immigration, which previous Liberal Democrat election campaigns had chosen not to major on.

The net loss of six seats seemed like a terrible disappointment on the night (with ten seats missed by less than a thousand votes) but this was softened by the new high watermark in terms of vote share (23 per cent). With hindsight, two factors prevented the Conservative overall majority that I expected. First, Labour did well enough with their own incumbency protection programme to deprive the Conservatives of many of the gains that they might have made (just as Liberal Democrats had done in key marginal seats like Torbay). Second, I was surprised by the relative weakness and inconsistency of the Conservatives' national messaging. The Liberal Democrats aimed to get into a position of power. But, with Gordon Brown as leader, Labour was never likely to do well enough to make a coalition with the Liberal Democrats a very serious option. The result left the Liberal Democrats in a position of power but with little real choice of coalition partners and thereby unable to exercise the balance of power between competing options. Nevertheless, the party that was always criticised as the recipient of protest votes has in the end become a party of power across the UK.

Notes

1. The 'Owenite' SDP was formally wound up after the humiliation of polling only a third of the votes of the Monster Raving Loony Party in the Bootle parliamentary by-election of May 1990. I identified this by-election as being one of considerable significance because the party had to contend with both 'continuing Liberal' and 'continuing SDP' candidates. By almost taking second place and humiliating Owen's party into disbanding, this helped the Liberal Democrats clear the path to a breakthrough in the Eastbourne by-election in October of that year.

2. My decision to fight the Eastbourne by-election to win was initially opposed by Paddy Ashdown, whose first thought was that we should not contest it (see *Ashdown Diaries*, Vol. I, and Ashdown's memoirs *A Fortunate Life*).
3. The most comprehensive account of this period is in Greg Hurst's book, *Charles Kennedy – a Tragic Flaw*.
4. See Andrew Russell and Ed Fieldhouse, *Neither left nor right? The Liberal Democrats and the electorate* for more on this – the most comprehensive side of the Liberal Democrats to date.

References

Ashdown, P. (2000) *The Ashdown Diaries Volume 1: 1988–1997*. London: Penguin.
Ashdown, P. (2009) *A Fortunate Life*. London: Aurum.
Crewe, I. and King, A. (1995) *The SDP: the Birth, Life and Death of the Social Democratic Party*. Oxford: Oxford University Press.
Denver, D. T. and Hands, G. (1997). *Modern Constituency Electioneering: Local Campaigning in the 1992 General Election*. London: Frank Cass.
Holme, R. and Holmes, A. (1998) 'Sausages or Policemen?' in Crewe, I., Gosschalk, B. and Bartle, J. (eds) *Political communications: Why Labour won the General Election of 1997*. London: Frank Cass.
Hurst, G. (2006) *Charles Kennedy: A Tragic Flaw*. London: Politico's.
Rennard, C. (2002) 'The Liberal Democrat campaign', in Bartle, J., Atkinson, S. and Mortimore, R. (eds) *Political Communications: The General Election Campaign of 2001*. London: Frank Cass.
Rennard, C. (2007) 'A new high water mark for the Liberal Democrats', in Wring, D., Green, J., Mortimore, R. and Atkinson, S. (eds) *Political Communications: The General Election Campaign of 2005*. Basingstoke: Palgrave Macmillan.
Russell, A. and Fieldhouse, E. (2005) *Neither left nor right? The Liberal Democrats and the electorate*. Manchester: Manchester University Press.

Part V
Campaigning

13
'This Election will be Won by People not Posters'... Advertising and the 2010 General Election

Chris Burgess

The potency of the poster

Political parties have deployed posters in every election since the beginning of the twentieth century. Despite their ubiquity, posters have often been overlooked by those seeking to analyse and understand the electoral role of different media, notably television and more recently the internet (Downey and Davidson, 2007; Scammell and Semetko, 1995). Exceptions to this include work by the historian James Thompson as well as Rose's groundbreaking study of campaign publicity (Rose, 1968; Thompson, 2007). Although the Nuffield studies have regularly featured posters, they are often only featured or mentioned in passing to illustrate key messages of successive campaigns. Of the limited analysis that does exist, there is a consensus that outdoor advertising is no longer as important as it once was (Butler and Ranney, 1992). This is in part explained by the intensification and diversification of political communication, whereby the process of influencing voters has become more complex (Lees-Marshment, 2008; Norris, 2007; Scammell, 1995). Where posters have been used they have often been devised to attract and maximise news media attention, a technique that can provide more publicity than the original posters when they are displayed as part of a conventional campaign (Franklin, 2004). Thus, although this is the most enduring form of election advertising, its influence – such as it is or may be – has arguably changed over the course of the last hundred years. Regardless of how posters have changed, they nevertheless remain an important part of campaigns, and one worth considering because of cost, not to mention their longevity.

Posters were an important as well as interesting feature of the 2010 General Election. During the lead-up to the formal campaign the Conservatives targeted marginal seats with outdoor advertising from January onwards, whereas Labour and the Liberal Democrats, deprived of the necessary funds, were unable to respond in kind. The Tories continued to comfortably outspend their rivals once the election had been called. Lack of resources meant that the other parties attempted to reply through poster launches largely designed for the television cameras as well as by deploying mobile as well as online billboard advertisements. The internet provided campaigners with a new forum for the release of their campaign messages. Moreover, the visibility of these images extended beyond party websites, courtesy of the blogosphere and newspaper coverage. This new online medium did, however, prove to be a mixed blessing, given that specially designed websites provided extensive opportunities for voters to vandalise the authentic posters. Consequently, anyone with internet access had the ability to subvert the meaning of any message produced by one of the parties. These 'new' posters were potentially effective in terms of both cost and impact because they could be so easily distributed. This chapter offers a detailed case study of the posters used by the major parties during the 2010 election by exploring the images produced, their usage and their relation to wider campaign objectives.

Conservatives

Campaigning for the 2010 election began months, if not years, before Gordon Brown's formal announcement of polling day. Preparations by the Conservatives began almost as soon as David Cameron had become Conservative leader in 2005. Cameron subsequently appointed his key adviser Steve Hilton as head of party strategy and later made Andy Coulson the Tories' Director of Communications in July 2007. Soon afterwards, the agency EURO RSCG was awarded the Conservatives' advertising contract in October the same year. The firm would have been known to Coulson through their previous work for the *News of the World*, the newspaper he used to edit. The decision to appoint a new firm to devise the campaign meant a break with the M&C Saatchi company that had overseen the party's efforts in each of the three previous (and unsuccessful) elections. However, the relationship with the brothers was to be rekindled nearer polling day.

Predictably, Labour's handling of the economy featured prominently in Conservative poster campaigns, which highlighted Britain's indebtedness and attempted to blame this on the Prime Minister. As early as January 2009, the party was pursuing this line with copy such as *Dad's Nose, Mum's Eyes, Gordon Brown's Debt* (Figure 13.1), a striking visual image that featured on 260 billboard sites around the country and was also, as was now obligatory, posted online. The same initiative featured an accompanying YouTube video of the same baby relating the same message. The advert attracted some media attention following its launch (Churcher, 2009). It was the opening phase of what would become a long-running effort to hold Brown responsible for the precarious state of the government's finances. This preparedness to repeat an economic message ad nauseam echoed the anti-Labour tax bombshell prior to and during the 1992 election, the last previous Conservative success. The debt issue resurfaced in December of 2009 with *Gordon Brown's Debt. Hasn't it grown?*, a poster featuring a child writing the numbers of the increasingly large national debt on a whiteboard. Like the previous advertising, the imagery both humanised and infantilised the deficit crisis by highlighting that the scale of the problem was so large that future generations would likely carry the responsibility for tackling it.

Figure 13.1 Published by the Conservative party

A month after they had tried to humanise the debt crisis, the Conservatives attempted to do the same for their leader. In what was effectively the opening image of the Tories' pre-election campaign, the party released the *We can't go on like this. I'll cut the deficit, not the NHS* poster (Figure 13.2) on 4 January as part of a New Year initiative to promote David Cameron's virtue as a caring but determined Prime Minister in waiting. Despite the need for possibly drastic action, the message to key 'middle ground voters' was that the NHS would be safe from cuts (Watt, 2010). Cameron's face was emblazoned across the advertisements and his open-necked shirt underlined his desire to present a less formal politician; inevitably comparisons were made with the approach of Tony Blair and his similar appearances in party publicity, including his manifesto. Cameron's *We can't go on like this* poster appeared on a thousand sites, but an unintended consequence of it was to draw attention to the alleged distortion of the leader's image, which, critics claimed, appeared unnaturally lacking in the usual skin tone, thereby suggesting careful editing had been applied. The advertisement was also subjected to a litany of more direct attacks both online and off. While unkind slogans were daubed on the outdoor version of the image, similarly rude things were legally and more readily applied to the same copy courtesy of internet sites that enabled users to commit acts of political vandalism from the comfort of their own homes.

Judged by impact on the wider news media, perhaps the most prominent of the online election sites in 2010 was mydavidcameron. com. It gave visitors the opportunity to critique official Conservative material by recreating it with new textual features, either written or

Figure 13.2   Published by the Conservative party

visual. The website received 252,641 hits in its first six weeks alone and was widely reported in the mainstream media (Driver, 2010; Fisher, 2010). However, although entertaining, particularly to commentators on the liberal left, it should not be overlooked that this online mockery, as well as the offline direct action variant, would have been seen by far fewer uncommitted voters than the original posters, and herein lies the potentially enduring appeal of this most traditional platform to party strategists. Yet initiatives such as mydavidcameron.com can be effective in changing elite perceptions, and it is perhaps noteworthy that the Conservatives scaled back expenditure on billboards and Cameron did not feature on another for several months (Fisher, 2010). A demonstration of this change in approach came with *R.I.P Off. Now Gordon Wants £20 000 when you die*, released on 9 February in both on and offline formats, although the latter was only in a modest, even perfunctory, eighteen sites around the country. The advert attacked an alleged Labour plan to tax people upon their death in order to pay for the care they received during old age. The play on words was quite arresting, but the sentiment divided opinion, with even commentators in the right-wing *Spectator* commenting that it was 'dispiriting to see this brand of political communication [is] spreading' (Hoskin, 2010). More predictably, Health Secretary Andy Burnham denounced the poster: 'If the Conservative Party had a shred of decency they would withdraw this flippant distasteful poster. Posters with gravestones are grubby and desperate. This is a craven attempt to frighten the most venerable in society. David Cameron should be ashamed of such black propaganda' (quoted in Richardson, 2010).

Other Conservative advertising was more positive. Midway through February, the party launched its second major billboard campaign, aimed at those who had not previously supported them. Three different versions of *I've never voted Tory before* posters went up on 1,500 sites. Each featured a different protagonist: Julie from Llandudno, Ian from Congleton (Figure 13.3) and Danielle from Brighton. The same voters also featured prominently in officially circulated YouTube videos, Party Election Broadcasts and the Conservative manifesto. This multiplatform marketing was an attempt to identify the party with representatives of the kinds of voter it deemed representative of those target groups it felt it had to reach and cultivate. This was nothing new, as had been demonstrated in 1959 when campaign strategists had circulated press advertisements asking 'what does a Conservative look like?' featuring what were presented as supporters not traditionally associated with the party.

Figure 13.3   Published by the Conservative party

The ubiquity of election posters and other related imagery has led to the creation of specialist commentary such as that provided by political advertising blogger Benedict Pringle. Reviewing the various early Conservative efforts, Pringle suggested that, cumulatively, *We can't go on like this*, *R.I.P Off* and *I've Never voted Tory before* were a schizophrenic collection that arguably revealed a lack of coherence in the party's overall message (Pringle, 2010a). The presentation of this case was not, of course, helped by the subversion of the imagery, be this off or online; the prominence of such vandalism led to some speculation as to whether this kind of activity could effectively undermine and possibly signal the end of the poster as a serious campaign medium (Mcsmith and Norris, 2010). That said, adverse reactions to this kind of advertising did at least generate more publicity for the Conservatives. Furthermore, although vandalised posters provided the news media with subversive and often amusing imagery, the same material was also seen, unblemished, by thousands of uncommitted voters living in marginal seats way beyond the metropolitan hub. By contrast, mydavidcameron.com was largely designed and colonised by the political cognoscenti, particularly of a liberal left bent, and it is debatable what, if any, influence the 1,200 images created on the site in its first six weeks had on the wider campaign.[1]

Prior to the formal election campaign there had been media speculation over the direction of the party's strategy, and this had often focused on the supposed differences between Cameron's key advisers, Steve Hilton and Andy Coulson. Hilton was widely assumed to be the counsel for a more nuanced, progressive-sounding message, while the former redtop newspaper journalist Coulson was often associated with a more trenchant, populist approach to campaigning. Divisions within

Figure 13.4   Published by the Conservative party

the hierarchy were highlighted during the election when the party recommissioned M&C Saatchi to work on their message while simultaneously retaining the services of their official agency. The Saatchis' motto 'brutal simplicity of thought' evidently provided the blueprint for a hard-hitting major campaign that ran across 850 sites from late March (Pringle, 2010b). The advertising consisted of seven images, each featuring the smiling face of Gordon Brown with one of the following accompanying slogans: *I let 80000 criminals out early vote for me. I took billions from pensions vote for me. I doubled the national debt vote for me. I doubled the tax rate for the poor vote for me. I lost £6 billion selling off Britain's gold vote for me. I caused record youth unemployment vote for me* (Figure 13.4) and, finally, *I increased the gap between rich and poor vote for me.* Lord Bell, who had worked for Margaret Thatcher, believed the posters would 'hold Labour to account, hit them where it hurts and evoke memories of Labour Isn't Working, which was such a successful campaign', the latter a strategy he had been directly involved in creating (Shipman, 2010).

The Conservatives continued with their more robust messaging right up to the day before Gordon Brown called the election, with George Osborne launching *Brown's recovery plan*, a poster in which two large boots are located in a vast inhospitable tundra with one of them moments from treading on a green shoot of 'recovery'. Leading blogger Tim Montgomerie likened the striking imagery to the 1992 Conservative 'Double Whammy' poster, itself an attack on Labour's economic policies (Montgomerie, 2010). The boots image was part of a concerted campaign to brand an intended rise in National Insurance as a 'jobs tax'. During its formal launch, two party aides in Gordon Brown and Alistair Darling masks donned the requisite footwear and then proceeded to dance on some green shoots to the tune of Nancy Sinatra's song 'These boots are made for walking' (PA, 2010).

During the closing weeks of the election the Conservatives attempted to maintain their momentum by launching new publicity initiatives designed to reach as many of the less committed as possible. On 19 April, nine new illustrations specifically designed for the outside of phone boxes appeared, and these deployed a number of visual icons more associated with the left than the right. An image of shaking hands in *Social Responsibility Not State Control* was more redolent of trade union imagery. Similarly, *People Power* (Figure 13.5) was evocative of a protest-style politics. But, like the rest of the series, these posters were designed to underline Cameron's call for a 'Big Society', a key theme of a Conservative campaign that had emphasised the importance of community-spiritedness and voluntarism. This theme was more explicitly addressed in another of the adverts that revisited and reworked a phrase previously attributed to Margaret Thatcher. This resulted in the slogan 'There is such a thing as society. It's just not the same as the state'. This copy, like the other visual texts, accompanied a simple Vote Conservative tag rather than the party's official tree logo (Pringle, 2010c).

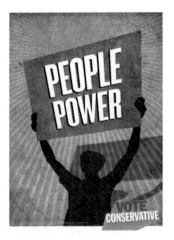

Figure 13.5   Published by the Conservative party

Figure 13.6   Published by the Conservative party

The day after the phone box adverts appeared, five more robust post-ers were distributed on 500 sites. Each featured David Cameron in dynamic pose, once again without tie or jacket and with sleeves rolled up, suggesting he was ready for the task ahead. The different texts, all in stark white lettering, were *Let's have national citizens service for 16 year-olds, Let's fund new NHS cancer drugs, Let's stop Labour's jobs tax, Let's scrap ID cards*, and, strongly echoing populist newspaper campaigns against so-called benefit scroungers, *Let's cut benefit for those who refuse work* (Figure 13.6). The latter poster generated most comment, with the ConservativeHome blog praising the release of an advert that outlined policy (Montgomerie, 2010). Similarly, another right-wing commenta-tor applauded the blunt message: 'I imagine it will play with the many voters who are frustrated at the unfairness and inconsistencies of the welfare system' (Hoskin, 2010). Overall, the bluntness of this copy was redolent of the kind of attack campaigning attributed to Andy Coulson rather than the 'Big Society' theme more associated with Steve Hilton (Jeffrey, 2010). But, arguably, this supposed dichotomy within the par-ty's message was overstated, in that all of this publicity was supportive of the main Conservative case that people needed to be more self-reliant. Aside from this, it was noteworthy that Cameron once again featured prominently in party advertising, and this was in part a response to Labour's satirising of him for being out of touch (see below).[2]

The Conservatives were also tactical in their use of advertising. Following a heated row between Cameron and Brown over the alleged lies concerning benefit cuts for the elderly in Labour campaign leaflets during the second Prime Ministerial Debate, the Tories felt compelled to issue a response *Did I lie about that dodgy leaflet,* an image that depicted Brown's head on the body of Vicky Pollard, a notoriously unreliable character from the popular BBC comedy sketch show *Little Britain.* Media coverage ensured this advert received wider publicity than would have been the case for text that was only available online.

Labour

When Labour campaign manager Douglas Alexander said that '[T]his election will be won by people, not posters', this was perhaps more a statement of hope, given his party's precarious finances meant it was unable to mount the kind of advertising offensive seen in the previous election of 2005 (Alexander, 2010). Alexander argued that word of mouth would matter in what would be a networked rather than a traditional media campaign. This view was promoted by Labour's official advertisers, Saatchi & Saatchi, the iconic firm formerly led by the eponymous brothers but which, following their forced departure in 1995, had gone on to win the account of a party they had once famously attacked in a succession of previous elections. The agency suggested that generating a conversation among consumers was more important than repetitive exposure in the forging of brand identities. Here social networking would be an important option, as well as being cheaper than more traditional forms of marketing promotion. Somewhat paradoxically, however, the party did not exploit the potential for producing online posters to the same extent as the Conservatives.

The Saatchis had originally won Labour's contract in September 2007, months after Gordon Brown had entered 10 Downing Street and during a period when there was fevered speculation as to whether he might call a snap election. The decision had been influenced by the firm producing an eye-catching poster, *Not flash, just Gordon,* depicting the new Prime Minister as an authentic politician who was his own man (Figure 13.7). Brown's apparent indecision over whether to go to the country to seek his own mandate led to considerable adverse media commentary and made his advertisers' task all the more formidable. For this and various other reasons, the new premier's public opinion ratings never recovered.

Despite Brown's perceived unpopularity, as judged by feedback in the form of polling and journalistic reportage, Saatchi & Saatchi still chose to use the leader's image, and, following on from their earlier *Not Flash, Just Gordon,* he continued to take a prominent place in official advertisements. Brown was presented as solid, dependable and not quixotic, in

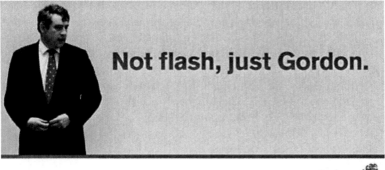

Figure 13.7   Published by the Labour party

Figure 13.8   Published by the Labour party

an obvious comparison with Cameron and a more oblique contrast with Tony Blair. Consequently, following the release of the Conservatives' *We can't go on like this*, Labour responded with *Building a foundation. Wearing it*, which simply counterposed a flattering photograph of Brown with the allegedly airbrushed image of Cameron (Figure 13.8).

Prior to the third leaders' debate the party launched a further poster featuring a large portrait of the Labour leader and two smaller ones of his Conservative and Liberal Democrat rivals. The appearance of the latter in official advertising was further recognition of Nick Clegg's impact on the campaign. It was instructive that the slogan accompanying the three politicians was *'substance vs. style'*, a reference to something Brown had himself brought up in the live Prime Ministerial debates in an attempt to diminish his opponents. The poster also stated the time and location of the third encounter, due to take place later that evening.

Saatchi & Saatchi had long sought to promote the essence of Brown as a no-nonsense politician, and this approach had been emboldened by media reports of so-called bullygate in February 2010, which suggested the Prime Minister had intimidated staff and reduced some of them to tears. Echoing the slogan associated with the soft drink Irn Bru, Saatchi & Saatchi had proposed running a poster emphasising Brown's gruff persona entitled *Made in Scotland from girders*. Party strategists were not so enthusiastic about this particular imagery, and it did not appear (Watt, 2010). However, in a moment of mockery actually mimicking life, the *Guardian* April Fool's day edition featured a poster masquerading as official copy, which depicted a menacing-looking Gordon Brown peering from the shadows along with an utterance aimed at Cameron contained in the tag line *Step Outside Posh Boy* (Priol, 2010).

The online mockery of Conservative posters by sites such as mydavidcameron.com encouraged Labour to commission ideas from its own supporters. In late March, the leading blog Labourlist published an advert that requested activists to design adverts for the party and cited Shepard Fairey, designer of the famous Obama *Hope* poster, as an inspiration (Smith, 2010). The initiative led to the distribution of one image that did make an impression, *Don't let him take Britain back to the 1980s*. The copy was produced by Jacob Quagliozzi, a 24-year-old sympathiser from St Albans, and superimposed the head of the Tory leader on the body of Gene Hunt, a fictional police detective from popular BBC television series *Ashes to Ashes*. Quagliozzi claimed his aim had been to 'remind the public that David Cameron has failed to change the Conservative party and show the threat they would pose to young people' (Quagliozzi, 2010). But the poster was problematic because Hunt was, like the Thatcherite Eighties setting for the drama, an ambiguous entity open to different interpretations, or perhaps none, given some voters would have not have experienced either phenomenon. Though prone to bending the law to achieve results, the detective was popular with audiences, who also saw him acting courageously in support of his junior colleagues.

On viewing Labour's Gene Hunt poster, Cameron jokingly offered to fund more of them, because he sensed they might actually promote the Conservatives' case. Cameron believed that there were millions of people, 'in the country who wish it was the 1980s and that police were out feeling collars and nicking people instead of filling in forms' (Cameron, 2010). The Tories then countered the day after the Labour original appeared with the same reasonably flattering image of Cameron sitting on the bonnet of Hunt's high-performance car, accompanied by a new slogan courtesy of the policeman's catchphrase *Fire up the Quattro* and appended with *It's time for change*. The foot of the poster mockingly declared: *Idea kindly donated by the Labour Party*.

The most ambitious and extensive Labour advertising launch came in the closing stages of the campaign. Gordon Brown and his leadership team presented a series of posters with the slogans, in childlike written text: *Don't forget to Vote Labour, Mum. Vote Labour, Gran. Vote Labour for us. Go on Grandad vote Labour.* The imagery emulated the Conservatives' earlier poster *Dad's Nose, Mum's Eyes* and was an explicit appeal to the electorate to think about their children's futures. The image of Brown and his team surrounded by supporters with the posters as the backdrop was a consciously staged media event to generate publicity for a more optimistic message. The initiative was, however, undermined when a man distracted by some heckling of the launch drove his Volkswagen into a bus stop as Peter Mandelson was addressing those present. The noise of the vehicle's impact and the subsequent imagery provided a symbol for those journalists inclined to talk of the party's campaign as a car crash. Asked whether he thought the incident was an omen for the outcome of the election, Mandelson replied 'I don't agree.'

Liberal Democrats

The Prime Ministerial Debates provided Nick Clegg with an ideal opportunity to appeal directly to the public. Furthermore, the predictions of a hung parliament in which his party would likely have the decisive say on who would become the next government ensured that Clegg would likely attract more attention than previous Liberal Democrat leaders. The party had been able to mount an extensive billboard advertising campaign in 2005, and partly used this to extol the virtues of Clegg's predecessor Charles Kennedy. Although similar funds were not available this time, the Liberal Democrats saw and used the potential of the internet as a method of publicising their message. They demonstrated the value of this approach by launching a new party, the 'Labservatives', through a series of advertising images designed by the agency Iris and communicated via social networking sites. The campaign, which was not branded as Liberal Democrat, attempted to generate a national dialogue about the similarities and failings of the other two main protagonists. The spoof party had its own logo, cynical tag line *For more of the same* and leader 'Gorvid Camerown'. Despite being a parody, the Labservatives subsequently deployed the tropes associated with a genuine campaign, such as a Party Election Broadcast and the inevitable website as well as posters (Figure 13.9). The Liberal Democrats followed up their spoof party campaign by releasing *Tory VAT bombshell* (Figure 13.10). The poster was another parody, this time of the Conservatives' celebrated 1992 advert *Labour's tax bombshell*. Like other publicity material, the image did not actually feature on billboards except for its official launch, a now well-established device to generate wider media coverage.

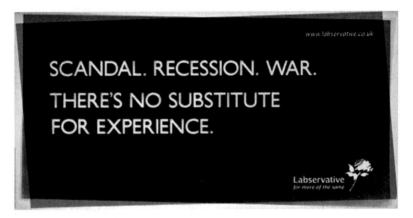

Figure 13.9   Published by Liberal Democrats

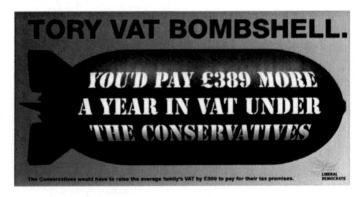

Figure 13.10   Published by the Liberal Democrats

Conclusion

The Conservatives were the only party who could afford to fund a sustained, nationwide billboard campaign in 2010. Arguably, their efforts were not especially memorable if judged by their impact and compared with historical precedence. Yet this expenditure demonstrated the enduring appeal of the traditional medium of posters in a multimedia age and, more specifically, their ability to reach the confirmed as well as less committed kinds of voter. The Conservatives' outdoor advertising promoted several themes. There were positive messages relating to Cameron himself and his so-called Big Society initiative. Other copy was of the more traditional 'knocking' variety and focused on Gordon Brown. This and other material also formed part of a concerted attempt to promote certain images in conventional news reporting and was why many of the poster launches were designed as eye-catching media events. The billboard format is, however, undergoing significant change, with the increasing popularity of digital outdoor technologies that enable parties to 'post' bills for days, or even hours, at a time. The electronic reproduction of these images has inevitably made them a feature of online campaigning, and this was greatly in evidence in the 2010 General Election with the launch of sites such as MyDavidCameron. com, a Labour supporting initiative whose creativity and innovativeness helped counteract the Conservatives' official campaign. The poster is far from spent as a means of modern political communication.

Notes

I would like to thank Dominic Wring, Philip Cowley and Steven Fielding for their comments and to Richard Huntingdon and Benedict Pringle for talking to me about the posters produced during the 2010 election.

1. Statistic taken from mydavidcameron.com: http://mydavidcameron.com/ about/stats1 (accessed 18 October 2010).
2. Thanks for Benedict Pringle for pointing this out to me.

References

Alexander, D. (2010) ' "This election will be won by people, not posters": The Douglas Alexander interview' (internet), Labour List, posted 24 March 2010, http://www.labourlist.org/election-won-by-people-not-posters-douglas-alexander-interview (accessed 19 October 2010).
Butler, D. and Ranney, A. (1992) 'Conlusion', in Butler, D. and Ranney, A. (eds) *Electioneering: A Comparative Study of Continuity and Change*. Oxford: Clarendon Press.
Cameron, D. (2010) quoted in 'Labour's Ashes to Ashes scores own goal' (internet), *Telegraph*, posted 3 April 2010, http://www.telegraph.co.uk/news/

election-2010/7550214/Labours-Ashes-to-Ashes-poster-scores-own-goal.html (accessed 1 October).

Churcher, J. (2009) 'Cameron: "New babies born with £17,000 debt"' (internet), *Independent*, posted 12 January 2009, http://www.independent.co.uk/news/uk/politics/cameron-new-babies-born-with-pound17000-debt-1316615.html (accessed 13 October 2010).

Downey, J. and Davidson, S. (2007) 'The Internet and the UK General Election', in Wring, D., Green, J., Mortimore, R. and Atkinson, S. (eds) *Political Communications: The General Election Campaign of 2005*. Basingstoke: Palgrave Macmillan.

Driver, C. (2010) 'Now these Cameron posters have DEFINITELY been airbrushed ...' (internet), *Daily Mail*, posted 14 January 2010, http://www.dailymail.co.uk/news/article-1243254/Tax-breaks-richest-3-000-estates-Because-I-m-worth--Spoof-posters-mock-David-Camerons-election-campaign.html (accessed 17 October 2010).

Eaton, G. (2010) 'New Tory poster swerves to the right' (internet), *New Statesman*, 20 April 2010, http://www.newstatesman.com/blogs/the-staggers/2010/04/refuse-work-poster-cameron (accessed 7 October 2010).

Fisher, J. (2010) 'Party Finance: Normal Service Resumed?' in Geddes, A. and Tonge, J. (eds) *Britain Votes 2010*. Oxford: Oxford University Press.

Franklin, B. (2004) *Packaging Politics: Political Communications in Britain's Media Democracy*. London Hodder.

Hoskin, P. (2010) 'A poster that cuts to the chase' (internet), *Spectator*, posted 20 April, http://www.spectator.co.uk/coffeehouse/5928608/a-poster-that-cuts-to-the-chase.thtml (accessed 7 October 2010).

Jeffrey, S. (2010) 'New Tory campaign poster – let's cut benefits' (internet), *Guardian*, 20 April 2010, http://www.guardian.co.uk/politics/blog/2010/apr/20/1 (accessed 7 October).

Lees-Marshment, J. (2008) *Political Marketing and British Political parties*. 2nd edn. Manchester: Manchester University Press.

McSmith, A. and Morris, N. (2010) 'Web satires trigger Tory ads rethink' (internet), *Independent*, posted 15 February 2010, http://www.independent.co.uk/news/uk/politics/web-satires-trigger-tory-ads-rethink-1899541.html (accessed 17 October 2010).

Montgomorie, T. 'Labour taxes and debt will crush the economy warns new Tory poster' (internet), Conservative Home, posted 5 April 2010, http://conservativehome.blogs.com/thetorydiary/2010/04/labour-taxes-and-debt-will-crush-the-economy-warns-new-tory-poster.html (accessed 17 April 2010).

Montgomorie, T. 'What other positive messages would you like to see on Tory posters?' (internet), Conservative Home, posted 20 April 2010, http://conservativehome.blogs.com/thetorydiary/2010/04/what-other-positive-messages-would-you-like-to-see-on-tory-posters.html (accessed 7 October 2010).

Norris, P. (2007) 'A Virtuous Circle: Political Communications in post-industrial societies', in Negrine, R. and Stanyer, J. (eds) *The Political Communications Reader*. Abingdon Routledge.

PA (2010) '*Labour will stamp on recovery, insist Tories* (internet), *Independent*, posted 5 April 2010, http://www.independent.co.uk/news/uk/politics/labour-will-stamp-on-recovery-insist-tories-1936408.html (accessed 10 October 2010).

Pringle, B. (2010a) 'I've Never Voted Tory' (internet), Benedict Pringle Commentary on political advertising; from Amnesty to Zanu-PF, posted

16 February 2010, http://politicaladvertising.co.uk/2010/02/16/ive-never-voted-tory/ (accessed 3 October 2010).

Pringle, B. (2010b) 'Conservative Poster – 80,000 Criminals Out Early and others'(internet), posted 29 March 2010, Benedict Pringle Commentary on political advertising; from Amnesty to Zanu-PF, http://politicaladvertising. co.uk/2010/03/29/conservative-poster-80000-criminals-out-early (accessed 3 October 2010).

Pringle, B. (2010c) 'Conservative posters on phone boxes' (internet), Benedict Pringle Commentary on political advertising; from Amnesty to Zanu-PF, posted April 19 2010, http://politicaladvertising.co.uk/2010/04/19/ conservative-posters-on-phone-boxes/ (accessed 3 October 2010).

Priol, O. (2010) 'Labour's election strategy: bring on no-nonsense hard man Gordon Brown' (internet), *Guardian*, posted 1 April 2010, http://www.guardian.co.uk/politics/2010/apr/01/labour-gordon-brown-hard-man (accessed 12 October 2010).

Quagliozzi, J. (2010) quoted on the Labour party website, http://www2.labour. org.uk/dont-let-him-take-britain-back-to-the-1980s,2010-04-03 (accessed 10 October 2010).

Richardson, M. (2010) 'Tories' Latest Campaign Poster' (internet), Sky News Blog, 9 February 2010, http://blogs.news.sky.com/boultonandco/Post:a935dcf5-4cc7-4e3b-8a32-d2bdc268911a (accessed 17 October 2010).

Rose, R. (1968) *Influencing Voters: A study in campaign rationality.* Faber and Faber.

Scammell, M. (1995) *Designer Politics: How Elections Are Won.* New York: St Martin's Press.

Scammell, M. and Semetko, H. A. (1995) 'The British Experience', in Lee Kaid, L. and Holtz-Bacha, C. (eds) *Political Advertising in Western Democracies: Parties & Candidates on Television.* California: Sage.

Shipman, T. (2010) 'Tories turn fire on "dishonest" Brown as May vote looms' (internet), posted 4 January 2010, *Daily Mail*, http://www.dailymail.co.uk/ news/article-1240404/Tories-turn-dishonest-Brown-May-vote-looms.html (accessed 5 October 2010).

Smith, A. (2010) 'PeoplePosters: Your ad on the streets of Manchester and London', (internet), posted 28 March 2010, Labour list, http://www.labourlist. org/peopleposters-your-ad-on-the-streets-of-manchester-and-london (accessed 19 October 2010).

Thompson, J. (2007) 'Pictorial Lies', *Past and Present*, 197: 177–210.

Watt, N. (2010a) 'David Cameron promises more NHS cash for poorer areas' (internet), *Guardian*, posted 4 January 2010, http://www.guardian.co.uk/ politics/2010/jan/04/cameron-promises-nhs-cash-protect-spending (accessed 1 October 2010).

Watt, N. (2010b) 'Selling Gordon Brown: how Saatchi tried to market the former PM' (internet), *Guardian*, posted 24 September 2010, http://www.guardian.co.uk/politics/2010/sep/24/brown-years-saatchi-sells-gordon (accessed 19 October 2010).

14
Constituency Campaigning in 2010

Justin Fisher, David Cutts and Edward Fieldhouse

Introduction

The importance and electoral impact of campaigning at constituency level is now widely accepted. A variety of different research teams have repeatedly demonstrated the electoral benefits of well-organised and intense election campaigns at constituency level in Britain, despite using different methodological approaches and measures of campaign strength (see, for example, Denver et al., 2003; Fieldhouse and Cutts, 2008; Pattie et al., 1995; Whiteley and Seyd, 1994). Fisher and Denver (2008) have also shown how the campaign at constituency level has become increasingly modernised. Modernisation – the utilisation of devices such as telephones and computers – has become core to campaigning, becoming more prevalent than traditional-style campaigning (though not necessarily matching the latter's electoral benefits) (Fisher and Denver, 2009).

In this chapter we consider first the strategies employed by the three principal parties in their campaigning at constituency level before examining an important new development in campaigning – the incorporation of new media. Data are drawn from a survey of all electoral agents of the five major parties in Great Britain – the Conservatives, Labour, Liberal Democrats, Plaid Cymru and the Scottish National Party (N=1,993).[1] One thousand and seventy-nine valid responses were received – an overall response rate of 54 per cent, together with interviews with party officials and local agents. In this chapter, we focus only on the three British parties: the Conservatives, Labour and the Liberal Democrats. Details of responses by party are shown in the Appendix.

Target seats and targeting strategies: a moving feast

All three parties, as would be expected, had target seats and specific targeting strategies. However, what has emerged over recent elections is not so much a binary measure of whether or not a seat is a target, but particular categories of target. In other words, there is a group of seats which are identified as targets, but the emphasis placed upon different subgroups will not necessarily be identical. Nor will it be static – depending on political and electoral circumstances, seats may move in or out of the core group. A good example of this occurred during the short campaign. After the television debates, when the Liberal Democrat poll rating soared and Labour's fell well below 30 per cent, a shift was made in the Conservatives' national direct mail strategy away from marginals being fought with the Liberal Democrats towards seats where the Conservatives were fighting Labour, but where the party had previously felt it had less chance of winning. However, changing a seat's target status mid-campaign may have a limited effect. While national campaigns may now be able to adapt relatively quickly (see Fisher, 2010), it is much more difficult at local level to shift resources as swiftly.

Importantly, each party arrived at the designation of its targets in different ways. The Conservatives were perhaps the most traditional in this respect, with targets being based principally on seat marginality, though some consideration was also given to the effects of first-time incumbency and the local government situation. They identified around 160 seats within four divisions. The 'premier league' consisted of thirty-eight seats, ones that the party expected to gain without significant effort. More important were the first and second divisions – seats the party would need to focus upon if it were to have any chance of power. The third division consisted of seats that were within the party's range, but which the party would only be likely to win if the electoral picture were going very well. The party began to focus on the target seats from 2006, and had a specific target seats operation as part of the wider Field Campaigns department at Conservative Central Office. A team of Campaign Directors was appointed from the existing field staff, and these individuals were focused solely on target seats. This role was a progression from the Area Campaign Directors (ACDs) following a restructuring in 2005, such that the Campaign Directors were less concerned with particular geography than the ACDs had been, and more with clusters of seats, of which each had between around eight and fifteen to look after. Target seats were actively monitored by the

Campaign Directors, who reported back to the national office weekly during the long campaign and then every night in the short campaign period. The party actively encouraged Campaign Directors to recruit supporters as well as members, and in this respect they had some success. The party had less success, however, in persuading members in safer or hopeless seats to campaign in targets – as one party official put it, 'we continue to find it a challenge.'

Labour had 145 targets. It, too, had four divisions of seats, but its Field Operations unit designated targets and their divisional position in a more elaborate way. Following the June 2009 elections, all local parties were assessed by the national party in respect of their work rate and voter contacts made, and target seats were then identified using propensity modelling. This technique applied four criteria: the level of activity in the local party, the electoral performance in various elections since 2005, the notional majority, and the existence of any particular political circumstances (such as hospital closures or expenses). All criteria were given a score, with the model then predicting the result. The aim of the targeting ultimately became the avoidance of a Conservative majority, and so almost all targets were defensive, the exceptions being a few Liberal Democrat marginals, seats lost in 2005 to independent or minor party candidates, and one of the seats in Scotland lost in a by-election during the Parliament.

The Liberal Democrats had a comparatively large number of target seats, including all their own seats plus a further 37 (mainly Labour-held) seats that the party hoped to gain; ninety-nine in total. Liberal Democrat targeting was based on prior local performance in both national and local election performance, candidate quality, doorstep returns and seat marginality, and was buoyed by the inroads made in 2005 together with the reality of the Conservative resurgence. The party clearly felt that Labour seats were the ones where the party was most likely to make gains, and seats were selected for targeting in some cases two years before the election, though some of these new targets lacked a local infrastructure (Kavanagh and Cowley, 2010: 237). In support of the target seats, there was a special unit at national level, as well as campaign and regional organizers for each of these seats, who had received significant training in preparation.

Of course, to some extent the parties' targeting strategies interlocked. Yet, for all parties, there were also seats upon which they were focusing that were not targeted by either of the other two parties – this was most true of the Liberal Democrats. The bulk of activity occurred in around 158 seats where two or more parties were focusing their efforts. Only seven of these were targeted by all three parties, and by far the most prevalent battleground was between the Conservatives and Labour – around 105 seats.

Constituency campaigning at the national level

A significant trend in recent elections has been the growing integration of national and constituency campaigns, such that Fisher and Denver (2008) suggest that the constituency campaigns may become more significant than the national 'air war'. At the very least it is clear that the 'ground' and 'air' wars have become progressively more integrated, with constituency campaigns increasingly supported by efforts at national level through activities such as direct mail and telephone voter identification – especially in target seats (Fisher et al., 2007). The 2010 election campaigns represented a continuation of these developments.

The Conservatives

The Conservatives went into the campaign in excellent financial shape, meaning that significant investment could be made in national efforts to support the constituency campaigns (Fisher, 2010). Direct mail was used heavily as a campaign technique, targeted at both key seats and key voters within them. Some sixteen million pieces of mail were delivered between January 2010 and the election, plus a further four million pieces of more 'localised' direct mail during the short campaign (Kavanagh and Cowley, 2010: 236). The message in many of these leaflets was, however, more of a national one than a local one, often focusing on the choice between David Cameron and Gordon Brown. Locally produced literature was closely monitored by the national party – every item required clearance from the centre, with a particular sensitivity towards candidates making any spending commitments. The use of direct mail was supported nationally by extensive telephone voter identification. The party had a call centre in its Millbank headquarters of around forty lines which had operated from the beginning of the year. In addition, it had regional call centres in Coleshill and Bradford, and encouraged volunteers from marginal seats also to make use of these facilities, dubbed GENEVA – the general election volunteer agency.

The database upon which the direct mail and telephone voter identification were based had been collected over some years. The party had developed a new computer software operation called MERLIN, with a view to gaining complete visibility of all local databases. It had been hoped that the central party would be able to add MOSAIC demographic data and exchange information easily between central and local databases, so that quick adjustments to campaign strategies could be made. This approach was broadly successful. However, the speed at which the national party could gain visibility of the local campaigns was hampered somewhat by the fact that the party was still relying on central party staff entering the data gathered from the constituencies by hand.

Unlike the other two main parties, the Conservatives' superior financial strength meant that the party could make significant use of billboard posters. The poster sites were bought as a package, with the vast majority appearing in the party's target seats – as one party official put it: 'There's no point putting them in bloody Beaconsfield, is there?' The first significant campaign began at the turn of the year, featuring a personalised message from David Cameron, and was followed by a series of posters aimed at electors who had not voted Conservative previously. However, as the campaign went on, the level of spending on billboard advertising was scaled back and more national expenditure was devoted to the use of direct mail (Fisher, 2010).

Visits from leading national figures also followed this targeted strategy. On average, target seats received four visits during the campaign, compared with less than one visit on average in safe seats. Somewhat puzzlingly, however, hopeless seats received an average of one and a half visits – a surprisingly high number both in absolute terms and compared with safe seats. Yet, as Fisher and Denver (2008: 816–7) show, this is a familiar pattern for the Conservatives, also occurring in previous elections.

The Conservatives' greater financial strength also provided a significant advantage over the other two main parties in the greater ability of the central party to support local parties in the lead-up to the campaign. Typically, while the party has always had more full-time agents than the other parties, they have tended to be based in the wealthier, safe seats. This time, the national party was able to make grants available to local parties in target seats to help employ agents if the local association was unable to fund the position itself. The central party began to recruit and train agents from around the beginning of 2006; and, from around thirty months before the election, local associations in target seats were required to submit a campaign plan which included a bid to fund specific activities. If the bids were successful, the national party would then allocate ring-fenced money to fund activities such as local surveys, newsletters and communications, local direct mail and database-building. Local activity was monitored by Campaign Directors, and the result was that local associations in target seats would ideally be much better prepared for the election campaign.

In terms of new media, there was not a huge central investment in the campaign, in part because the national party had a relatively limited database of email addresses and mobile telephone numbers. Social media sites such as Facebook were used, but were generally organised locally. The national party did, however, seek as far as possible to monitor local Facebook and Twitter activity to ensure that no inappropriate pledges were being made.

Labour

At national level, Labour found itself to be in a particularly poor financial state and could only spend a limited sum on the campaign (Fisher, 2010). The most significant direct impact on constituency campaigning was that far fewer campaign organisers were in place on the ground, and that they took up their positions far later. Whereas in 2005 it had been more common to have special organisers in place some two years before the election, in 2010 many were only appointed – either on short-term contracts or by secondment from the national office – at the beginning of the year.

Labour, however, still made much use of direct mail and telephone voter identification to support its constituency campaigns using a new online database system called Contact Creator. Built by Experian, it contained the whole of the electoral register together with MOSAIC demographic data. The key development for this campaign was the ability for all local parties to upload canvass returns and contact details in real time, and over 500 constituency Labour parties signed up for this system, for which they paid a small fee. This allowed the national party to produce daily reports on how each individual campaign was performing, whereas in 2005 the national party had had only one snapshot of canvass returns, produced when all the local parties had submitted their returns on disk. The use of this Contract Creator database allowed the party to fine-tune where direct mail was sent and who received telephone calls on a daily basis, and shift the emphasis of the campaigns accordingly. Indeed, Labour even had an iPhone application, which enabled members to make calls to key voters in target seats as determined by the Contact Creator database.

Labour also used the regularly updated records on constituency-level activity to incentivise parties in the build-up to the campaign. In target seats, parties that made more contacts (guided and advised by the national party based on the database records), held more street stalls and engaged in high-visibility activity were given additional free direct mail from the national party. This formed part of a general strategy in respect of constituency campaigns, namely that the national party wanted to take on the responsibility of arranging printing and postage so that constituency parties could concentrate on face-to-face activity such as knocking on doors. To that end, almost all of the leaflets were printed through the national system, and nearly three-quarters of constituencies delegated the printing and arrangement of the FREEPOST candidate's address (to which all candidates are entitled) to the national party. The result was that the FREEPOST leaflets were all delivered only three days after the Prime Minister had visited the Palace to seek a dissolution of Parliament. Overall, in the period after 1 January, some eight to ten million pieces of direct mail were sent (including 3.5 million in the last two weeks).

The direct mail operation was supported by telephone voter identification, which focused almost exclusively on target seats. However, Labour's poor financial position also limited this activity to some extent. The party's national telephone bank in Gosforth employed far fewer callers (around fifty) than had been the case previously (there were around 200 in 2001). Nevertheless, the Contact Creator database meant that more effective use could be made of 'late money' – donations made during the campaign. Within two days, money could be utilised to send direct mail, use telephone voter identification and transport volunteers into target seats. Indeed, the transportation of volunteers was a further example of the integrated systems that the national party had developed for fighting the campaigns in the constituencies. Individuals who joined the party or volunteered online would be put in touch with local coordinators, who would call them in an effort to boost campaigns in key seats. Labour's campaigning was also highly focused in terms of visits by leading national figures. Target seats received four visits on average, compared with a mean of one visit in safe seats and less than one in hopeless seats.

While at the national level there was some investment in new media campaign methods (Fisher, 2010), the use of new media was mainly regarded by Labour as being principally about journalists (promoting stories) and providing supporters with information. However, local parties were also provided with an Interactive Web Creator. The national party provided local parties with localised websites, which were able to capture all local contacts and then feed these data directly into the Contact Creator database. In addition, local Facebook pages were encouraged, though not monitored by the national party.

The Liberal Democrats

Like the other two parties, the Liberal Democrats made significant use of direct mail to support their target seats. Some twenty million pieces of direct mail were sent from January to the election, with around nine million during the short campaign alone (Kavanagh and Cowley, 2010: 237). At local level, parties were presented with templates for their leaflets with particular style options available. The national party attempted to monitor their use in target seats, though the party could not be sure if the templates were used in all seats. In support of the direct mail, regional phone banks were established across the country. A large phone bank in East Anglia had been set up in 2009 and others followed. These phone banks principally made calls to target seats.

As in 2005, tours by the party leader were another significant form of campaigning in support of target seats. While the 2005 tour had been based principally around Charles Kennedy (Fisher, 2005: 184), in 2010 various leadership and senior figures took part (Nick Clegg, Vince Cable, Chris Huhne, Charles Kennedy, Paddy Ashdown and Menzies Campbell), presumably reflecting Nick Clegg's relatively low profile prior to the leaders' debates. On average, target seats received two visits from such national figures during the campaign, whereas non-target seats very rarely hosted any senior figures.

In terms of new media, Twitter and Facebook were used heavily by the national party. Candidates were encouraged to have a presence on Twitter and Facebook, but were also offered advice and training on what not to put in Tweets or in Facebook updates. This effort was reflected in the level of new media activity in target seats, where Liberal Democrat activity was higher than both Labour and the Conservatives (see Table 14.6) and gave some credence to the claim of a Liberal Democrat official that 'we won the digital war at the General Election.'

The varying intensity of the campaigns at the constituency level

Campaigning at the constituency level includes many aspects, and, as demonstrated in previous studies (see, for example, Denver and Hands, 1997), overall campaign intensity is best illustrated by the creation of an index, which incorporates all of the core components of a constituency campaign: preparation, organisation, manpower, use of computers, use of telephones, polling day activity, use of direct mail, level of doorstep canvassing, leafleting, and now e-campaigning. Given the growth of e-campaigning, this has been added to the overall index. The intensity index is calculated using a Principal Components Analysis (PCA) of all the core indicators of constituency campaigning. The PCA suggests that one factor is sufficient to represent the variance in the original variables and produces factor scores, which are then standardised around a mean of 100. This process allows easy comparisons between parties as well as the target status of seats.

The first step is to evaluate the distribution of campaign intensity by party and by target status. Table 14.1 illustrates the mean campaign indexes for each party overall and then by seat status. First, it is clear (as is usual) that the Conservatives had the strongest campaigns overall, with the Liberal Democrats having the weakest. However, overall strength only tells part of the story. What is more important is that the strongest campaigns take place in the target seats. As Fisher and Denver (2008) have shown, for example, while the Liberal Democrats have always been much weaker overall, they have been very successful in fighting their strongest campaigns where they were needed most, and therefore moving to a level of campaign development that is on a par with that of the Conservatives, despite the significant disparity in overall resources (see also Fieldhouse and Cutts, 2008).

To test this further, we disaggregate the data by the target status of the seat: Targets (seats that a party is seeking to gain or defending, often with a small majority), Held Not Target (seats that the party holds comfortably), and Not Held Not Target (seats in which the party has very little chance of winning). Given that campaigns at constituency level are unable to react as quickly as at national level, there is unlikely to be significant variation between the divisions of target seats in terms of local activity. For that reason, we use a single category of target seat in this analysis. Table 14.1 illustrates once again that the Liberal Democrats were successful in channelling their campaign resources effectively, the intensity of the campaigns in their target seats being higher than that of Labour and almost as high as the Conservatives. Elsewhere, the results are pretty much as expected for both the Conservatives

Table 14.1 Overall campaign intensity by party and target status

	All	Held Not Target	Target	Not Held Not Target
Conservative	111	115	140	92
Labour	101	116	133	77
Liberal Democrat	91	*	139	83

Notes: Details of numbers of cases and the construction of the index for this and all tables can be found in the Appendix

*In this and subsequent tables, all Liberal Democrat seats were regarded as targets. There are therefore no Liberal Democrat seats in the Held Not Target category

and Labour. Nevertheless, this represents something of a change for the Conservatives, who have historically struggled to focus their efforts effectively. Indeed, perhaps the principal surprise is the relative strength of Conservative campaigning in its hopeless seats (Not Held, Not Target) – possibly reflecting the enthusiasm of Conservative supporters in an election in which the party had a realistic chance of overall victory.

Traditionalism, modernisation, e-campaigning and e-organisation

To get a better idea of more detailed patterns in the campaign it is worth examining different forms of campaigning in more detail. Previous work has shown how campaigns have been shifting from more traditional approaches, based on volunteer labour, towards more modern approaches, which utilise telephones, computers and direct mail (Fisher and Denver, 2008, 2009). This has been a function of both the general decline in membership and the relative fall in the costs associated with the use of such technology.

Preparation and effort in campaign activities

As a first step, we evaluated the level of effort put into different campaign techniques. Respondents were asked to indicate the degree of effort that had gone into these activities on a five-point scale, such that a higher score indicates more effort. Of course, not all activities require equal effort, but the data can nevertheless be taken as an indicator of the relative importance afforded to different activities. Table 14.2 illustrates the mean effort put into a range of activities in the year before the campaign proper began. For all parties, the distribution of leaflets was

Table 14.2   Mean effort in year before election (1 = low, 5 = high)

Mean	Con	Lab	Lib Dem	All
Leaflets	3.9	3.3	3.3	3.5
Street Stalls	2.0	2.1	1.5	1.9
Resident Surveys	3.1	2.3	2.5	2.6
Target Specific Groups	2.5	2.4	2.1	2.3
Media Coverage	3.2	3.0	2.6	2.9
Website	3.5	2.9	3.1	3.1
Social Network Sites	2.2	2.1	2.1	2.1

the most significant activity. Interestingly, however, the operation and maintenance of a website was second most important across all parties, suggesting that constituency parties were now seeing the web as an important tool of communication. All three parties also focused considerable attention on getting media coverage, while the Conservatives and Liberal Democrats made significant use of resident surveys. By way of contrast, the use of social networking sites was afforded a much lower level of effort (as were the much more traditional street stalls).

A further indication of the relative importance of different campaign activities is illustrated in Table 14.3. Here, respondents were again asked to indicate on a five-point scale how much effort was devoted to a range of activities during the campaign itself. Table 14.3 shows the mean scores for each party, where a higher score again indicates most effort. As with the longer-term campaigning, all three parties afforded the most effort, by some margin, to the distribution of leaflets (including the candidate's election address). This was followed, for the two larger parties, by traditional doorstep canvassing. What is also apparent, however, is that, as with the pre-campaign effort, a website was again deemed to be very important – all parties put a significant effort into operating and maintaining one.

However, other forms of e-campaigning were apparently deemed far less significant in the parties' campaigns. The effort put into emailing voters and using social networking and video or image-sharing sites was far lower than for established campaign techniques such as direct mail and doorstep canvassing for all parties. The importance of websites is

Table 14.3   Mean effort during campaign (1 = low, 5 = high)

Mean	Con	Lab	Lib Dem	All
Leaflets	4.6	4.4	4.2	4.4
Doorstep Canvassing Voter Identification	3.6	3.2	2.6	3.1
Doorstep Canvassing Introduce Candidate	3.6	3.2	2.4	3.0
Telephone Canvassing	2.2	2.5	1.8	2.2
Election Address	4.5	4.1	4.0	4.2
Emailing Voters	1.9	1.6	1.6	1.7
Organising Postal Votes	3.0	2.6	2.1	2.5
Campaigning for Postal Votes	3.0	2.6	2.4	2.7
Targeting Groups	2.4	2.5	2.2	2.4
Media Coverage	3.2	2.9	2.7	2.9
Maintaining Website	3.1	2.8	2.9	2.9
Social Networking Sites	2.0	2.0	2.1	2.0
Video/Image Sharing Sites	1.5	1.4	1.4	1.4

the exception here, but, by and large, e-campaigning was not nearly as prominent in terms of campaign efforts as many had predicted.

The balance of campaigns: continuing modernisation?

In order to examine this relative emphasis in campaigns we use scales that capture overall activity levels of traditionalism, modernisation and e-campaigning (details of scale creation are shown in the Appendix). As with the broader measure of campaign intensity, this allows the production of overall measures as well as the disaggregation by seat status.

Just as with overall levels of campaign intensity, we would expect most kinds of activity to take place in target seats and least in hopeless seats. By and large, we would also expect seats that parties hold, but that are not targets, to score somewhere in between, in part because safe seats tend to have higher levels of membership or local wealth (Fisher, 2000; Fisher et al., 2006). Of course, parties are not completely free to distribute resources without constraint – volunteer labour, for example, is notoriously hard to make mobile, thus leading the intensity of some campaigns in safe seats where there are large memberships to be surprisingly high. More modern campaign techniques should, however, be easier to distribute efficiently, since they are more mobile. Nevertheless, analysis of the distribution of such efforts has previously shown predicted patterns for Labour and the Liberal Democrats – traditional activity being more likely to take place in target seats – though not for the Conservatives (Fisher and Denver, 2009).

Table 14.4, however, reveals that the Conservatives in 2010 appeared to have overcome this problem – for all three parties, traditional campaigning (which includes volunteer labour, leafleting and posters) was highest in target seats. Indeed, perhaps the only puzzle is why Conservative traditional campaigning was relatively high in other seats as well. The level in safe seats (Held Not Target) is relatively easy to

Table 14.4 Traditional campaigning by party and target status

	All	Held Not Target	Target	Not Held Not Target
Conservative	112	117	131	97
Labour	99	117	124	78
Liberal Democrat	92	*	130	85

Note: *In this and subsequent tables, all Liberal Democrat seats were regarded as targets. There are therefore no Liberal Democrat seats in the Held Not Target category explain – safer seats tend to have higher membership, and, even if some of their members campaign in more marginal constituencies, a significant proportion will continue to engage in traditional methods in safe seats – especially with the party being relatively popular. More difficult to explain is the relatively high level of traditional activity in 'hopeless' seats – much lower than in target seats, but nearly as strong as Labour's level overall. Perhaps the reason for this was the high expectation of a Conservative win, which boosted party morale even in hopeless seats. Certainly, the same phenomenon was observed in Labour's hopeless seats in 1997 (Fisher and Denver, 2009: 201).

Table 14.5 illustrates patterns in respect of campaign intensity using modern techniques, including the use of telephone, direct mail and computers. And, as expected, the use of modern techniques is most prevalent in target seats and least prevalent in hopeless seats. Indeed, both these data and those on traditional campaigning illustrate the continued success of the Liberal Democrats in successfully channelling their resources into their target seats – in both cases, the scores compare very favourably with the other two parties, being higher than Labour in respect of targeted traditional campaigning and very slightly higher than the Conservatives in respect of modern campaigning in these seats.

One of the key developments expected in the campaign was the use of e-campaigning. The growth of such technologies, along with their widespread use in the US Presidential elections in 2008, led many to suggest that e-campaigning would be particularly significant in this election. Indeed, coverage of e-campaigning before the election gave the impression that this could even be the dominant form. As Tables 14.2 and 14.3 suggest, however, parties seemed to put less effort into such techniques than the pre-election hyperbole might have suggested (see also Chapter 15). Nevertheless, it is still worth examining the distribution of parties' overall e-campaigning efforts. As with traditionalism and modernisation, a scale was constructed (details in the Appendix) and then scores disaggregated by seat status. The results are shown in Table 14.6.

Table 14.5   Modern campaigning by party and target status

	All	Held Not Target	Target	Not Held Not Target
Conservative	105	105	131	91
Labour	102	116	135	79
Liberal Democrat	95	*	132	88

Note: *In this and subsequent tables, all Liberal Democrat seats were regarded as targets. There are therefore no Liberal Democrat seats in the Held Not Target category

A number of key observations can be made. First, unlike traditionalism and modernisation, Labour's level of e-campaigning was lower than that of both the Conservatives and the Liberal Democrats, suggesting that the latter did indeed make particular efforts in this area. Second, while familiar patterns are apparent in terms of target seats recording most activity, the differentiation in intensity between targets and non-targets in the case of the Conservative and Labour parties is not nearly as marked as in the case of modern campaigning techniques. The same is not as apparent for the Liberal Democrats (though the gap is smaller than in the case of both modern and traditional techniques). This suggests two things – first, that the costs of e-campaigning are relatively low, so that more campaigns can utilize them with less regard for seat status. Second, it may imply that e-campaigns were regarded as being less important than other techniques and so less effort was put into targeting such resources.

Such points become easier to gauge if we produce a net score of parties' modern and e-campaigning efforts. Since both are measured on the same scale, the net levels can be calculated by simply subtracting the level of e-campaigning from that of modern campaigning. This produces a score such that a negative figure is indicative of more e-campaigning relative to modern campaigning and vice versa. The results are shown in Table 14.7. What is very clear is that the two explanations are both supported. For all three parties, modern campaigning dominates in safe

Table 14.6　E-campaigning by party and target status

	All	Held Not Target	Target	Not Held Not Target
Conservative	104	101	112	104
Labour	97	98	104	93
Liberal Democrat	101	*	121	97

Note: *In this and subsequent tables, all Liberal Democrat seats were regarded as targets. There are therefore no Liberal Democrat seats in the Held Not Target category

Table 14.7　The balance of modern and e-campaigning by party and target status

	All	Held Not Target	Target	Not Held Not Target
Conservative	1	4	19	−13
Labour	5	17	31	−14
Liberal Democrat	−6	*	11	−9

Note: *In this and subsequent tables, all Liberal Democrat seats were regarded as targets. There are therefore no Liberal Democrat seats in the Held Not Target category

Table 14.8   E-organisation by party and target status

	All	Held Not Target	Target	Not Held Not Target
Conservative	99	98	108	96
Labour	102	112	120	89
Liberal Democrat	99	*	121	95

Note: *In this and subsequent tables, all Liberal Democrat seats were regarded as targets. There are therefore no Liberal Democrat seats in the Held Not Target category

seats, and particularly in target seats. Similarly, e-campaigning dominates in 'hopeless' seats. And, while it is true that the Liberal Democrats produce a negative score overall, this is to be expected given that the party has more 'hopeless' seats than the other two parties. In summary, then, e-campaigning was widespread in all three parties' campaigns, but, while its relatively low cost meant it took place in more constituencies, it was apparently not a priority campaigning tool.

A separate aspect of the use of e-technology is how it is used within parties. And, as with almost all organisations, email has become the principal form of communication for parties – as one party official said, 'we live on email'. However, recent developments mean that it is also worth examining the distribution of e-organisation within constituency campaigns. Again, a scale was constructed and details can be found in the Appendix. The results are shown in Table 14.8 and, although much e-communication is ubiquitous, familiar patterns still emerge in respect of the relative intensity of e-organisation in target, safe and hopeless seats, though this is more marked for Labour and the Liberal Democrats than for the Conservatives. What is also apparent is that all parties engage in similar levels of e-organisation overall, with Labour, untypically, engaging marginally more.

Conclusions

Constituency campaigning in the 2010 General Election represented both continuity and change. Some broad trends continued. First, national and constituency campaigns continued to be strongly integrated, with significant efforts being made at national level to support the campaigns at local level. Indeed, the distinction between the 'ground' and 'air' wars becomes increasingly difficult to disentangle. Second, the use of 'modern' campaign techniques continued to grow, although Labour did appear to acknowledge explicitly that much could be gained from face-to-face contact in the constituencies by urging local parties to engage in such activities while the national party focused on the distribution of leaflets.

However, there were also some changes. The Conservatives were much more successful than in previous years in differentiating the level of activity in target seats compared with safe and hopeless seats, suggesting perhaps that the most potent benefit of Lord Ashcroft's work with the party was improved targeting – at least in terms of devoting most effort to such seats. A second change was the development of e-campaigning. There were certainly high expectations of the impact of e-campaigning, but the evidence at constituency level was that, in general, parties were still wedded to other techniques and that e-campaigning was given a much lower priority. As one party official said, 'there was a whole lot of bullsh*t built on the back of the Obama campaign...', suggesting that one of the problems with e-communication was that 'nobody read the f***ing thing.' That said, e-campaigning had obvious appeal to parties with lower incomes, and the results at both national and constituency level suggest that the Liberal Democrats were keener advocates than the other two parties.

Overall, constituency campaigning in 2010 was highly targeted, integrated with the national party and focused much more on techniques such as direct mail than techniques using new media. Indeed, while it is likely that e-campaigning will develop further and become more important as a campaigning tool in constituencies, that time has not yet come, and it is evident that the hyperbole surrounding such techniques before the election was not justified.

Appendix

Responses

The numbers of responses for each party by target status were as follows:

	All	Held Not Target	Target	No Target Not Held
Conservative	288	111	57	120
Labour	387	129	73	185
Liberal Democrat	353	*	50	303

Note: *In this and subsequent tables, all Liberal Democrat seats were regarded as targets. There are therefore no Liberal Democrat seats in the Held Not Target category

Calculation of campaign intensity index

Responses to the questions below are grouped into the following core components of constituency campaigning: Preparation, Organisation,

Manpower, Computers, Polling Day Activity, Telephones, Direct Mail, Canvassing, Leaflets and E-Campaigning. These groups are then entered into a Principal Components Analysis, which produced one component.

Group	Question
Preparation	How prepared – Jobs
Preparation	How prepared – Campaign funds
Preparation	How prepared – Main committee rooms
Preparation	How prepared – Local committee rooms
Preparation	How prepared – Electoral register
Preparation	How prepared – Election address
Preparation	How prepared – Printing
Preparation	How prepared – Identifying supporters
Preparation	Started serious planning
Preparation	Use of previous canvass records
Organisation	Percentage of constituency covered by active local organisations
Organisation	How long ago knew responsible
Organisation	Delegated duties – Canvassing organiser
Organisation	Delegated duties – Postal votes
Organisation	Delegated duties – Candidate aide
Organisation	Delegated duties – Computer officer
Organisation	Local organisers or sub-agents
Manpower	Number of campaign workers
Manpower	Number of campaign helpers on polling day
Computers	Delegated duties – Computer officer
Computers	Use of computers – Direct mail
Computers	Use of computers – Canvass returns
Computers	Use computerised electoral register
Computers	Computers used to compile knock-up lists
Computers	Election software provided by party HQ
Polling Day Activity	Good morning leaflets delivered
Polling Day Activity	Voters knocked up on polling day
Polling Day Activity	Percentage of constituency covered
Polling Day Activity	Number of campaign helpers on polling day
Polling Day Activity	Volunteers sent into your constituency
Telephones	Used telephone canvassing in constituency
Telephones	Outside canvassing
Telephones	Use telephone canvassing
Telephones	Telephone canvassing organised from outside constituency
Telephones	Voters contacted by telephone on polling day
Direct Mail	Leaflets targeted at particular groups
Direct Mail	Direct mail used to target individual voters
Canvassing	Percentage of electorate canvassed
Canvassing	Percentage of electorate telephone canvassed?
Leaflets	How many regionally/nationally produced leaflets distributed
Leaflets	Total number of locally produced leaflets

Continued

Continued

Group	Question
E-Campaigning	Pre-election campaign – Operating and maintaining a website
E-Campaigning	Pre-election campaign – Using social networking sites
E-Campaigning	Contact voters in the constituency by text message
E-Campaigning	Make use of Twitter to communicate with voters
E-Campaigning	Use of computers – Emailing voters
E-Campaigning	Local party and candidate website
E-Campaigning	Campaign effort – Maintaining website
E-Campaigning	Campaign effort – Emailing voters
E-Campaigning	Campaign effort – Social networking sites
E-Campaigning	Campaign effort – Video/image sharing sites
E-Campaigning	Voters contacted by text on polling day
E-Campaigning	Voters contacted by email on polling day

Calculation of other indexes

Responses to the questions below were included in the calculation of the following scales:

Traditionalism

- No. of posters distributed
- No. of nationally or regionally produced leaflets distributed
- No. of locally produced leaflets distributed
- Percentage of electorate canvassed on doorstep
- No. of campaign workers
- Knocked up by party workers
- No. of polling day workers

Modernisation

- Amount of direct mail sent
- Percentage of electorate telephone canvassed
- Used computers
- Had computerised electoral register
- Used party software
- With website
- Knocked up by telephone
- Used computers for knocking-up lists

E-Campaigning

- Pre-election campaign – Operating and maintaining a website
- Pre-election campaign – Using social networking sites
- Contact voters in the constituency by text message

- Make use of Twitter to communicate with voters
- Use of computers – Emailing voters
- Local party and candidate website
- Campaign effort – Maintaining website
- Campaign effort – Emailing voters
- Campaign effort – Social networking sites
- Campaign effort – Video/image sharing sites
- Voters contacted by text on polling day
- Voters contacted by email on polling day

E-Organisation

- Contact campaign workers in the constituency by text message
- Computers used to maintain web pages
- Computers used to email campaign workers
- Computers used for targeted direct mail
- Computers used to keep records of canvass returns

Notes

Research for this chapter was funded by the Economic and Social Research Council. Grant Number RES-000-22–2762.

1. As is customary, no candidates from the major parties (in this case, Labour and the Liberal Democrats) contested the seat of the Speaker.

References

Denver, D. and Hands, G. (1997) *Modern Constituency Electioneering*. London: Frank Cass.
Denver, D., Hands, G., Fisher, J. and MacAllister, I. (2003) 'Constituency Campaigning in Britain 1992–2001: Centralisation and Modernisation', *Party Politics*, 9: 541–59.
Fieldhouse, E. and Cutts, D. (2008) 'The Effectiveness of Local Party Campaigns in 2005: Combining Evidence from Campaign Spending and Agent Survey Data', *British Journal of Political Science*, 39: 367–88.
Fisher, J. (2000) 'Small Kingdoms and Crumbling Organisations: Examining the Variation in Constituency Party Membership and Resources', *British Elections & Parties Review*, 10: 133–150.
Fisher, J. (2005) 'Campaign Finance', in Geddes, A. and Tonge, J. (eds) *Britain Decides: The General Election of 2005*. Basingstoke: Palgrave, 170–186.
Fisher, J. (2010) 'Party Finance – Normal Service Resumed?' *Parliamentary Affairs*, 63: 778–801.
Fisher, J. and Denver, D. (2008) 'From Foot-Slogging to Call Centres and Direct Mail: A Framework for Analysing the Development of District-Level Campaigning', *European Journal of Political Research*, 47: 794–826.

Fisher, J. and Denver, D. (2009) 'Evaluating the Electoral Effects of Traditional and Modern Modes of Constituency Campaigning in Britain 1992–2005', *Parliamentary Affairs*, 62: 196–210.

Fisher, J., Denver, D. and Hands, G. (2006) 'Party Membership and Campaign Activity in Britain: The Impact of Electoral Performance', *Party Politics*, 12: 505–19.

Fisher, J., Denver, D., Fieldhouse, E., Cutts, D. and Russell, A. (2007) 'Constituency Campaigning in 2005: Ever More Centralization?' in Wring, D., Green, J., Mortimore, R. and Atkinson, S. (eds) *Political Communications: The British General Election of 2005*. Basingstoke: Palgrave, 79–92.

Kavanagh, D. and Cowley, P. (2010) *The British General Election of 2010*. Basingstoke: Palgrave.

Pattie, C. J., Johnston, R. J. and Fieldhouse, E. A. (1995) 'Winning the Local Vote: The Effectiveness of Constituency Campaign Spending in Great Britain, 1983–1992', *American Political Science Review*, 89(4): 969–83.

Whiteley, P. and Seyd, P. (1994) 'Local Party Campaigning and Voting Behaviour in Britain', *Journal of Politics*, 56: 242–51.

15
Below the Radar? Online Campaigning at the Local Level in the 2010 Election

Rosalynd Southern and Stephen Ward

Despite a growing agreement that local campaigning has increased in importance over the past three elections, there have been few concerted studies of one of the main innovations during that time – online campaigning. The received wisdom has been that the internet has played very little role at the constituency level, with candidates and parties failing to exploit its possibilities and the audience for any online offerings being limited to party hacks, journalists and political geeks. However, recently, studies from other democracies have indicated that the internet is beginning to make an impact, in terms of both challenging the standardised top-down nationally controlled campaign model (Zittel, 2009) and, possibly, even providing electoral benefits to candidates (Gibson and McAllister, 2006, 2008; Sudulich, 2009; Sudulich and Wall, 2010).

In the run-up to the 2010 General Election there was considerable media speculation that the internet, and especially the rapid rise of social networking tools, might have some influence on the conduct and outcome of the election. However, after a couple of weeks of the campaign the same newspapers were declaring that the internet had failed to make any mark, although little evidence was provided to assess its role properly (Gibson et al., 2010a). This chapter, therefore, attempts to provide some of this evidence in the context of candidate campaigning online. In particular, we examine: patterns of online competition – who went online and where; the extent to which candidates personalised their campaigns and engaged in dialogue with the electorate through so-called Web 2.0 tools (blogs, Twitter, YouTube and Facebook); and whether online campaigning offers any move away from traditional campaigns and any impact on electoral competition.

UK constituency campaigning: renewed importance?

Over the past two decades a renewed consensus has emerged that constituency campaigns still matter and that local campaigning is, in fact, becoming increasingly important (Denver and Hands, 2001; Denver et al., 2003; Fisher and Denver, 2009; Johnston and Pattie, 2003; Seyd and Whiteley, 2003). Those studying campaign communication from a longer-term historical perspective have referred to the emergence of new era of campaigning, where the local level is seen as regaining some of its pre-war importance (Blumler and Kavanagh, 1999; Farrell and Webb, 2000; Norris, 2000). Broader technological and societal changes are seen as being drivers for the shifts in the campaign focus. For example, the fragmentation of the media since the late 1980s has led some to argue that the national television-centred campaign that has predominated since the 1960s is beginning to erode. This, along with the breakdown of traditional cleavage structures and partisan support for parties, has led to growing volatility and a less reliable core vote, meaning that parties have had to seek new techniques to appeal to an increasingly fickle public.

Beyond these broad studies of the evolution of campaign communication is more empirically focused research concentrating directly on the parties' campaign efforts. According to Fisher et al. (2005), such studies tend to highlight three broad shifts around local campaigns. First, there has been an increasing focus on key target seats where party resources (finance, staff and volunteers), and campaign efforts are selectively deployed in those seats that parties deem vital to their chances of success. Thus elections are now centred on the battle to win the key marginal constituencies. Second, constituency campaigning has become increasingly professionalised, with parties deploying ever more sophisticated campaign machinery – targeted direct mailing and advertising, telephone canvassing, opinion polling focus groups, database-building and information surveillance – added to traditional efforts of canvassing, door-knocking and leafleting (Fisher and Denver, 2009). Third, constituency and local campaigning matters: local campaigning has effects where parties deploy their campaign resources, be it in terms of increased turnout, or higher party vote share in targeted constituencies.

Within this broad consensus around the importance of local campaigning there are, however, some differences in emphasis, notably about how far successful constituency campaigns are really a reflection of local campaign activity. Denver and Hands (2001) have argued that, while constituency campaigning has become more important, this more accurately reflects the success of nationally coordinated campaigning in which party HQs have increased their control over constituency campaigns via targeting resource deployment. Alternatively, others (Seyd and Whiteley, 2003; Whiteley and Seyd, 2002) have pointed towards the continuing importance of more traditional local party campaign activity, arguing that electoral success is still, in part, dependent on having a strong presence on the ground that enables a greater intensity of campaigning. Other debates also remain around the impact of local campaigning, such as the circumstances in which local spending and communication matter (Jackson and Lilleker, 2004; Johnston and Pattie, 2009), or whether, in the age of permanent campaigning, incumbent MPs can build any advantage over challenger candidates.

The internet and local campaigning: potential impacts

The emergence of the internet has been seen as both challenging and intensifying trends in constituency campaigns. Initially, at least, internet campaigning was often viewed as an antidote to the centralised, professionalised marketing approach that has dominated election campaigns over the past two decades or more. Yet it has been suggested that the role of the internet is more likely to accelerate some of the changes in electioneering that pre-date its emergence. These debates about the impact and role of the internet tend to concentrate on three areas (organisation, content/style, and competitiveness of campaigns):

- Organisation – decentralising campaign control? The fragmentation of the media arguably means that the command and control model of campaigning is less effective, with parties needing to exploit the multiplicity of channels. However, in addition, new technologies offer opportunities for individual candidates to decentralise campaigns through providing a variety of relatively cheap tools to build a stronger presence outside the iron grip of party HQ (Norris, 2000). With minimal resources, candidates can now highlight their own viewpoints, messages, voting records and personality via new ICTs on a continuous basis. What is more, the proliferation of such communication channels and the speed of communication mean that it is more difficult for national parties to monitor and keep control of them. Yet, despite the decentralising possibilities, others have questioned whether candidates or local parties are really best placed to take advantage of such possibilities (Smith, 1998, 2000). Resources (skills and finance) still mean that party HQ is likely to be best placed to adopt high-tech campaigns and set the boundaries for local parties (Ward and Gibson, 2003).

- Content and style – challenging professionalisation? It's not just the way in which campaigns might be run but also the content and style of campaigns that could be altered by the rise of new technologies. We have already noted the possibilities for candidates and local parties to localise and personalise their campaigns more effectively. However, more radically, it could be suggested that the whole style of political communication might be affected, especially by social networking tools (Kalnes, 2009). In particular, the broadcast model of communication is challenged as voters come to expect greater degrees of dialogue and interactivity fostered, in part, by new technologies (Coleman, 2005; Williamson, 2010a). Indeed, some campaigners have argued that successful Web 2.0 campaigns will need to cede some control over the message to their audience (Christiansen and Roberts, 2009). Although the web might allow such diversification, several studies have indicated that, rather than increasing interactivity, the growth of web-based technologies is more likely to intensify data-gathering on, and surveillance of, voters to improve the marketing and targeting of party messages (Crabtree, 2010; van Onselen and van Onselen, 2008; Ward, 2005).

- Competitiveness – enhancing pluralism? One of the earliest ideas in the internet campaigns literature was the notion that online tools would enhance pluralism (Bimber, 1998) and increase the competitiveness of elections by challenging the dominance of mainstream parties and candidates (Corrado and Firestone, 1996; Selnow, 1998). The post-war era had seen increasingly sophisticated and expensive campaigns that tended to benefit resource-rich larger parties. Similarly, the development of the 'permanent campaign' allowed some incumbents to use office to gain name recognition and promote their record. Initially, it was thought that the relatively low level of resources required to run online campaigns, and the ability to bypass traditional media editors, would disproportionately benefit outsider or independent candidates and parties (Corrado and Firestone, 1996; Norris, 2000). Sceptics, however, countered by arguing that this line of argument overestimated the influence and reach of the net, while underestimating the continuing importance of resources (Bimber and Davis, 2003; Davis, 1999; Margolis and Resnick, 2000). Furthermore, it ignored the realities of the political environment and the rules of the electoral contest (electoral system, electoral threshold, media rules etc.) which in many countries eroded the ability of independents or outsiders to challenge effectively (Ward et al., 2008).

Online campaigning at the local level in the UK

Concerted studies of constituency-level online campaigning have been relatively limited thus far. Nevertheless, several trends can be highlighted from the existing research. First, there has been significant, if patchy, growth of candidates campaigning online over time. In 2005, the percentage of candidates with an online presence more than doubled to 37 per cent, with significantly higher percentages among main parties (Ward and Gibson, 2003; Ward et al., 2008). This was despite the fact that many commentators and politicians suggested that the internet was of relatively little importance in the campaign (Ward, 2005).

The pattern of competition online is not unexpected. Studies from 2005, and also between campaign periods, suggest that marginals see a greater range of activity, with the possibility of an additional 'me too' effect; that is, the presence of a leading candidate encourages other candidates to follow suit (Lusoli and Ward, 2005a; Sudulich and Wall, 2010). Moreover, in 2005, one could detect hotspots of web activity (Cambridge, Bristol, Leeds), not only reflecting the profile of individual candidates but also suggesting that the broader demographics of the constituency were influential in driving candidates online. Middle-class, urban/suburban constituencies with large student populations were especially likely to see increased web activity.

In terms of patterns of party competition, there is not much to suggest that challengers or minority parties gain any sustained advantage at the constituency level. Although the Liberal Democrats have often tended to be the initial pioneers with web technology, be it websites, blogs or Facebook, other main parties have generally caught up reasonably quickly (Williamson, 2008; Williamson et al., 2010). Indeed, in 2005, it was the Conservatives who led on the basis of simple web presence. As for non-parliamentary parties, with the exception of the Greens, very few of their candidates could be found online (Ward et al., 2008).

Arguments about the web leading to more personalisation of content, or decentralising the party message, are more contradictory. Although there have been instances of candidates going off-message (Ward and Gibson, 2003) and increased willingness of some candidates and MPs to adopt a more personalised approach through blogs (Francoli and Ward, 2008), there are also plenty of counter-trends. In general, candidates tend to self-censor their message anyway, and increasingly parties have provided templated website options or standardised design packages, some with party content produced nationally by the party– a trend also detected in Canada and Australia (Gibson et al., 2008; Smith and Chen, 2009). The Labour Party initially pioneered their web-in-a-box template, which provides a base level of professional web presence for local parties and MPs. However, in the run-up to 2005, the Conservative Party also provided a template for local parties with minimal standard content.

In both 2001 and 2005, parties and candidates were reluctant to engage in dialogue with voters, tending to see the costs as outweighing any benefit (Ward and Gibson, 2003; Ward et al., 2008). Hence, there were few opportunities for interactivity via either websites or email newsletters. The overall view of web campaigning (from the party perspective) at the local level was that it was of marginal importance at best. Most commentators felt that the web lacked a sufficient audience to be of much use; a view backed up by 2005 post-election survey data indicating that only 3 per cent of voters had visited a party or candidate site (Ward and Lusoli, 2005). Furthermore, it was also argued that systemic features in the UK eroded the value of web campaigning locally. Geographically, most UK constituencies are comparatively small-scale, and candidates expressed the view that traditional personal methods of campaigning (door-knocking, leafleting, street meetings) were more effective than email or websites (Ward, 2005).

While the experience of local campaigning so far has been relatively limited, in the run-up to the 2010 campaign there were suggestions that the internet might play a much greater role than previously, especially given the potential unpredictability of the outcome. Initially, there was considerable discussion in the media of the notion of an internet election,[1] just as there had been in 2001 and 2005 (Wring and Ward, 2010). Commentators looked enthusiastically towards the US and Obama's high-profile and savvy use of the internet and speculated whether the UK would see similar adoption of technology during the campaign. The expectation of a significant role for the internet was also built on the growth and increasing appeal of the technology itself. Since the previous campaign, the web had grown to reach a mass audience of around 70 per cent of the British public (Dutton et al., 2009). The political blogosphere, which was in its infancy in 2005, had become a central fixture of the Westminster landscape. What gained most attention, however, was the explosion of social media tools, notably Facebook and

Twitter. By late 2008, around 25 per cent of MPs had a Facebook site and about 10 per cent already had a Twitter account (Williamson, 2008). A further Hansard Society study indicated that there had been another surge among prospective parliamentary candidates in 2009, although most were still accused of being in broadcast mode rather than promoting real dialogue with voters (Williamson et al., 2010).

Research questions and methods

The aim of this chapter, then, is to examine the role of the internet at the local level in the context of debates about constituency campaigning. Hence, we investigate three main areas:

- Competition: what was the level of online activity among candidates and what was the pattern of party competition online? Did the Conservative Party maintain its dominance in terms of web presence from 2005? Did outsider parties make any impact? How far do marginality and incumbency matter in terms of web presence?
- Organisation: how far can we detect any localisation of campaigning, or is it still tempered by national influences (e.g. has the templating of online content continued?)
- Content/style: were candidates exploiting opportunities to personalise their message and engage in dialogue with electorate? In particular, to what extent did they adopt Web 2.0 tools and did this really lead to greater levels of openness and interactivity?

By way of conclusion, we also reflect on whether the net is likely to make much of a difference to campaigning at the local level.

In order to examine these questions we look, in particular, at two broad types of web campaigning: candidates' personal web presence and candidates' use of Web 2.0 technologies, such as Twitter, Facebook and blogging. Looking at web presence gives us an indicator of the extent of the localisation of web campaigning, particularly when we break this down into different types of web presence (see below).

Examination of candidates' personal campaign websites was done in the first week of the campaign, and the websites of each of the 2,425 candidates from the six largest parties (Labour, Conservatives, Liberal Democrats, UK Independence Party, Green Party and British National Party) standing in England were recorded.

The sites were categorised into three types: (1) a personal profile on a central party page; (2) a personal site that took the form of a template designed and endorsed by the central party organisation (so-called web in a box); and (3) an individually designed, independent site.

Due to time constraints and a desire to capture the most data possible for Web 2.0 use, this was limited to the 172 'most marginal' seats in England. This was selected using Ralling and Thrasher's notional majorities and taking into account the predicted 5 per cent national swing away from Labour. Any 'ultra-marginal' (less than 5 per cent swing needed to unseat incumbent) Labour-incumbent seat was removed (as these more than likely would not be the focus of the Labour campaign, having been given up for lost), and then all the seats up to and including a marginality of 12 per cent were included in the sample. Selecting each candidate from these seats gave a sample size of 770. For each of the 770 candidates, their use of the five most popular forms of Web 2.0 (Facebook, Twitter, YouTube, blogging and Flickr) was recorded.

Additionally, we also aimed to ascertain not only whether candidates were using these new technologies but whether they were using them to their full potential. One of the main advantages of using Web 2.0 in campaigning is its potential to engage directly with voters in a more interactive way than had been possible before with other types of web campaigning, thus providing us with a further indication of whether a new style of election campaign communication is emerging. When we collected the data for this part of the study, for each application that each candidate was using, four levels of use were recorded: static, active, open and interactive.

First, a binary measure of simply whether or not they were using each application was recorded. The number of updates for each type of Web 2.0 was also recorded in order to be able to gather whether the candidate was actively using it, and, if so, how regularly. Furthermore, it was noted whether the candidates' pages allowed comments. This was to capture whether they were open to feedback from their potential voters. Lastly, any actual responses to comments were gathered. This showed a true interaction and engagement with a potential constituent via Web 2.0 in a way that simply allowing comments would not. Responding to comments took the candidate into the 'Interactive' category.

Results

Internet presence in constituency campaigning: overall adoption trends

Table 15.1 shows the overall percentages of candidates' use of both different types of personal web presence and different types of Web 2.0

Table 15.1   Overall levels of web use

Personal Site	
No Website Found	13.80%
Profile on Party Page	39.40%
'Web in a Box'	16.00%
Independent Design	30.70%
Type of Web 2.0	
Facebook	41.80%
Twitter	33.90%
YouTube	33.10%
Blog	35.00%
Flickr	7.80%

technology. Drawing out the findings for personal websites, it is clear that the majority of candidates in England did make use of some form of web presence as part of their campaign. Only 13.8 per cent had no web presence whatsoever. However, this masks the extent to which the web presence of candidates was truly localised or independent, since well over half the candidates (56 per cent) used either a standardised page on the central party website (the most popular choice) or a 'web in box' style template. Just less than a third of candidates adopted their own independent design websites. One other striking feature is the relatively slow growth of web campaigning (at least in terms of basic presence). Although our figures here are not directly comparable to the previous 2005 study, if we exclude the central party page profiles, around 46 per cent of candidates managed their own site compared with a figure of around 37 per cent in 2005.

One possible explanation for the prevalence of simple profile pages may be down to campaign resources. The central party will fund and host the main party site and any pages on it. This means that a candidate will have to devote none of his or her own personal campaign budget and resources to a personal site on a central party page. For candidates with limited funds for their campaign, this is a cost-effective (indeed, free) way of acquiring a professional-looking personal campaign web space. While the popularity of web in a box type websites appears to be declining, they may still appeal to the less tech-oriented candidates who want a professionalised web presence but perhaps lack skills, resources or motivation to create and fully develop their own.

When assessing social media tools, it is worth remembering that most hadn't really entered the public domain in 2005 but are now being adopted rapidly by political campaigners. Only blogging had really made a mark before 2005, but was largely ignored by candidates in the last election. Our data from marginal constituencies suggest that the new tools have been adopted more quickly than previous Web 1.0 tools. Facebook, in particular, seems to have been popular, although all the so-called Web 2.0 tools (with the exception of Flickr) have seen significant minority adoption. Given the nature of social media, at face value, this might appear to confirm greater levels of personalisation and interactivity in constituency-based campaign; however, as we shall see later, the evidence is not necessarily so clear-cut.

Party competition online

Table 15.2 shows candidates' use of each different type of website, by party. Drawing out some general patterns from the data, one noticeable trend is that there is little evidence of increased online competitiveness from minor parties. The idea that the web provides some sort of resource-free level playing field is not borne out by the evidence. A candidate from one of the three main parties is more likely to have a professionally designed website than a candidate from one of the three smaller parties. Hence, 57.7 per cent of Conservative candidates and 43.2 per cent of Labour candidates had a personal website compared with only 3.2 per cent of BNP candidates and 7.9 per cent of Green candidates. Again, this follows a similar pattern to previous elections. Resources are clearly part of the explanation; the Liberal Democrats had fewer target seats to aim at, while the Greens, UKIP and BNP were focusing their resources and campaigns on just one or two seats where they believed they had a chance of making an impact, and to some extent this is reflected in the patterns of web presence.

Table 15.2   Type of personal website by party

	No Website	Party Profile	'Web in a Box'	Independent
BNP	69.0%	27.8%	0.0%	3.2%
Cons	0.9%	25.8%	15.6%	57.7%
Greens	21.6%	63.0%	7.5%	7.9%
Labour	20.5%	15.0%	21.4%	43.2%
LDs	6.3%	40.9%	27.3%	25.4%
UKIP	9.1%	73.3%	6.2%	11.3%
Total	13.8%	39.4%	16.0%	30.7%

Breaking the figures down by party reveals other notable trends in relation to competition and campaigning by the main parties. First, as in 2005, the Conservatives established a clear lead. Virtually all their candidates had some form of web presence. Moreover, Conservative candidates were more likely to have developed their own personal presence. Second, by contrast, over a fifth of Labour Party candidates were absent from the cyberspace campaign (almost level-pegging with the Greens in terms of a proportion of their candidates having no site). Some of this can be explained by the high number of personal profile pages that had been set up on the central party page in the candidate's name but remained empty. So, although a space was created for each candidate to set up a profile, it seems that submitting something for this space was not enforced in the same way that it clearly was for the Conservative, Liberal Democrat or even the UKIP site. Finally, while traditionally the Liberal Democrats have often been seen as the most enthusiastic and among the earliest adopters of web technology (Gibson and Ward, 1998; Ward and Gibson, 2003; Williamson et al., 2010), the 2010 figures suggest this lead is lost when it comes to election periods.

Looking more specifically at Web 2.0 campaigning (Table 15.3), the overall trends of adoption by technology seem to be reflected in party use, with the notable exception again being the BNP candidates. Twitter and Facebook didn't seem to hold much appeal for them, whereas their level of use of YouTube beats that of the Liberal Democrats and is similar to Labour.

Overall, the Conservatives had the highest level of use of Web 2.0. Well over half of their candidates had some sort of personal blog, which is almost double the level of Liberal Democrats blogging. They were the only party showing any sort of significant use of Flickr, and their use of YouTube is the highest of any party by a fair amount. Labour edges

Table 15.3 Use of Web 2.0 by party

	Twitter	Facebook	Blog	YouTube	Flickr
BNP	4.0%	8.0%	20.0%	36.0%	0.0%
Cons	44.0%	52.1%	58.0%	45.6%	17.9%
Greens	20.9%	38.4%	30.2%	24.4%	2.3%
LDs	44.5%	51.8%	32.3%	35.4%	7.3%
Labour	45.8%	54.2%	40.5%	37.5%	8.9%
UKIP	8.5%	11.3%	9.9%	14.9%	0.0%
Total	33.9%	41.8%	35.0%	33.1%	7.8%

them out of first place on Twitter and Facebook, but not to any significant degree.

The party with the lowest level of Web 2.0 use is the BNP. This is perhaps to be expected, due to the open nature of some types of Web 2.0 and the hostility there is towards this party. This is reflected in the results, showing that the less 'interactive' types of Web 2.0 are more popular with BNP candidates. The types where comments, for example, can be controlled were most popular. Most BNP blogs required one to sign up and sign in before a comment could be left on the site.

The Green Party were the best of the small parties in their level of Web 2.0 use. This fits in with their image as a progressive party with a young support base as well as their more grass-roots structure. However, if a traditionally young support base should equal a high level of Web 2.0 use, it seems that the Liberal Democrats, with their numerous student supporters, go somewhat against this pattern, as they do not top Labour on use of a single type of Web 2.0. So it may be that it is the culture of the party that drives uptake of Web 2.0 tools, rather than the demographic make-up of the expected supporters.

Personalisation and interactivity?
Web 2.0 and levels of engagement

Perhaps the most striking pattern to emerge from the table below (Table 15.4) is the large number of candidates that used the different technologies but did not actually update them more than once a week during the campaign. This would seem to suggest that a lot of candidates wanted to 'be seen' using the new forms of campaigning but were not committed to using the technology to its full potential or to actively engage with potential voters. Many of these pages remained unchanged throughout the campaign, acting as little more than a 'glorified cyber-leaflet'. In fact, for nearly every type of Web 2.0 except

Table 15.4 Levels of engagement by type of Web 2.0

	Facebook	Twitter	Blog	YouTube
No Use of Type of Web 2.0	58.2%	66.1%	65.0%	66.9%
Use but No Updates (Static)	17.0%	8.8%	8.5%	15.6%
Regular Updates (Active)	13.4%	6.6%	9.1%	12.9%
Very Regular (Active)	11.4%	18.4%	17.4%	4.6%
Allow Comments? (Open)	27.0%	–	19.5%	19.8%
Responds to Comments (Interactive)	9.2%	17.8%	1.3%	–

blogging, there were more candidates who used the application but did not update it than who made regular updates. For Facebook, 17 per cent were 'Static' compared with 13.4 per cent making regular updates, and of those using YouTube 15.6 per cent were 'Static', whereas only 12.9 per cent made regular updates.

However, when the two categories of 'Regular Updates' and 'Very Regular Updates' are combined, it is clear that more candidates were updating their pages than were keeping their profiles static. For instance, taking Facebook as an example, 17 per cent of those using this type of Web 2.0 for their campaign did not update during the past week. However, 24.8 per cent made either Regular (one or two) or Very Regular (three or more) updates in the past week. Regarding blogging, although 8.5 per cent of candidates who had a blog for campaigning made no blog posts during the past week, 25.5 per cent of blog users made either Regular (one post in the past week) or Very Regular (two or more posts in the past week) updates.

So, although it is clear that a relatively large proportion of candidates were using Web 2.0 in an ineffective or superficial manner, there were more candidates who were actively and regularly updating their pages throughout the campaign. However, simply making regular or even very regular updates is in many ways no different from certain forms of older, Web 1.0 types of campaigning, such as sending out an email newsletter. Indeed, often a lot less effort will have gone into a Facebook wall update or a Tweet than into a campaign e-newsletter. The flow of information is still largely one-way and top-down, from candidate to potential constituent. The real test of whether candidates were unlocking Web 2.0's full potential lies in their willingness to engage with their potential voters, either by allowing them to give feedback or by interacting with them fully by replying to that feedback. This is where the 'Open' and 'Interactive' variables are important.

Observing these two categories (Open and Interactive) and taking the two types of Web 2.0 where they are directly comparable, a rather stark pattern emerges. First, regarding Facebook, although 27 per cent of candidates allowed their 'Friends' to leave comments on any updates, only 9.2 per cent of them replied to these comments. For blogs, although 19.5 per cent of candidates allowed the readers of their blog to leave a comment, only 1.3 per cent read and replied to those comments. It is clear from these figures that the vast majority of candidates using Web 2.0 during their campaign were either unaware of how to use the technology to its full potential or were uninterested in doing so. One extreme example of this was a UKIP candidate who repeatedly 'tweeted' when he had no followers of his Twitter account.

Overall, the picture that emerges is that, although larger number of candidates overall were 'using' Web 2.0 during their campaign, very few of them used the technology in the way it was intended – to actively engage in a two-way flow of information, over the web, with supporters, followers and possible future voters.

Taking into account levels of engagement by party, the patterns above do somewhat mirror the general use of Web 2.0 in Table 15.3. For Facebook, UKIP and the BNP had the lowest percentage of candidates who responded to comments left on their Facebook wall, with only 2.1 per cent of UKIP candidates and no BNP candidates falling into this category. The Liberal Democrats performed best in this category, with 15 per cent of candidates responding to comments compared with the 9.2 per cent overall average. The Conservative and Labour candidates were in second and third place, with 11.7 per cent of Conservative candidates and 10.5 per cent of Labour candidates responding to comments. Green Party candidates were placed below the three main parties, but still did slightly better than the overall figure, with 9.3 per cent of them responding to comments. Nevertheless, the clear pattern is that the larger parties were better at being interactive via Facebook (Table 15.5).

Examining the results for Twitter, there is a very similar pattern of use to Facebook. No BNP candidates, and 2.1 per cent of UKIP candidates, responded to Tweets: the same percentage of UKIP candidates as responded to Facebook comments. Once again, the Liberal Democrats had the highest proportion of candidates who interacted, with 29.2 per cent of them responding to Tweets. The Conservatives follow, with 22.8 per cent of their candidates responding to Tweets, and, as for Facebook, Labour are in third place, with 14.3 per cent of their candidates responding to Tweets, slightly ahead of the Greens, 14.0 per cent of whose candidates responded to Tweets. From these results, it is clear that use of Facebook and Twitter, by party, follow largely similar patterns.

For blogging, when regarding the overall figure for Response to comments, the Green Party and the Conservatives outperform the rest, with 2.2 per cent and 3.0 per cent compared with the 1.3 per cent total figure. Labour are only slightly below the total, with 1.2 per cent, but the Liberal Democrats perform rather poorly, considering their position as the third largest party, with only 0.6 per cent of candidates surveyed responding to comments on their blogs. Perhaps more predictably, no candidates from either UKIP or BNP responded to comments. With the exception of the Green Party, the larger parties were more Interactive

Table 15.5   Levels of engagement by type of Web 2.0 by party

	BNP	Cons	Greens	LDs	Labour	UKIP	Total
Facebook							
No updates past week	92.0%	72.1%	71.8%	64.9%	70.8%	94.2%	75.2%
Regular updates	8.0%	14.5%	17.6%	13.2%	18.0%	5.1%	13.4%
Very Regular updates	0.0%	13.3%	10.6%	21.9%	11.2%	0.7%	11.4%
Open For Comment	0.0%	32.1%	26.7%	38.8%	34.0%	5.7%	27.0%
Responds to Comments	0.0%	11.7%	9.3%	15.0%	10.5%	2.1%	9.2%
Twitter							
No Updates	96.0%	67.3%	82.6%	66.7%	67.5%	92.3%	74.9%
Regular Updates	0.0%	8.8%	3.5%	4.0%	13.1%	2.8%	6.6%
Very Regular	4.0%	23.9%	14.0%	29.3%	19.4%	4.9%	18.4%
Responds to Tweets	0.0%	22.8%	14.0%	29.9%	14.3%	2.1%	16.8%
Blogging							
No past week	84.0%	55.6%	73.0%	71.3%	76.8%	92.3%	73.5%
Regular Posts	8.0%	13.6%	6.7%	9.8%	11.9%	1.4%	9.1%
Very Regular posts	8.0%	30.8%	20.2%	18.9%	11.3%	6.3%	17.4%
Open for comment	12.0%	26%	25.8%	24.4%	14.9%	9.2%	19.5%
Responds	0.0%	3.0%	2.2%	0.6%	1.2%	0.0%	1.3%
YouTube							
No updates	88.0%	80.5%	83.1%	76.2%	83.9%	89.4%	82.5%
Regular Updates	4.0%	14.8%	10.1%	17.1%	13.1%	9.2%	12.9%
Very Regular Updates	8.0%	4.7%	6.7%	6.7%	3.0%	1.4%	4.6%
Open for rating/ comment	28.0%	16.0%	19.8%	26.8%	20.8%	13.5%	19.8%

than the smaller ones, following a similar pattern to Facebook and Twitter, but the Liberal Democrats buck the trend for this type of Web 2.0, being the most interactive party for both Facebook and Twitter but falling well short here by coming in fourth place.

Lastly, examining the use of YouTube during the campaign shows rather different trends than for other types of Web 2.0. It should be noted here that, due to the way YouTube is used, there was no very reliable way of checking whether candidates might have responded to comments made to their videos. Therefore the highest level of engagement for YouTube is 'Open'. However, taking this highest level of use, the BNP are the party with the highest percentage of YouTube users who are open for comment and rating, at 28.0 per cent, in contrast to the other types of Web 2.0, where they exhibited the lowest percentage of high-level use. The Liberal Democrats are in second place, with 26.8 per cent of their candidates exhibiting the highest level of use. Labour's candidates are in third place with 20.8 per cent, followed by the Greens at 19.8 per cent. Perhaps most surprising is the figure for the Conservative candidates' use of YouTube. In terms of 'Openness' the Conservatives are in either first or second place for every other type of Web 2.0, but for YouTube they are second to last, at 16 per cent only outperforming UKIP (who are last or second to last on every other type of Web 2.0 for 'Openness') at 13.5 per cent.

It does not seem very clear why this should be, but it may be the nature of YouTube. It is not a social networking site, and so many candidates may have simply not thought about receiving feedback via YouTube. YouTube is not particularly well suited to a two-way flow of information; it is set up more as a platform to simply post clips onto rather than have 'conversations' – more suited to a top-down, one-way style of campaigning. This may have been why YouTube proved popular with the BNP. On YouTube, a video can still be watched without the comments overshadowing it, whereas on Twitter or Facebook a BNP candidate's wall/feed would be potentially overrun with negative comments.

Conclusions

Fifteen years on from its emergence in the UK, internet campaigning seems to support, rather than challenge, findings in the broader constituency campaign literature. Overall, new technologies have tended to accelerate many of the trends in constituency campaigning that were present before the internet emerged. Although we have seen increasing usage of web technologies and apparently rapid adoption of some of the Web 2.0 tools, their impact is somewhat tempered by a variety of factors. First, strikingly, the majority of candidates, barring a page on the national party website, still do not attempt to campaign online. Second, the internet is reinforcing the distinction between marginals/target seats and other constituencies where the web campaign is less intense. Third, the extent of localisation or decentralisation is limited by templated sites and standardised content, although this has reduced since 2005. Nevertheless, some online campaigning may give the appearance of localisation but is in fact driven primarily from the centre. Fourth, any decentralisation of campaigns via websites, email and social media is being more than countered by the increasing sophistication of database-driven campaigning, largely coordinated and controlled from the centre (Crabtree, 2010). Fifth, while the rapid adoption of Facebook, Twitter and blogs might suggest more diversification and a new style of communications, further analysis suggests that, as yet, most candidates have only cautiously adopted the technology, perhaps taking a 'wanting to be seen' rather than 'wanting to engage' approach. Finally, as Ward noted in 2005, there are also systemic limitations on internet campaigning in the UK. Despite the consistent (often unfavourable) comparisons in the media with the US, the political, social and media environment, as well as the electoral geography, of the UK mean that web tools are unlikely to be exploited to the same extent or in the same way.

In light of this, some might ask whether online constituency campaigning matters very much. Certainly, simply running a sophisticated online campaign, with added Web 2.0, is no guarantor of electoral success. As others have noted, there are plenty of candidates who won plaudits for their online efforts but did worse than one might expect, while others who did nothing online increased their votes (Williamson, 2010b). Nevertheless, survey evidence indicates that the numbers visiting party sites in 2010 (including candidate sites) increased five-fold from 2005, with around 15.5 per cent claiming to have accessed online party sites, suggesting that the audience is no longer insignificant (Gibson et al., 2010b). In addition, as Williamson found in the run-up to the 2010 campaign, there is now an increasing expectation, among younger voters especially, that politicians should be engaging online, even if voters remain suspicious of their motives for doing so. Although, unsurprisingly, the internet campaign might have failed to live up to the over-hyped expectations promoted in the press, there are increasing reasons to believe that not adopting the technology risks missing out on potential benefits such as message amplification, mobilisation of activists and organisational support, which contribute indirectly to successful campaigns.

Note

1. See, for example, John Harris, 'Welcome to the first internet election', *Guardian.co.uk*, 17 March 2010 (accessed on 21 May 2010); Patrick Wintour, 'The internet will be a giant force in election campaign says Lord Gould', *Guardian.co.uk*, 1 April 2010 (accessed on 21 May 2010); Jon Swaine, 'Facebook and Twitter to have unprecedented impact', *Telegraph.co.uk*, 6 April 2010 (accessed on 21 May 2010); Matt Warman, 'Never underestimate the power of the internet', *Telegraph.co.uk*, 7 April 2010 (accessed on 21 May 2010).

References

Bimber, B. (1998) 'The Internet and Political Transformation: Populism, Community and Accelerated Pluralism', *Polity*, 31(1): 133–160.

Bimber, B. and Davis, R. (2003) *Campaigning Online: The Internet and US Elections.* Oxford: Oxford University Press.

Blumler, J. and Kavanagh, D. (1999) 'The Third Age in Political Communication: Influences and Features', *Political Communication*, 16: 209–30.

Christiansen, K. and Roberts, M. (2009) 'Respect, empower and include: the new model army', in Anstead, N. and Straw, W. (eds) *The change we need: What Britain can learn from Obama's victory.* London: The Fabian Society.

Coleman, S. (2005) 'New mediation and direct representation: reconceptualizing representation in the digital age'. *New Media & Society*, 7(2): 177–98.

Corrado, A. and Firestone, C. (1996). *Elections in Cyberspace: Toward a new era in American Politics.* Washington DC: Aspen Institute.

Crabtree, J. (2010) 'Cameron's Battle to Connect', *Wired*, March.

Davis, R. (1999) *The Web of Politics.* New York: OUP.

Denver, D. and Hands, G. (2001) 'The fall and rise of constituency campaigning', in Bartle, J. and Griffiths, D. (eds) *Political Communications Transformed: from Morrison to Mandelson.* Basingstoke: Palgrave.

Denver, D., Hands, G., Fisher, J. and MacAllister, I. (2003) 'Constituency campaigning in Britain 1992–2001: Centralisation and Modernisation', *Party Politics*, 9(4): 541–59.

Dutton, W., Helsper, E. and Gerber, M. (2009) *The Internet in Britain 2009.* Oxford Internet Surveys, Oxford Internet Institute, University of Oxford.

Farrell, D. and Webb, P. (2000) 'Political Parties as Campaign Organizations', in Dalton, R. and Wattenberg, M. (eds) *Parties without Partisans.* Oxford: Oxford University Press, 102–28.

Fisher, J. and Denver, D. (2009) 'Evaluating the Electoral Effects of Traditional and Modern Modes of Constituency Campaigning in Britain 1992–2005', *Parliamentary Affairs*, 62(2): 196–210.

Fisher, J., Denver, D., Fieldhouse, E., Cutts, D. and Russell, A. (2005) 'Constituency Campaigning in the 2005 British General Election'. Paper presented to the EPOP conference, University of Essex.

Francoli, M. and Ward, S. J. (2008) '21st Century Soapboxes? MPs and their Blogs', *Information Polity*, 13 (1/2): 21–39.

Gibson, R. K. and McAllister, I. (2006) 'Does Cybercampaigning Win Votes? Online Political Communication in the 2004 Australian Election', *Journal of Elections, Public Opinion and Parties*, 16(3): 243–64.

Gibson, R. K. and McAllister, I. (2008) 'Do Online Election Campaigns Win Votes? The 2007 Australian *YouTube* Election.' Paper presented at the Annual Meeting of the American Political Science Association, 28–31 August, Boston.

Gibson, R. K. and Ward, S. J. (1998) 'UK Political Parties and the Internet: Politics as Usual in the New Media?' *Harvard International Journal of Press/Politics*, 3(3): 14–38.

Gibson, R. K., Lusoli, W. and Ward, S. J. (2008) 'Nationalizing and Normalizing the Local? A Comparative Analysis of Online Candidate Campaigning in Australia and Britain', *Journal of Information Technology and Politics*, 4(4): 15–30.

Gibson, R. K., Ward, S. J. and Williamson, A. (2010a) 'Introduction: Whatever happened to the Internet?' in Gibson, R. K., Ward, S. J. and A Williamson (eds) *The Internet and Election 2010: putting the small p back into politics.* London: Hansard Society, 1–4.

Gibson, R. K., Cantijoch, M. and Ward, S. J. (2010b) 'Citizen Participation in the e-campaign', in Gibson, R. K., Ward, S. J. and Williamson, A. (eds), *The*

Internet and Election 2010: putting the small p back into politics. London: Hansard Society, 5–16.

Jackson, N. and Lilleker, D. 'Just public relations or an attempt at interaction? British MPs in the press, on the web and in your face'. *European Journal of Communication*, 19(4): 507–34.

Johnson, R. and Pattie, C. (2003) 'Do canvassing and campaigning work? Evidence from the 2001 General Election in England', in Rallings, C., Scully, R., Tonge, J. and Webb, P. (eds) *British Elections and Parties Review XIII.* London: Frank Cass.

Johnston, R. and Pattie, C. (2009) 'MPs' Expenditure and General Election Campaigns: Do Incumbents Benefit from Contacting their Constituents?' *Political Studies*, 57(3): 580–91.

Kalnes, O. (2009) 'Political Parties on Web 2.0: The Norwegian Case'. *Journal of Information Technology Politics*, 6(3): 251–66.

Lusoli, W. and Ward, S. J. (2005) 'Logging On or Switching Off? The Public and the Internet at the 2005 General Election', in Coleman, S. and Ward, S. (eds) *Spinning the Web: Online Campaigning during the 2005 General Election.* London: Hansard Society, 13–21.

Margolis, M. and Resnick, D. (2000) *Politics as Usual? The Cyberspace Revolution.* London: Sage.

Norris, P. (2000) *A Virtuous Circle.* New York: Cambridge University Press.

Selnow, G. (1998) *Electronic Whistle-stops: The Impact of the Internet on American Politics.* Westport: Praeger.

Seyd, P. and Whiteley, P. (2003) 'Local party campaigning and voting behaviour in Britain', *Journal of Politics*, 56: 242–51.

Smith, C. (1998) 'Political Parties in the Information Age: from mass party to leadership organization', in Snellen, I and van de Donk, W. (eds) *Public Administration in the Information Age: A Handbook.* Amsterdam: IoS Press.

Smith, C. (2000) 'British Political Parties: Continuity and Change in the Information Age', in Hoff, J., Horrocks, I. and Tops, P. (eds) *Democratic Governance and New Technology.* London: Routledge, 57–70.

Smith, P. J. and Chen, P. J. (2009) 'A Canadian E-lection 2008? Online media and Political competition'. Paper presented to Canadian Political Science Association Conference, Ottawa, 27–29 May.

Sudulich, M. L. (2009) 'Do ethos, ideology, country and electoral strength make a difference in cyberspace? Testing an explanatory model of parties' websites'. Paper presented to ECPR Joint research workshops, Lisbon, 14–19 April.

Sudulich, M. L. and Wall, M. (2010) 'Every little Helps Cyber campaigning in the 2007 Irish General Election', *Journal of Information Technology and Politics*, 7(2): 340–55.

van Onselen, A. and van Onselen, P. (2008) 'On message or out of touch? Secure web sites and political campaigning in Australia', *Australian Journal of Political Science*, 43(1): 43–58.

Ward, S. J. (2005) 'The Internet and 2005 Election: Virtually Irrelevant?' in Geddes, A. and J. Tonge (eds) *The Nation Decides: The 2005 General Election.* Palgrave: Basingstoke, 188–206.

Ward, S. J. and Gibson, R. K. (2003) 'Online and On message? Candidate Websites in the 2001 General Election', *British Journal of Politics and International Relations*, 5(2): 188–205.

Ward, S. J. and Lusoli, W. (2005) 'From Weird to Wired? MPs, the Internet and Representative Politics in the UK', *Journal of Legislative Studies*, 11(1): 57–81.

Ward, S. J., Gibson, R. K. and Lusoli, W. (2008) 'Not Quite Normal? Parties and the 2005 UK Online Election Campaign', in Davis, R., Owen, D., Taras, D. and S.J. Ward, S. J. (eds) *Making a Difference? Internet Campaigning in Comparative Perspective*. Lanham' MD: Lexington Books, 133–60.

Whiteley, P. and Seyd, P. (2002) *High Intensity Participation*. Michigan: University of Michigan Press.

Williamson, A. (2008) *MPs Online: Connecting with Constituents*. London: Hansard Society.

Williamson, A. (2010a) *Digital Citizens and Democratic Participation*. London: Hansard Society.

Williamson, A. (2010b) 'Inside the Digital Campaign', in Gibson, R. K., Ward, S. J. and Williamson, A. (eds) *The Internet and Election 2010: putting the small p back into politics*. London: Hansard Society, 17–26.

Williamson, A., Miller, L. and Fallon, F. (2010) *Behind the Digital Campaign: An exploration of the use, impact and regulation of digital campaigning*. London: Hansard Society.

Wring, D. and Ward, S. (2010) 'The Media and the 2010 Campaign: the Television Election?', *Parliamentary Affairs*, 63(4): 802–17.

Zittel, T. (2009) 'Lost in Technology? Political Parties and Online Campaigning in Germany's Mixed Member Electoral System', *Journal of Information Technology and Politics*, 6(3/4): 298–311.

Part VI
Media

16
Playing by the Rules: The 2009 MPs' Expenses Scandal

Jennifer vanHeerde-Hudson

The limited impact of the biggest Parliamentary scandal in 200 years

In May 2009, *The Daily Telegraph* began publishing uncensored details of expenses claims made by members of the UK House of Commons. Although the vast majority of those submitted were within the rules governing parliamentary allowances, various claims, including some for gardening and cleaning services, plasma TVs, toilet roll holders, £500,000 for the five abstentionist Sinn Fein MPs and even Hob Nob biscuits, triggered public fury and indignation. Against the backdrop of the banking and financial crises and the persistent economic downturn, MPs were caught up in what then Prime Minister Gordon Brown called the 'biggest parliamentary scandal for two centuries'.[1]

The fallout of the MPs' expenses scandal was not limited to a few serious offenders. Vilified in the press, many of those implicated announced this would be their last parliamentary term within days of the *Telegraph*'s revelations. In total, 148 MPs stood down before the May 2010 General Election, including cabinet and ministerial resignations, but the biggest scalp was that of Speaker Michael Martin, the first speaker to resign in some 300 years following criticism of his handling of the ensuing crisis.

Properly understood, the expenses scandal, and the public anger that arose as a result, was not about castigating politicians as criminals or indeed criminal behaviour in the true sense of the term; of the millions of claims submitted, only a very small number of MPs were accused of criminal wrongdoing.[2] What was perceived to be especially problematic was the lack of transparency and accountability that governed the parliamentary allowances scheme. That MPs had apparently sought to keep expenses details from being disclosed, and were essentially free to regulate their own activities, reinforced for many of the public a belief that politicians and those in Parliament were 'out of touch' with the lives of 'ordinary' British citizens and subject to a different set of rules and standards.

The public's reaction to the *Telegraph's* revelation was, with few exceptions, disgust and outrage. Unlike other political crises that often fail to capture the public imagination, some 95 per cent of voters surveyed in June 2009 had heard of the scandal, with 91 per cent being angered by it, and 82 per cent feeling that MPs who were implicated in the expenses scandal should resign immediately. Moreover, survey data suggested that the public overwhelmingly disagreed with the sentiment that the scandal was somehow unimportant (Clarke *et al.*, 2009). Nearly one year on from the crisis, evidence from a YouGov (2010) survey showed that only a small fraction of the public thought the expenses scandal a minor matter that had been exaggerated by the public; 83 per cent suggested it was a major scandal that shamed Parliament.

The expenses crisis was a major media story of the last parliament, which at its height even rivalled the drama of the Blair/Brown saga as well as the ongoing fallout from the economic crisis. Arguably the first indication of the scandal's electoral impact came in June 2009 with the results of the European elections. With the expenses scandal still fresh in voters' minds, turnout (34.7 per cent) was down nearly four percentage points compared with 2004. Here it was largely Labour voters who stayed at home, with nearly one million fewer supporters going to the polls. Consequently the party bore the brunt of public anger and polled third behind the Conservatives and the UK Independence Party (UKIP). For the first time in nearly 100 years Labour polled behind the Tories in Wales – a traditional party stronghold.

The impact of the MPs' expenses scandal on the 2010 General Election was less obvious than some had predicted. Recent work by Clarke *et al.* (2009) has shown that, while the scandal did influence vote choice, the impact of expenses was mitigated by 'pulse-decay', essentially the time between the unfolding of events in the spring of 2009 and the election in May 2010. This finding of a 'dissipating effect' echoes previous work on the impact of scandals on the vote, although it tells us less about for whom the issue was important, not to mention their subsequent behaviour. Most recently, Pattie and Johnston (2010) have argued that, while public anger had declined little since the initial revelations, the impact on the election was relatively minor.

In this regard, the MPs' expenses scandal bears some resemblance to the scandal involving members of the US House of Representatives. In September 1991, the General Accounting Office revealed that many Representatives had written over 8,000 overdrafts on personal chequeing accounts held with the House bank. Because the bank had covered cheques members wrote on overdrawn accounts, it had, in effect, enabled the politicians to benefit from interest-free loans (Dimock and Jacobson, 1995; Jacobson and Dimock, 1994). Although the House originally resisted disclosing the list of offenders, it eventually capitulated and the names of those members who had issued the cheques were made public. The fallout from the scandal resulted in a record number of retirements and a decline in congressional approval ratings, although the impact of the scandal on the subsequent elections in November 1992 has been shown to be limited (Banducci and Karp, 1994; Dimock and Jacobson, 1995).

The lack of a direct electoral impact on the 2010 General Election was partly demonstrated by the relatively poor showing of independent candidate and high-profile celebrity broadcaster Esther Rantzen in the Luton South constituency previously represented by Margaret Moran. Moran's £100,000 claim in relation to a second home in Hampshire that was some distance from her seat as well as from Westminster had been the focus of much discussion and had led to Rantzen declaring her intention to contest the seat. The MP's subsequent decision to stand down in 2010 removed much of the rationale for the celebrity's candidature; nevertheless, she carried on her campaign in Luton, but ultimately failed. But, unlike previous high-profile interventions involving independent candidates, Rantzen lost her deposit.

Arguably the more substantial impact of the expenses scandal has been on public perceptions of MPs' probity and levels of trust in them and in Parliament. A recent report by the Hansard Society (2010) noted that trust in politicians has not fallen measurably since the expenses scandal, as the percentage of respondents saying they trust politicians either 'a great deal' or 'a fair amount' was down by just 1 per cent from the number who did so in 2004. However, more respondents (6 per cent) say they trust politicians 'not at all' than in previous years. Thus, according to their report, the expenses scandal has not contributed to a significant decline in trust in politicians, as this was already at low levels. If trust is relatively stable, what does appear to have suffered is belief in the probity of Members of Parliament. There is ample survey evidence to suggest that the public think that MPs spend their time furthering personal and career interests (50 per cent) (Hansard Society,

2010), are unprincipled (47 per cent), are more interested in serving their own personal interests (66 per cent), dishonest (48 per cent), and out of touch with the day-to-day lives of their constituents (70 per cent) (YouGov, 2010). The long-term consequences of the expenses scandal may be unknown, but the damage to the reputation of MPs and Parliament more generally is well documented.

The remainder of this chapter details the unfolding of the expenses scandal as a major news media story that dominated the political agenda for an inordinate length of time. The piece also analyses correlates of involvement in the expenses scandal and, similarly to Stewart (1994: 521), who examined factors that 'could tempt members of that party to use a public institution for private gain', assesses whether and how expenses claims made by MPs varied according to party, seniority, or electoral security, to explore which MPs were more likely to have been implicated in the expenses scandal.

A scandal unfolds

The disclosure of MPs' expenses claims was nothing short of a perfect storm that dominated media coverage in the weeks that followed the *Telegraph's* initial revelations. However, the origins of the scandal date back to 2004, when Heather Brooke, an investigative journalist, began making requests to the House of Commons Freedom of Information Office to release information concerning MPs' expenses. In January 2005, with the Freedom of Information Act (2000) in place, Brooke made several requests for information relating to MPs' travel, second homes and staff, but was rebuked following personal interventions from Michael Martin, which ultimately contributed to his resignation as Speaker in May 2009.

In 2006 the Information Commissioner, Richard Thomas, considered three related requests – one from Brooke and two from journalists at the *Sunday Times* and *Sunday Telegraph* – to release expenses details on key members, including a number of cabinet and shadow cabinet members, Prime Minister Gordon Brown and Conservative Party leader David Cameron. The Commissioner ordered a partial release of the information requested, but Parliament intervened and the requests were passed on to the Information Tribunal on appeal. The Tribunal upheld the Commissioner's decision, but again Parliament intervened, this time taking the decision to the High Court, which found in favour of the requesters and released the data in May 2008. Parliament made one final attempt to exempt itself from FOI legislation, but the motion encountered significant opposition in the House. Ultimately, Parliament agreed to disclose information regarding expenses claims in June 2009.[3]

Parliament's publication of expenses claims was, however, spectacularly thwarted by the *Telegraph's* acquisition of a disk containing millions of non-redacted claims dating back to 2004. John Wick, a former SAS officer, sold the disk to the *Telegraph* for £300,000 with two important conditions: first, that the *Telegraph* had just ten days to start publishing the details of MPs' expenses claims and, second, that the alleged abuse of expenses would not be used for partisan purposes, but would expose what was believed to be systematic abuse of parliamentary allowances (Winnett and Rayner, 2009).[4] News of expenses claims for some of the Labour party's most senior MPs first went public on evening news programmes on 7 May; the next morning the *Telegraph* published detailed expense claims for the Prime Minister, Chancellor Alistair Darling and several members of the cabinet. For three days, the *Telegraph* focused exclusively on expense claims from MPs in the Labour party, until 10 May, when the paper turned its attention to the Tories for two days before releasing information on claims for members of all political parties.

'Are we only allowed to buy things in the 99p store?'[5]

The expenses scandal was the result of what was perceived to be widespread inappropriate use of a system to compensate MPs for costs incurred while carrying out their parliamentary duties. In addition to their annual salary, MPs could claim for expenses for staff wages, IT provision, travel, stationery/postage, and costs associated with running their constituency office. MPs residing outside inner London were also entitled to claim costs associated with buying and furnishing second homes, and the day-to day-costs of maintaining these, under the Additional Cost Allowance (ACA) scheme.[6] The scheme allowed MPs to claim up to £24,000 annually for mortgage interest, gardening and cleaning expenses, utilities and council tax. In addition, MPs were entitled to keep the profits from selling taxpayer-subsidised second homes and forgo any capital gains taxes.

Of the millions of claims made by MPs, only a small number were in violation of the rules governing allowances. However, it was those claims and practices within the rules – and indeed the rules themselves – that became the focus of public ire and political action. Detailed reports of the range of expense claims prompted both amusement and disgust.

Some of the more widely reported claims included Sir Peter Viggers' floating duck house, Douglas Hogg's moat cleaning expenses, Margaret Beckett's £600 hanging baskets and potted plants, and Michael Gove's lavishly furnished home. Of the more sizeable claims, David Chaytor and Elliot Morley received £13,000 and £16,000, respectively, for interest payments against mortgages that allegedly no longer existed, while their colleague Jim Devine is alleged to have used false invoices for cleaning services. All three soon to be ex-MPs were charged with false accounting in connection with their parliamentary expenses claims, and, despite their mounting a legal challenge claiming that expenses claims fall under the protection of parliamentary privilege, the Supreme Court has upheld the charge and the cases are being heard in Court.

A good deal of press coverage highlighted the extensive practice of 'flipping' – the practice of re-designating one's second home to maximise claims related to maintenance, refurbishment or mortgage interest under the ACA allowances. While re-designating a second home did not violate rules governing expenses, it was the belief that many MPs had used the system to their advantage that invited public ire. Ed Balls and Yvette Cooper, both cabinet ministers in the previous government, were referred to the parliamentary sleaze watchdog for the way in which they designated their second homes; Alistair Darling was shown to have flipped his second home four times; and Hazel Blears switched her designated second home three times in a single year. Married MPs Andrew MacKay and Julie Kirkbride both resigned after coming under intense pressure for claims nearing £250,000 on separate second homes. Other high-profile controversies included Barbara Follett, married to writer and best-selling author Ken Follett, who claimed £25,000 for private security patrols at her home. Similarly, another of the wealthiest MPs, Shaun Woodward, received nearly £100,000 in mortgage interest on a million-pound flat he owned.

Finding themselves facing an unprecedented onslaught of public fury, MPs responded to the allegations differently. Although a number chose to defend their actions as being within the rules of the allowances system, many made immediate and conciliatory apologies – which included offers to repay any transgressions highlighted by the *Telegraph*. And, as noted above, many MPs chose to stand down rather than contest the 2010 General Election. Perhaps unwisely, Tory MP Anthony Steen told a reporter that much of the public fury over his expenses was the result of plain old 'jealousy' for the fact that his house, for which he claimed just under £90,000 in expenses over four years, resembles Balmoral.[7]

The response from the political parties was far more conciliatory. Conservative party leader David Cameron was widely judged to have best read and responded to the public mood, calling for shadow ministers and backbenchers to pay back expenses identified by the *Telegraph* some five days after the initial revelations. Although Gordon Brown soon followed suit, some in the Labour party and the press saw a missed opportunity for him to exploit an advantage. Labour's so called 'star chamber', a disciplinary panel set up by its National Executive Committee to adjudicate claims brought against the most serious offenders, was meant to ensure that the party retained control over which candidates would stand in 2010 and de-selected Anne Moffat, Jim Devine, Frank Cook and Ian Gibson, among others. However, the party's desire to be seen to be doing something partly rebounded when Gibson, who felt particularly hard done by and received some sympathetic media treatment, immediately resigned his seat to force a by-election that his party subsequently lost.

The Fees Office, which was responsible for processing parliamentary expenses claims, had neither the remit nor the resources to monitor the tens of thousands of expenses receipts submitted each year. Consequently, the allowances system was self-policing: MPs were free to establish the types and limits of allowances they could claim, with little external oversight. In response to the scandal, all three main parties publicly supported an independent investigation into Member's ACA claims, resulting in some £1.3m in repayments and the creation of the Independent Parliamentary Standard Authority (IPSA) to establish and administer new rules governing parliamentary expenses. Inter alia, the new rules limit expenses claims for second homes, require MPs to submit receipts for claims of any size, and abolished resettlement grants (worth tens of thousands of pounds) for MPs who have lost their seat or retired. However, IPSA has recently announced that, while it will publish individual MPs' claims, it will not publish the corresponding receipts, citing poor value for taxpayer's money. While the new system has come under heavy criticism from some MPs, many accept that it goes some way to restoring public confidence and trust by taking control over expenses away from MPs themselves and placing this in the hands of an independent body.

Using a public institution for private gain? Analysis of expenses claims and controversies

The next section examines MPs' expenses claims for the 2005–10 Parliament.[8] The data come from four principal sources: expense claims for 2007–9, Sir Thomas Legg's review of past Additional Cost Allowance claims, the Electoral Commission's 2001 and 2005 General Election reports and a content analysis of newspaper reports on expenses in the two weeks that followed the *Telegraph*'s revelations. Two measures of claims are used: first, the average of total claims made for 2007–8 and 2008–9,[9] and, second, the amount an MP was asked to repay following Legg's review of ACA claims. The two variables provide important but distinct measures of the types of claims members make on allowances. The first measures the extent to which MPs use the allowances they have available to them; the second variable taps the extent to which Members were understood to have made claims that were perceived to be problematic for various reasons. This was a complex issue, because, as many MPs implicated in the scandal argued in their own defence, they were simply claiming what 'the rules allowed'. However, the said irregularities were not uniformly distributed across each of the nine categories of expense, but were concentrated in the Additional Costs Allowances. But simply looking at total ACA claims raised issues to do with validity, as is the case with the first measure: the amount of claims is not necessarily an indicator of abuse. The amount MPs were requested to repay following Legg's review of past ACA claims, therefore, helps sifts out those claims that were not contentious from those that were.

Following Stewart (1994), the explanatory variables are grouped into two categories: the first associated with the MPs' institutional position (party membership, seniority, chamber status and marginality); and the second associated with their individual circumstances (age, sex and wealth). One potential set of explanations for variation in expense claims stems from characteristics of individual MPs. First among these is wealth. To the extent that expense claims are associated with financial hardship, we would expect wealthier MPs to claim less in expenses, particularly ACA expenses. To measure wealth, I use an ordered variable that captures sources of income in addition to MPs' parliamentary salary.[10] Using the *Register of Members' Interests*, four sources were coded: remunerated directorships, remunerated employment, land and property, and registrable holdings. MPs reporting no interests across these four categories were coded 0.[11] A further factor is age. As noted in Stewart (1994: 525), this captures a number of factors 'that are difficult to measure but may be related to expense claims'. Here, young MPs, who are likely to have fewer assets than their more senior colleagues, may be more likely to rely on expenses, particularly ACA–related, that fund the cost of running a second home and weekly allowances for food.

Finally, despite a priori evidence to suggest that men and women rely on different judgements in making business-related decisions (Betz *et al.*, 1989) – which may affect how and the extent to which MPs use their allowances – how gender affects expenses claims is less clear. Although Bampton and Maclagan's (2009) evidence shows that women employ an 'ethic of care' in decision-making and consequently are more likely to engage in moral behaviour, Dawson (1992: 24) demonstrates that, where decisions affect 'one's personal conscience such as padding an expense account', women behave similarly to men. This suggests two hypotheses: first, that average expenses for male and female MPs are statistically indifferent; and, second, because women's social norms reinforce a sense of 'following the rules', they are less likely to abuse expenses. In other words, female MPs may claim just as much as their male counterparts, but they are less likely to engage in 'abusive' behaviour.

The second group of explanatory variables focuses on MP's institutional position and the extent to which institutional privileges affect MPs' use of parliamentary allowances. These variables are similar to those employed by Stewart (1994: 525), and test the extent to which 'involvement in the scandal was prompted by the arrogance of power' and institutional security. Party membership is dummy variable coded 1 if the MP was a member of the Labour party, 0 otherwise. Status measures political or policy influence within the chamber and is a dummy variable coded 1 if the MP held the position of cabinet minister, shadow cabinet minister, chair of a permanent select committee or speaker/deputy speaker. Seniority is measured as the total number of years of service in the House of Commons. Marginality is measured as the average of the percentage difference between the first and second-place parties in the 2001 and 2005 General Elections. For those MPs elected after the May 2005 General Election, I used the average of the difference between the first and second-place parties for the 2005 General Election and the by-election results.

Table 16.1 shows the top claimers for 2007–8 and 2008–9 for total expenses claims. The average claim for 2007–8 was £144,207, and £147,762 in 2008–9. Table 16.1 shows that MPs Michael Connarty, Fabian Hamilton, Eric Joyce and Mohammad Sarwar are consistently high claimers, while Philip Hollobone, Dennis Skinner, Desmond Swayne and Alan Williams are among the lowest. Perhaps surprisingly, so is former Speaker Michael Martin, who, in his role as former Speaker, is entitled to live in a grace and favour mansion and is also entitled to the additional cost allowance. In terms of electoral impact, there is no relation to high/low claims and outcome. Only one of the sixteen

Table 16.1 'Saints and sinners': highest and lowest total expense claims for 2007–8 and 2008–9

	MP	2007–8	General Election Result	MP	2008–9	General Election Result
Top ten highest claims						
1	Joyce, Eric	187,334	Won	Sarwar, Mohammad	192,987	Did not stand
2	Connarty, Michael	183,466	Won	Godsiff, Roger	189,338	Won
3	Carmichael, Alistair	176,190	Won	Robertson, Angus	188,164	Won
4	Wallace, Ben	175,523	Won	Alexander, Danny	187,625	Won
5	Sarwar, Mohammad	174,882	Did not stand	Connarty, Michael	187,032	Won
6	Kennedy, Charles	174,232	Won	Joyce, Eric	186,548	Won
7	Anderson, David	173,556	Won	Hamilton, Fabian	184,071	Won
8	Borrow, David	172,706	Lost	Allen, Graham	183,487	Won
9	McGovern, James	171,989	Won	Meale, Alan	182,933	Won
10	Hamilton, Fabian	171,824	Won	Doran, Frank	182,139	Won
Bottom ten lowest claims						
1	Hollobone, Philip	47,737	Won	Russell, Bob	14,968	Won
2	Skinner, Dennis	66,933	Won	Hollobone, Philip	46,931	Won
3	Martin, Michael	74,522	Resigned	Johnson, Boris	48,477	Did not stand
4	Williams, Alan	80,526	Did not stand	Martin, Michael	56,067	Resigned
5	Taylor, Richard	86,484	Lost	Marshall, David	58,069	Won
6	Winterton, Nicholas	89,133	Won	Skinner, Dennis	68,245	Won
7	Sharma, Virendra	93,052	Won	Howell, John	70,559	Won
8	Swayne, Desmond	94,753	Won	Bercow, John	86,344	Won (Speaker)
9	Winnick, David	96,202	Won	Swayne, Desmond	90,273	Won
10	Dobson, Frank	97,840	Won	Williams, Alan	91,689	Did not stand

(Note: MPs in italics denote bottom ten in both 2007–8 and 2008–9)

highest claimers (four MPs appeared in both 2007–8 and 2008–9 lists) lost their bid for re-election, with only Sarwar standing down. As in the US House Banking Scandal, many of the most serious offenders stood down prior to the general election, and, in doing so, prevented voters from potentially punishing the highest claimers. Of the lowest claimers, Richard Taylor lost his Wyre Forest seat, Alan Williams did not stand, and Boris Johnson also did not stand, as he was elected Mayor of London in 2008. Somewhat ironically, former Speaker Michael Martin, one of the lowest claimers in both 2007–8 and 2008–9, resigned over his handling of the expenses crisis.

Although the disclosure of MPs' expenses by the *Telegraph* was intended to hold all parties accountable for their behaviour, there was some disquiet within Labour that focusing on their party for the first three days had created a perception among some of the public that this was a problem created by and endemic to their MPs. Although the Tories did get their turn four days later, the move to concentrate on Labour first was deemed by some to reflect the *Telegraph*'s long and favourable relationship with the Conservative party. This chapter does not examine public perceptions as to which party's MPs claimed more and were responsible for most of the controversy, but seeks, rather, to determine whether expense claims made in 2007–9 differ systematically by gender, party, seniority and electoral security or marginality of the constituency.

Table 16.2a and b show the results of independent samples t-tests for each grouping, by total claims and by expenses MPs were asked to repay as a result of the Legg review. The data in Table 16.2a show that in every case there is a statistically significant difference in the mean total expenses claimed. With respect to party differences, Labour MPs (£149,167) claimed more on average than other parties' MPs (£142,240). When just the two main parties are compared, the difference in mean claims is even larger. On average Labour MPs claimed £149,167 and Conservative MPs claimed £138,582 ($t = -6.64$, $p = 0.000$).

The data also show gender differences in average claims made over the period, with female MPs claiming £3,000 more on average than their male counterparts. Average expenses claims also differed by seniority and the marginality of the constituency the MP represented. Senior MPs – those serving more than fifteen years in the House of Commons – claimed £6,000 less on average compared with more junior MPs.[12] Finally, MPs from marginal constituencies claimed £3,000 more than MPs from non-marginal constituencies. Both of these latter two findings run somewhat contrary to how we might expect junior and more vulnerable MPs to behave.

Table 16.2a Tests of difference for total claims

	Mean	Std Dev	t	Sig
Men	145,449	18,767	−2.01	0.05
Women	148,452	13,638		
Labour	149,167	15,988	4.86	0.001
Other	142,240	19,400		
Low Seniority	148,305	16,802	−4.49	0.001
High Seniority	141,707	19,228		
Marginal (≤10%)	148,628	17,324	−2.01	.05
Not Marginal (>10%)	145,238	18,069		

Table 16.2b Tests of difference for expenses repaid

	Mean	Std Dev	t	Sig
Men	1,796	4,208	−0.114	0.91
Women	1,850	5,316		
Labour	1,558	3,569	−1.43	0.15
Other	2,096	5,243		
Low Seniority	1,453	3,802	2.40	0.02
High Seniority	2,469	5,348		
Marginal (≤10%)	1,700	4,554	0.315	0.75
Not Marginal (>10%)	1,837	3,959		

Table 16.2b shows the results of independent samples t-tests examining differences among groups in terms of the amount MPs were requested to pay back. With respect to party differences, other party members were asked to pay back more on average than Labour MPs, suggesting that, while Labour MPs claimed more on average, they were less likely to abuse their claims. However, the mean difference is not statistically significant. Again, however, when just Labour and Conservative MPs are compared, Conservative MPs were asked to pay back more, approximately £1,000 on average (£2,566) than Labour MPs (£1,558) (t = 2.06, p = 0.04). As shown in Table 16.2a, female MPs claimed more on average and were also asked to pay more back; however, the difference between male and female MPs was less than £60 and not statistically significant. Table 16.2b tells a different story with respect to seniority and

marginality. In this case more senior MPs were asked, on average, to pay back more than £1,000 (p=0.02), with those MPs representing safe seats being asked to pay back just over £100 (p=0.76).

Thus far the data suggest significant differences in the amount MPs claimed by party, gender, seniority and electoral security; however, these differences are not robust when examining the amount repaid. In terms of party differences, there is some evidence to suggest that Labour did indeed make more use of allowances than did MPs from other parties; however, Labour were seemingly more responsible in their claims in the first instance. Neither finding is likely to please the public, but whether one agrees with the allowances system or not – and many didn't – claims by most Labour MPs were determined to be within the rules. What factors, however, explain variation in total expenses over 2007–9? Table 16.3 shows the results of claims as a function of Members' institutional position and individual characteristics. With regard to the latter, only age was a significant predictor of expense claims, with older MPs claiming less than their younger colleagues. Being male and being wealthier are positively related to expense claims; however, neither of these variables reaches traditional levels of significance. In terms of MPs' position within the chamber, the data suggest that seniority, marginality and status are negatively related to total claims made; however, only

Table 16.3 Determinants of expense claims, 2007–9

	b	t	p<|t|
Age	−395.6 (98.28)	−4.03	0.001
Male	1,061.1 (1,771.74)	0.60	0.54
Wealth	13.35 (717.37)	0.02	0.98
Labour	9,466.1 (1,643.20)	5.76	0.00
Status	−1,401.6 (1790.24)	−0.78	0.43
Marginality	−130.24 (60.34)	−2.16	0.03
Seniority	−224.14 (113.40)	−1.98	0.49
Constant	168,125.7	34.91	0.00

marginality is statistically significant (p=0.03). The longer MPs have sat in the Commons and the more marginal their constituencies, the less likely they are to claim as much in expenses. The same is true for those MPs holding high-ranking or prestigious positions. Finally, on average Labour MPs were more likely to claim higher expenses than MPs from other political parties (p=0.001).

While the data in Table 16.3 demonstrate those factors that contribute to making higher claims, Table 16.2a and b show that claiming more doesn't necessarily indicate exploitation of the allowances system. Determining who were perceived to have transgressed over their expenses requires a dependent variable that better taps the extent to which claims that were made were in apparent contravention of the rules governing parliamentary allowances. Because a vast majority of the claims that featured in the *Telegraph*'s revelations were ACA claims (which was the focus of Sir Thomas Legg's review), I use the amount MPs were asked to pay back as the dependent variable to measure whether their expense claims were problematic.[13] Although Legg's review was criticised, particularly by MPs who perceived Legg to be applying a different set of rules and standards to existing claims, the measure provides a good indication of those MPs whose activities were controversial. Legg's review shows that repayments were required of those MPs who did break the rules by claiming both capital and mortgage interest when only interest was allowable, by submitting duplicate claims, for over-claiming against set limits, or for simple 'accounting' errors.

Table 16.4 presents the results of two models, the first using repayments as the dependent variable, and the second using repayments interacted with press mentions of an individual MP's expenses claims. Of the three explanatory variables related to total claims – age, marginality, and Labour party membership – none are found to be significantly related to repayments. Indeed, age reverses signs from the first model, but status and marginality remain negatively signed. Wealth is positively signed and statistically significant, which runs counter to the stated hypothesis. Rather than less wealthy members using expenses to supplement their incomes, it is in fact the wealthiest MPs who are more likely to have been queried over their parliamentary allowances. The results show that, on average, male MPs repaid less than female MPs; however, the relationship is not statistically significant. Of the four institutional variables, only seniority, which is positively related to repayments, is statistically significant. Thus, the evidence suggests that, counter to many of the hypotheses, it was not younger, less well-off MPs who made use of parliamentary allowances, but precisely those

Table 16.4 Determinants of abuse of Additional Claims Allowance (ACA)

	Model 1			Model 2		
	B	**t**	**p<|t|**	**b**	**t**	**p<|t|**
Age	17.69 26.81	0.66	0.51	18.10 98.38	0.18	0.85
Male	−629.5 492.70	−1.28	0.20	−2,770.3 1,807.82	−1.53	0.12
Wealth	548.7 196.80	2.79	0.005	2,206.1 722.10	3.06	0.002
Labour	−69.6 443.76	−0.16	0.87	−712.22 1,628.27	−0.44	0.66
Status	−79.3 477.63	−0.17	0.86	897.3 1,752.54	0.51	0.60
Marginality	−18.3 16.27	−1.13	0.25	−56.7 59.72	−0.95	0.343
Seniority	68.4 30.79	2.22	0.027	338.5 112.98	3.00	0.003
Constant	335.7	0.26	0.79	−13.26	−0.00	0.998

MPs who had been in Parliament for some time and had more opportunities to supplement their income.

The second model employs a modified dependent variable, repayments interacted with the number of press citations each MP received in the two weeks following the *Telegraph*'s initial disclosure. A citation was coded in instances where the MP's expenses, either explicitly or implicitly, were alleged as problematic. As coverage of the scandal dominated media reports, the variable was intended to analyse those expense claims that were perceived to be the most outrageous or extravagant, even though the amount the MP was asked to repay may have been small.[14] Using this measure, the results are similar to model 1, with wealth and seniority statistically significant predictors of repayments. Interestingly, the sign on status moves from negative in model 1 to positive in model 2, which likely reflects the press paying more attention to higher-profile MPs' expenses claims than to those of a purely representative sample.

Conclusions

The chapter explored the dynamics of the expenses crisis and the way in which the story developed into a major media-driven scandal throughout 2009 and beyond. Revelations in the *Telegraph* day after day dominated the political agenda and ensured the previously less than prominent issue of MPs' expenses became headline news. Critically, much of this coverage routinely focused on relatively trivial sums in terms of the money claimed, but which were simultaneously promoted as symbols of a culture of excess. The discussion then sought to evaluate and explore the specifics of the case through exploration of three empirical questions: do claims differ systematically by party, seniority, electoral security or gender; what factors explain variation in expenses claims; and finally, given the widespread nature of the controversial practices documented by the *Telegraph*, what factors explain why some but not all MPs became embroiled in the expenses scandal? The evidence suggests differences among all groups in terms of total claims for the 2007–9 period; however, only seniority is statistically significant with respect to repayments.

As the party in power, Labour had the most recent opportunity to reform the allowances system, but institutional inertia and parliamentary tradition proved to be powerful bulwarks against such change. Furthermore, the detailed evidence shows that Labour Members claimed more than other party representatives in terms of their overall expenses. However, when compared with MPs of other parties, especially their Conservative counterparts, Labour MPs featured less in what subsequently became the scandal. Leaving partisanship aside, other factors are useful when exploring those who featured prominently in the story. Senior MPs were, for instance, prone to claiming less on average than their younger colleagues, but were also more likely to have been implicated in the parliamentary allowances scandal. In terms of gender there was little difference; male MPs claimed slightly more, but were less likely to have been censured, than their female counterparts.

Finally, turning to another factor, the parliamentarians' own levels of income, is instructive, because this was something of an indicator in relation to the likelihood of the Member to make claims that were later queried. Here there is something of an apparent paradox, in that it was more likely to have been the wealthier MPs who were asked to pay back more of what they had claimed. Consequently, many of those who had additional earnings from remunerated work, property or investments were also more likely to have been implicated in the crisis. The proposed remedy that MPs be paid more to provide them with sufficient recompense is perhaps misjudged, given it tended to be richer Members who were perceived to have transgressed in relation to some of their claims. Ultimately, this demonstrates the usefulness of reviewing available evidence and analysing data that were often overlooked in some of the more sensationalist reporting of the original scandal.

Appendix

A. Measurement of variables

PARTY MEMBERSHIP: 1 = Labour; 0 = other.

SENIORITY: number of years served in the House of Commons.

MARGINALITY: the average of the percentage difference between the first and second-place parties for the 2001 and 2005 General Elections. The average of the percentage difference between the first and second-place parties for 2005 and the by-election results was used to calculate marginality for MPs elected in by-elections.

AGE: age of MP at 31 December 2009.

STATUS: dummy variable coded 1 if MP held (cabinet) ministerial role, shadow (cabinet) minister, chair of permanent select committee, or speaker/deputy speaker; all else = 0.

SEX: Male = 1; Female = 0

WEALTH: ordered variable (0–4) indicating the number of additional income opportunities MPs have. Cases were coded 0 if MPs had no reported interests in the following four categories: remunerated directorships, remunerated employment, land and property, and registrable holdings. See *Register of Members' Interests* (from May 2005 to 16 June 2008) (2008) for more information on reporting requirements for each of the categories.

EXPENSES: Average of total amount claimed for expenses in 2007–8 and 2008–9.

REPAID: Amount MP was requested to repay per Sir Thomas Legg's review of previous ACA payments. The value is the amount requested after a review of any appeals made by MPs against the Legg report.

REPAID*MENTIONS: As above, multiplied by the number of mentions a Member received in newspaper reports in the two weeks following the *Telegraph*'s initial report. Items were coded that suggested a Member's claim(s) was/were inappropriate, abusive, illegal or extravagant. The following papers were sampled: *The Independent, The Independent on Sunday, Daily Telegraph, The Sunday Telegraph, The Guardian, Observer, The Times, The Sunday Times, The Sun, News of the World, The Daily Mirror, The Mirror on Sunday, Daily Star, The Sunday Star, Daily Express, Express on Sunday, Daily Mail* and *The Mail on Sunday*. Number of citations = 425.

B. Correlation matrix for explanatory variables

	1	2	3	4	5	6	7
1. Age	1.00						
2. Male	0.05	1.00					
3. Wealth	0.07	0.19	1.00				
4. Labour	0.17	−0.21	−0.39	1.00			
5. Status	−0.07	0.05	0.10	−0.11	1.00		
6. Marginality	0.19	0.02	0.08	0.39	0.12	1.00	
7. Seniority	0.66	0.16	0.16	0.03	0.10	0.27	1.00

Notes

I would like to thank Adrian Blau, Justin Fisher and Meg Russell for their helpful advice, and Oisin Gilmore and Nina Kaysser for their research assistance.

1. Viner, K. Interview with Gordon Brown, 20 June 2009, *The Guardian Online*, http://www.guardian.co.uk/politics/2009/jun/20/gordon-brown-interview/print (accessed 18 August 2010).
2. Three MPs have been charged under the Theft Act for expenses claims: Elliot Morley, Jim Devine and David Chaytor. Lord Hanningfield also faces six charges for submitting dishonest claims.
3. See http://www.public-standards.org.uk/Library/Background_Paper_No_2__Timeline_of_ Events.pdf for a complete timeline to the expenses scandal.
4. The *Telegraph*'s revelations were not the first to be brought to the public's attention. Leaks from the disk had emerged in February 2009, including Jacqui Smith's claim for pornographic films, published by the *Sunday Express*, and Tony McNulty claiming his parents' home as his second home, thereby qualifying for allowances under the ACA.
5. Michael Connarty, MP, Linlithgow and East Falkirk, 21 May 2009, http://www.telegraph.co.uk/news/newstopics/mps-expenses/5330641/Best-quotes-on-the-Telegraphs-MPs-expenses-investigation.html?image=1 (accessed 28 August 2010).
6. The ACA is not available to MPs representing inner London constituencies. They are, however, eligible to receive a London supplement worth approximately £3,000.
7. See Telegraph.co.uk, 21 May 2009, http://www.telegraph.co.uk/news/newstopics/mps-expenses/5362605/MPs-expenses-Anthony-Steen-claims-people-just-jealous-of-his-large-house.html (accessed 21 August 2010).
8. The sample size (N=645) does not equal the number of seats in the House of Commons, as members who died were excluded from the analysis. Members elected through by-elections were included where data was available.
9. Expense claims for 2007–08 are for the period of 1 April to 31 March. I sample 2007–8 and 2008–9 expense claims as indicators of claims for the whole of the 2005–10 Parliament. The mean claim for 2007–8 was £144,188, and £147,763 for 2008–9 (t=−7.038, p<0.001) Although expense claims were higher in 2008–9, there is some suggestion that MPs were already cutting

back on expenses in speculation that the disk containing expense claims was in circulation.

10. In 2007, MPs' salaries were approximately £61,500, with those MPs taking on additional responsibilities in the House earning significantly more.

11. See *Register of Members' Interests* (2008) for specific reporting requirements. I have excluded gifts/benefits (UK), overseas gifts/benefits and overseas visits; although they provide in-kind benefits, they are not an additional source of income. As noted in the Register, it is not intended to be an indicator of a MP's wealth, but to provide transparency and accountability. Because neither the Register nor any other data source captures wealth, the measure is weaker on validity.

12. To create groups for comparison, I split seniority at the mean value of fifteen years. Marginal constituencies are considered marginal if the average difference between the first and second-place party in the 2001 and 2005 General Elections is ≤10 per cent.

13. One option in measuring the dependent variable would be to use average ACA claims for 2007–8 and 2008–9. However, this measure suffers similar problems of validity to the 'claims' variable; claiming more doesn't necessarily mean the claims were made in breach of the rules.

14. As noted in the Legg review, over £55 million was paid out to MPs (ACA claims) during 2004–9; of that £11 million was called into question, but only £1.3 million was repaid (Legg, 2010: 25). This measure is not without criticism, as the press focused in large part on high-profile MPs rather than a representative sample.

References

Bampton, R. and Maclagan, P. (2009) 'Does a "Care Orientation" Explain Gender Differences in Ethical Decision Making? A Critical Analysis and Fresh Findings', *Business Ethics: A European Review*, 18(2): 179–191.

Banducci, S. and Karp, J. (1994) 'Electoral Consequences of Scandal and Reapportionment in the 1992 House Elections', *American Politics Quarterly*, 22(1): 3–26.

Betz, M., O'Connell, L. and Shepard, J. (1989) 'Gender Differences in Proclivity for Unethical Behavior', *Journal of Business Ethics*, 8(5): 321–4.

Clarke, H., Sanders, D., Stewart, M. and Whiteley, P. (2009) 'Public Reaction to the MPs Expenses Claims Scandal: Evidence from the BES-CMS'. Paper presented at the Elections, Public Opinion and Parties Conference, University of Strathclyde.

Dawson, L. (1992) 'Will Feminization Change the Ethics of the Sales Profession'? *Journal of Personal Selling and Sales Management*, Winter: 21–32.

Dimock, M. and Jacobson, G. (1995) 'Checks and Choices: The House Bank Scandal's Impact on Voters in 1992', *Journal of Politics*, 57(4): 1143–59.

Electoral Commission (2001) *Election 2001: The Official Results*. London: Politico's Publishing.

Electoral Commission (2006) *Election 2005: Constituencies, Candidates and Results*. London: Electoral Commission.

The Guardian (2010) MP Expenses claimed, 2008-09, http://www.guardian.co.uk/news/datablog/2010/feb/04/mps-expenses-claims-full-list#data (accessed 9 August 2010).

Hansard Society (2010) *Audit of Political Engagement 7: The 2010 Report with a Focus on MPs and Parliament*. London: Hansard Society.

House of Commons (2008) *Register of Members' Interests*. London: The Stationery Office Limited. http://www.publications.parliament.uk/pa/cm/cmregmem/080616/080616.pdf (accessed 24 August 2010).

House of Commons: Members Estimate Committee (2010) *Review of Past ACA Payments: First Report of Session 2009-10*. London: The Stationery Office Limited.

Jacobson, G. and Dimock, M. (1994) 'Checking out: The Effects of Bank Overdrafts on the 1992 House Election', *American Journal of Political Science*, 38(3): 601–24.

Legg, T. (2010) House of Commons Members Estimate Committee: Review of Past ACA Payments. House of Commons. London: The Stationary Office Limited.

Pattie, C. and Johnston, R. (2010) 'The Electoral Impact of the 2009 MPs Expenses Scandal'. Working Paper. University of Sheffield.

Stewart, C. (1994) 'Let's go Fly a Kite: Correlates of Involvement in the House Bank Scandal', *Legislative Studies Quarterly*, 19(4): 521–35.

Winnett, R. and Rayner, G. (2009) *No Expenses Spared*. London: Bantam Press.

YouGov (2010) 'YouGov/The Sun: Survey Results', http://today.yougov.co.uk/sites/today.yougov.co.uk/files/TheSun_BrokenBritain.pdf (accessed 21 November 2010).

17

The Transformation of Campaign Reporting: The 2010 UK General Election, Revolution or Evolution?

Ivor Gaber

Introduction

This chapter argues that the 2010 election represented a transformative moment in the reporting of British general election campaigns. Some of the changes were incremental – going back over several previous elections – but some were dramatic and specific to the 2010 campaign. The single most important reason why 2010 was a totally different campaign to report was because of the advent of the leaders' televised debates. The debates not only had a dramatic impact themselves but also, by their intensification of attention on the leadership issue, played an important part in making 2010 a virtually policy-free campaign. However, there were other major developments – more incremental – that also had an important impact on the daily business of election campaign reporting in 2010.

In summary, these developments were, first, that significant changes had been taking place in the way that the parties had been organising their media campaigns during previous elections, and this trend accelerated in 2010. These changes included the way that parties used press conferences, news releases, regional tours and big events. Second, there was a heightened effort by the parties to increase their unmediated contact with the electorate, most of which takes place far away from the prying eyes of the news media. And, third, the intensification of the news process continued unabated. This intensification relates not just to the amount of information available to journalists, but also to the speed with which they are able to disseminate news and the variety of dissemination outlets they now have at their disposal. All these factors contributed to making the 2010 campaign election reporting, but not as we know it.

That was then...

A sense of this change can be garnered from two metaphorical snapshots. The first comes from the 2010 election, and it would show a tweeting, blogging, web-posting political reporter struggling to keep up with all the news coming at him or her during the hectic days, and nights, of the campaign and also struggling to disseminate it. The second is the reporter, leading a more ordered, almost sepia-like, existence during the 1979 campaign, the last time Labour was ejected from office. This was a time when there was no breakfast-time television, no twenty-four-hour TV and radio news, and no mobile phones, and the internet was no more than a twinkle in the eye of military planners and IT enthusiasts.

The 1979 campaign reporter's day started early, with the first of the then daily press conferences (usually conducted by the party leaders) beginning at 7.30 in the morning at Liberal Party Headquarters; from there it was on to Labour's press conference at 8 am and finally to the Conservatives at 8.30. The conferences served three purposes. First, they enabled the parties to establish (not always with a great deal of success) their 'theme for the day'. Second, they gave reporters a chance to quiz politicians about the latest gaffes, leaks or attacks from other parties. And, third, they provided the TV reporters with their first pictures of the day – these pictures would have included not only the press conferences, but also the party leaders and their entourages undergoing the highly staged process of boarding the campaign 'battle bus' to start the day's campaigning.

This daily photo-opportunity was designed, in the absence of breakfast-time or twenty-four-hour news, to provide pictures for use in the lunchtime news bulletins. And the rest of the campaign day was similarly based around the broadcasters' news bulletins, which, in addition to lunchtime, included early evening news shows and the 'flagship' bulletins at 9 or 10 pm. The parties responded to the broadcasters' requirements by drawing up campaign planning grids. These grids sought to establish a daily campaign theme, which, in theory at least, would be outlined at the morning press conference, encapsulated by the party leader visiting a relevant location for the lunchtime bulletin, presented as a more substantial story for the early evening bulletin (probably involving an interview), and then rounded up for the flagship bulletins, possibly by means of a speech from the party leader reiterating the day's campaign message. Newspaper reporters found themselves increasingly trailing in the wake of their broadcasting colleagues as campaigns came to be more and more dominated by the rhythms of television news – consistently shown to be the public's most used and trusted source of election information.

And this is now ...

Fast forward now to the 2010 election, when there were virtually no early morning press conferences, battle buses were rarely seen, very few set-piece speeches were delivered and political reporters were able to access much of the campaign via their Blackberrys or iPhones and file their stories from their laptops and iPads. The 2010 election reporter's day also began early; reporters would use their mobile phones to catch up on the overnight news from the parties, the major news sites, the Facebook groups and the key tweeters and political bloggers, not to mention perusing messages and queries from their offices, while at the same time listening to BBC Radio 4's *Today* programme and/or the 5Live *Breakfast Show*. Over coffee and toast our reporter would be keeping his or her eye on Sky News and the BBC's News 24 with another eye on the laptop, checking for updates. In fact, on the days when none of the leaders' debates were taking place, the 2010 election reporter could stay at his or her breakfast table, keeping up with all the campaigning news and information while at the same time filing copy, adding to his or her blog, sending a tweet, posting something on Facebook or even recording a podcast.

The party press conferences – which by 2010 were not being held on a daily basis – didn't need to be attended in person because Sky and the BBC carried them live, and provided the instant analysis as well. The same went for major speeches by the party leaders. Only the need to get some local 'colour' or to attend the leaders' debates might drag the reporter away from his or her desk. These debates, which in 2010 were held in three locations outside London, might or might not have illuminated the electorate, but they did at least ensure that campaign reporters occasionally forsook their desks for the lure of the so-called spin rooms – the makeshift press offices at the debate locations that were used by the parties for face-to-face briefings with the journalists after the debates.

The demise of the press conferences

One of the most obvious signs of the changed nature of campaign reporting in 2010 was the demise of the regular morning press conferences that used to be the centrepieces, or at least the starting points, of the election campaign day. It would be a mistake to suggest that there was a direct cause/effect relationship between the introduction of the leaders' debates and the ending of the morning press conference ritual; change had been in the air for some time. The origin of the early morning press conferences goes back to 1959, when Labour, faced with a hostile press and a seemingly impregnable governing Conservative Party, introduced them in an attempt to gain some control over the day's news agenda.[1] There had been press conferences during previous campaigns, but they had been essentially operational briefings – the leader will be visiting such and such a constituency tomorrow – rather than the central focus of the campaign day. Between 1964 and 2001 the early morning press conference became a key part of the campaign. Martin Linton, a former Labour MP and political correspondent, writing about the 1983 campaign, observed:

> The press conference remains the most important event of the campaign day and, even if much of what is said is quickly lost, the main story of the day is still likely to have had its origins in the morning press conference. (Linton, 1986: 150)

Although, as another political journalist has noted, even from the outset the parties were not the unalloyed enthusiasts for these conferences that they might have appeared to be:

> The influence of the morning press conferences began to decline almost immediately after their successful beginning in 1959, becoming 'ordeals to be endured with minimal harm'. (Rosenbaum, 1997: 138)

Press conferences were not just an opportunity for the parties to try to set the news agenda for the day; they also provided them with an occasion for defending themselves against attacks from their opponents and launching attacks of their own. For journalists the morning press conferences provided a daily moment when they were able to challenge the politicians on virtually any issue that took their fancy. And, as press conferences became ever more geared towards television, they also assumed a symbolic value – a well-run press conference, in which questions were dealt with competently, conveyed the sort of positive image that parties were keen to promote. Conversely, a badly run conference gave out very negative messages, a classic example of this being during

Labour's 1983 campaign when it appeared that – mid-campaign – their party leadership had debated who should be leading the campaign.

By 2001 neither Labour nor the Tories were holding press conferences every day of the campaign; indeed, on the eve of the 2005 election one of Labour's key campaign organisers, Douglas Alexander, was ruminating that:

> Labour must find new ways to communicate directly with the electorate, reviewing its old techniques such as poster campaigns, battle bus tours, photo opportunities and question and answer sessions. (Negrine and Lilleker, 2002: 314)

However, when it came to the 2005 campaign, while both Labour and the Conservatives announced that they would no longer be holding their regular morning conferences, the Liberal Democrats continued, and in a matter of days the other two were forced to resume the early morning follies (Kavanagh and Butler, 2005: 69). In 2010, there were again discussions about whether press conferences should be held at all. In the event they were held, but very much on an ad hoc basis. Indeed, there was not one single day during the campaign when all three parties held a morning press conference; and those that were staged looked, to many journalists, somewhat anachronistic and irrelevant. As Adam Boulton and Joey Jones of Sky News have noted, the press conferences '...felt as if journalists and politicians alike were going through the motions, as if the whole campaign pantomime had become redundant' (Boulton and Jones, 2010: 78–9).

The Liberal Democrats did stick to the daily routine and held press conferences on most days. Labour held just ten over the four weeks of the campaign (and of these only three were fronted by Gordon Brown) and the Conservatives virtually abandoned them altogether. They held just three conventional conferences, but also organised a series of either 'manifesto' or 'contract' launches – most of these were fronted by David Cameron, and they more or less achieved for the Party all the positives of a press conference without too many of the negatives.

The main negative that all parties have confronted is that, whatever might be the party's chosen 'theme of the day', the journalists' questioning almost immediately hones in on the latest gaffe, leak, internal division or adverse opinion poll. For reporters, press conferences were an effective way of challenging the politicians, but for the parties they became increasingly counterproductive. A further problem was that, in addition to journalists not 'playing by the rules', the parties sometimes didn't either. This author recalls leaving a Conservative Party press conference during the 1997 election campaign and being handed a press release by Labour Party staff waiting outside, which contained a detailed rebuttal of the policy announcements made just a few moments ago by the Tories. Labour had monitored the Tories' conference on television and then ensured that they would be denied any opportunity of setting the news agenda in the absence of a Labour counterblast. This set parties thinking about the advantages of continuing to play by these particular rules.

Blogger Mark Pack, as a former Liberal Democrat campaign adviser, thinks that the heyday of the early morning press conferences had already passed, but that their further decline diminishes the quality of the democratic process:

> This election continued, and accelerated, the death of the morning press conference cycle. They were never perfect means of politicians and journalists interacting, but they did give journalists the chance to pin politicians down when there was bad news in the air. Without the fixed rendezvous in the diary, it is easier for politicians to dodge journalists and in the end that's bad for politics as it relies on robust, but fair coverage with journalists asking questions directly of the main players. (email communication, 4 October 2010)

The decline of the news release

If the passing of the early morning press conferences was one signal of how 'traditional' reporting of election campaigns was being transformed, another was the demise of one of the other mainstays of election coverage, the news release. In campaigns past the parties saw them as an important part of the armoury to be deployed in the daily battle for the news agendas. In 2010 party news releases suffered much the same fate as the daily press conferences, summed up succinctly by the *Daily Mirror's* Associate Editor, Kevin Maguire, who told the author during the campaign 'I can't remember the last time I looked at one of the party's campaign press releases' (private conversation, 4 May 2010).

In 2010 even the very notion of what comprised a news release was becoming problematic. Up until then, even though the mode of delivery might have changed (from paper, to fax, to email, to website posting), what constituted a release was not in doubt. However, by 2010 the party press teams were not just communicating with journalists by use of the news release but were making extensive use of Facebook, YouTube, Twitter, SMS messaging and other social media. Sometimes these messages might be described as conventional press releases distributed by other means, but on other occasions they were either a one-sentence rebuttal, or a link to a Party Election Broadcast on YouTube, or an announcement of a 'flash press conference' (as unscheduled briefings became known). The volume of conventional news releases issued by the parties halved between 2005 and 2010. During the 2005 campaign Labour issued 126 releases, the Conservatives 111 and the Liberal Democrats 113. In 2010 the equivalent figures were sixty-four, sixty-five and sixty-eight (Gaber, 2006). And not only did the number of releases halve between 2005 and 2010, but, as discussed later in this chapter, their subject matter bore increasingly little relevance to the central concerns of the electorate.

Information overload

If the parties' conventional means of communicating with the media – press conferences and news releases – were in decline, other means, as indicated, were more than taking their place. Reporters' daily email inboxes would usually be full to overflowing with party messages; all the main parties ran active campaign websites and Facebook groups, and made extensive use of the micro-blogging site Twitter – as did the bloggers, the citizen journalists and the mainstream journalists themselves (Gibson et al., 2010; Painter, 2010; Newman, 2010).

Newspaper reporters were as enthusiastic in their uptake of the new means of getting and sending information as were the new media exponents. Steve Richards, Chief Political Commentator of the *Independent*, says that for journalists this is all very positive; he is less sure about its impact on the politicians themselves:

> This was an election of tweeting and blogging and this completely transformed the dynamics of the campaign. Political leaders can now get sense of how well they are doing on the media within seconds of a broadcast interview ending from the blogs and tweets. It is an extraordinary and important new dimension to election campaigns. It's good for us journalists but what it does for the minds of politicians I am less sure. It must lead to panic and a loss of self-confidence. It's going to need tough political leaders to cope. (Richards, 2010a)

During the campaign Andrew Sparrow wrote a daily election blog for the *Guardian* newspaper. 'If journalism is the first draft of history,' he writes, 'then live blogging is the first draft of journalism. It's not perfect, but it's deeply rewarding...and it beats sitting on a battle bus' (Newman, 2010: 17). Sparrow estimates that he blogged around 14,000 words a day and he describes his own role as keeping abreast of the news those people who shared his passion for politics but who didn't have ten hours a day to spare monitoring television, the press or the internet. According to Sparrow, his page received more than 100,000 page views at the start of the campaign, rising to 450,000 page views on the day of 'Bigotgate'[2] and two million page views and 335,000 unique users in the aftermath of the results themselves (ibid.).

Of all the new tools at the disposal of reporters in the 2010 campaign, Twitter was the most important. Channel Four News presenter Krishnan Guru-Murthy has described Twitter

> ...almost as a wire service, in that so many journalists and news organisations and politicians are now on Twitter using it to get their material out very quickly, sometimes quicker than online or air. (ibid.: 19)

The *Daily Telegraph*'s online political journalist Edward Roussel believes that Twitter is now a vital part of any journalist's toolkit:

> It has great immediacy. It is a very fast platform and the way it forces people to condense their views into 140 characters is quite brilliant. It forces people to cut right to the chase. It is a fantastic journalistic tool...We're in an environment now where it is all about instant gratification. People want to know what is happening straight away and they would rather know what is happening in a short pithy way than an hour later in a thought through way. (ibid.: 15)

BBC political correspondent Jon Sopel has been reporting for the BBC for almost thirty years. In the 2010 campaign he became a Twitter convert. He describes how it transformed his experience of interviewing politicians:

> I would ask a question and look at my Twitter account and Charlie Whelan [a Labour spin doctor] had already tweeted about it or Eric Pickles [leading Conservative politician] says no Jon that's not right. It's unbelievable – everything is happening instantly. What is

different is the ability of all the participants, all the key players to be having their say. (ibid.: 18)

Indeed, many journalists who covered the frantic coalition negotia-tions between the Conservatives and Liberal Democrats in the days after the Election recall how it was the moment when William Hague, the Conservative's chief negotiator, tweeted that he was going back into the talks with the Liberal Democrats that they realised just how indis-pensable Twitter had become as a primary source of news (Richards, 2010a).

Michael Crick, the Political Editor of BBC TV's *Newsnight* pro-gramme, has noted how news distribution has speeded up phenom-enally, for both journalists and audiences; this has in itself presented new dangers:

> The daily churn of events is getting faster and faster because of 24-hour news and the role of the online media, especially Twitter. However this can mean that journalists are faced with an over-whelming pressure to pluck the low-hanging fruit of immediate, personality-related stories on easy subjects, at the expense of longer-term, detailed, sometimes investigative work, based on policy issues and subjects that are hard for everyone – journalists and audiences alike – to comprehend. (email communication, 11 November 2010)

Shane Greer, the Executive Editor of *Total Politics* magazine, also sees some dangers in this new information-rich environment. He argues that the speed and quantity of the information now circulating online is forcing mainstream journalists to cut corners:

> Whereas before the news cycle could be measured in hours, in the last election we came to measure it in minutes. In addition to this, mainstream media reporters are themselves under increasing pres-sure to deliver up to the minute news online... stories are moving faster than ever and mainstream journalists are pressured to ensure they don't fall behind, but those same journalists are under pressure to ensure their stories stand up. As a result, whilst a story has moved on in the blogosphere or on Twitter the mainstream media is often scrambling to double-source something that's already in the public arena. Clearly, this creates pressure on journalists to bend the rules, to take risks and report stories before they have been fully verified. (email correspondence, 11 October 2010)

Where did all the policy go?

A particular – and arguably unique – problem facing reporters during 2010 was the almost complete lack of substantive policy debate between the parties, leading to what this author has described as a 'hollowed out election' campaign (Gaber, 2011). Three main causal explanations can be advanced. First, the leaders' debates squeezed out the time and attention available for coverage of policy and, instead, increased the media's focus on the issue of leadership and the personal qualities of the party leaders. Second, a process of ideological convergence between the three main parties – which has been underway for some time – reached a high-water mark in 2010 as Labour continued to occupy the centre ground staked out by Blair and Brown; the Conservatives, under Cameron, pressed on with their efforts to lose their 'nasty party' label; and the Liberal Democrats, led by one of the authors of the 'Orange Book', shifted to the right. Hence the centre ground became a little crowded.

The third factor explaining the 'hollowed out' election, and one peculiar to 2010, was that none of the three major parties wanted to address, in any meaningful way, the two issues that the polls showed were overwhelmingly rated the most important by the electorate – namely how to tackle the UK's deficit and immigration. All three parties agreed that public spending would have to be cut, but none was prepared to elaborate as to how this was to be achieved. As Sky News' Political Correspondent Glen Oglaza noted at the time: 'Economy? This is the key issue of this election. It is remarkable really how little we have heard about it' (Oglaza, 2010). This observation was echoed from the other side of the campaign piste by Labour's Deputy Head of News, Tom Price, who said: 'We were aware that some journalists thought that none of the parties were giving them sufficient details about where any proposed cuts might fall' (interview, 2 July 2010). Indeed, there is not a single reference to the phrase 'cuts in public expenditure' in any of the parties' election news releases; and only the Liberal Democrats gave any indication, and then only in the most general of terms, as to where public expenditure cuts might fall (Gaber, 2011).

There was a similar reluctance to discuss immigration. The former Labour minister, Frank Field, commented: '...despite brief mentions in the manifestos, immigration is the issue that dare not speak its name' (Field, 2010). The parties tiptoed around this issue partly out of fear of being labelled 'racist' but also because there was some anxiety that publicising this issue would boost the electoral prospects of the far right British National Party.[3] Even the Conservatives, the party that might have expected to have benefited most from a discussion about immigration, did not post a single news release about immigration throughout the campaign (Gaber, 2011). Hence, reporters faced a situation in which the two major issues of public concern were virtually absent from the campaign – perhaps it was little wonder that the leaders' debates and then Gordon Brown's encounter with a disillusioned Labour voter in Rochdale – dubbed 'Bigotgate' – came to occupy so much of their time and attention during the campaign.

A final factor that contributed to this absence of policy discussion was the sheer quantities of opinion polls that deluged political reporters – no fewer than ninety-three separate polls were published during the four weeks of the campaign, providing an almost endless supply of 'horse race' material, at the expense of discussion of policy issues. In 1979 just twenty-six polls were published during the campaign, making the horse race less easy to predict and certainly less easy to write about.

Reaching past the media

The relationship between politicians and the media has long been portrayed as one of an ongoing struggle for power between two great competing armies (Barnett and Gaber, 2001). This battle has been chronicled in forensic detail by, among others, the former BBC political correspondent Nicholas Jones, who between 1995 and 2001 published a series of books whose very titles give a flavour of this war: *Soundbites and spin doctors: how politicians manipulate the media – and vice versa, Sultans of Spin: the media and the new Labour Government* and *The Control Freaks: how New Labour gets its own way* (Jones, 1995, 1999, 2001). While there has been this understandable focus on 'spin', and the attempts by political parties to manage the media, behind this lies a trend, first identified by scholars two decades ago, of a rise in the phenomenon of seeing election campaigns not as episodic discrete events, but in the context of a much larger political marketing strategy involving strategic communications, branding, reputation management and all the other tools deployed by the commercial marketeers (see, for example, Lees-Marshment, 2004; Lilleker et al., 2006). This involves parties taking a much broader approach to the business of communicating with voters, seeing them, indeed, as consumers at least as much as voters, and hence downplaying the role of the media in this process; although it's worth noting that, just because the parties seek to body-swerve past the media as they seek to communicate directly with voters, this does not mean that the media can therefore be discounted when analysing the effectiveness of political marketing strategies and tactics (Savigny and Temple, 2010).

Nonetheless, parties have increasingly sought to find ways of bypassing the media, and, although the output of political reporters might be having a profound impact on how party messages are being received and interpreted, this is an activity that is difficult for reporters to track. This trend of what might be termed a subterranean campaign began in earnest in 2001, when Labour and the Conservatives began to make use of consumer data bases such as MOSAIC in order to understand and segment the electorate with a view to targeting specific voters in specific marginal constituencies. With the use of direct mail, it was estimated that in one such constituency target voters received up to eleven items of personalised mail from the two main parties during the four weeks of the 2001 campaign.[4]

This trend continued in 2005, when 21 per cent of electors reported receiving a personal letter from one of the three main parties (compared with 14 per cent in 2001), a further 7 per cent were telephoned (compared with 5 per cent) and 3 per cent reported receiving email (1 per cent in 2001) (Kavanagh and Butler, 2005: 168). Kavanagh and Cowley, in their study of the 2010 campaign, quote a Liberal Democrat campaigner who dubbed it the 'Direct mail campaign...more paper delivered to more houses than any campaign in British history'. During the campaign Labour reportedly delivered 7.4 million letters to voters and the Conservatives eight million. Kavanagh and Cowley also report that the parties made much greater use of phone banks to canvass potential supporters, much of this being done by members from their own homes using software and numbers downloaded from the parties' own social media sites. They report that between 1 January and polling day Labour, for example, made half a million voter contacts by phone (Kavanagh and Cowley, 2010: 232). All of this amounts to massive campaigning activity taking place away from the prying eyes of the media, thus heightening the sense of 'What's going on out there?'

This trend, which in 2005 came to be known as the 'air war' and the 'ground war', was even more pronounced in 2010. The air war was the national battle fought out on the television screens and in the national newspapers – which in 2010 was enlivened by the leaders' televised debates. However, it was the ground war – the parties' direct contact with the electors – that absorbed more of the parties' time, money and attention. In 2005 this battle was fought largely by means of phone and direct mail, and on the doorstep. In 2010 these means of contact were supplemented by email, SMS messaging, Twitter, Facebook and other forms of social media. The problem, at least from the journalists' perspective, was that all this additional combat took place way below their own radar. Lynton Crosby, who ran the Conservatives' campaign in 2005, observed then:

> Many media commentators do not see much of the real campaign these days. It does not take place on the TV, on the radio or even in newspapers. It is the local activity on the ground that really counts – letters to voters, postcards, newsletters, telephone canvassing, doorknocking. (Miller, 2005)

In 2010 the 'ground war' intensified. One indicator of this is the amount of resources the parties devoted to advertising in the national media. On that measure 2010 was noteworthy:

> This election was remarkable for the absence of party political advertising. The Liberal Democrats, alone among the parties, invested in press advertising with a one-page insertion in *The Times* (5 May) with Nick Clegg offering a personal guarantee. ... This was by some distance the slightest show of political advertising in modern campaigns. It compares to 35 pages of party advertising in 2005. (Scammell and Beckett, 2010: 304)

A sense of the 'real campaign' taking place elsewhere was felt by journalists even in 2005. Andy Bell, Political Editor of Channel Five News, wrote:

> I was based in Westminster throughout the campaign and by the last 10 days that became uncomfortable. It was like sitting in a command bunker far removed from the battle while ever-more interesting rumours filtered back from the front line. (Bell, 2005)

Much the same experience was reported in 2010 when national political correspondents again had that sense that somewhere out in the country the tectonic plates might be shifting, about which they were blissfully unaware. Although for Steve Richards of the *Independent* this merely added to the fun of reporting the campaign:

> Reporting the election as a whole was weird. It was very hard to get a hold of. It was so shapeless but exciting and, for the first time in many years, it was unpredictable. (Richards, 2010a)

The leaders' debates

But in one aspect, if no other, the 'air war' remained important in 2010 – that aspect being the televised leaders' debates, which dominated the campaign in a way that no other media phenomenon has dominated any recent election campaign before. As Labour's campaign organiser Douglas Alexander correctly predicted before the campaign proper began, the debates altered '... the choreography of the traditional UK election campaign' (Wintour, 2010). Kavanagh and Cowley echoed this view (although they failed to note that Alexander had anticipated the debates' impact): '...the debates had a much greater impact on the rhythm and feel of the campaign than almost anyone had predicted' (Kavanagh and Cowley, 2010: 158).

The three leaders' time and attention were dominated by the debates. Much of the weekend prior to the debate-day on Thursdays was taken up with preparations, then through Monday to Thursday they divided their time between campaigning and further preparation, and on Friday they dealt with the aftermath (ibid.: 176). The debates similarly dominated the lives of the reporters covering the campaign. Tuesdays were spent filing preview pieces for Wednesday's papers and programmes. On the Wednesday reporters would travel to the out-of-London debate locations and file from there on the prospects for the following day. On Thursday they would report the debate and its immediate aftermath, on the Friday they would write and produce more reflective pieces, and then come the weekend they were once again looking forward to the next debate. In such a situation it is hardly surprising that most other aspects of normal campaign reporting suffered. As the *Observer*'s political columnist, Andrew Rawnsley, put it: 'The debates sucked the oxygen out of all the other campaign events and focused too much attention on the trivialities of personality' (Rawnsley, 2010: 726).

On the other side of the fence – the party press offices – the debates also dominated the campaign. One Labour Party press officer reported that: 'The silence of the Labour press office on the days of the debates was eerie with all media at the "extraordinary political village" of the debate sites' (Thorogood, 2010). The very fact of the debates meant that, for the middle three weeks of the campaign, the party leaders, and their advisers, devoted much of their time, and most of their emotional energy, to preparing for the televised confrontations. This left little opportunity to build campaigns around other issues. As Jonny Oates, Director of Communications at the Liberal Democrats, put it, 'Once they began, the debates dominated. We had planned to have more set-piece events but in the event the debates became the big story' (interview, 27 July 2010).

Before the campaign began there was some expectation that the four-and-a-half hours of debate between the party leaders – staged on major television channels at prime time – should ensure that a discussion of policy would assume a greater importance in the 2010 campaign than had previously been the case, but that was not to be. The debates represented a classic case of presentation trumping substance. There are a number of reasons why this was so; the most obvious one being their sheer novelty. Given that it was the first time in more than fifty years, since the 'the first TV election', that such televised confrontations were taking place, it was hardly surprising that they attracted so much attention. And this attention was dramatically heightened when, following the first debate, the poll ratings of the Liberal Democrats jumped six points, not because of any particular Liberal Democrat policy resonating with the public, but because of favourable reaction to party leader Nick Clegg's on-screen performance.

Another factor was simply that the debates consumed so much media time and space that they drove out other aspects of the campaign (the volcanic ash cloud that brought world aviation to a halt during the period of the campaign also competed strongly with the election for media attention). Understandably, the media is only ever going to devote a certain amount of space and time to the election, and, if a large amount of this is taken up by the debates, that leaves so much less for coverage of policy issues. But the debates' domination of the campaign was explained, not just by the amount of time and space they occupied, but, as Sky News' Adam Boulton and Joey Jones suggest:

> ...the overwhelming media narrative was taken up by the debates – who had won, who had lost (and how badly) and how things might be different next time round. (Boulton and Jones, 2010: 79)

However, not all political reporters were convinced that the debates were unambiguously positive in terms of their impact on the campaign. The *Independent*'s Steve Richards feared that they could have a long-term distorting impact on the conduct of politics, and not just at election times:

> I really do worry that the prospect of leaders' debates affecting both the sort of leaders political parties might go for; and also that during campaigns content will be all but wiped out. The rhythm of politics, almost from now to the next election, could be determined by the

prospect of who will do best in the next series of leaders' debates. (Richards, 2010a)

The debates' domination is reflected in the press coverage of the campaign. Scammell and Beckett found that in the 2005 election articles about the party leaders accounted for 13 per cent of all front-page election stories and 14 per cent of all election editorials. The comparable figures for 2010 were 40 per cent of front pages and 30 per cent of editorials – a doubling of press coverage of leadership issues. Commenting on this, the authors write:

> ... the TV debates led directly to two highly distinctive characteristics of this election. First, this was an extraordinarily leader-focussed contest, even by recent standards of personalised campaigns. It was not just that the debates themselves intensified attention to the leaders and their performances; it was also that they cast a presidential framing over the entire contest. (Kavanagh and Cowley, 2010: 296)

If the parties were concerned about the intense focus on leaders, only the Labour Party sought to do something about it. They wrote to the Conservatives and the Liberal Democrats to see if they would join them in an approach to the broadcasters to express concern, but when the approach was rebuffed they published extracts from the letter. It argued that the focus on the debates had 'dramatically reduced' the airtime given to policy issues. They went on to claim:

> ... that whilst our manifestos were fully, fairly and properly covered, since then the usual specialist examination of specific policy areas has not been done. If the public are not exposed to the different policy details and arguments which we are presenting, we are concerned that you will not be fulfilling your traditional duty of explaining and probing the plans of all the main parties ... If the public don't hear the arguments, we believe that, despite the impact of the debates, many will still be in the dark as to the differences between our plans and values. (Labour Party, 2010)

Such concerns are not shared by Sky News' Adam Boulton, who believes that the debates encouraged more policy discussion than in the past and that their overall impact on the campaign was positive:

> Media coverage of the 2010 was transformed by the debates. For the first time TV did what it does best – take a live event into millions

of viewers simultaneously. Doing for politics what Sky has done for sports and what talent contests have done for live entertainment. (email communication, 4 October 2010)

But Boulton goes on to make a significant observation that goes wider than the impact of the debates on the reporting of the campaign and bears more on the supposed ongoing battle between the 'old' and 'new' media. Prior to the election there was, as there has been before every election since 1997, much speculation as to whether this would be the 'first' internet election. (See Gibson et al., 2010; Painter, 2010; Newman, 2010.) Boulton takes a different tack, noting that in the battle before last – the one between newspapers and broadcasters – to establish which was the primary medium for reporting elections, the outcome had been uncertain. The 2010 debates, he claims, established that it was television that was the prime site for the reporting of the campaign:

> In general the papers did not devote as much space or effort to election coverage in 2010 as in previous elections. For the first time I cannot recall a single print interview or article which impacted on the work I was doing. The many very intelligent people involved in print journalism are in 'transition', they will doubtless re-group and come back with imaginative, and insightful ways to revalidate their coverage. But I do not expect newspapers will ever again be the primary and dominant force of political coverage – the electronic media will not give up that role. (email communication, 4 October 2010)

Boulton's observation focuses on a crucial debate that has been largely unresolved ever since the 1959 election, most frequently identified as the first television campaign: what is the central site of contestation in modern election campaigns? Is it television, which the public consistently reports as its most used and most trusted source of news about politics,[5] or is it the national press, which still claims to be the most 'influential' (Wilby, 2010)? For, while Adam Boulton is probably right in arguing that – because of the leaders' debates – 2010 represented a new high point in television's domination of an election campaign, it could equally be argued that it was the newspapers' subsequent interpretation of these debates, combined with the instant polling, that most shaped public perceptions of the winners and losers. It is arguable whether such a question can ever be satisfactorily resolved, for asking voters to evaluate whether they were more influenced by watching the debates or by subsequently reading about them requires them to make a judgement of Solomon.

Self-evaluation of the impact of various media is invariably influenced by those very media themselves, and therefore does little more than measure a measure, hence serving no useful analytical purpose.

Hence, writing the obituary of the political influence of the press, as Boulton does, is perhaps a touch premature. Newspapers in the UK still have significant readerships. Despite falling circulations, an average of around nine million copies of national newspapers are sold every day (read by, on average, 2.5 people). A further ten million unique users access national newspaper websites on a daily basis.[6] However, the press's influence is based on far more than simply the number of readers.

In most newsrooms, including broadcast and online, newspapers still play a key role. Not only have most journalists seen or read the papers before arriving at work, but the press's news agenda still plays a crucial role in deciding the day's main stories. As the veteran journalist Peter Wilby observes: 'For all the warnings of declining sales, press headlines continue to obsess politicians and influence the running order of TV and radio news' (Wilby, 2010). And this is the crucial point – newspapers retain their predominant position as opinion-formers, not because they possess any intrinsic worth, and not even because of the relatively high number of readers they retain, but because politicians, and crucially, other journalists, think they are important. The American sociologist Michael Schudson has noted that the power of the mass media lies not in their direct influence on the public but in the perception of opinion-formers and decision-makers that the public is influenced by the mass media (Schudson, 1995).

There is another, mundane but important, point to be made. Newspapers are durable and accessible in a way that TV and radio news coverage is not – at least not as easily. Opinions expressed in print usually have greater impact than those broadcast. For Steve Richards of the *Independent* this was an ongoing frustration:

> For a decade on Sundays I presented a political programme early on GMTV, went straight to Broadcasting House to review the newspapers on Michael Parkinson's Radio 2 show, and in the evenings took part in a weekly debate with another columnist on BBC News 24. Quite often I did not meet anyone who had watched or heard a single word...Media and politics are in a state of flux but influence, power and indispensability lie as much with the written word as it ever did. (Richards, 2010b)

Whether, come the next election, the press continues to exercise this hold over both the public and public opinion-formers remains a moot point. However, if, as seems likely, the leaders' debates are continued, the broadcasters (pace Adam Boulton) will again be able to claim that they are the main stage upon which the election is being fought. But their colleagues in the press will know that, in terms of the performances, they are the critics – and, as any theatrical impresario will tell you, it's the critics, rather than the performers, who determine the public's reaction to the, in this case, electoral drama unfolding.

Notes

1. For a fuller account of the role of party press conferences see Thorogood, 2010.
2. This is the name given to Gordon Brown's much-publicised encounter with a disillusioned Labour voter in Rochdale; Brown's negative reactions about the voter were inadvertently captured by a Sky News microphone.
3. This is based on a number of private conversations with party press officers who, as far as this topic was concerned, did not wish to be identified – another indication of the sensitivity of the topic.
4. First noted in 'The Hidden Campaign', Channel Four News item, 28 April 2001.
5. Audience research for the BBC, the ITV and latterly Ofcom demonstrates that television news is consistently the public's main and most trusted source of political news.
6. Figures taken from the Audit Bureau of Circulation, http://www.pressgazette.co.uk/section.asp?navcode=161 (date accessed 22 November 2010).

References

Barnett, S. and Gaber, I. (2001) *Westminster Tales: the 21ˢᵗ century crisis in political journalism*. London: Continuum.

Bell, A. (2005) 'The election: a dog's breakfast', *British Journalism Review*, 16(2): 7–1.

Boulton, A. and Jones, J. (2010) *Hung Together: The 2010 Election and the Coalition Government*. London: Simon and Schuster.

Field, F. (2010) 'Anger over immigration could "spread to the streets" if it is not debated', *Daily Telegraph*, 13 April.

Gaber, I. (2006) 'Dislocated and distracted: media, parties and voters in the 2005 General Election Campaign, *British Politics*, 1(3).

Gaber, I. (2011) 'The Hollowed-Out election or where did all the policy go?' in *Journal of Political Marketing* (in press).

Gibson, R., Williamson, A. and Ward, S. (eds) (2010) *The internet and the 2010 election: putting the small 'p' back in politics?* London: Hansard Society.

Jones, N. (1995) *Soundbites and Spin Doctors: how politicians manipulate the media – and vice versa*. London: Indigo.

Jones, N. (1999) *Sultans of Spin: the media and the new labour government*. London: Victor Gollancz.

Jones, N. (2001) *The Control Freaks: how New Labour gets its own way*. London: Politico's.

Kavanagh, D. and Butler, D. (2005) *The British General Election of 2005*. Basingstoke: Palgrave Macmillan.

Kavanagh, D. and Cowley, P. (2010) *The British General Election 2010*. Basingstoke: Palgrave Macmillan.

Labour Party (2010) http://itn.co.uk/c395010bd5e5b2f3f1e4abf69083dd8f.html, 26 April 2010 (accessed 30 November 2010).

Lees-Marshment, J. (2004) *The Political Marketing Revolution: Transforming the government of the UK*. Manchester: Manchester University Press.

Lilleker, D., Jackson, N. and Scullion, R. (2006) *The marketing of political parties: Political marketing at the 2005 British General Election*. Manchester: Manchester University Press.

Linton, M. (1986) 'Political parties and the press in the 1983 campaign', in *Political Communications: The General Election Campaign of 1983*. Cambridge: Cambridge University Press.

Miller, D. (2005) 'Election spin mostly underground', Spinwatch, http://www.spinwatch.org, quoted in 'Dislocated and Distracted: Media, Parties and the Voters in the 2005 General Election Campaign', in *British Politics*, 2006, 1: 344–66.

Negrine, R. and Lilleker, D. (2002) 'The Professionalisation of Political Communication', *European Journal of Communication*, 17(3): 305–23.

Newman, N. (2010) '#UKelection 2010, mainstream media and the role of the internet: how social and digital media affected the business of politics and journalism', Working Paper, Oxford Reuters Institute for the Study of Journalism.

Oglaza, G. (2010) Sky News 28 April 2010, quoted in Thorogood, M. 'Labour's press conferences and the national news agenda in the 2010 General Election', MA dissertation.

Painter, A. (2010) *A Little More Conversation, A Little More Action: Orange's digital election analysis*. London: Orange.

Rawnsley, A. (2010) *The End of the Party*. London: Penguin Books.

Richards, S. (2010a) 'That was the political reporting year that was', talk at City University, London, 9 December 2010.

Richards, S. (2010b) 'Blogging: the power of the instant opinion', *The Independent*, 16 December 2010.

Rosenbaum, M. (1997) *From Soapbox to Soundbite*. Basingstoke: Palgrave Macmillan.

Savigny, H. and Temple, M. (2010) 'Political Marketing Models: The Curious Incident of the Dog that Doesn't Bark', in *Political Studies*, 58: 1049–64.

Scammell, M. and Beckett, C. (2010) 'Labour No More: The Press', in Kavanagh, D. and Cowley, P. *The British General Election of 2010*. Basingstoke: Palgrave Macmillan.

Schudson, M. (1995) *The Power of News*. London: Harvard University Press.

Thorogood, M. (2010) 'Campaign 2010 – the death of the morning press conference?' Unpublished MA dissertation, City University, London.

Wilby, P. (2010) 'Future tense but press powers on', in *New Statesman*, 20 December 2010: 26.

Wintour, P. (2010) 'Party leaders agree TV election debate rules: Negotiators thrash out 76-point pact on format Nationalists and smaller parties angry at exclusion', *Guardian*, 3 March 2010.

18
Reporting the 2010 General Election: Old Media, New Media – Old Politics, New Politics

David Deacon and Dominic Wring

To say that the media are central to modern election campaigning may be axiomatic, but there are specific reasons why the media are particularly significant in British general elections. Britain still has a very unitary political system, only partially tempered by political devolution. It also has centralised and nationally orientated news media whose dominance is arguably increasing, as pressures on regional news broadcasting intensify and cost-cutting, conglomeration and falling circulation undermine the vitality of the local press. The coexistence of these factors is a recipe for a highly media-centred political culture.

One measure of this is how frequently the role and significance of the media has been a matter of electoral controversy in Britain. For example, in the 1980s and early 1990s there was considerable discussion about the anti-Labour excesses of the Tory-supporting press. In 1992 there were competing allegations of BBC anti-Conservative bias and government attempts to use the Corporation's imminent charter review to exert undue control over its journalism. In 1997, there was extensive debate about the sudden and considerable swing of national press opinion behind Labour under Tony Blair. In contrast, in recent general elections there has been a marked absence of any significant media controversies, beyond routine complaints about journalists' cynicism and parties' spin control-freakery. By 2005, even the presence and qualified allegiance of the so-called Tony Press became an accepted, rather unremarkable, feature of the political landscape.

However, in the 2010 General Election media issues were back on the electoral agenda with a vengeance, for three reasons. First, there was considerable excitement about the potential impact that online media could have on the communication, conduct and outcome of the campaign. Second, for the first time in a British general election the leaders of the three main political parties agreed to participate in three prime-time live televised debates. Third, there was a major realignment of national press opinion towards David Cameron and the Conservative party – a long recidivist swing that began officially in September 2009 when the *Sun* newspaper timed its formal editorial renunciation of New Labour to coincide with Gordon Brown's conference speech to his party.

Interest was further stimulated by the potentially contradictory effects of these coincidental developments. For example, the blogosphere, new social media and other direct forms of digital communication were seen by some as offering a challenge to the traditional opinion-leading power of the national press – although few went as far as Kerry McCarthy, Labour's 'Twitter Czar', whose claim 'Labour doesn't need the *Sun*. We've got Twitter' attracted ridicule and incredulity in equal measure. Others anticipated that the staging of three televised leaders' debates would place the broadcasters back at the centre of the campaign, providing opportunities for the leaders to talk 'over the heads' of a resurgent Tory press and offering a focal point for an inclusive national conversation about the leaders and their policies, thereby 'exposing the deficiencies of new media' (Chadwick, 2010: 17).

This chapter considers the validity of these claims in the context of a wider information audit of the interpretative and evaluative dimensions of mainstream national news coverage of the 2010 campaign. This is the latest in a series of content analyses of general election news coverage conducted by the Loughborough Communication Research Centre (LCRC)[1] since 1992 (Deacon et al., 1998, 2001, 2005). One of the purposes of the discussion in this chapter is to consider the extent to which trends identified in 2010 can be seen as compounding or confounding previous patterns in election reporting.

Party presence

The degree of parity in the airtime and print space allocated to political competitors during campaigns is a perennial concern as it offers the most obvious, if basic, measure of reporting balance. Table 18.1 provides a comparison of the number of appearances and amount of direct quotation allocated to the main parties and leaders in 2010. Comparative figures are also provided from the LCRC's 2005 election content analysis, which used very similar sampling and coding procedures (see Deacon et al., 2006: 230).

Table 18.1 Party appearances and quotation time by election campaign and media sector

Broadcast

	Appear (%)		Quote (%)	
	2010	2005	2010	2005
Labour Leader	17	12	16	14
Labour other	17	23	22	24
Cons Leader	16	13	13	13
Conservative other	11	17	14	19
Lib Dem Leader	15	9	12	9
Liberal Democrat other	9	15	13	13
Other Party	14	11	10	8
(Base N)	(1,259)	(1,441)	(55,334)	(46,393)

'Quality' press

	Appear (%)		Quote (%)	
	2010	2005	2010	2005
Labour Leader	20	15	25	7
Labour other	24	35	20	39
Cons Leader	18	10	20	19
Conservative other	16	21	13	20
Lib Dem Leader	14	6	16	6
Liberal Democrat other	6	10	4	4
Other Party	2	4	2	5
(Base N)	(1,626)	(2,505)	(44,107)	(56,337)

Mid-market press

	Appear (%)		Quote (%)	
	2010	2005	2010	2005
Labour Leader	21	20	19	18
Labour other	18	38	14	29
Cons Leader	20	13	36	28
Conservative other	14	17	16	15
Lib Dem Leader	19	4	12	3
Liberal Democrat other	8	6	3	5
Other Party	1	2	0.3	2
Base (N)	(640)	(506)	(15,008)	(14,419)

Popular press

	Appear (%)		Quote (%)	
	2010	2005	2010	2005
Labour Leader	25	21	22	39
Labour other	16	35	18	29
Cons Leader	27	13	35	19
Conservative other	11	17	12	7
Lib Dem Leader	18	5	12	2
Liberal Democrat other	3	8	1	2
Other Party	1	1	0.3	1
Base (N)	(955)	(765)	(16,438)	(20,967)

Notes: up to five political actors could be coded per item. All percentages are rounded and may not add up to 100. The base N for 'appear' = total number of politicians coded; the base N for Broadcast media = total politician speaking time in seconds; the base N for all press = total number of quoted words

The findings show that in the recent campaign there was a marked reduction in the so-called incumbency effect: the tendency for the party in office to command greater media prominence in coverage as a result of their executive authority. In 2010, Labour accounted for 39 per cent of all politician appearances coded in the news sample, a 9 per cent reduction from the previous election. The Conservatives increased their share of appearances by 3 per cent to 33 per cent, but the biggest gainers were the Liberal Democrats, who raised their presence by 5 per cent to 22 per cent overall. The main reason for the latter's increase was a marked reduction in the two-party squeeze in press coverage. Regulations on broadcast coverage of the main parties have always secured the third party a significant minority presence on television and radio, but in the 2010 campaign the non-regulated press also could not treat the party as being of only peripheral importance.

The composition of Liberal Democrat exposure in 2010 changed as it increased. In 2005, 39 per cent of Liberal Democrat references were to their then leader, Charles Kennedy. In 2010, Nick Clegg accounted for 71 per cent of the party's appearances. This increased dominance of the party leader was also evident with the other two main parties, albeit less dramatically. In 2010, Gordon Brown accounted for 51 per cent of all Labour appearances, and David Cameron for 60 per cent of the Conservatives'. These compare with figures of 33 per cent for Tony Blair and 38 per cent for Michael Howard in 2005. Overall, the three main party leaders in 2010 claimed 56 per cent of *all* references to party politicians.

Figure 18.1 charts the extent to which leadership appearances dominated national reporting over the last four British general elections.

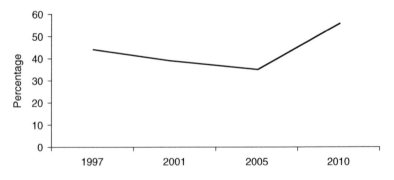

Figure 18.1   Frequency of main leaders' appearances as a percentage of all politician appearances (all media) (1997–2010)

The results show that the 2010 campaign was by far the most 'presidentialised' of recent times, confounding what had previously been an election-on-election reduction in the leaders' prominence. On the basis of content analysis alone, it is only possible to speculate as to the reasons for this, but, in our view, a combination of factors probably explains the shift. The 2010 election was recognised as being one of the closest contests for more than thirty years, presenting a distinct possibility of political change and a very significant power-broking role for the third main party. In such a febrile and uncertain environment, one would expect media attention to gravitate to the main political leaders, as spin-doctors and journalists contested the various leaders' strengths and failings. Whereas in previous elections there had been no likely alternative to Tony Blair, in 2010 none of the party leaders could be ignored, however much they might be disparaged. Furthermore, the 'presidentialisation' effects in the 2001 and 2005 campaigns were mitigated by the politics of the then Labour leadership, in which Gordon Brown's power and influence as Chancellor of the Exchequer meant he commanded a significant slice of media comment, reducing Blair's dominance. In 2010, Brown stood alone. But the most significant probable explanation for the change was the impact of the televised leadership debates, whose purpose was to bring the main party leaders into the media spotlight, both literally and figuratively.

Follow the leader

For all the talk of a politically disaffected and disconnected citizenry, the three ninety-minute televised leadership debates of the 2010 campaign certainly captured public attention. The first debate on ITV1 on 15 April was seen by 9.68 million viewers, gaining more audience share than the popular soap operas *Coronation Street* and *EastEnders*.[2] Viewing figures were reduced for the second debate held a week later on Sky News and broadcast simultaneously on BBC News 24, producing a composite viewing audience of 3.6 million. But, once the debate returned to a terrestrial platform on BBC1 on 29 April, the viewing figures recovered to 7.43 million. As Wring and Ward (2010) comment, 'Cumulatively these represented huge, unprecedented audiences for general election-related broadcasting of any kind; during this period the most popular television news bulletin attracted 5.56 m viewers' (2010: 218).

Just as the debates attracted public attention, so they became a major discussion point in national news. Not surprisingly, the broadcasters sought to make the most of these debates as they unfolded, developing presentational and feedback techniques that sought to capture the impact, drama and instantaneity of the debates. BBC, Sky and ITV used 'worm polling' techniques, first developed in New Zealand election reporting, to track the 'real time' responses of a select group of viewers to the leaders' statements and performance. Broadcasters also used 'sentiment tools' to track the tone and tenor of comments posted via social media such as Twitter and Facebook. Several TV correspondents posted immediate responses and appraisals on their blogs, even before delivering their verdicts on air (see Chadwick (2010) for a useful overview of these developments). These represented just the tip of the iceberg of broadcast analysis and commentary, and, of course, the fascination with the content and impact of the debates extended to other media as well. In our study, one in four of all articles sampled were found to contain some reference to the leadership debates, with citation levels in broadcast exceeding those in the press, but not to any dramatic extent.

Despite this widespread media interest in the debates, their attention was not sustained. Table 18.2 shows a monotonic reduction in coverage from first debate to last, with the first debate attracting nearly half of all the media commentary. To some extent, this difference can be explained as a sample frame artefact, in that there was greater time available for commentary on the earlier debates to accumulate. However, a reduction is also evident, even if one restricts sampling to the days of each debate and the two following weekdays. Fifty-nine per cent of all election items produced during this three-day period for the first debate made some reference to it. For the second debate this figure reduced to 45 per cent, and for the final debate the proportion of citation dropped even further to 35 per cent.

The intensity of media interest in the first debate can in part be explained by the unprecedented nature of these media events, which had been mooted in previous elections but had always been stymied by the failure to secure cross-party agreement. But it was not novelty alone

Table 18.2 Share of leadership debate coverage devoted to each encounter

	Broadcast %	Quality %	Mid-market %	Popular %
First	48	52	47	49
Second	27	25	22	27
Third	24	16	16	17
Various	0	8	16	7

that drove the first debate to the apex of the news agenda. This occasion marked the beginning of 'Cleggmania', whereby the assured performance of the Liberal Democrat leader and the positive bounce that followed in his party's opinion poll rankings drove him to the centre of the campaign and even led to speculation that the Liberal Democrats might become the main opposition party.

Table 18.3 compares the overall media evaluations made of the leaders' performances in the debates. When coding these variables, we were not only interested in those occasions when journalists opined openly about the success or otherwise of a candidate, but also when they dispassionately attributed success or failure by relaying external evidence or the opinions of others. The results show that most journalists hedged their bets when appraising the performance of the two main party leaders, with most evaluations being either mixed, neutral or unclear in their direction. This equivocation was less evident in the treatment of Nick Clegg, whose positive ratings far exceeded those of the other leaders.

Table 18.3 Media evaluations of the main party leaders

		All %	Broadcast %	Quality Press %	Mid- market %	Popular Press %
Brown	Positive	8	9	6	3	13
	Negative	20	14	14	33	26
	Mixed/ unclear/ no evaluation	72	77	80	64	61
	(Number of cases)	(389)	(118)	(102)	(63)	(106)
Cameron	Positive	21	15	20	29	23
	Negative	10	4	12	6	15
	Mixed/ unclear/ no evaluation	70	81	68	65	62
	(Number of cases)	(391)	(120)	(103)	(63)	(105)
Clegg	Positive	38	41	53	34	21
	Negative	8	2	5	11	15
	Mixed/ unclear/ no evaluation	54	57	42	55	64
	(Number of cases)	(406)	(126)	(112)	(62)	(106)

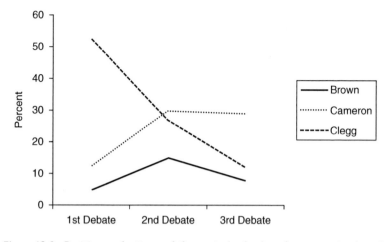

Figure 18.2   Positive evaluations of the party leaders' performances in the tel-evised debates (all media)

These overall ratings mask the extent to which media assessments of the leaders' performances shifted debate-by-debate. Figure 18.2 examines how the proportion of positive ratings for the participants shifted throughout the debates, and shows that, after the first burst of Cleggmania, positive evaluations of Cameron's performance exceeded those of Clegg's to a considerable extent in the last debate.

This reversal may be explicable in terms of the actual performance of the leaders across the three events. Certainly, many commentators felt that Cameron raised his presentational game significantly in the last two debates. Nevertheless, it is difficult to escape the conclusion that the shift also reflects a change in the editorial direction and focus of many news organisations, particularly those with more open partisan proclivities. It is to these matters that the discussion now turns.

The uncertain return of the Tory press

Table 18.4 compares the stated editorial declarations of the national press in 2010 with 2005. The columns indicating the endorsement are based on close analysis of the various newspapers' editorial endorse-ments in the final week of the campaign. Obviously these statements are only one dimension of the given title's political output, but they are highly significant nonetheless. Editorials of this kind are typically self-conscious and lengthy, detailed statements. Moreover, they are the

Table 18.4 Editorial declarations and circulations of the national newspapers: 2005 and 2010

	2005			2010		
Dailies	**Party**	**Strength**	**Circulation**	**Party**	**Strength**	**Circulation**
Guardian	Labour	Weak	0.34	Lib Dem	Moderate	0.29
Times	Labour	Weak	0.51	Conservative	Weak	0.51
Telegraph	Conservative	Strong	0.87	Conservative	Moderate	0.68
Financial Times	Labour	Weak	0.38	Conservative	Weak	0.39
Independent	Lib Dem	Moderate	0.23	Lib Dem	Moderate	0.19
Mail	Conservative	Strong	2.3	Conservative	Strong	2.1
Express	Conservative	Strong	0.87	Conservative	Strong	0.67
The Sun	Labour	Weak	3.26	Conservative	Strong	3
Mirror	Labour	Strong	2.29	Labour	Strong	1.57
Star	None	–	0.85	None	–	0.82
Weeklies						
Observer	Labour	Moderate	0.42	Lib Dem	Moderate	0.33
Independent on Sunday	Lib Dem	Weak	0.18	None		0.17
Sunday Times	Conservative	Weak	1.35	Conservative	Strong	1.14
Sunday Telegraph	Conservative	Strong	0.65	Conservative	Strong	0.51
Mail on Sunday	None	–	2.37	Conservative	Strong	1.98
Sunday Express	Conservative	Strong	0.84	Conservative	Strong	0.57
News of the World	Labour	Weak	3.64	Conservative	Strong	2.91
Sunday Mirror	Labour	Strong	1.53	Labour	Strong	1.12
The People	Labour	Moderate	0.9	None	–	0.53

result of discussions involving the most senior executives, the composition varying between newspapers but involving a selection of editors, leader-writers and possibly proprietors (Firmstone, 2008). Table 18.4 indicates both the political affiliations of the papers and the strength of their support. 'Strong' indicates a paper whose support was unconditional, 'Moderate' describes an editorial with some qualification of the allegiance, and 'Weak' relates to the most tepid and conditional of endorsements. Figures 18.3 to 18.5 collate the 2010 data according to aggregate circulation, political affiliation (by circulation) and strength of affiliation (by circulation) and compare these with all other British general elections since 1992.

The results show two major changes in 2010, against a long-term decline in national press circulation figures (see Figure 18.3). First, there was a major switchback in editorial opinion towards the Conservatives (see Figure 18.4). Second, there was a recovery in the strength and stridency of press opinion (see Figure 18.5). As we have argued elsewhere, one of the defining features of the so-called Tony Press between 1997 and 2005 was the conditionality of its support. Press opinion essentially became de-aligned rather than realigned during this period (see Deacon and Wring, 2002). But, if this equivocation reduced significantly in 2010, there was no straightforward reversion to the Labour-bashing of the early 1990s. The complexity of the campaign caused by the sudden emergence of a telegenic third figure required Conservative advocates to fight on two fronts, thereby dividing their focus.

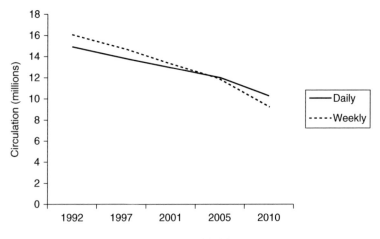

Figure 18.3   National press circulation (1992–2010)

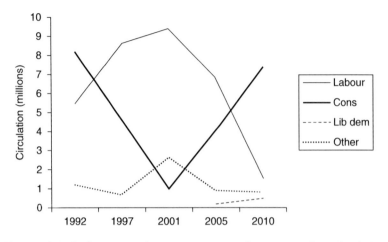

Figure 18.4 Daily national press party endorsements by circulation (1992–2010)

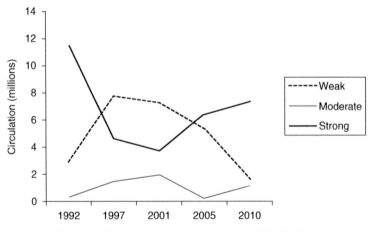

Figure 18.5   Strength of partisanship by circulation (1992–2010)

Certainly, there was a marked mobilisation of Conservative press opinion against Nick Clegg and his party after the first debate, which explains at least partly the reduction in positive media evaluations of the Liberal Democrat leader over the final two debates. Just before the second debate, the *Daily Telegraph* claimed Clegg had received improper payments from party donors ('Nick Clegg, the Lib Dem donors and Payments into his

Private Account; EXCLUSIVE: Donor Cash Mystery', *Daily Telegraph*, 22 April 2010: 1). This topic briefly surfaced during the second debate on Sky when raised by the debate's moderator in apparent contravention of the rules governing the programmes. At the same time the *Daily Express* attacked the Liberal Democrats' policy on immigration ('CLEGG'S CRAZY IMMIGRATION POLICY; 2.5 m on dole but he wants jobs for asylum seekers', *Daily Express*, 22 April 2010: 1) and the *Sun* ridiculed Clegg's preparations for the debate, leaking details of a misplaced party document that outlined his strategy ('LIB DEMS LOSE PLOT; CLEGG AIDE LEFT SECRETS IN BACK OF CAB: Leader told to be more like David Cameron in telly debates. Campaign chief urges him to gloss over nukes policy: Warning in dossier: Don't act weird like PM. Be Normal', the *Sun*, 21 April 2010: 4–5). The most extraordinary attack came from the *Daily Mail* on the day of the second debate. Under the headline 'CLEGG IN NAZI SLUR ON BRITAIN', the paper dragged up a piece written for the *Guardian* by Nick Clegg in 2002, in which he claimed German society had come to terms with the legacy of World War Two more effectively than the British. In the front page article, the paper's deputy political editor fulminated against 'an astonishing attack on our national pride'.

Such was the intensity of these attacks that even Labour's chair of electoral strategy, Peter Mandelson, was moved to criticise them as 'disgusting and classic smears…straight out of the Tory party' (*Guardian*, 23 April 2010). Others argued that the crudity and vituperative nature of these attacks did not so much reveal the Tory press rediscovering the potency of its voice as indicate its dismay and disorientation. For example, the *Guardian* ran a piece on the day of the second debate that claimed 'Cleggmania' had set off 'raw panic' in right-wing media outlets and quoted John Lloyd, director of journalism at the Reuters Institute for the Study of Journalism at Oxford University, who commented: 'Clearly, the newspapers and editors who are ideological Tories are suffering from a howl of rage, now that what had seemed to be a shoo-in has turned into the risk of a hung parliament.'[3]

Interpreting the campaign

Direct evaluations of election protagonists of this kind are just one dimension by which the media can influence the direction and outcome of elections. Just as significant are the ways in which journalists frame the campaign – the issues they focus upon and those they neglect. This can be termed as the *interpretative* dimension of reporting, and is also important, as it provides some measure of the richness and diversity of the informational diet provided by the news media during these crucial political periods.

In recent times, some commentators have noted the tendency of election coverage to concentrate on the process rather than the substance of politics, by emphasising the strategies and personalities of politicians rather than engaging with policy complexities (e.g. de Vreese, 2008; Esser et al., 2001; Plasser and Lengauer, 2008). This epiphenomenal fixation in the media has not escaped the attention of British politicians. For example, in the 2001 General Election, both Tony Blair and his Communications Director Alastair Campbell separately condemned the media's failure to address 'real issues' in their coverage and their fixation with 'process not policy' (see 'Labour May Re-Think Labour's Backdrops', the *Guardian*, 10 May 2001: 7). The leadership debates stirred similar concerns in 2010, when Labour sought to recruit cross-party signatories to a letter to the major news broadcasters raising concerns about the impact of the leadership discussions on election news content. Both opposition parties declined to sign, but Labour sent the complaint anyway, writing: 'We believe that the Leadership debates are good thing and an important part of the General Election but we do believe that an unintended consequence of the attention they get has been a lack of policy scrutiny and discussion that was normal in previous election coverage. We think the public are being short-changed by the focus on process not policy' (25 April 2010).

Table 18.5 gives an overview of the interpretative dimensions of the election coverage by ranking the most to least prominent themes found in the content analysis sample. At first sight the finding that 43 per cent of themes dealt with 'electoral process' seems to lend credence to Labour's concerns. However, the LCRC's 2005 election news analysis found almost exactly the same levels of process coverage in campaign reporting (Deacon et al., 2005). Although the precise details of this category changed in 2010 as a result of the leadership debates, in broader terms they seem to have only consolidated what is now a chronic propensity in election news reporting.

In the context of a major and perpetuating global financial crisis, it is not surprising that 'Economy' and 'Taxation' were the most prominent substantive topics in campaign reporting overall, being particularly evident in broadcast and 'quality' press coverage. In contrast, the fallout from the MPs' expenses scandal that rocked Parliament in the months preceding the election reverberated more strongly in the more popular sections of the press, with 'Impropriety/Standards' accounting for 14 per cent of the themes in the mid-market papers and 10 per cent of those in the popular

Table 18.5   Main themes in election news

	All %	Broadcast %	Quality Press %	Mid-market Press %	Popular Press %
Electoral Process	43	43	40	37	53
Economy	9	10	11	6	6
Taxation	7	7	8	4	5
Impropriety/ Standards	6	3	5	14	10
Immigration, Race, Asylum	5	5	3	10	5
Constitutional	4	4	6	4	1
Media and ICTs	4	8	1	0	0.1
Public Services	4	4	4	4	2
Business	2	2	4	1	1
Defence Military	2	2	2	1	2
Education	2	2	2	2	2
Employment	2	2	2	3	2
Social Security	2	1	2	2	4
Crime	1	1	1	2	2
Europe	1	1	2	3	1
Women's Issues	1	1	1	3	3
NHS	1	1	1	3	0.4
Environment	1	1	1	1	0.1
Northern Ireland	0.3	0.5	0.2	0	0
Foreign Policy	0.2	0.1	0.4	0	0
Health	0.2	0.1	0.2	0.6	0.3
Housing	0.2	0.1	0.3	0	0
Transport	0.2	0.2	0.3	0.4	0
Agriculture	0.1	0.1	0.1	0	0
Local Government	0.1	0.1	0.1	0	0
Arts	0.1	0	0.4	0	0
(number of themes)	(4,635)	(2,045)	(1,390)	(504)	(696)

Notes: up to three codes could be entered per item. Percentages = number of themes coded per category / total number of themes * 100. Percentages above 0.5% are rounded and may not add up to 100

press. (For broadcast and quality press coverage, the figures were 6 and 3 per cent respectively.) Once again, these patterns should not be seen as new or unique. For example, in the 1997 General Election coverage, charges of political 'sleaze' – a conflated condemnation of politicians' private indis-cretions and public impropriety – commanded similar levels of attention and were far more prominent in the popular press (see Deacon et al., 1998: 138–140). This tends to suggest that these news outlets habitually incline to a more individuated and negative perception of politics and politicians, but what differed in 2010 was that these accusations of impropriety did not map clearly onto the party political contest. Opprobrium against unaccountable, freeloading politicians was dispensed across the political spectrum, unlike the 'sleaze' scandals of 1997, which mainly implicated the Conservative party. This general tone of disdain, even disgust, was exemplified by a commentary piece in the *Sunday Express* in the final week of the campaign, which commented: 'These men and women who make pronouncements about our lives, day in, day out, have discovered that the moral high ground is a dark and lonely place, especially when you are caught with your trousers around your ankles' ('Love them or hate them, we have a duty to vote', the *Sunday Express*, 2 May 2010).

Media coverage of immigration, race and asylum issues during general elections in the UK has been a perennially controversial matter. For instance, in 1992, the Conservative party was criticised for running a series of alarmist stories about Labour's immigration policies in the last week of the campaign (Billig and Golding, 1992), and in the lead-up to the 2001 General Election both main parties accused their opponents of 'playing the race card' for the purposes of political advantage. This led the Commission for Racial Equality to request that all parties sign a 'compact of good practice' undertaking that they would not recklessly emphasise asylum, race or immigration issues for political gain (*Guardian*, 15 March 2001: 10). In 2010, these matters did not feature so prominently, with the sole and notable exception of the mid-market papers, the *Daily Express* and the *Daily Mail*, which placed at least twice as much emphasis on these matters as any other media.

Immigration, race and asylum issues were late entrants into the media election debate, only gaining significant prominence towards the last days of the campaign. The trigger was a memorable and excruciating meeting between the Prime Minister and a member of the public, Gillian Duffy, during a visit to Rochdale on 27 April 2010. After a testing exchange, during which Mrs Duffy claimed people from Eastern Europe were 'flocking' to Britain, the pair parted amicably. But when Brown returned to his car he forgot to remove his Sky TV microphone and journalists were able to eavesdrop on Brown's candid view of Mrs Duffy and the photo-opportunity. Describing the encounter as 'a disaster' and criticising his aides for having arranged it, Brown dismissed Duffy as 'just a sort of bigoted woman that said she used to be Labour'. The gaffe stimulated an immediate media feeding frenzy: Mrs Duffy was tracked down and her shock and outrage captured on camera, as was the Prime Minister's dismayed reaction as his unguarded comments were played back to him at the BBC radio station. The rumpus was so immediate and intense that Brown had no choice but to visit Mrs Duffy at her home to offer a lengthy and unconditional apology. After forty minutes, he emerged from her house and through a rictus grin declared himself a 'penitent sinner' to the serried ranks of journalists and news crews gathered in Mrs Duffy's front garden.

'Bigotgate', as it became known, dominated media coverage for a few days. Much of the commentary focused on what it revealed about Brown's personality, his state of mind and its emblematic significance for Labour's faltering campaign. However, a proportion of the debate also considered evidence for Duffy's concerns about immigration and whether her remarks constituted bigotry. The *Daily Mail* and *Daily Express* were unequivocal in their position, repudiating Brown's label unconditionally (e.g. 'IF THIS WOMAN'S A BIGOT THEN I'M PROUD TO BE ONE TOO', the *Daily Mail*, 29 April 2010; 'Labour are the real immigration bigots', the *Daily Mail*, 29 April 2010; 'Gillian Duffy Asked the Questions we All Want Answered', the *Daily Express*, 30 April 2010). Figure 18.6 compares the daily average number of news items that referred to immigration, race and asylum issues prior to the Duffy encounter (7–26 April) with the average number on the day of the event and the three days

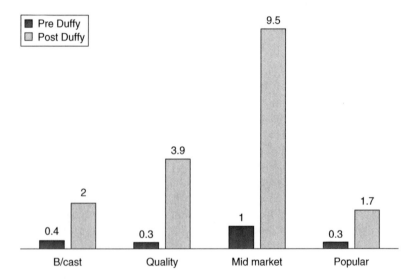

Figure 18.6 Average number of items referring to 'Immigration/Asylum/Race' before and after the Gillian Duffy controversy (by media category)

Notes: 'Pre-Duffy' period = weekdays between 7 April and 27 April; 'Post-Duffy' period = 28 April – 30 April. Averages = total number of items that had 'Immigration/Asylum/Race' as a theme / number of days * number of media outlets included under each media grouping.

after (27–30 April). The triggering effect across all media sectors is stark, but most dramatic in the mid-market tabloids, who used the event as a licence to bring the issue, a long-standing concern of theirs, to electoral prominence.

Significant absences

When considering the thematic contours of the campaign it also important to note issues that were marginalised or ignored. The significance of these absences becomes particularly evident when one considers the topics that have dominated political and media debate in Britain since the election. In the context of a comprehensive spending review announced in November 2010, the Conservative/ Lib Dem coalition government has implemented a raft of radical and highly contentious reforms to social welfare and the public expenditure, intended both to achieve steep reductions in national indebtedness and to redefine the terms of the social contract. These policies include: exponential increases in university tuition fees, the abolition of universal child benefits, a major defence review, the introduction of a universal welfare credit scheme with powerful penalties for claimants who refuse opportunities to take up employment, a fundamental restructuring of National Health Service budgeting and management, changes to penal policy, and the removal of council tenants' rights to retain indefinite occupancy of public housing. All of these policies relate to subject areas that were marginalised during the campaign itself: themes related to 'public services' accounted for 4 per cent of coverage; 'Education', 2 per cent; 'Social Security', 2 per cent; 'Defence/Military', 2 per cent; 'NHS', 1 per cent; 'Crime', 1 per cent; and 'Housing', 0.2 per cent'. Moreover, this tendency seems to have perpetuated since the election. As the chief political commentator of the *Independent* recently observed:

> Because we've been focusing so much on the novelty of the coalition, the dynamics within the coalition, there's been less focus, I think, on the degree of change they're trying to bring about. They're trying to recast the relationship between the state and the citizen in ways that I think have as radical a scope as the '45 government. And they're moving I think faster than the Thatcher government in '79. In the first six months of this coalition there has been sweeping change on a scale that I think has been underestimated because of the novelty of the coalition itself. (Steve Richards, *Today*, BBC Radio 4, 20 December 2010)

The absence of policy debate during the election becomes even more evident when one breaks these subject categories down further. For example, the government's plans to triple university tuition fees in England have sparked mass demonstrations and instances of civil disorder since their announcement. This is already shaping up to be one of the most controversial and divisive issues of the coming parliament. The news media were fully aware that major plans were afoot before the election, as the Labour government had set up the Browne Review of Higher Education funding in 2009 and both main parties had indicated their intention to implement its main recommendations regarding tuition fees. The Liberal Democrats, in contrast, had made the abolition of first degree tuition fees a cornerstone of their manifesto. Also, in the last weekend of the campaign, a source involved in the Browne committee leaked details to the *Sunday Times* about the direction of Browne's 'hawkish' thinking, and projected fee levels of £7–£14,000 per annum. The week before the leak, the head of the National Students' Union accused the main parties of engaging in a 'conspiracy' to suppress debate about the issue during the campaign (*The Times*, 20 April 2010: 10).

Table 18.6 provides the results of an additional analysis keyword search of the Nexis newspaper digital archive to quantify the number

Table 18.6   Number of articles and main emphasis of national press items referring to 'tuition fees' (7 April – 6 May)

	'Quality'	Mid-market	Popular
Tuition Fees as main focus	8	3	
Tuition Fees as secondary focus	18	3	1
One sentence reference	23	9	6
Main emphasis			
Labour record/plans	11	2	3
Conservative plans	1	2	1
Liberal Democrat plans	16	6	3
Other party plans	4	1	
Cross-party comparison/collusion	4		
Public concern/debate	5		
University management demands	3	1	
Student union demands	1	1	
Browne review	1		
Other issues	3	2	

Notes: the count is based on a keyword search of daily newspaper content held on the Nexis database. The newspapers sampled were: the *Guardian*, *Times*, *Independent*, *Telegraph*, *Mail*, *Express*, *Mirror* and *Sun*. The keyword used was 'tuition fees'.

and main emphasis of daily national newspaper articles that made any reference, in any section, to 'tuition fees' during the campaign. The search identified only eleven items across all newspapers that had tuition fees as their main focus, twenty-two that referred to the issue in a subsidiary context and thirty-eight that mentioned it in one sentence or less. In terms of their focus, the largest proportion of these articles addressed the Liberal Democrats' manifesto commitment to the revocation of tuition fees, which they have since reneged upon. The next most prominent category related to Labour's previous record on tuitions and their proposals. Conservative plans received less coverage than those of the minority parties. If there was a cross-party conspiracy to keep tuition fees off the political agenda, it is difficult to escape the conclusion that, in media terms at least, it was extraordinarily effective.

The first internet election?

'2010 is the UK's first ever social media election.' Richard Allan, Facebook's Director of European Public Policy

If one were to take some pre-election commentary seriously, analysing mainstream media coverage of the recent UK general election is becoming, or may have already become, a redundant exercise. In the months preceding the campaign, a steady stream of news articles and public statements speculated that 2010 would see the first internet election in the UK, in which ever more fractal and unpredictable online communication would take centre stage in the communication of the election (e.g. 'How the 2010 election will be won by blogs and tweets', the *Observer*, 3 January 2010; 'Welcome to the first E-election', the *Guardian*, 17 March 2010). There was nothing new in these claims; indeed, by our reckoning, this is the fourth time that 'first internet general election' has been declared in the UK.[4] But, if the refrain was familiar, there seemed to be stronger grounds for assuming that 2010 might prove a tipping point. The five years since the last election have seen the explosion of the 'blogosphere' and social media Facebook, YouTube, Twitter, and other online social networking forums. Moreover, all the political parties were making considerable long-term investment in their digital strategies, and this trend was given a significant impetus by Barack Obama's astute use of new media in his successful bid for the US Presidency in 2008 (Cain Miller, 2008; Haynes and Pitts, 2009).

As the campaign countdown began, journalistic anticipation intensified about the impact of new media in the campaign. For example, in early March the *Independent* asked: 'With just two months to go, when will the internet election take off?' (1 March 2010: 43). One reason for this enthusiasm lay in the potential opportunities new media forums offered for disrupting the parties' tight choreography of their campaigns, allowing journalistic opportunities to find and amplify the comments of careless or recalcitrant party members who strayed off message. And it did not take long before an opportunity arose. In early April the Scottish *Sun* newspaper downloaded and published the Tweets of Stuart MacLennan, Scottish Labour candidate for Moray, in which he personally abused opposition politicians, boasted about his alcoholic intake, referred to older people as 'coffin dodgers' and on one occasion described a member of the public he was sitting opposite on a train as having a face like 'an old boot'. Most of the tweets were posted before MacLennan became a candidate, but, as the controversy grew, Labour were forced to sack him. In response, MacLennan offered a contrite apology for being 'very, very silly'.

We have already noted the significance of the internet and social media as a supplement to the televised leadership debates, but as part of our media audit we also quantified the extent to which news items appearing in the mainstream 'offline' media had their origins in 'online' media, along the lines of the MacLennan controversy. Despite the pre-election hype, only a small minority of items betrayed any such connections. 'Twitter' was only referred to in 1.2 per cent of items; 'Facebook', 0.4 per cent; 'blogs', 1.9 per cent. We recognise that the influence of the internet may have been more significant in other domains of campaign communication (e.g. e-campaigning, cyber-activist subversion of party publicity, direct canvassing, etc.) and that divisions between new and old media are no longer clear and can be overstated. Nevertheless, these findings suggest that in media terms the claims of an internet election were unfounded, and that the ties that bind the mainstream news organisations to the blogosphere and social media remain tenuous.

Concluding remarks

The political complexity and competitiveness of the 2010 election were mirrored in its mediation. National broadcasters found a new and influential basis for asserting their importance in the electoral process, via the televised debates, at the same time as many sections of the national press abandoned years of cognitive dissonance and reconnected their implicit conservatism with open support for the Conservative party. In the battle for influence that followed, the broadcasters clearly shaped the narrative of the campaign by elevating the status of the Liberal

Democrat leader and preventing the Tory press from returning to habit-
uated patterns of attack against Labour. In this contest, online media
struggled to gain a foothold. Where they did have influence, this was in
a way that supplemented rather than subverted the mainstream media.
In 2010 Britain, 'big media' still rule the roost, and the wait for the first
internet election continues.

The results of our analysis also reveal similarities across media sectors
that raise questions about their democratic performance. As with other
recent elections, one is struck by the narrowness of the range of voices
that participated in media discourses, which in 2010 was more limited
than ever. In terms of issue coverage, too, journalists' fascination with the
manoeuvrings and machinations of the electoral process once again
restricted the room for detailed discussion of the difficult policy choices
that confronted the country. 'Bigotgate' may have demonstrated the
aggression and irreverence of the British media, but, although a couple
of newspapers took the opportunity to advance their editorial concerns
about immigration, it was ultimately a media frenzy about a personal
and strategic faux pas. Elsewhere, the media failed to focus much attention on policy matters of ongoing or imminent significance. This was
not entirely their own fault, as there is plenty of circumstantial evidence that the political parties sought to divert and sequester debate
on difficult issues, such as higher education funding. Nonetheless, it
suggests a collective failure of imagination, ambition and independence
which left the electorate poorly positioned to anticipate the scale, sever-
ity and radicalism of the statecraft that was to follow.

Notes

1. The 2010 content analysis sampling time period began on 7 April and ended
   on 6 May 2010 (the day of the formal commencement of the campaign
   and polling day, respectively). Sampling was restricted to weekday coverage published during this period (i.e. Monday to Friday). The programmes
   covered in the broadcast sample were: BBC1, 10 pm news; ITV, *News at Ten*;
   BBC2, *Newsnight*; Channel 4, 7 pm news; Channel 5, 7 pm news; Sky News,
   9–9.30 pm; BBC Radio 1, *Newsbeat*; BBC Radio 4, *Today* (7.30–8.30 am). The
   newspapers covered in the sample were: the so-called quality press – the
   Guardian, the *Independent*, *The Times*, the *Daily Telegraph* and the *Financial
   Times*; the 'mid-markets'– the *Daily Mail* and the *Daily Express*; and the 'populars', comprising the *Sun*, the *Mirror* and the *Star*. Any item that made a
   clear reference to the 2010 UK General Election was coded. Where the item
   referred to the election in an incidental way, only the section that discussed
   the election was coded. The entire content of the broadcast sample was analysed. For the newspaper sample, all election-related content in the following

302 David Deacon and Dominic Wring

sections was coded: (1) the front page; (2) the next two pages of any general
news coverage; (3) the first two pages of any specialist section assigned to
the coverage of the campaign; (4) the page containing and facing the paper's
leader editorial. The rationale here was to concentrate our analysis on the pri-
oritised news arenas in the press. The authors wish to acknowledge the dedication of our coding team: Fred Attenborough, Emily Harmer and Ian Taylor.
We also would like to thank our colleagues Peter Golding, James Stanyer,
John Downey, Michael Billig and Jonathan Potter for supporting the research
project.
2. Figures from the Broadcasting Audience Research Board. There were also
other debates featuring front bench politicians debating their subject areas
mainly on the BBC during the election. Channel 4 broadcast a Chancellors'
debate just before the campaign began.
3. An anecdote that lends some credence to this interpretation was an impromptu
confrontation in the *Independent* newspaper's headquarters between editor-
in-chief Simon Kelner and Rupert Murdoch's son and key lieutenant James,
who was accompanied by Rebekah Brooks, the former *Sun* editor who manages their News International firm's UK papers. Kelner had not invited the
pair, who subsequently barged into his office and forcefully remonstrated
with him about an *Independent* advertisement with the headline 'Rupert
Murdoch Won't Decide this Election. You Will.' Although the protagonists'
own media were reluctant to dwell on the episode, other journalists saw it as
highly newsworthy, and Channel 4's political correspondent Cathy Newman
broadcast an account of what had happened from inside the headquarters
of the *Independent*. If nothing else, the encounter between Kelner and his
critics revealed the sensitivity of Murdoch executives to the charge that they
were seeking to influence the election outcome. Furthermore, as former *Sun*
editor David Yelland saw it, the confrontation reflected unease within the
company at the emergence of the Liberal Democrats as potential partners in
government. As Yelland argued, the third party had previously been largely
ignored by papers belonging to Murdoch's News International group, and
he interpreted the confrontation with Kelner as a sign of concern inside the
media company that the apparent surge in support for the third party might
damage their Conservative allies' position (Yelland, 2010).
4. For one of the earliest examples of this kind of claim, see North (1997). For
critical appraisals of these claims in the last two UK general elections, see
Downey (2001) and Downey and Davidson (2005).

References

Billig, M. and Golding, P. (1992) 'The Hidden Factor: Race, the News Media and
the 1992 Election', *Representations*, 31(4): 36–8.
Cain Miller, C. (2008) 'How Obama's Internet Campaign Changed Politics', *New
York Times*, 7 November.
Chadwick, A. (2010) 'Britain's First Live Televised Party Leaders' Debate: From
the News Cycle to the Political Information Cycle', *Parliamentary Affairs*,
64(1): 1–21.

De Vreese, C. H. (2008) 'Media in the Game of Politics: Effects of Strategic Metacoverage on Political Cynicism', *The International Journal of Press/Politics*, 13(3): 285–309.

Deacon, D. and Wring, D. (2002) 'Partisan Dealignment and the British Press', in Bartle, J., Mortimore, R. and Atkinson, S. (eds) *Political Communications: the British General Election of 2001*. London: Frank Cass, 197–211.

Deacon, D., Golding, P. and Billig, M. (1998) 'Between Fear and Loathing: National Press Coverage of the 1997 British General Election', in Denver, D., Fisher, J., Cowley, P. and Pattie, C. (eds) *British General Elections and Parties Review*. London: Frank Cass, 135–149.

Deacon, D., Golding, P. and Billig, M. (2001) ' "Real Issues" and Real Coverage in the 2001 Campaign', *Parliamentary Affairs*, 54(4): 666–7.

Deacon, D., Wring, D., Billig, M., Downey, J., Golding, P. and Davidson, S. (2005) *Reporting the 2005 UK General Election: A Study Conducted on Behalf of The Electoral Commission*. Loughborough: Loughborough University.

Deacon, D., Wring, D. and Golding, P. (2006) 'Same Campaign, Differing Agendas: Analysing News Media Coverage of the 2005 General Election', *British Politics*, 1: 222–56.

Downey, J. (2001) 'In search of the net election', *Journalism Studies*, 2(4): 604–10.

Downey, J. and Davidson, S. (2005) 'The internet and the 2005 UK General Election', in Deacon, D., Wring, D., Billig, M., Downey, J., Golding, P. and Davidson, S. (eds) *Reporting the 2005 UK General Election*. Loughborough: Loughborough Communication Research Centre: 60–71.

Esser, F., Reinemann, C. and Fan, D. (2001) 'Spin-Doctors in the United States, Great Britain and Germany. Meta-communication about media manipulation', *Harvard Journal of Press/Politics*, 6: 16–45.

Firmstone, J. (2008) 'The editorial production process and editorial values as influences on the opinions of the British Press towards Europe', *Journalism Practice*, 2(2): 212–29.

Haynes, A. and Pitts, B. (2009) 'Making an Impression: New Media in the 2008 Presidential Nomination Campaigns', *Political Science & Politics*, 42: 53–8.

North, A. (1997) 'My vote for wired winners and losers; After the first Internet election which Web sites came first past the post?' *The Independent*, 6 May 1997: 5.

Plasser, F. and Lengauer, G. (2008) 'Television campaigning Worldwide', in Johnson, D. (ed.) *Routledge Handbook of Political Management*. London: Routledge, 256–70.

Wring, D. and Ward, S. (2010) 'The Media and the 2010 Campaign: the Television Election?' in Geddes, A. and Tonge, J. (eds) *Britain Votes 2010*. Oxford: Hansard Society.

Yelland, D. (2010) 'Nick Clegg's rise could lock Murdoch and the media elite out of UK politics', *Guardian*, 19 April.

19
Genre and the Mediation of Election Politics

Kay Richardson, Katy Parry and John Corner

This book's focus on the role of traditional (mass) and new (online) media in the unfolding of events across the general election period will be developed in the present chapter through an exploration of forms of mediation beyond news, in non-journalistic genres across the mediascape. The relevance of this study follows from its approach to the positioning of 'politics' within the broader context of political culture, rather than the more specific one of political knowledge. To introduce a cultural framing in this context is to recognise that public interest in political affairs has a variable character, and that citizens access the 'political' in different forms and at different levels. Undoubtedly, they access politics as information and opinion, mediated 'officially' via news journalism and associated editorial comment, and less officially via online sources, in ways explored by other contributors to this volume. They also access it through comedy programmes, drama, newspaper cartoons, reality television, blogs, online forums, Twitter streams and satiric newspaper columns, many of which are designed to offer pleasure as much as, or more than, to enhance their understanding of the electoral stakes and perhaps mobilise them to electoral action.

Despite the broader terms of cultural engagement at work here, material of this kind works alongside other mediations in constructing knowledge and feelings about the sphere of politics and its values. The genres that offer these gratifications operate differently at different positions on the 'elite'/'popular' spectrum of taste, and are of interest to us when they rely on substantive thematic content with a specifically political focus, in whole or in part. In doing so, they contribute to the character of discourse about politics in ways that are specific to times and places. Our study thus belongs within what can be described as the 'cultural turn' in the political communication field, a more comprehensive placing of mediation within the broader settings of social values and expressivity. The work of such writers as John Street, Liesbet van Zoonen, Jeffrey Jones and Gianpetro Mazzoleni testifies to the history, and strength, of this academic development, across a number of Western democratic states (see, e.g., Corner and Pels, 2003; Jones, 2005; Mazzoleni, 2009; Street, 1997; van Zoonen, 2005).

The account presented here of mediated politics during the general election campaign forms part of a more extensive British case study of mediation 'beyond the news' throughout 2010, auditing the range of available materials at a number of different points in the annual political cycle (see Corner et al., 2011). Whereas previous research on 'non-news' political texts have tended to focus on particular genres such as cartoons (Seymour-Ure, 2001) or TV drama (van Zoonen, 2003; Corner and Richardson, 2008, 2009), a distinctive feature of this current research is its attempt to explore expressive characteristics across a generic range. During any general election campaign, politics is centre stage for the national mainstream media, and various modes of ostensibly 'civic' consideration inform much of their practice. Yet high-profile electoral events also provide the resources for mediations that take politics deep into the territory of popular culture. In the 2010 General Election, it was such events as the (planned) Leaders' Debates and the (unplanned) 'Bigotgate' gaffe that provided key anchor points around which non-news genres discursively orchestrated their own textualities, according to their own criteria of relevance, value and interest. In what follows, we demonstrate some of the variation that we discovered in April/May 2010. For our approach, an understanding of how meaning derives from the articulation of textual 'content' within parameters of textual 'form' is of particular importance, and has informed our use of *genre* as the organisational basis of this article. It is to the concept of 'genre' that we now turn.

Genre

The notion of 'genre' is a relatively unfamiliar one within the literature on political communications, although, as the above-mentioned 'cultural turn' in international work continues, this is likely to change. One reason for its absence is that established work in the area, particularly on media and elections, has been centrally, if not exclusively, concerned with the modes of political journalism. Here, although there are important variations in formal organisation and market demographics to be registered, ideas of generic-level variation might seem beside the point given the relative singularity of focus. However, since our own project centrally involves drawing comparisons and contrasts across very different ways of representing politics in speech, image and writing across diverse media, ideas of the generic are at the core of our approach. Recognising, if only approximately, what 'kind' of thing a given item of mediation belongs to informs a sense of what kind of formal 'rules' it might follow in its construction, what kinds of satisfaction it might give and what kind of criteria might be most appropriate to judgements of its qualities. In relation to politics and the political, it provides an indication of the expressive range, scope and level of detail likely to be found and the modes of address and tones that will be employed. Notions of genre provide basic templates both for media practice and for media use. Although in their more intensively commercialised varieties they have been regarded as formulaic constraints on creativity, they are better approached analytically as frameworks enabling certain types of discursive work to be done effectively, building on recognised precedents but allowing originality. An example that demonstrates an occasion when the political world and a commercialised variety of television genre collided rather uncomfortably was Gordon Brown's appearance on the celebrity chat show *Life Stories with Piers Morgan* in February 2010, in which he talked with great emotion about the death of his daughter in front of a studio audience that included his tearful wife. Appearing within a television genre associated with celebrity revelations opened up novel space for the incumbent prime minister to show his 'human' side, but it also highlighted just how far Brown had moved, from conventional political television, into a popular form of programming with its own distinctive 'rules' and highly stylised qualities. The idea of generic 'affordance' may be used to register this positive capacity.[1]

The generic system is constantly being modified by new options as a result of broader market and technological as well as aesthetic shifts, and, as we shall show, within Britain it is still strongly overdetermined by the differentiations of social class. In what follows, we give attention to three areas of electoral mediation occurring outside the frame of political journalism, in which varied forms of speech, image and writing are explored respectively – in broadcast talk, political cartoons and newspaper sketch-writing.

Contexts of non-news political talk in broadcasting

This section focuses on political talk in broadcast genres other than journalism, moving from radio through to television, across dialogic and monologic modalities, and from contexts calling for performances of 'self' to those where dramatised actorly performances of 'others' are required. Detailed analysis is offered on extracts from *The News Quiz* and *This Week*, with briefer comments on formats deployed in *Bremner, Bird and Fortune*.

The News Quiz is a long-running comedy panel show on BBC Radio Four.[2] Series 71 was on air throughout the 2010 General Election and afterwards, and Episode Four, recorded on 7 May, in the nervous hiatus between the vote on 6 May and the formation of the new coalition government on 11 May, offers some relevant illustrations of the approach.

The basic generic format involves getting the four panellists to answer a series of cryptically worded questions on topical events, starting with the most newsworthy ones, which are frequently political. The contestants are expected to produce witty performances as they elaborate their replies; this is managed interactively, giving the talk a conversational joke-making tenor and drawing the studio audience into its sociability: the broadcast audience is invited to appreciate the good-humoured ambience. On 7 May, the first question was 'Why are we waiting?' – a reference to the indeterminacy of the election outcome and the negotiations then under way among the political parties. The four panellists (Jeremy Hardy, Francis Wheen, Sue Perkins, Jack Dee) found humour in the waiting game itself (if they wait in the pub, it will be not a 'hung parliament' but a 'hungover' parliament) and also from the broadcast mediation of the election night. One aspect of the BBC's election night coverage invited particular derision from the panellists: rather than reporting from a conventional studio setting, political interviewer Andrew Neil broadcast his segments from a lavish party boat on the Thames, soliciting comments on the political developments from incongruous combinations of celebrities:

Wheen:
...they had this weird thing with Andrew Neil, the great boulevardier, they kept cutting away to him, and he said, 'And now here to discuss the fiscal crisis we have Joan Collins and Martin Amis [...] Completely randomly chosen juxtapositions. Bruce Forsyth and Simon Schama, discussing the constitutional implications of a hung parliament!

The ridicule is here directed at the BBC, not at politicians, and it is mildly satirical. There is critical substance too behind Jeremy Hardy's mockery of how the election's outcome was rhetorically appropriated in some of the commentary, as if it were the product of group deliberation rather than diverse individual preferences:

> Hardy:
> I like the idea that the British public have spoken and come to this decision, so the British public have all come together and decided that the best thing would be to have a completely impotent Tory government that can't do anything, and to give the Lib Dems a kicking even though they really like them.

Contingent circumstances such as the indeterminate election result offer local opportunity to display the endemically ridiculous nature of political leadership as such. Political personalities come in for a lot of teasing, and the kind of humour on offer is very characteristic of British political satire more generally, in a history that goes back to the 'classic' 1960s *That Was The Week That Was* (BBC 1961–2).[3] Although our account here cannot do justice to the vocal performances of the panellists, one important resource in their largely affectionate ridicule of individuals is the production of caricature-imitations of politicians' *talk*, so that Mandelson is offered up through the prism of the sultry–sexy 'roué' voice of actor Leslie Phillips, and Gordon Brown through an exaggerated rendering of his Scottish accent, deep pitch and grainy delivery.

If the mode of *The News Quiz* is primarily dialogic, that of our next example is primarily monologic. *This Week* belongs to the overall genre of 'talk show', as a weekly late night politics programme on BBC1, hosted by Andrew Neil. During the election campaign its frequency was increased to twice weekly. In addition to Neil himself, the show normally features two regulars and various guests in a studio. But it also finds time for short films shot on location, billed as 'Take of the Week', each presented by a different expert or celebrity. The filming allows some scope for visual creativity, but it is the monologic lecture discourse, partly to camera and partly in voiceover, that is the dominant ingredient in the multimodal mix (which also includes some music). This monologic format is relatively unusual in current affairs programming, corresponding closely to the written style of the opinion-piece format found in the comment section of the quality press, and re-presented here as broadcast talk. During the election campaign, presenters of this slot included writer Will Self, BBC economics correspondent Robert Peston, former MP turned broadcaster Michael Portillo, newspaper columnist Andrew Rawnsley and chat show host

Richard Madeley. We shall draw on Madeley's three-minute film for purposes of demonstration.

Deploying his signature droll style, Neil introduces the film as being about politics and the cult of celebrity, following the first televised Leaders' Debate, which was Nick Clegg's big media opportunity. The film is shot on Hampstead Heath, offering its own symbolic value as 'the natural habitat of the British leftie–liberal'. Madeley's lecture works the 'X-factor politics' motif, which is not offered as a sustained analogy, but as a powerful image for glossing what had happened as a result of that debate.[4]

> We've been living in the age of celebrity for quite a long time now. And it's still in the ascendant. So the moment that the X-Factor met politics, live, on ITV One television – vvvvooom!

As a professional speaker, Madeley is able to animate these statements with dramatic timing and stress, to deliver a more emotionally engaging variant of what was not an original observation about the crossover area between popular culture and politics. Three minutes is long enough for him to develop an argument about the power of the media to elevate style over substance in the era of celebrity politics (he suggests that Clegg got his facts wrong and didn't say much in the debate) and draws the piece to a strong conclusion, albeit one which was later to be confounded by actual events:

> For the first time, then, in British electoral history, a single TV event, one television programme, has not only changed the course of an election, but potentially, the course of British political history. It's quite extraordinary. Can you think of any event, over the course of the last fifty years, that's had such an enormous effect on a single party's fortunes, overnight? Because I can't. But that's what happens when the X-factor on television meets the X-factor in the ballot box.

Along with cinema, television has often been used for the production of dramatic narratives with political subject matter. Some of these have been fully fictional. For instance, *The Amazing Mrs Pritchard* (BBC1, 2006) was a drama series about what happens when an 'ordinary' person suddenly becomes Prime Minister after forming a new political party which sweeps into power (see the critical discussion in Corner and Richardson, 2008). Other dramas have involved the fictionalised telling of 'true' stories. Here, *The Deal* (Granada for Channel 4, 2003) is a much-cited example, exploring the relationship between Tony Blair and Gordon Brown over a number of years and focusing on the arrangements made between them regarding the leadership of the Labour Party and the period for which Blair would serve as Prime Minister before stepping down. For a general overview of political drama on British television, including examples taken from the history of its development since the 1960s, see Corner and Richardson (2009). The production schedules required by both these kinds of drama, along with other factors, meant that none concerning the election were aired during the election period itself (although the turn of events clearly offers rich possibilities for future treatment). However, brief dramatised performances were offered as part of comedy in a way that is significant for our overall concern with generic range. For instance, the embryonic dramatisation evident in the spontaneous vocal caricatures of *The News Quiz* (see above) was seen in much fuller form in political impressions. For the election, Rory Bremner produced his characteristic sustained, scripted impersonations of politicians on Channel Four's *Bremner, Bird and Fortune: The Daily Wind Up. The Daily Wind Up* was an adaptation of the regular *Bremner, Bird and Fortune* programme in a three-part series, across three days in election week, with serious intent though mediated largely through comedy. The performance skills of Bremner are recurrently deployed in generic formats built on both stand-up and sketch comedy models. For this mini-series a 'street theatre' mode was also offered, in which Bremner participated in local campaigning as 'Peter Mandelson', 'William Hague' and 'Gordon Brown', interacting with real politicians such as George Osborne as well as with real voters in 'vox pop' moments. Bremner's unscripted impersonations here were sufficiently broad not to be regarded as exercises in deception, and the satirical impulse is weaker in these reality sketches than it is in his studio routines. The Bremner mini-series also provided one of the few loci for dramatised performance of *fictional* characters during the election. For these, no impersonation is required, only actorly characterisation, with an emphasis on easily recognisable social types. In the second episode, the series' familiar 'dinner party' set makes its appearance. In this scenario, John Bird, John Fortune, Frances Barber and Pauline McLynn portray two metropolitan couples whose self-interested motives and values emerge from under postures of civic high-mindedness, and who thus satirise a recognisable middle-class populism. The *visual* affordances of the audiovisual mode, of course, work differently in the stand-up routines, the street theatre sketches and the dinner party material.

While the impact of Bremner's stand-up act is enhanced only by his own physical and facial movements, and the background required for the middle-class dining room scenario can be satisfied by appropriately clothed actors and an appropriately dressed studio set, the vox pop interactions, which depend on the perception that the conversations are unscripted and that some of the participants are genuine members of the public, require the authentication of the real streets of provincial English places, such as Alderley and Salford. The application of a dramatic modality here provides a way of engaging with contemporary political events through a practice that is distinctive both in the immediacy provided by the imitation and in the 'realism' of the setting.

Visual voodoo: political cartoons in the newspapers

Martin Rowson, regular cartoonist for *The Guardian* and the *Daily Mirror*, has referred to the art of caricature as 'a type of voodoo – doing damage to someone at a distance with a sharp object' (2009: 153). The caricaturing of political leaders in editorial (or political) cartoons is merely one element of the imaginative capacities of this graphic form: by drawing on dimensions of fantasy, reality, allegory and metaphor, the political cartoon can offer a unique appraisal of political people, behaviours, events and structures via a diverse range of visual styles, attitudes and moods, often with comic effect. This section looks, then, at the political cartoon, an illustrative form of political commentary originating as a regular newspaper item in the late nineteenth century, and now stabilised as a daily multiple-column feature within the leader and comment sections of the 'quality' newspapers, and less consistently within the pages of the mid-market and tabloid titles.[5] Regularly printed in colour across all newspapers, this primarily pictorial mode often integrates text, in titles, captions, speech bubbles and labelling of content (both to aid identification and to draw out allegorical connections). As a more recent development, political cartoons are also available in digital form via the newspapers' sister websites, with *The Guardian*'s cartoons regularly garnering around 100 viewer reactions in the few days that the pages are open to comments. The internet has increased visibility for cartoonists' work at a time when scarce employment opportunities had led some authors to fear the decline of the political cartoon alongside the shrinking readership of traditional quality newsprint (see, e.g., Danjoux, 2007; Seymour-Ure, 2001).

Political cartoons have an ephemeral quality, often making elliptical references to topical subjects and news events, which might prove difficult to appreciate fully in the subsequent years or months. Conversely, the sharp observations of a cartoonist can endure beyond the life cycle of a news story, or even a political career, with certain caricatures recurring and becoming familiar to regular readers. Despite the often instantaneous and brutal 'bite' recognised in a momentary glance, only those acquainted with the particular cartoonist's stylistics, favoured cultural allusions and recurring tropes are likely to pick up on the full array of meanings and insinuations. Rather than explicate further on the broad generic and thematic features found during the election period, we now present four cartoons as illustrative examples, with analysis focused on aspects of visual design and the varied modes of engagement with political realities.

An election campaign period offers a particularly fruitful time for visual satirists; as political candidates strive to promote their identities and characters in order to gain public recognition and approval, cartoonists concurrently subvert, distort and exaggerate character traits to humorous effect (Conners, 2005; Edwards, 2001; Seymour-Ure, 2001). Yet portrayals of distinct moments in the campaign and political caricature can also extend to implications concerning the nature of institutions or structures, in spite of the limitations of the static visual frame.

In the cartoons we have audited, there is, not surprisingly, an emphasis on *political persons*, in particular the three party leaders, thereby making personal characterisation and caricature a principal depictive mode. Chris Riddell's cartoon on the first Leaders' Debate, printed in the *Observer* (18 April 2010), pictures the leaders in a boxing ring, drawing on a sporting metaphor which highlights the unusual participation of *three*, rather than two, opponents (Figure 19.1). With finely observed facial likenesses, rather than grotesque caricature, the two larger figures of Brown and Cameron are bruised and bloody following the bout, while a sprightly, unharmed Clegg is awarded victory by an off-frame referee. In placing the leaders in a boxing ring, post-fight, Riddell critiques the reductive quality of the post-debate analysis, focused on declaring a 'winner' in terms of performance rather than offering any detailed dissection of the policies put forward. He also satirises the moveable definition of 'winning', which is dependent on the infantilised perspective adopted by each party (here represented by the leaders in their party colours (red, blue and yellow shorts)).

Where Richard Madeley, in the example cited above, had questioned the rise of 'X-factor politics', alluding to televised popular culture, here the metaphorical domain of sport also highlights the campaign as a contest between individuals (with the surrounding darkness accentuating

Figure 19.1   Chris Riddell, *Observer*, 18 April (glove details are Clunk, Eton, Vince)
© Guardian News & Media Ltd 2010

the solitary focus on the three leaders). In terms of textual elements, aspects of each leader's personality are condensed into a slogan on the wristbands of their gloves: Brown's 'clunk' referring to his 'clunking fist' as coined by Tony Blair in his election-as-boxing metaphor back in 2006; Cameron's 'Eton' a reminder of his privileged past; and Clegg's 'Vince' referring to Vince Cable, at this stage the deputy leader of the Lib Dem party held in relatively high regard by the general public. The cartoon has no printed title, but each leader has a speech bubble, with a repetitive structure: Brown, 'I won because Posh Dave looked plastic and sounded fake...'; Cameron, 'I won because grumpy Gordon couldn't land a knockout punch...'; Clegg, 'I won because I have nothing to lose!' Whereas the two main party leaders point to each other's perceived weakness with verbal caricature and name-calling, Clegg delivers a victorious phrase that simultaneously undercuts his own achievement. The words inject a level of ambiguity into the cartoon; these are not the words that Clegg would choose to speak, but instead represent the reaction in the critical press to his surprisingly assured performance and apparent popularity. Read at face value, Clegg's victory is depicted as hollow; he really did have 'nothing to lose', being the lesser-known political leader suddenly given equal billing in the political 'ring'. On the other hand, the battered, knock-kneed Brown and Cameron are clearly the losers in this depiction, their claims for victory insincere or deluded. As Seymour-Ure has noted (2001: 348), cartoonists often draw on a political leader's television image, 'confident that they share it with their audience', and the dominance of the Leaders' Debates is likely to have intensified the influence of the televised campaign upon cartoon portrayal during this election period.

Our next cartoon directly comments on the power of television to raise the public profile of political leaders, and we include it here due to its contrasting visual style and cultural allusions (Figure 19.2). Again the setting is imaginary, but in this case the fairytale story of Pinocchio and his creator Geppetto provides the inspiration, along with Clegg's new-found standing as a 'real politician' – alluded to here as substantiated by his equal billing in the debates. The fairytale genre of literature is a densely allegorical form of storytelling, and here the recognisable features are utilised, with the top-left title imitating the beginning of the story, 'When you wish upon a star ...', the scenery a simple wooden house with stars in the sky. But, unlike the depictions of political persons in the cartoon above, Rowson uses the devices of exaggeration and distortion (in the dark eyes and large lips of Vince Cable as Geppetto), politicians depicted as animals (Cameron as the fox), or as inanimate objects

Figure 19.2   Martin Rowson, *Guardian*, 19 April
© Guardian News & Media Ltd 2010

(Clegg as a wooden Pinocchio). The 'fat cat' beside Cameron, peering in at the window, is also a condensed representation for high-earning, big business interests who have close relationships with political leaders; his proximity to Cameron and possible interest in Clegg providing a neat visual device that implies potential developments in the tale, as Clegg progresses on his journey of self and political discovery.

The political figures are not so easily recognisable to those readers with only a passing interest in politics, and Rowson also rewards a familiarity with the Pinocchio story and its own sinister undercurrents. Rather than appearing overjoyed with Clegg's transformation, Cable is depicted as shaking the boy-Clegg, an elder father-figure who has lost control of his creation or 'puppet': 'The Tellyfairy's promise has come true! You have turned into a real politician!' A promise coming true is a usually a celebratory proclamation in the fairytale genre, here subverted by Rowson into a more ambivalent statement, imbued with a cynicism directed at the nature of mediatised politics. Rowson's use of Pinocchio to depict Nick Clegg is perhaps the most vivid example of innovation during this period, a symbolic construct that was devised for portraying the electoral campaign but one which worked even better for portraying the activities of the government that followed.

Editorial cartoons in the broadsheets have received criticism for their elitist qualities, often requiring high levels of topical knowledge, recognition of political character traits and a wider literary or cultural understanding in order to decipher their meanings. Although digital access to editorial cartoons may now be starting to challenge Seymour-Ure's earlier claim that cartoonists such as Mac in the *Daily Mail* reach 'a readership of about the same size as all the broadsheet cartoonists added together' (Seymour-Ure 2001: 353), it is still the case that those cartoons aimed at the mid-market newspaper readership reach a considerable audience and offer interesting points for comparison with the 'qualities'. The example by Mac below (Figure 19.3) presents a quieter form of cartoon, with simplicity of composition, strong use of symbolism, and sparing use of colour or text. This cartoon accompanied a front page editorial on the eve of the election (5 May 2010), filling the top half of the page while the headline read, 'Vote DECISIVELY to stop Britain walking blindly into disaster', with the capitalised 'decisively' also in red type. Such prominent positioning for the cartoon is unusual, although front page editorials are familiar during the final days of the election campaign. The political message is unambiguous in this case; a blind Britannia walks to the edge of the cliff, into the thunderstorms of a 'hung parliament'. In the opposite direction, to the

Figure 19.3   Mac, *Daily Mail*, 5 May
© Stan McMurtry (Mac)/Daily Mail 2010

right of the frame, the sun shines on 'strong government'. In employing the traditionalist female personification of Britannia, Mac signals a visual appeal to national pride, here depicted in immediate peril, rather than resplendent and proud. Eschewing caricature and captioning, Mac's tone is a serious one, contingent on the editorial's direct message, which is to 'vote Conservative' and avoid the prospect of the 'shabby compromises' of a coalition government. The two options are presented as clearly opposed, a condensation of a political argument that fears a Labour–Lib Dem coalition and hopes for an outright win for the Conservatives; albeit an argument expressed in non-party terms as a choice between 'hung parliament' and 'strong government', thereby raising the sense of crisis to an institutional rather than party-political level.

Our final cartoon exemplifies a finely drawn, enigmatic style of comment, alluding to the formation of coalition government as a marriage between party leaders Cameron and Clegg (Figure 19.4). The cartoon contains no direct reference to either political person, yet the metaphor of romance was heavily, and often heavy-handedly, utilised across the mediascape during this post-election period (Parry and Richardson, forthcoming). Christian Adams' cartoon for the *Telegraph* provides a subtle portrayal, one in contrast to the many other depictions of the coalition as a civil partnership, marriage, or showbiz coupling, by adopting a wry take on the 'political honeymoon' period. The signifiers

Figure 19.4   Christian Adams, *Telegraph*, 15 May
©Telegraph Media Group Limited, 2010

in the cartoon all allude to two lovers (honeymoon suite, champagne,
a red rose, 'do not disturb' sign), yet the political content (an already-
lit bomb) sneaks into the cartoon's serene setting through its place-
ment under the trolley tablecloth. Very much a 'cartoonish' bomb in
its appearance, here it is labelled with the potential problems for the
new coalition (Tax, Europe, Cuts, National Insurance). The mood in
this example is whimsical rather than cynical, with elements of farce
introduced as an inherent dimension of coalition politics.

Cartoons clearly provide a distinctive generic format for representing
election politics. Although they are individually authored, they work
within the broad political identity of their newspaper context and often
attempt both to be provocative and yet to pick up on currents of feeling
and judgement circulating both among specific readerships and then
more broadly in the culture. Their particular emphasis on visual personification, together with their symbolic licence, freely extending to
fantasy, makes for an instructive complement to the written and spoken
formats we have collected.

The political colourists: sketch-writing

Another practice involving the routine mediation of the political, a practice in which, again, generic factors are distinctive and significant, is

the work of the 'colourists' who write regular accounts of Parliamentary and political life for many British newspapers. However, the way they do this is at some remove from the predominant forms of news journalism, having a primary commitment to entertaining through the kinds of caricature and the (often elaborate) conceits through which they render the people and events that constitute 'the scene'. In this sense, they can be likened to cartoonists (Hoggart, 2010a), although the detail with which they can assemble their portrayals within a narrative frame and the range of evaluative commentary that they can bring to bear are of a different order.

Political sketches, the core of 'colour' writing, have a long history, traceable back to the days when attendance at Parliamentary sessions was not possible for writers and therefore speculation and imaginative invention were necessary (Richardson and Corner, 2011 forthcoming). Over the last fifty years, sketch-writing has undergone a number of major shifts as a cultural practice, reflecting in part radical changes both in the nature of official political culture and in the broader popular culture within which newspaper writing makes its address to readers.[6]

In looking at how examples of written sketches contributed to the mediation of the election, we engaged with two, related, dimensions of their generic character. These might be labelled tone and positioning. Tone indicates the kinds of mood established in the writing through its use of tactics of description and address. A dominant characteristic of tone in a lot of the work we examined, across different authorial styles, was the sense of amused, curious and often condescending detachment with which it observed the different 'spectacles' of the election as well as its more intimate, 'glimpsed' moments, a detachment which it invited the reader to share. By positioning we mean both the kinds of normative alignment or disjunction with the political structure, processes and issues established by the writers and that anticipated with their readers. These accounts, permeated as they are with a sense of the theatrical, and often farcical, character of political business, rarely shift to defined terms of criticism (in the manner, say, of political columnists or of some satirical approaches). Their positioning is also generically framed as a confident one at the level of both the personal grounding and the social articulation, taken up without argument in a manner often suggesting assumed peer relations with those elites whose practices they 'sketch'.

Our first example is from the *Daily Telegraph*, on 16 April, the day after the first of the televised Leaders' Debates had taken place. It is the opening of a piece by sketch-writer Andrew Gimson.

Punches flew as the job interview turned nasty

THREE middle-aged men last night submitted themselves to a job inter-view, with the selection panel consisting of many millions of voters, minus anyone who popped out to make a cup of tea or turned over to watch Welcome to Lagos on BBC Two.

Almost at once the three candidates started to fight among themselves. Like pumped-up boxers, they hurled punches regardless of how this might appear to the viewers.

Personally we enjoyed the fight, even if it went on for longer than was strictly necessary. Adversarial politics is a vital part of our tradition, and brought out the differing characters of the three men far better than an uninterrupted exchange of high-minded platitudes would have done.

Gordon Brown tried without much success to hide how furious he is at being forced to reapply for the job.

Gimson starts his piece by immediately employing a principal device of the sketch-writer, the diminishing of 'the political' as a sphere of action by a description that transforms it into emphatically lowly terms. As readers, we are asked to consider a job interview which turns into a punch-up, and the first, short sentence of the title plunges us into a con-templation of this (highly public) affray. In another characteristic move for this genre, however, Gimson notes his own personal enjoyment in watching the contest, noting the less productive alternative in which the three men might have exchanged 'high-minded platitudes'. Within the strategically reductive terms of the account, these are presented as the *only* options for contemporary political behaviour. Gordon Brown, within this view, is an angry middle-aged man suffering the indignity of having to reapply for his job. Both the politicians and the event are reframed, to their great disadvantage.

Our second example is taken from the writer Ann Treneman, at the time the only woman among the political sketch-writers on the major dailies. This is taken from her piece in *The Times* on 8 May, two days after Election Day, when, in the light of the inconclusive elec-tion results, speculation began about the series of alliances that might develop between the Conservatives, or just possibly Labour, and the Liberal Democrats.

Loves me, loves me not: Clegg and the dating game

Spare a thought for Little Nicky Clegg. He had believed he was a contender. But now, the morning after the nightmare before, he was merely a pretty

> *face lusted after by the other two for their own selfish reasons. Thus he did the only thing he could: he played hard to get. For yesterday we saw three men playing a very public game of power dating.*

As noted in the previous section, the Clegg–Cameron alliance attracted commentary framed in erotic terms, as a 'civil partnership', for instance, but also with more hostile phrasing: right-wing commentator Richard Littlejohn elaborated on the romantic metaphor, coining the coalition formation as a 'Brokeback Mountain-style love-in', and ominously ending his column: 'The honeymoon stops here' (Littlejohn, 2010). This was widely taken up in those genres that have scope for imaginative development, particularly after the Number 10 press conference of 12 May (projected within the erotic/marital frame as a 'wedding day'). Here, Treneman describes a 'dating game' in which Clegg is placed as the woman in relation to two suitors. Later in the piece, this idea is developed further:

> *Our love-hate triangle now moves to Downing Street where Gordon is fuming. He disliked Nick, but he hated Dave. How dare they talk of love! Such was his fury that he knew he had to do the hardest thing of all - act. Thus at 12.40pm, Gordon strode out of No 10. He looked straight into the camera (and thus into the eyes of Nick) and did all but throw himself at Nick's feet. He even told Nick that he respected him (yes he did, even though everyone who has ever dated knows that this is a bad line). Then he gushed about their wonderful new life together.*

Here, the language and narrative are taken straight from the pages of popular romantic fiction, although, as also in the case of the Gimson example earlier, the figurative analogy is not simply a comic embellishment worked upon the political behaviour it describes; it is used to illuminate aspects of this behaviour.

Our final example is taken from *The Guardian* of 19 May, following the first day of the Parliamentary session with the new Government. It is the opening of a sketch by Simon Hoggart, one of the most celebrated of writers in this genre and one who has offered valuable commentary on its history and stylistic conventions (Hoggart, 2010a, b).

Lib Dems Get a Feel for Posh Seats

The Commons looked much the same yet weirdly different. What were Alistair Darling and Harriet Harman doing on the left, and the Tories on the right? Why were so many Lib Dems sprinkled among them? The place was full of familiar faces, yet many were entirely different, as if a failing soap opera had decided to replace a third of the cast overnight.

Almost everyone was in bubbling, devil-may-care mood. No wonder – apart from the newbies, these are the survivors who have crawled safely to shore. Relief can create slight hysteria.

Here, the high space of politics, the chamber of Commons, becomes the low space of soap opera (a 'failing' soap opera too). Hoggart's writing works to place the reader within the immediacy of his assumed disorientation. His apparent lack of understanding as to why things look 'weirdly different' gives the political changes that have occurred a sharpness that a more conventional account, drawing on the knowledge of the previous weeks, would not. The description is not only physical and spatial; with its references to 'mood', to 'survival' and to 'hysteria', it reaches inside the subjective world of professional politics.

All three of the pieces from which we have cited can be judged to have an 'affectionate' alignment with what they observe of electoral events as well as a 'critical' one. The absurdity of what is happening is projected gently and can quickly be retrieved for a serious judgement if necessary, as in Gimson's remarks about the importance of adversarial relations between the parties. Sketch-writing offers a distanced, often bemused view of the 'theatre of politics' – its places, events and characters – and builds on this physicality (for instance, Hoggart's 'posh seats' above) to make indirect points about political value. Its way of 'bearing witness' to electoral events is reductive, but the reductions are designed (again, as in cartoons) to identify some of the core dynamics at work. Unlike some of the other work we examine here, its descriptive detail, elaborative wit and tones of social confidence make it a genre likely to have an appeal limited by social class and education, one that has less purchase on those whose dominant relation to the political class is defined either by disconnection or by anger.

Concluding remarks

In our full study of how British politics in 2010 was articulated across the media, we engage with a wide variety of generic forms, only a selection of which have been explored briefly here. We have shown how these forms work to 'theme' and 'place' the political in very different ways, among other things locating official politics, and the political class, within terms that include criticism and derision as well as affirmation.

Going 'beyond the news' raises many questions on the established political communication agenda, albeit in a revised form – for instance, questions about knowledge and the relation between understanding and
action. It also puts a sharp emphasis on questions of political *feeling*, on
how the affective dimension of the political is encountered through a
sense of the dramatic, the ironic, the farcical and the outrageous. This
dimension cannot be explored by textual study alone, and we believe
that our current work with respondent groups will take us further into
an understanding of this core component of political subjectivity.

For the purposes of the present chapter, it is the representations of
electoral politics across a range of generic treatments that hold particular interest: a moment with distinctive opportunities, both for direct
public engagement in politics and for heightened visibility of political
figures across the mediascape. Whether in the ventriloquising of politicians' voices in the *News Quiz*, Rory Bremner's 'acting out' of political
personae and mimicry of street-level campaigning, or the astute caricaturing of political leaders' qualities by cartoonists and sketch-writers,
these examples offer a small dip into the imaginative and expressive
affordances found across the range of media genres that, we argue, play
an integral role in the mediation of British political culture. Election
periods bring to the fore issues of representation (in both the political
sense and the media sense), a time when aspects of the 'political' cut
across and sometimes deeply into the 'form' and 'content' of various
genres. In offering a brief overview of the cross-generic range of election
coverage in 2010, this project hopes to make a start in encouraging a
more inclusive approach, adaptable for future election studies, in which
there is sensitivity to a range of very different ways of using language
and images for conveying ideas about political values, practices and
structures.

Notes

1. The concept of 'affordance' can be traced back to the work of J. J. Gibson in the
   psychology of perception (Gibson, 1979), though Oliver (2005) suggests that
   it has been extended so far from its original use in a variety of research contexts as to have outlived its usefulness. In the 2000s this concept was drawn
   into the general field of multimodal social semiotics (Kress, 2003), where
   the focus has been on the potentialities of communicative modes (speech,
   writing) and of technologies (the computer, the mobile phone) rather than
   on those of genres. Its applicability to genre rests on the fact that genres offer
   relatively stable modal configurations that form the basis of textual production and interpretation.

2. This series is the 'older sister' of the TV show *Have I got news for you*, though reaching a much smaller and more elite audience. During a series run, each episode goes out weekly (Fridays at 6.30 pm, repeated Saturdays at 12.30 pm). Comedian Sandi Toksvig is the current host; the rest of the cast is not fixed from week to week, though there are some regulars.
3. For further history of broadcast political comedy with specific reference to television, see Crisell (1991) and Duguid (2003). Political humour on radio has not attracted academic attention in its own right, though *The Men From the Ministry* (BBC radio 1962–77) occasionally attracts a passing comment.
4. *The X-Factor* (ITV, 2004–present) is a high-profile television talent contest, which goes out on a Saturday evening and is watched by very large audiences who phone in to vote for their favourite acts. The least popular acts are eliminated weekly until only the series' winner remains.
5. Within this audit period, *The Guardian*'s regular editorial cartoonists were Steve Bell, Martin Rowson and Phil Disley, with Chris Riddell for the *Observer*. The *Telegraph* cartoonists are Christian Adams, Nicholas Garland and Michael Daley. Peter Brookes and Morten Morland are political cartoonists for *The Times*. Mac (Stan McMurtry), Michael Heath and Robert Thompson provide cartoons for the *Mail*, while David Trumble, Andy Davey and Tom Johnston draw for the *Sun*. Kerber and Black provide daily cartoons within the editorial section of the *Daily Mirror*, although these are smaller single-column 'pocket' cartoons.
6. There were five sketch-writers regularly contributing to the national press at the time of the election: Simon Hoggart (*Guardian*), Ann Treneman (*Times*), Quentin Letts (*Daily Mail*), Andrew Gimson (*Telegraph*) and Simon Carr (*Independent*).

References

Conners, J. L. (2005) 'Visual Representations of the 2004 Presidential Campaign: Political Cartoons and Popular Culture References', *American Behavioral Scientist*, 43(3): 479–87.

Corner, J. and Pels, D. (2003) *Media and the Restyling of Politics*. London: Sage.

Corner, J. and Richardson, K. (2008) 'Political culture and television fiction: *The Amazing Mrs Pritchard*', *European Journal of Cultural Studies*, 11(4): 387–403.

Corner, J. and Richardson, K. (2009) 'Political values and television drama', paper for the Politics and Drama panel at the 2009 Political Studies Association Annual Conference, http://www.psa.ac.uk/journals/pdf/5/2009/Corner.pdf (accessed 14 March 2011)

Corner, J., Richardson, K. and Parry, K. (2011, forthcoming) 'Political culture and the mediascape: a British case study', *Interactions* 1(3) (sections of earlier draft working paper at http://www.liv.ac.uk/communication-and-media/Staff/politicalculture.htm (accessed 14 March 2011)).

Crisell, A. (1991) 'Filth, Sedition and Blasphemy: The Rise and Fall of Television Satire', in Corner, J. (ed.) *Popular Television in Britain*. London: BFI.

Danjoux, I. (2007) 'Reconsidering the Decline of the Editorial Cartoon', *PS: Political Science & Politics*, 40(2): 245–8.

Duguid, M. (2003). 'TV satire: political humour from TW3 to HIGNFY', http://www.screenonline.org.uk/tv/id/946719/ (accessed 3 December 2010).

Edwards, J. L. (2001) 'Running in the shadows in campaign 2000: Candidate metaphors in editorial cartoons', *American Behavioral Scientist*, 44(12): 2,140–51.

Gibson, J. (1979) *The Ecological Approach to Visual Perception*. Boston: Houghton Mifflin.

Hoggart, S. (2010a) 'Prime Ministers I have known', *The Guardian*, 8 October 2010.

Hoggart, S. (2010b) *A Long Lunch: My stories and I'm sticking to them*. London: John Murray.

Jones, J. (2005) *Entertaining politics: satiric television and political engagement*. Plymouth: Rowman and Littlefield.

Kress, G. (2003) *Literacy in the new media age*. London: Routledge.

Littlejohn, R. (2010) 'The new politics? More like Brokeback Mountain', *Daily Mail*, 14 May: 17.

Mazzoleni, G. (2009) *Politica pop. Da 'Porta a porta' a 'L'isola dei famosi'* (with Sfardini, A.). Il Mulino, Bologna.

Oliver, M. (2005) 'The problem with affordance', *E-learning*, 2(4): 402–13.

Parry, K. and Richardson, K. (forthcoming) 'Political imagery in the British General Election of 2010: The curious case of "Nick Clegg"' *British Journal of Politics and International Relations*.

Richardson, K. and Corner, J. (2011 forthcoming) 'Sketchwriting, political "colour" and the sociolinguistics of stance' *Journal of Language and Politics*, 10(2).

Rowson, M. (2009) 'Dark Magic', *Index on Censorship*, 38(1): 140–164.

Seymour-Ure, C. (2001) 'What Future for the British Political Cartoon?', *Journalism Studies*, 2(3): 333–55.

Street, J. (1997) *Politics and popular culture*. Philadelphia: Temple University Press.

Van Zoonen, L. (2003) 'After Dallas and Dynasty we have... Democracy': Articulating Soap, Politics and Gender', in Corner, J. and Pels, D. *Media and the Restyling of Politics*. London: Sage, 99–116.

Van Zoonen, L. (2005) *Entertaining the Citizen: When Politics and Popular Culture Converge*. Boston: Rowman and Littlefield.

20
Conclusion: Time for Change?

Simon Atkinson and Roger Mortimore

Some general elections are quickly forgotten, mere milestones along the way of the country's political odyssey. Others can be turning points – and not necessarily only those that result in a change of government.

> The defeat of 1983 ... was without question the defining event of postwar Labour politics. 'Defining' is not a word used lightly, for it was this election, and the events leading up to it, that seared into the electoral consciousness of almost every voter in Britain an image so negative, so destructive, so alienating that it has taken 14 years, three leaders and a totally remade party to eradicate it.

This was the verdict of Philip Gould, writing in the 1997 volume in this series, just after the first and most dramatic of Labour's three election victories (Crewe et al., 1998: 4).

The 2010 General Election brought the next change of government – with the Conservatives returning to power after a period of time in opposition which will have felt just as painful as Labour's doldrums in the 1980s and early 1990s were to Philip Gould and his colleagues. Both parties went through periods when there was a very real question as to how they could ever regain enough support to take power again, going through policy reviews and various leaders along the way.

But perhaps it remains to be seen whether 2010 proves to be a defining election or only a stepping stone to a more decisive change of national direction some time in the future. Certainly, there are a number of other things that will be remembered about this election. Most notable, of course, is the novelty of a coalition government, which emerged after an unprecedented period of negotiations and uncertainty following the electorate's inconclusive verdict.

The period preceding the campaign set the scene, and it is striking to see that many of the contributors to this volume start their commentaries well before the official launch on 6 April. This is hardly surprising, given that the run-up included the 'Election That Never Was' of autumn 2007, which saw the party machines, the media and the pollsters marching up to the top of the hill before marching down again.

Then, rather than enjoying a pre-election boom, the rhetoric about how best the country could share the spoils of growth was quickly jettisoned as Britain experienced a recession that was as sharp as it was unexpected – part of a broader global financial crisis whose longer-term impact is still far from clear.

Throughout this final period, it was clear that we had the interesting twin dynamics of an unpopular Labour government accompanied by a distinct lack of enthusiasm among the electorate for the Conservative Party or, indeed, David Cameron. Time for change it may have been, but the decision was ultimately given in a grudging, qualified way – and the signs were certainly there before the spring of 2010.

The result was an election campaign that was perhaps the most exciting for many years. As we see from many of the contributions in this volume, while events were still unfolding few felt that they could say with any certainty what exactly what was going to happen next or, indeed, what the outcome would be. The mood of the electorate, the way the parties fought their campaign, the impact of the debates, and the novelty and uncertainty associated with the rise of social media all played their part in this.

In almost all respects, except the long-anticipated ejection of the incumbent government, the course of the election was very different from that of 1997, the last occasion on which a change in power had taken place. But what of the way the parties fought the election and communicated with the voters? How different from 1997 was that?

In one sense, it would hardly be surprising that the changes in political communications since 1997 were more dramatic than we might normally expect to see in the lifespan of a single government: those same years have seen probably the biggest changes in citizens' everyday communications habits over any thirteen-year period since Victorian times. The mobile phone, even in 1997 only just beginning to break out of the luxury bracket, is now effectively universal. Multi-channel television has become the norm, while DVD boxed sets and catch-up services such as the BBC's iPlayer are beginning to erode the collective community experience of simultaneous viewing. The vast majority of the voting public have internet access, which most use regularly, and the emergence of social media – though yet to reach their full potential – has revolutionised the public's ability to interact with each other, and to access political (and other) news information directly, unfiltered by the traditional news media.

Yet political communications do not necessarily evolve in the same way or at the same pace as changes in wider communications habits. The changes that have occurred in election campaigning in recent times have not necessarily been predictable. Looking back at what was being said in 1997, we get a foretaste of how election campaigns might be about to change.

> The launch of special election sites on the World Wide Web (WWW) such as Online Magic's GE'97, and those of the BBC, the *Daily Telegraph* and the *Guardian* received extensive coverage on radio and television news and in the print media. Tony Blair and Paddy Ashdown each took to the Internet for an online question and answer session, more than 50 MPs were accessible through electronic mail (e-mail) and the Conservatives and Liberal Democrats transmitted their party political broadcasts on their Internet pages. Drawing analogies with the US presidential election campaign, Michael Martin, the creative director of Online Magic, declared that the Internet would 'provide a significant new forum for debate' in the United Kingdom. (Ward and Gibson, in Crewe et al., 1998: 93)

The need to spell out 'World Wide Web' and 'electronic mail' in the passage quoted above serves as a reminder of just how the landscape changed during Labour's time in office. But, even then, the expectation that elections would increasingly move online was clear. Yet, thirteen years on, the internet, so routine a part of everyday life for most of the British public, remains almost a sideshow in electoral campaigning terms.

It was still the 'old' media, not the new, that were overwhelmingly dominant in the 2010 campaign – though, as several of the contributors' chapters discuss, the way in which these media cover elections, and in which the candidates use them to campaign, are constantly evolving. The biggest talking points of the election were the television debates, with the main distraction being Gordon Brown's 'Bigotgate' blunder, also directly caused by television. (It was the transmission of his private comments by a forgotten television microphone that caused that crisis.) The impact of the press was perhaps slightly less, but that seemed unlikely a few months before the election, when the MPs' expenses scandal was the topic of the day, driven by the leaked information published in the *Daily Telegraph*. And, as we discuss elsewhere, much of the tone of the campaign was set by the opinion polls, many more than ever before (see Chapter 7 by Kellner et al.) both charting the 'horse race' during the campaign and reporting reaction to the leaders' debates – and most of the polls were commissioned by and reported in the newspapers and on TV.

It was mainly the traditional media, too, which (picking up on a remark by Gordon Brown's former pollster, Deborah Mattinson) promoted the idea that this might be the 'Mumsnet election'. This was perhaps the clearest case of the internet making a mark on the campaign, and all the party leaders found it worth their while to make time to be 'interviewed' by a Mumsnet forum. But the parties' targeting of voters is making increasing use of geodemographic methods (Experian's MOSAIC) that classify voters by their physical addresses rather than their online activities, once again picking up on the tried-and-tested, but not new, techniques of commercial marketing – although, as Fisher et al. discuss in Chapter 14, even that is far from fully implemented.

The new media are, perhaps, making their mark by contributing to the secondary influence of television, as the programmes – in this case the debates – affect the opinions of those who have not watched them (as discussed in the chapter by Coleman et al. and measured in Chapter 5 by Hawkins and Lawes). Their impact is spread not only by word of mouth and by news reporting, but in blogs, by Twitter and clips on YouTube and similar services. But there were few obvious instances of new media initiating, rather than merely disseminating, significant campaign events. Perhaps the closest was the website where users were invited to deface Conservative campaign posters with new images or slogans (as detailed in Chapter 13 by Chris Burgess). Yet even this was inspired by one article in a newspaper and later popularised by others.

Trends in political communications, it seems, are not driven by developments in communications technology and media practices more generally, or even by methods of campaigning proven successful in other countries, but by political developments. The biggest innovation in the 2010 campaign was the introduction of TV debates, fully fifty years after the USA had the same. That this leap was taken had, as Chapter 2 by Ric Bailey and Chapter 3 by Adam Boulton and Tom D.C. Roberts both show, nothing to do with technology and everything to do with politics. Similarly, looking back to 1997, it has been the open adoption of political marketing techniques that has evoked most discussion, with policy development led by focus group findings and, once Labour was in power, the concept of government as the 'permanent campaign'. (In fact, these were little discussed in the Political Communications volume at the time – though see Ward and Gibson, pp. 97–8, and Worcester, pp. 56–7, both in Crewe et al., 1998). Again, these developments were decades behind the parallel developments in commercial marketing, but needed political change – the ascendancy of 'New Labour' within the Labour Party – to bring them into the electoral sphere.

In some other respects, campaigning practice has proved, if not entirely resistant to change, at least prone to drag its feet. At constituency level, the focus remains on the marginal constituencies, and on the 'ground war' rather than the 'air war' (although, as Fisher et al. in Chapter 14 argue, the two are becoming increasingly indistinguishable). In fact, even as technological advances steadily make the reach of the national campaign potentially more effective, the importance of the local campaign is being reasserted and recognised once more.

Given this, it is interesting that local online campaigning has remained so low-key (see the detailed survey in Chapter 15 by Southern and Ward). Should we be surprised at the failure of local issues to take hold in an election where they might, more than on any other recent occasion, have been expected to be paramount? The expenses saga (as detailed by Hudson in Chapter 16) should have given the voters unusually large incentives to pick and choose between their local candidates. Moreover, the closeness of the election put a premium on the promotion of tactical voting. The internet offered unparalleled opportunity to organise local campaigns, cutting the cost both figuratively (in terms of time and effort) and literally (removing the existing restraint on campaigning imposed by the expenses regulations). Yet there were only sporadic signs that it was making any difference.

Mobile internet access and the advent of social media offer other possibilities, and scattered candidates have made limited local use of Twitter, Facebook and similar developments. Yet it would be hard to point to a single constituency where even their most enthusiastic advocates could claim a direct impact on the outcome, except of course for the case of the unfortunate candidate sacked by his party before nominations had opened for 'tweeting' indiscreetly.

Nevertheless, some changes have proved beyond the power of the competing parties to resist, and, as Fisher et al. recount in Chapter 14 of this volume, the use of 'modern' campaign techniques at local level is growing, albeit slowly. In fact, 'modern' techniques in this context means mainly the use of computers, direct mail and the telephone. It seems incredible now that as late as 1997 Denver and Hands (in Crewe et al., 1998) found it worthwhile to include a table on computer use by local campaigns, because appreciable numbers of campaigns still made no use of them! That is unthinkable now, even if they are used for nothing more complicated than generating address labels. What has really changed, though, is greater sophistication in the approach to targeting particular voters, allowing these not-very-new methods of contact to better fulfil their potential.

Another new feature of the current landscape is the lack of (or lack of interest in) set-piece speeches. The Philip Grould cited in our introduction, for example, references Major's 'don't bind my hands' speech, and Blair speeches in Scotland and Stevenage, giving specific dates to help us understand key moments. Aside from Gordon Brown's unfortunate experience in Rochdale, it feels difficult to identify anything particularly interesting coming from the traditional 'battle bus' style campaigning we have all become used to, and little sign that this is a temporary phenomenon. Even Brown's relatively passionate eve of poll speech to the London Citizens' conference was overshadowed by yet another intervention from a protester.

As far as the national campaign planners are concerned, the driving desire is to maintain control over the course of events and power to set the agenda. At the same time, there are clear signs that that many voters would prefer exactly the opposite. One reason, perhaps, why campaigners have been slow to embrace the possibilities offered by new technology is the way mobile communications, the internet and new social media have made it much more difficult to plan and control their messaging using the campaign approaches that have been tested and refined throughout the post-war period.

This is a theme taken up in Chapter 17 by Ivor Gaber – who reminds us of the decline of the week-by-week 'election grid' through which the parties, in theory at least, planned the agenda they wanted to get across as they built momentum prior to polling day. A party might make the wrong choices or get the wrong messages across, but it felt (and arguably was, at least to some extent) in control. Suddenly this is much less the case, a development unexpectedly exacerbated by the introduction of the leaders' debates, which so dominated the election as to reduce the period when the parties could fight to set the agenda to a couple of days each week. We see this too in the decline in the use of press releases and press conferences, which were so integral to the established model of campaigning.

We can see the reaction to this process in the highly restrictive conditions that the parties imposed on the TV debates. The rare moments in past elections where the Prime Minister of the day has been confronted by an 'ordinary voter' stand out in the memory, and no doubt bring out campaign strategists in a cold sweat. The debate rules, apparently aimed above all at preventing any meaningful interaction with the studio audience, are evidence that such moments are still feared.

But in that case, what did Labour and the Conservatives think they could achieve by agreeing to the debates? Their introduction was certainly not inevitable. The tastes of the public can to some extent influence, but can certainly not dictate, how the campaign is fought – public demand alone could not have forced the debates to take place if the leaders had been unwilling. (Or was it simply that, being a format with such a superficial resemblance to the increasingly ubiquitous 'reality TV' game shows, they felt its time had finally come as a means of reinvigorating public engagement with politics?)

What is telling, though, is how both Labour and the Conservatives seem to have misunderstood the consequences of this development: once the debates were in place it was in the hands of the public, not of the parties, how they reacted to it. Arguably, for either party even to have agreed to a debate in which the Liberal Democrat leader had equal status was a major tactical error. But, certainly, it was no secret that the modern public is impatient with 'spin' and 'Punch and Judy politics', takes an interest in the personal element and would hope to be convinced how to vote on a man-to-man or man-to-woman basis. That it was only Nick Clegg's advisers who apparently instructed their man to address the camera directly shows little appreciation by the bigger parties of what the voters would expect to get from the debates.

The nature and impact of the debates must therefore go down in the 'to be continued' category as we look ahead to next time. On what terms will they take place? Will the novelty have worn off among the electorate, making them less powerful? Will the parties deploy different tactics in terms of how they put their leaders across in the most telling manner?

What else will change before we have another change of government? We can only guess how technology might have moved on in another few years' time, and the uses that elections will make of it may be even less predictable. If, in 1997, we had known of the technological changes to come, surely few would have expected that the obsession of the parties, the Tories in particular, with the billboard poster would survive to 2010. Perhaps the mydavidcameron.com 'airbrushed for change' experience will finally relegate posters from the front line of campaigning in the future. Or perhaps not.

Similarly, in 1997, few expected the 'low turnout' of 71 per cent (Crewe et al., 1998: xvii) to represent something of a high-water mark a little over a decade later. The elections since then have presented the parties, pollsters and pundits with new challenges in understanding an electorate that, while professing to be no less interested in politics, is certainly less motivated to actually turn out in the same numbers; that, again, could continue to present new challenges in the future. Looking ahead, the new experience of coalition government makes predictions about the future even more precarious; so, too, may an amended electoral system if the public votes to adopt it.

So it is far from clear what we should expect the contributions to future books in this series to cover, or which aspects of political communications today will seem extraordinary in a few years' time. Election campaigning is very much a law unto itself. Perhaps the only thing that is certain is that there is sure to be something that surprises us.

Reference

Crewe, I., Gosschalk, B. and Bartle, J. (eds) (1998) *Political Communications: Why Labour Won the General Election of 1997*. London: Frank Cass.

Appendix

The Prime Ministerial Debates

For the first time in British general election the leaders of the three main parties took part in three televised debates, one held during each of the three weeks prior to polling day. The encounters were governed by an extensive list of 76 guidelines:

1. The objective is to select an audience which is broadly a demographic cross section of the country.
2. The audience to be made up of roughly 200 people, subject to venue capacity.
3. ICM has been appointed as an external recruitment agency and the methods of recruitment are based on their expert advice. In broad terms, we will aim to:
4. Recruit within a 30 mile radius of the host city, mindful of administrative borders on either side of that radius based on the revised ICM list of constituencies.
5. Recruit according to gender, age, ethnicity and social class to best reflect the broader voting-age population. The recruitment procedure will be transparent, and its methodology will be available to the parties for comment.
6. Ensure around 80% of the audience is made up of voters who express a voting intention at the time of recruitment.
7. These will be subdivided into ratios which reflect a ratio of 7 Labour, 7 Conservative, 5 Lib Dem. The political ratios will take precedence over the demographic in the final selection of the audience by ICM.
8. Within the 80% (see point 6) the broadcasters retain the right to recruit some audience members who express an intention to vote for smaller parties.
9. Ensure that around 20% of the audience will be undecided but will be politically engaged. ICM's definition of undecided voters to be the basis of this selection.
10. Reserve a small number of seats for participants from outside the ICM selected audience, whose questions have been pre-submitted and selected by the broadcaster's editorial panel. The broadcasters may use a variety of methods to encourage the submission of such questions from across the UK in the build up to the debates.
11. The number of questions from outside the ICM selected audience will be a maximum of four per debate.
12. Over-recruit by a small margin to accommodate 'drop outs' or 'no shows'.
13. Issue audience members with a protocol of rules, including security procedures for entry and conduct during the debates. The protocol will be agreed by the parties.

Audience role

14. The objective is to ensure maximum debate between the party leaders – the distinctive characteristic of these programmes – whilst allowing the audience's voices to be heard directly posing questions.
15. Each broadcaster will nominate a panel to choose the questions for its debate. The panel's membership will be public, but they will meet in private.
16. Each selection panel will include a member to oversee compliance. List of names of panel members will be published.
17. The objective of each panel shall be to ensure fair question selection in order to frame a balanced debate within the rules of our agreements.
18. The panel will meet confidentially in the weeks running up to their debate.
19. All questions submitted by the ICM selected audience will be seen by a member of the panel. Email questions will be sifted and a selection given to the panel.
20. Initially, each panel will sift through a selection of questions drawn from those submitted by members of the public.
21. They will narrow down their selections in a series of meetings up to and including the day of the debate.
22. Each panel will have five to seven members, including a designated chair who would have a casting vote if necessary.
23. The panel cannot be quorate with fewer than three of its members present.
24. In selecting its questions, the panel will take full account of the following:
25. Each question will be relevant to all three party leaders.
26. No question shall focus on one party or one leader.
27. All questions will be based on election issues.
28. Audience members will be made aware of these rules before submitting their final questions.
29. Half the programme will be based on the agreed theme. Within that portion of the programme, a maximum of three questions will be selected on a single sub-theme (as listed in point 65 of this document).
30. Half the programme will be un-themed. In this portion of the programme, a maximum of two questions will be selected on a single subject.
31. The range of questions chosen will reflect the broadcasters' legal and compliance responsibilities for due impartiality and fairness.
32. The panel will use its editorial judgement to select questions and will take into account factors such as the prominence of certain issues in the campaign, the distinctiveness of the different parties' policies on election issues, voters' interest and issues relevant to the role of the Prime Minister.
33. Within these rules, the editorial independence of the panel shall be paramount, because each broadcaster is answerable to its regulator for its programme content.
34. Questions may be selected by the editorial selection panel up to the start of the debate.
35. The selected questions will not be shown to anyone outside the editorial team in advance of the programmes.
36. Members of the audience will ask their questions. The moderator will ask the leaders to respond. The moderator may read email questions.

37. All questions will be addressed to and answered by all three leaders.
38. The audience members will be restricted to asking the selected questions.
39. There will be an option of viewer involvement via emails read by the moderator.
40. In order to maximise the time available for viewers to hear the leaders discussing election issues with each other, the studio audience will be asked not to applaud during the debate. There will be opportunities to do so both at the beginning and at the end of each programme.

Structure of programme

41. The programme will start with all three leaders on set and standing at their podiums.
42. The moderator will have a podium/desk and will move within a small area to allow eyeline with the audience and the leaders.
43. The moderator will introduce the leaders.
44. The first half of the programme will be on the agreed theme but with the agreement of all the parties, in case of a major national or international event not included in the theme of the debate, the moderator will ask the leaders for their reaction to the development at the start of the programme before moving on to the theme.
45. The time taken for the reaction to such an event will be added to the time available for the themed part of the debate, unless the event is clearly part of the theme of the debate, in which case the reaction will be counted as part of the time allotted to the theme.
46. Each leader will make an opening statement on the theme of the debate lasting for 1 minute. After the three opening statements the moderator will take the first question on the agreed theme. There will be closing statements of 1 minute 30 seconds from all three leaders at the end of the 90 minutes.
47. Each leader will have 1 minute to answer the question.
48. Each leader will then have 1 minute to respond to the answers.
49. The moderator may then open the discussion to free debate between the leaders for up to 4 minutes on merit.
50. The length of the debate on each question will be decided by the programme editor.
51. The programme editor will use their best endeavours to keep to the 4 minute time allowance but it may need to be extended in the interest of equality of treatment.
52. Questions will be taken on the theme until around half way through the programme, depending on timing and ensuring fair treatment of all three leaders.
53. At the end of the themed period, the moderator will open the debate to general questions selected by the broadcaster's panel from the audience or via email.
54. The same timing format will apply to the general questions i.e. each leader will have 1 minute to answer the question. Each leader will then have 1 minute to respond. The moderator will then open the discussion to free debate between the leaders for up to 4 minutes on merit.

55. There will be a clock indicating the time remaining for statements, answers to questions and responses. This will be visible to the candidates and moderator but not to the audience in the debate or on screen.
56. The order of speakers, based on an agreed grid, has been determined by the parties drawing lots.
57. At the end of the programme the three leaders will shake hands.

Role of the moderator

58. To moderate the programme.
59. To keep the leaders to the agreed time limits.
60. To ensure free-flowing debate being fair to all candidates over the course of the programme.
61. To ensure fairness on the direction of the programme editor.
62. To seek factual clarification where necessary.
63. It is not the moderator's role to criticise or comment on the leaders' answers.
64. The candidates accept the authority of the moderator to referee the rules on stage and ensure a free flowing, fair debate conducted within the agreed rules.

Themes

65. Order of themed debates. The order of the themes for the first half of each programme was determined by the broadcasters drawing lots. The order is as follows:
    1. Domestic affairs including but not exclusively: NHS; Education; Immigration; Law and Order; Family; Constitution; Trust in politics; Political reform;
    2. International affairs including but not exclusively; International relations; Afghanistan; Iraq; Iran; Middle East; UK defence; International terrorism; Europe; Climate change; China; International Development
    3. Economic affairs including but not exclusively: financing of public services; Taxation; Debt; Deficit; Public finances; Recession; Recovery; Banking and finance; Business; Pensions; Jobs;

Set

66. The leaders will stand at podiums throughout the debate. The positions of the three leaders during the debates are to be determined by agreement with all parties.
67. The moderator will have a podium/desk and will move within a small area to allow eyeline with the audience and the leaders.
68. Each broadcaster responsible for their own titles, music, branding etc.

Audience cutaways

69. The purpose of the programmes are for the viewers to see and hear the party leaders engaging in debate with each other and answering questions from

the audience. The audience is a key element of the programmes and has to be seen by the viewers but there will not be undue concentration of the reactions of individual audience members.

70. There will be a close up of the questioner while he/she is asking a question.
71. There will be no close-up cutaways of a single individual audience member while the leaders are speaking.
72. However if one of the leaders directly addresses an individual audience member, a close-up shot of that individual can be shown e.g. if a leader answers a question by directly addressing the questioner.
73. There may be group shots and wide shots of the audience during the programme.
74. The programme will be confined to events inside the debate studio.
75. Breaking News straps will not be put over live coverage of the debate. On news channels (Sky News, BBC News channel), the scrolling news tickers will offer other news but will not cover breaking news lines from the debates while the debates are taking place.
76. Each party will have the right to recall the negotiating panel made up of representatives from the broadcasters and the parties, during the campaign to discuss issues arising from the debates.

Index